P9-AOE-536

CAREERS AND OCCUPATIONS

LOOKING TO THE FUTURE

CAREERS AND OCCUPATIONS

LOOKING TO THE FUTURE

Catherine Dybiec Holm

INFORMATION PLUS REFERENCE SERIES
Formerly published by Information Plus, Wylie, Texas

GALE GROUP

Detroit
New York
San Francisco
London
Boston
Woodbridge, CT

CAREERS AND OCCUPATIONS: LOOKING TO THE FUTURE

Catherine Dybiec Holm, *Author*

The Gale Group Staff:

Editorial: John F. McCoy, *Project Manager and Series Editor*; Michael T. Reade, *Series Associate Editor*; Jason M. Everett, *Series Assistant Editor*; Rita Runchock, *Managing Editor*; Luann Brennan, *Editor*; Thomas Carson, *Editor*; Andrew Claps, *Editor*; Kathleen Droste, *Editor*; Nancy Matuszak, *Editor*; Christy Wood, *Associate Editor*; Ryan McNeill, *Assistant Editor*; Jeffrey Telford, *Assistant Editor*

Image and Multimedia Content: Barbara J. Yarrow, *Manager, Imaging and Multimedia Content*; Robyn Young, *Project Manager, Imaging and Multimedia Content*; Dean Dauphinais, *Senior Editor, Imaging and Multimedia Content*; Kelly A. Quin, *Editor, Imaging and Multimedia Content*; Leitha Etheridge-Sims, Mary K. Grimes, and David G. Oblender, *Image Catalogers*; Pamela A. Reed, *Imaging Coordinator*; Randy Bassett, *Imaging Supervisor*; Robert Duncan, *Senior Imaging Specialist*; Dan Newell, *Imaging Specialist*; Christine O'Bryan, *Graphic Specialist*

Indexing: Jennifer Dye, *Indexing Specialist*; Lynne Maday, *Indexing Specialist*

Permissions: Maria Franklin, *Permissions Manager*; Margaret Chamberlain, *Permissions Specialist*; Julie Juengling, *Permissions Specialist*

Product Design: Michelle DiMercurio, *Senior Art Director*; Kenn Zorn, *Product Design Manager*

Production: Mary Beth Trimper, *Composition Manager*; Gary Leach and Carolyn Roney, *Typesetting Specialists*; NeKita McKee, *Buyer*; Dorothy Maki, *Manufacturing Manager*

TABLE OF CONTENTS

PREFACE

Careers and Occupations: Looking to the Future is the latest volume in the ever-growing *Information Plus Reference Series*. Previously published by the Information Plus company of Wylie, Texas, the *Information Plus Reference Series* (and its companion set, the *Information Plus Compact Series*) became a Gale Group product when Gale and Information Plus merged in early 2000. Those of you familiar with the series as published by Information Plus will notice a few changes from the 1999 edition. Gale has adopted a new layout and style that we hope you will find easy to use. Other improvements include greatly expanded indexes in each book, and more descriptive tables of contents.

While some changes have been made to the design, the purpose of the *Information Plus Reference Series* remains the same. Each volume of the series presents the latest facts on a topic of pressing concern in modern American life. These topics include today's most controversial and most studied social issues: abortion, capital punishment, care for the elderly, crime, health care, the environment, immigration, minorities, social welfare, women, youth, and many more. Although written especially for the high school and undergraduate student, this series is an excellent resource for anyone in need of factual information on current affairs.

By presenting the facts, it is Gale's intention to provide its readers with everything they need to reach an informed opinion on current issues. To that end, there is a particular emphasis in this series on the presentation of scientific studies, surveys, and statistics. This data is generally presented in the form of tables, charts, and other graphics placed within the text of each book. Every graphic is directly referred to and carefully explained in the text. The source of each graphic is presented within the graphic itself. The data used in these graphics is drawn from the most reputable and reliable sources, in particular from the various branches of the U.S. government and

from major independent polling organizations. Every effort was made to secure the most recent information available. The reader should bear in mind that many major studies take years to conduct, and that additional years often pass before the data from these studies is made available to the public. Therefore, in many cases the most recent information available in 2000 dated from 1997 or 1998. Older statistics are sometimes presented as well, if they are of particular interest and no more-recent information exists.

Although statistics are a major focus of the *Information Plus Reference Series* they are by no means its only content. Each book also presents the widely held positions and important ideas that shape how the book's subject is discussed in the United States. These positions are explained in detail and, where possible, in the words of those who support them. Some of the other material to be found in these books includes: historical background; descriptions of major events related to the subject; relevant laws and court cases; and examples of how these issues play out in American life. Some books also feature primary documents, or have pro and con debate sections giving the words and opinions of prominent Americans on both sides of a controversial topic. All material is presented in an even-handed and unbiased manner; the reader will never be encouraged to accept one view of an issue over another.

HOW TO USE THIS BOOK

For most Americans, nothing shapes their lives more than work. From the beginning of adulthood until retirement, the world in which they live is a working world. Yet the working world is changing, and at a seemingly ever more rapid pace. Technology is changing the way businesses operate, service industries are replacing traditional manufacturing jobs, businesses are moving from downtown skyscrapers to suburban office parks, and more and more Americans are working from home or as temps rather than seeking traditional, long-term, careers. This book examines all of these trends and more, providing the latest information on what Americans do for a living, how much they earn, how they find work, and what other factors influences these key issues in every American's life.

Careers and Occupations: Looking to the Future consists of nine chapters and three appendices. Each chapter is devoted to a particular aspect of the American workforce. For a summary of the information covered in each chapter, please see the synopses provided in the Table of Contents at the front of the book. Chapters generally begin with an overview of the basic facts and background information on the chapter's topic, then proceed to examine sub-topics of particular interest. For example, Chapter 6: Earnings and Benefits begins with an overview of the average earnings of American workers. It then breaks down earnings over a number of categories, including gender, industry, and particular careers. The average starting salaries for college graduates is also discussed. After its examination of earnings, the chapter moves on to an overview of employee benefits in the United States. The typical benefits available at employers of different sizes is examined, as are the typical benefits offered in different industries. Health care benefits and retirement savings plans are then given special attention. Readers can find their way through any chapter by looking for the section and sub-section headings, which are clearly set off from the text. Or, they can refer to the book's extensive index, if they already know what they are looking for.

Statistical Information

The tables and figures featured throughout *Careers and Occupations: Looking to the Future* will be of particular use to the reader in learning about this issue. These tables and figures represent an extensive collection of the most recent and important statistics on the American workforce. For example, the average earnings for Americans of different genders and races, the current and projected size of the workforce, the distribution of the workforce across different industries in the past, present, and projected future, and the prevalence of drug testing policies among employers. Gale believes that making this information available to the reader is the most important

way in which we fulfill the goal of this book: To help readers understand the issues and controversies surrounding the American workforce, and reach their own conclusions about them.

Each table or figure has a unique identifier appearing above it, for ease of identification and reference. Titles for the tables and figures explain their purpose. At the end of each table or figure, the original source of the data is provided. The reader can also find the source information for all of the tables and figures gathered together in the Acknowledgments section.

In order to help readers understand these often complicated statistics, all tables and figures are explained in the text. References in the text direct the reader to the relevant statistics. Furthermore, the contents of all tables and figures are fully indexed. Please see the opening section of the index at the back of this volume for a description of how to find tables and figures within it.

In addition to the main body text and images, *Careers and Occupations: Looking to the Future* has three appendices. The first appendix is the Important Names and Addresses directory. Here the reader will find contact information for organizations that study the U.S. economy and workforce, or play an important role in setting the policies that affect them. The second appendix is the Resources section, which is provided to assist the reader in conducting his or her own research. In this section, the author and editors of *Careers and Occupations: Looking to the Future* describe some of the sources that were most useful during the compilation of this book. The final appendix is this book's index. It has been greatly expanded from previous editions, and should make it even easier to find specific topics in this book.

COMMENTS AND SUGGESTIONS

The editor of the *Information Plus Reference Series* welcomes your feedback on *Careers and Occupations: Looking to the Future* Please direst all correspondence to:

Editor

Information Plus Reference Series

27500 Drake Rd.

Farmington Hills, MI, 48331-3535

ACKNOWLEDGMENTS

The Gale Group thanks the following sources for permission to use their illustrations and information in Careers and Occupations: Looking to the Future.

Table 2.15, Spring, 1998. From "Profile of the Temporary Work Force," In *Contemporary Times*. National Association of Temporary and Staffing Services. Reproduced by permission.

The 1996 Job Security and Layoffs Survey, figure 2.7, 1996. From SHRM Issues Management Program. Society for Human Resource Management. Reproduced by permission.

The Gallup Poll Monthly, figure 2.8, 2000. Gallup Organization. Reproduced by permission.

Tables 9.1, 9.12, 9.13, May 2000. Economic Analysis Department. Dun and Bradstreet Corporation. Reproduced by permission.

Recruiting Trends, 1997-98, 27th Edition, table 6.6, December, 1997. Michigan State University. Reproduced by permission.

Business Starts Record, figures 9.1, 9.2 and table 9.2, Spring, 1996-97. Dun and Bradstreet Corporation. Reproduced by permission.

Business Failure Record, figure 9.3 and table 9.3, Fall, 1996-97. Dun and Bradstreet Corporation. Reproduced by permission.

CHAPTER 1
TODAY'S LABOR FORCE

The number of workers in the American civilian non-institutionalized labor force (not in the army, school, jail, or mental health facilities) grew rapidly over the past three decades, almost doubling from 75.8 million in 1966 to 139.4 million in 1999. The labor force includes those who are working part- or full-time or are unemployed, but actively looking for a job. During this period, the proportion of the population in the labor force rose from 59.2 percent to 67.1 percent. (See Table 1.1.) This growth was attributable to the entrance into the workforce of the post-World War II baby-boom children and the increase in the number and percentage of women entering the workforce. (See Chapter 2 for changes in the workforce.)

GENDER, AGE, RACE, AND ETHNIC ORIGIN.

In 1999, 76.7 percent of the male population and 60.7 percent of the female population 20 years and over participated in the labor force. A slightly higher percentage of whites were in the labor force (67.3 percent) than blacks (65.8 percent). Black women (66.1 percent) were somewhat more likely to be in the labor force than white women (59.9 percent), while a somewhat higher percentage of white men (77.2 percent) were in the labor force than black men (72.4 percent). More than two-thirds (67.7 percent) of those of Hispanic origin participated in the labor force—83.5 percent of the men and 57.7 percent of the women. (See Table 1.2.)

Americans were most likely to be working between the ages of 25 and 54. In 1999, 91.7 percent of men and 76.8 percent of women 25 to 54 years old were in the workforce. The percentage dropped to 67.9 percent for men and 51.5 percent for women among those 55 to 64 years of age. (See Table 1.3.) The proportion of men in the labor force in this age group generally has declined over the past few years, while the percentage of women has increased. In addition, a growing percentage of jobs held by the age group are part-time instead of full-time.

The low unemployment rate (2.7 percent in 1999) indicated among this older group in Table 1.3 reflects the fact that many of these older workers have given up looking for a job, are therefore not in the labor force, and are not counted among the unemployed. More than two of five adults who were not in the labor force were more than 65 years old.

Older workers leave the workforce for many reasons, ranging from disability to a genuine desire to retire. For many older people, however, leaving the workforce is not a voluntary act. Companies trying to cut expenses sometimes find it in their financial interest to force older, more highly paid workers into retirement and replace them with younger, lower-paid workers. The increasing desire of many companies to streamline their staffs, frequently by eliminating many middle-management positions, has had detrimental effects on this age group. They are frequently offered early retirement with some fringe benefits, but may be laid off with no benefits if they refuse early retirement. Older people are also more expensive to insure.

Student Workers

In 1995 one in four (26.2 percent) American high schoolers worked while going to school. Most (23.7 percent) worked part-time. In college, even more students worked (61.9 percent). Approximately 32 percent worked full-time, and 30 percent worked part-time. (See Figure 1.1.) In both high school and college, equal percentages of male and female students worked. According to the Bureau of Labor Statistics, 80 percent of high school students will hold at least one job before graduation.

The *Third International Math and Science Study* found that 61 percent of high school seniors worked an average of 3.1 hours daily. Only about 28 percent of seniors in other countries worked, and they averaged 1.2 hours daily. The combination of plentiful low-wage jobs in the service economy, young people's desire for con-

TABLE 1.1

Employment Status of the Civilian Noninstitutional Population 16 years and Over, 1966–2000

(Numbers in thousands)

| Year and month | Civilian noninstitutional population | Civilian labor force | | | | | | | | | Not in labor force |
| | | Number | Percent of population | Employed | | | | Unemployed | | | |
				Number	Percent of population	Agriculture	Nonagricultural industries	Number	Percent of labor force		
1966	128,058	75,770	59.2	72,895	56.9	3,979	68,915	2,875	3.8		52,288
1967	129,874	77,347	59.6	74,372	57.3	3,844	70,527	2,975	3.8		52,527
1968	132,028	78,737	59.6	75,920	57.5	3,817	72,103	2,817	3.6		53,291
1969	134,335	80,734	60.1	77,902	58.0	3,606	74,296	2,832	3.5		53,602
1970	137,085	82,771	60.4	78,678	57.4	3,463	75,215	4,093	4.9		54,315
1971	140,216	84,382	60.2	79,367	56.6	3,394	75,972	5,016	5.9		55,834
1972[1]	144,126	87,034	60.4	82,153	57.0	3,484	78,669	4,882	5.6		57,091
1973[1]	147,096	89,429	60.8	85,064	57.8	3,470	81,594	4,365	4.9		57,667
1974	150,120	91,949	61.3	86,794	57.8	3,515	83,279	5,156	5.6		58,171
1975	153,153	93,775	61.2	85,846	56.1	3,408	82,438	7,929	8.5		59,377
1976	156,150	96,158	61.6	88,752	56.8	3,331	85,421	7,406	7.7		59,991
1977	159,033	99,009	62.3	92,017	57.9	3,283	88,734	6,991	7.1		60,025
1978[1]	161,910	102,251	63.2	96,048	59.3	3,387	92,661	6,202	6.1		59,659
1979	164,863	104,962	63.7	98,824	59.9	3,347	95,477	6,137	5.8		59,900
1980	167,745	106,940	63.8	99,303	59.2	3,364	95,938	7,637	7.1		60,806
1981	170,130	108,670	63.9	100,397	59.0	3,368	97,030	8,273	7.6		61,460
1982	172,271	110,204	64.0	99,526	57.8	3,401	96,125	10,678	9.7		62,067
1983	174,215	111,550	64.0	100,834	57.9	3,383	97,450	10,717	9.6		62,665
1984	176,383	113,544	64.4	105,005	59.5	3,321	101,685	8,539	7.5		62,839
1985	178,206	115,461	64.8	107,150	60.1	3,179	103,971	8,312	7.2		62,744
1986[1]	180,587	117,834	65.3	109,597	60.7	3,163	106,434	8,237	7.0		62,752
1987	182,753	119,865	65.6	112,440	61.5	3,208	109,232	7,425	6.2		62,888
1988	184,613	121,669	65.9	114,968	62.3	3,169	111,800	6,701	5.5		62,944
1989	186,393	123,869	66.5	117,342	63.0	3,199	114,142	6,528	5.3		62,523
1990[1]	189,164	125,840	66.5	118,793	62.8	3,223	115,570	7,047	5.6		63,324
1991	190,925	126,346	66.2	117,718	61.7	3,269	114,449	8,628	6.8		64,578
1992	192,805	128,105	66.4	118,492	61.5	3,247	115,245	9,613	7.5		64,700
1993	194,838	129,200	66.3	120,259	61.7	3,115	117,144	8,940	6.9		65,638
1994[1]	196,814	131,056	66.6	123,060	62.5	3,409	119,651	7,996	6.1		65,758
1995	198,584	132,304	66.6	124,900	62.9	3,440	121,460	7,404	5.6		66,280
1996	200,591	133,943	66.8	126,708	63.2	3,443	123,264	7,236	5.4		66,647
1997[1]	203,133	136,297	67.1	129,558	63.8	3,399	126,159	6,739	4.9		66,837
1998[1]	205,220	137,673	67.1	131,463	64.1	3,378	128,085	6,210	4.5		67,547
1999[1]	207,753	139,368	67.1	133,488	64.3	3,281	130,207	5,880	4.2		68,385
Monthly data, seasonally adjusted[2]											
1999:											
April	207,236	139,086	67.1	133,054	64.2	3,341	129,713	6,032	4.3		68,150
May	207,427	139,013	67.0	133,190	64.2	3,290	129,900	5,823	4.2		68,414
June	207,632	139,332	67.1	133,398	64.2	3,330	130,068	5,934	4.3		68,300
July	207,828	139,336	67.0	133,399	64.2	3,278	130,121	5,937	4.3		68,492
August	208,038	139,372	67.0	133,530	64.2	3,234	130,296	5,842	4.2		68,666
September	208,265	139,475	67.0	133,650	64.2	3,179	130,471	5,825	4.2		68,790
October	208,483	139,697	67.0	133,940	64.2	3,238	130,702	5,757	4.1		68,786
November	208,666	139,834	67.0	134,098	64.3	3,310	130,788	5,736	4.1		68,832
December	208,832	140,108	67.1	134,420	64.4	3,279	131,141	5,688	4.1		68,724
2000:											
January[3]	208,782	140,910	67.5	135,221	64.8	3,371	131,850	5,689	4.0		67,872
February	208,907	141,165	67.6	135,362	64.8	3,408	131,954	5,804	4.1		67,742
March	209,053	140,867	67.4	135,159	64.7	3,359	131,801	5,708	4.1		68,187
April	209,216	141,230	67.5	135,706	64.9	3,355	132,351	5,524	3.9		67,986

[1] Not strictly comparable with prior years.

[2] The population figures are not adjusted for seasonal variation.

[3] Beginning in January 2000, data are not strictly comparable with data for 1999 and earlier years because of the introduction of revisions in the population controls used in the household survey.

SOURCE: *Employment and Earnings.* Bureau of Labor Statistics, Jan. 2000

sumer goods, and saving for college spurs the rising youth employment.

Many adults are concerned that high school students are working too many hours. They feel that the main "job" of young people is getting educated—not earning money. Laurence Steinberg, a psychologist at Temple University, in a 10-year survey (1985–95) of 20,000 high school students in California and Wisconsin, found that almost one-third of students who had jobs were often too tired to do their homework. Students who worked more than 20 hours per week earned lower grades and cut more classes than students who did not work or worked fewer hours.

TABLE 1.2

Employment Status of the Civilian Noninstitutional Population by Sex, Age, Race, and Hispanic Origin

(Numbers in thousands)

Employment status, sex, and age	Total		White		Black		Hispanic origin	
	1998	1999	1998	1999	1998	1999	1998	1999
Total								
Civilian noninstitutional population	205,220	207,753	171,478	173,085	24,373	24,855	21,070	21,650
Civilian labor force	137,673	139,368	115,415	116,509	15,982	16,365	14,317	14,665
Percent of population	67.1	67.1	67.3	67.3	65.6	65.8	67.9	67.7
Employed	131,463	133,488	110,931	112,235	14,556	15,056	13,291	13,720
Agriculture	3,378	3,281	3,160	3,083	138	117	742	734
Nonagricultural industries	128,085	130,207	107,770	109,152	14,417	14,939	12,549	12,986
Unemployed	6,210	5,880	4,484	4,273	1,426	1,309	1,026	945
Unemployment rate	4.5	4.2	3.9	3.7	8.9	8.0	7.2	6.4
Not in labor force	67,547	68,385	56,064	56,577	8,391	8,490	6,753	6,985
Men, 16 years and over								
Civilian noninstitutional population	98,758	99,722	83,352	83,930	10,927	11,143	10,734	10,713
Civilian labor force	73,959	74,512	63,034	63,413	7,542	7,652	8,571	8,546
Percent of population	74.9	74.7	75.6	75.6	69.0	68.7	79.8	79.8
Employed	70,693	71,446	60,604	61,139	6,871	7,027	8,018	8,067
Agriculture	2,553	2,432	2,376	2,273	118	99	651	642
Nonagricultural industries	68,140	69,014	58,228	58,866	6,752	6,928	7,367	7,425
Unemployed	3,266	3,066	2,431	2,274	671	626	552	480
Unemployment rate	4.4	4.1	3.9	3.6	8.9	8.2	6.4	5.6
Not in labor force	24,799	25,210	20,317	20,517	3,386	3,491	2,164	2,167
Men, 20 years and over								
Civilian noninstitutional population	90,790	91,555	76,966	77,432	9,727	9,926	9,573	9,523
Civilian labor force	69,715	70,194	59,421	59,747	7,053	7,182	8,005	7,950
Percent of population	76.8	76.7	77.2	77.2	72.5	72.4	83.6	83.5
Employed	67,135	67,761	57,500	57,934	6,530	6,702	7,570	7,576
Agriculture	2,350	2,244	2,182	2,094	112	96	621	602
Nonagricultural industries	64,785	65,517	55,319	55,839	6,418	6,606	6,949	6,974
Unemployed	2,580	2,433	1,920	1,813	524	480	436	374
Unemployment rate	3.7	3.5	3.2	3.0	7.4	6.7	5.4	4.7
Not in labor force	21,075	21,362	17,545	17,685	2,673	2,743	1,568	1,573
Women, 16 years and over								
Civilian noninstitutional population	106,462	108,031	88,126	89,156	13,446	13,711	10,335	10,937
Civilian labor force	63,714	64,855	52,380	53,096	8,441	8,713	5,746	6,119
Percent of population	59.8	60.0	59.4	59.6	62.8	63.5	55.6	55.9
Employed	60,771	62,042	50,327	51,096	7,685	8,029	5,273	5,653
Agriculture	825	849	784	810	20	18	91	92
Nonagricultural industries	59,945	61,193	49,543	50,286	7,665	8,011	5,182	5,561
Unemployed	2,944	2,814	2,053	1,999	756	684	473	466
Unemployment rate	4.6	4.3	3.9	3.8	9.0	7.8	8.2	7.6
Not in labor force	42,748	43,175	35,746	36,060	5,005	4,999	4,589	4,819
Women, 20 years and over								
Civilian noninstitutional population	98,786	100,158	82,073	82,953	12,203	12,451	9,292	9,821
Civilian labor force	59,702	60,840	49,029	49,714	7,912	8,224	5,304	5,666
Percent of population	60.4	60.7	59.7	59.9	64.8	66.1	57.1	57.7
Employed	57,278	58,555	47,342	48,098	7,290	7,663	4,928	5,290
Agriculture	768	803	729	765	19	17	85	88
Nonagricultural industries	56,510	57,752	46,612	47,333	7,272	7,646	4,843	5,202
Unemployed	2,424	2,285	1,688	1,616	622	561	376	376
Unemployment rate	4.1	3.8	3.4	3.3	7.9	6.8	7.1	6.6
Not in labor force	39,084	39,318	33,044	33,239	4,291	4,226	3,988	4,155
Both sexes, 16 to 19 years								
Civilian noninstitutional population	15,644	16,040	12,439	12,700	2,443	2,479	2,204	2,307
Civilian labor force	8,256	8,333	6,965	7,048	1,017	959	1,007	1,049
Percent of population	52.8	52.0	56.0	55.5	41.6	38.7	45.7	45.5
Employed	7,051	7,172	6,089	6,204	736	691	793	854
Agriculture	261	234	250	224	8	4	36	45
Nonagricultural industries	6,790	6,938	5,839	5,980	728	687	757	809
Unemployed	1,205	1,162	876	844	281	268	214	196
Unemployment rate	14.6	13.9	12.6	12.0	27.6	27.9	21.3	18.6
Not in labor force	7,388	7,706	5,475	5,652	1,427	1,520	1,197	1,257

NOTE: Detail for the above race and Hispanic-origin groups will not sum to totals because data for the "other races" group are not presented and Hispanics are included in both the white and black population groups. Beginning in January 1999, data reflect revised population controls used in the household survey.

SOURCE: *Employment and Earnings.* Bureau of Labor Statistics, Jan. 2000

TABLE 1.3

Employment Status of the Civilian Noninstitutional Population by Age, Sex, and Race

(Numbers in thousands)

Age, sex, and race	Civilian noninstitutional population	1999 Civilian labor force		Employed				Unemployed		Not in labor force
		Total	Percent of population	Total	Percent of population	Agriculture	Nonagricultural industries	Number	Percent of labor force	
Total										
16 years and over	207,753	139,368	67.1	133,488	64.3	3,281	130,207	5,880	4.2	68,385
16 to 19 years	16,040	8,333	52.0	7,172	44.7	234	6,938	1,162	13.9	7,706
16 to 17 years	8,060	3,337	41.4	2,793	34.7	107	2,686	544	16.3	4,723
18 to 19 years	7,979	4,996	62.6	4,379	54.9	128	4,251	618	12.4	2,983
20 to 24 years	17,968	13,933	77.5	12,891	71.7	332	12,559	1,042	7.5	4,034
25 to 54 years	118,198	99,414	84.1	96,228	81.4	2,009	94,219	3,186	3.2	18,785
25 to 34 years	37,976	32,143	84.6	30,865	81.3	648	30,218	1,278	4.0	5,833
25 to 29 years	18,339	15,517	84.6	14,836	80.9	318	14,519	681	4.4	2,822
30 to 34 years	19,637	16,626	84.7	16,029	81.6	330	15,699	597	3.6	3,011
35 to 44 years	44,635	37,882	84.9	36,728	82.3	782	35,946	1,154	3.0	6,753
35 to 39 years	22,379	18,937	84.6	18,345	82.0	388	17,957	592	3.1	3,441
40 to 44 years	22,256	18,945	85.1	18,382	82.6	393	17,989	562	3.0	3,311
45 to 54 years	35,587	29,388	82.6	28,635	80.5	580	28,055	753	2.6	6,199
45 to 49 years	19,324	16,330	84.5	15,904	82.3	341	15,563	426	2.6	2,994
50 to 54 years	16,263	13,058	80.3	12,731	78.3	239	12,492	327	2.5	3,205
55 to 64 years	23,064	13,682	59.3	13,315	57.7	422	12,893	367	2.7	9,382
55 to 59 years	12,747	8,895	69.8	8,656	67.9	234	8,422	239	2.7	3,852
60 to 64 years	10,317	4,787	46.4	4,659	45.2	188	4,471	128	2.7	5,530
65 years and over	32,484	4,005	12.3	3,882	11.9	283	3,599	124	3.1	28,478
65 to 69 years	9,281	2,137	23.0	2,065	22.2	120	1,945	72	3.4	7,144
70 to 74 years	8,540	1,116	13.1	1,088	12.7	81	1,007	29	2.6	7,424
75 years and over	14,663	752	5.1	729	5.0	82	648	23	3.0	13,911
Men										
16 years and over	99,722	74,512	74.7	71,446	71.6	2,432	69,014	3,066	4.1	25,210
16 to 19 years	8,167	4,318	52.9	3,685	45.1	188	3,497	633	14.7	3,848
16 to 17 years	4,143	1,732	41.8	1,437	34.7	84	1,353	295	17.0	2,411
18 to 19 years	4,024	2,587	64.3	2,249	55.9	104	2,145	338	13.1	1,437
20 to 24 years	8,899	7,291	81.9	6,729	75.6	259	6,470	562	7.7	1,608
25 to 54 years	57,870	53,093	91.7	51,496	89.0	1,467	50,029	1,597	3.0	4,776
25 to 34 years	18,565	17,318	93.3	16,694	89.9	497	16,198	624	3.6	1,248
25 to 29 years	8,931	8,283	92.7	7,949	89.0	249	7,700	334	4.0	649
30 to 34 years	9,634	9,035	93.8	8,745	90.8	247	8,498	290	3.2	599
35 to 44 years	21,969	20,382	92.8	19,811	90.2	569	19,241	571	2.8	1,587
35 to 39 years	11,026	10,287	93.3	9,999	90.7	301	9,699	288	2.8	739
40 to 44 years	10,942	10,095	92.3	9,811	89.7	269	9,543	283	2.8	848
45 to 54 years	17,335	15,394	88.8	14,991	86.5	401	14,590	403	2.6	1,942
45 to 49 years	9,444	8,532	90.3	8,302	87.9	240	8,062	229	2.7	912
50 to 54 years	7,892	6,862	87.0	6,689	84.8	160	6,528	173	2.5	1,029
55 to 64 years	11,008	7,477	67.9	7,274	66.1	297	6,977	203	2.7	3,531
55 to 59 years	6,123	4,799	78.4	4,671	76.3	160	4,511	128	2.7	1,324
60 to 64 years	4,885	2,678	54.8	2,603	53.3	136	2,466	75	2.8	2,207
65 years and over	13,779	2,333	16.9	2,263	16.4	222	2,041	70	3.0	11,446
65 to 69 years	4,279	1,218	28.5	1,177	27.5	94	1,083	40	3.3	3,062
70 to 74 years	3,776	657	17.4	642	17.0	64	578	15	2.3	3,119
75 years and over	5,724	458	8.0	444	7.8	63	380	14	3.1	5,266
Women										
16 years and over	108,031	64,855	60.0	62,042	57.4	849	61,193	2,814	4.3	43,175
16 to 19 years	7,873	4,015	51.0	3,487	44.3	46	3,440	529	13.2	3,858
16 to 17 years	3,917	1,606	41.0	1,357	34.6	23	1,334	249	15.5	2,312
18 to 19 years	3,955	2,410	60.9	2,130	53.9	23	2,107	280	11.6	1,546
20 to 24 years	9,069	6,643	73.2	6,163	68.0	74	6,089	480	7.2	2,426
25 to 54 years	60,329	46,321	76.8	44,732	74.1	542	44,190	1,588	3.4	14,008
25 to 34 years	19,411	14,826	76.4	14,171	73.0	151	14,020	654	4.4	4,585
25 to 29 years	9,408	7,235	76.9	6,888	73.2	68	6,819	347	4.8	2,173
30 to 34 years	10,003	7,591	75.9	7,284	72.8	83	7,201	307	4.0	2,412
35 to 44 years	22,666	17,501	77.2	16,917	74.6	212	16,705	584	3.3	5,166
35 to 39 years	11,352	8,650	76.2	8,346	73.5	87	8,259	304	3.5	2,702
40 to 44 years	11,314	8,850	78.2	8,571	75.8	125	8,446	279	3.2	2,464
45 to 54 years	18,251	13,994	76.7	13,644	74.8	179	13,465	350	2.5	4,257
45 to 49 years	9,880	7,798	78.9	7,602	76.9	100	7,501	197	2.5	2,082
50 to 54 years	8,371	6,196	74.0	6,042	72.2	78	5,964	154	2.5	2,175

TABLE 1.3

Employment Status of the Civilian Noninstitutional Population by Age, Sex, and Race [CONTINUED]

(Numbers in thousands)

Age, sex, and race	Civilian noninstitutional population	1999								
		Civilian labor force								
		Total	Percent of population	Employed				Unemployed		Not in labor force
				Total	Percent of population	Agriculture	Nonagricultural industries	Number	Percent of labor force	
Women (cont.)										
55 to 64 years	12,056	6,204	51.5	6,041	50.1	126	5,915	163	2.6	5,851
55 to 59 years	6,624	4,096	61.8	3,985	60.2	74	3,911	110	2.7	2,528
60 to 64 years	5,432	2,109	38.8	2,056	37.8	52	2,004	53	2.5	3,323
65 years and over	18,705	1,673	8.9	1,619	8.7	61	1,558	54	3.2	17,032
65 to 69 years	5,002	920	18.4	888	17.7	26	862	32	3.5	4,082
70 to 74 years	4,764	459	9.6	446	9.4	17	429	13	2.9	4,305
75 years and over	8,939	294	3.3	286	3.2	18	267	9	2.9	8,645

SOURCE: *Employment and Earnings.* Bureau of Labor Statistics, Jan. 2000

Researchers at the University of North Carolina's Injury Prevention Research Center concluded that student jobs, such as cashiers, sales clerks, and fast food service workers, are often not very challenging, and impose significant time pressure and stress. The researchers thought the students would benefit more from student activities and reading. Others claim that jobs challenge students and teach them greater responsibility.

Of the 301 students who responded to the survey by the Occupational Health Surveillance Program, Massachusetts Department of Public Health, 75 percent said they worked for spending money. Fifty percent wanted to buy something expensive, 33 percent were saving for future schooling, 23 percent helped support their families, and 2 percent were supporting themselves.

EDUCATION

The more years of education, the more likely the person will be part of the labor force and the less likely to be unemployed. College graduates had the highest labor force participation (79.9 percent) and the lowest unemployment rate (1.8 percent). On the other hand, those with less than a high school diploma had a labor force participation rate of 42.7 percent and an unemployment rate of 6.7 percent. Better-educated workers of any gender or racial group were also more likely to be in the labor force and employed. (See Table 1.4.) See Chapter 4 for more information on the relationship between labor force participation and education.

FAMILIES

In 1998, 82.6 percent of the nation's 70.2 million families had at least one employed person. Black families continued to be less likely to include an employed member (78.8 percent) than were either white or Hispanic families (82.9.percent and 84.7 percent, respectively).

(See Table 1.5.) It should be noted that these data include families that may have members who are beyond the generally accepted working age.

About 4.5 million families (6.4 percent of all families) had at least one person who was unemployed in 1998. Almost 71 percent of all families that included an unemployed person also contained at least one employed family member. White families were considerably less likely to have an unemployed person (5.6 percent) than were black (11.8 percent) or Hispanic (10.6 percent) families. (See Table 1.5.)

In 1998, in 28.5 million families, both the husband and wife worked. These employed couples comprised a little over half of all married couples (53.7 million) in 1998. There were 10.3 million "traditional" couples in which only the husband was employed outside the house. In another 2.8 million families, only the wife worked. (See Table 1.6.)

Married-couple families (83.9 percent) and families maintained by men (85.9 percent) were more likely to include an employed person than families maintained by women (75.7 percent). (See Table 1.6.) There were far fewer families with an unemployed member that were maintained by men (388,000) than women (1.3 million). (See Table 1.7.)

About eight of ten married-couple families (83.2 percent) with an unemployed member also contained at least one employed family member. In contrast, roughly half of the families with unemployment that were maintained by men (59 percent) or women (46.5 percent) also included an employed person. (See Table 1.7.)

In 1998 both parents were employed in 64.1 percent of married-couple families with children under 18 years old. In just 28.9 percent of two-parent families, the father, but not the mother, was employed. The proportion in which the father, but not the mother, was employed was

FIGURE 1.1

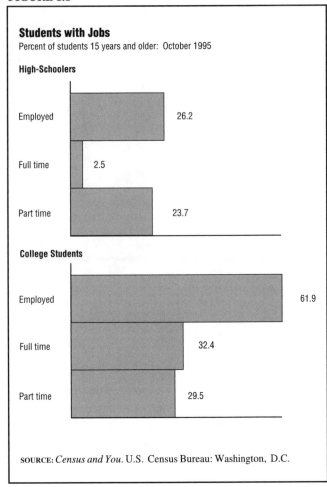

Students with Jobs
Percent of students 15 years and older: October 1995

High-Schoolers

Employed — 26.2

Full time — 2.5

Part time — 23.7

College Students

Employed — 61.9

Full time — 32.4

Part time — 29.5

SOURCE: *Census and You.* U.S. Census Bureau: Washington, D.C.

much higher among families with preschool children (under six years of age) (36.2 percent) than it was in families whose youngest child was six to 17 years old (22.8 percent). (See Table 1.8.)

In 1998 more than nine of ten fathers (94.6 percent) and seven of ten mothers (71.8 percent) were labor-force participants. Among the mothers, the participation rate for those who were unmarried (single, widowed, divorced, or separated) (76.7 percent), was similar to the rate for married mothers (70 percent). (See Table 1.9.)

In 1998 the unemployment rate of married mothers was 3.3 percent, compared to a 9.3 percent rate for unmarried mothers. The unemployment rate for mothers with preschool children (6.5 percent) continued to be higher than the rate for mothers whose youngest child was of school age (4.1 percent). (See Table 1.9.)

In 1997 more than half (57.9 percent) of all mothers of children under one year old were in the labor force. This proportion rose among mothers with children two years of age (65.8 percent). These proportions remained nearly the same in 1998, with 57.9 percent of all mothers with children under one year in the labor force and 64.4 of mothers in the labor force with children two years of age.

Unmarried mothers during 1997 with children under one year of age were somewhat less likely to be in the labor force (54.0 percent) than were married mothers with children the same age (59.2 percent). In 1998, 58.8 percent of unmarried mothers with children under one year were in the workforce, while 70.7 percent of unmarried mothers with children that were two years old were in the workforce. (See Table 1.10.)

THE WORKING POOR

In 1997, 35.6 million persons (13.3 percent of the population) lived at or below the official poverty level. Although the nation's poor were primarily children and adults who were not in the labor force, one in five (7.5 million persons in the labor force) were classified as "working poor." The working poor are individuals who spent at least 27 weeks in the labor force but whose income still fell below the official poverty threshold. (In 1996 the poverty threshold for one person was $7,995.) The poverty rate for those who worked for at least 27 weeks was 5.4 percent. (See Table 1.11.)

Over half of workers below the poverty level (52 percent) usually worked full-time, although full-time work substantially lowers a person's probability of being poor. Among persons in the labor force for 27 weeks or more, the poverty rate for those usually employed full-time was 4 percent compared with 11.9 percent for usually part-time workers. (See Table 1.11.) Only 7 percent of the workers below the poverty level actively looked for a job for more than six months in 1997, but ended up not working at all.

Gender, Race, and Age

Of all persons in the labor force for at least 27 weeks, more women (almost 4.0 million) than men (3.5 million) were poor. The poverty rate was higher for working women (6.7 percent) than men (4.9 percent), as fewer of them were in the labor force for more than half of the year. (See Table 1.12.)

While nearly three-fourths of the working poor were white workers, black and Hispanic workers continued to experience poverty rates that were more than twice the rates of whites. White working women (5.5 percent) and men (4.5 percent) in the labor force for more than half of the year were about equally likely to be poor. By contrast, black working women had a poverty rate of 14.6 percent, almost twice the rate of black working men (7.9 percent). (See Table 1.12.)

Younger workers were most vulnerable to being poor, particularly minority teenagers. High poverty rates among younger workers largely reflect the lower earnings and higher rates of unemployment associated with having relatively little education and work experience. (See Table 1.12.)

TABLE 1.4

Employment Status of the Civilian Noninstitutional Population 25 Years and Over by Educational Attainment, Sex, Race, and Hispanic Origin

(Numbers in thousands)

Educational attainment	Total		Men		Women		White		Black		Hispanic origin	
	1998	1999	1998	1999	1998	1999	1998	1999	1998	1999	1998	1999
Total												
Civilian noninstitutional population	171,983	173,746	81,986	82,657	89,997	91,089	144,900	145,992	19,384	19,761	16,134	16,644
Civilian labor force	115,779	117,101	62,494	62,903	53,285	54,198	97,206	98,025	13,168	13,540	11,232	11,563
Percent of population	67.3	67.4	76.2	76.1	59.2	59.5	67.1	67.1	67.9	68.5	69.6	69.5
Employed	111,855	113,425	60,497	61,032	51,359	52,392	94,330	95,316	12,324	12,771	10,615	10,985
Employment-population ratio	65.0	65.3	73.8	73.8	57.1	57.5	65.1	65.3	63.6	64.6	65.8	66.0
Unemployed	3,924	3,676	1,998	1,870	1,926	1,805	2,877	2,709	844	768	617	578
Unemployment rate	3.4	3.1	3.2	3.0	3.6	3.3	3.0	2.8	6.4	5.7	5.5	5.0
Less than a high school diploma												
Civilian noninstitutional population	29,375	28,337	13,975	13,388	15,400	14,948	23,557	22,765	4,459	4,247	7,138	7,189
Civilian labor force	12,561	12,110	7,711	7,347	4,850	4,763	10,146	9,815	1,785	1,684	4,191	4,226
Percent of population	42.8	42.7	55.2	54.9	31.5	31.9	43.1	43.1	40.0	39.6	58.7	58.8
Employed	11,673	11,294	7,238	6,921	4,435	4,372	9,510	9,235	1,579	1,488	3,889	3,926
Employment-population ratio	39.7	39.9	51.8	51.7	28.8	29.2	40.4	40.6	35.4	35.0	54.5	54.6
Unemployed	887	817	472	426	415	391	635	580	207	196	303	300
Unemployment rate	7.1	6.7	6.1	5.8	8.6	8.2	6.3	5.9	11.6	11.6	7.2	7.1
High school graduates, no college												
Civilian noninstitutional population	57,524	57,559	26,212	26,158	31,313	31,402	48,709	48,629	6,910	7,008	4,296	4,566
Civilian labor force	37,465	37,327	19,961	19,785	17,504	17,542	31,313	31,145	4,864	4,944	3,195	3,370
Percent of population	65.1	64.8	76.2	75.6	55.9	55.9	64.3	64.0	70.4	70.5	74.4	73.8
Employed	35,976	36,017	19,188	19,125	16,788	16,893	30,249	30,211	4,504	4,631	3,018	3,213
Employment-population ratio	62.5	62.6	73.2	73.1	53.6	53.8	62.1	62.1	65.2	66.1	70.2	70.4
Unemployed	1,489	1,310	773	661	717	649	1,064	934	360	313	177	158
Unemployment rate	4.0	3.5	3.9	3.3	4.1	3.7	3.4	3.0	7.4	6.3	5.5	4.7
Less than a bachelor's degree[1]												
Civilian noninstitutional population	42,261	43,358	19,488	19,997	22,773	23,360	35,643	36,349	5,042	5,318	2,934	3,049
Civilian labor force	31,412	32,115	15,860	16,212	15,552	15,903	26,211	26,621	4,000	4,219	2,373	2,437
Percent of population	74.3	74.1	81.4	81.1	68.3	68.1	73.5	73.2	79.3	79.3	80.9	79.9
Employed	30,477	31,209	15,415	15,778	15,062	15,430	25,527	25,944	3,795	4,032	2,282	2,356
Employment-population ratio	72.1	72.0	79.1	78.9	66.1	66.1	71.6	71.4	75.3	75.8	77.8	77.3
Unemployed	935	906	445	434	489	473	685	677	204	187	91	81
Unemployment rate	3.0	2.8	2.8	2.7	3.1	3.0	2.6	2.5	5.1	4.4	3.8	3.3
Some college, no degree												
Civilian noninstitutional population	29,526	30,111	13,883	14,192	15,642	15,919	24,715	25,077	3,768	3,895	2,120	2,205
Civilian labor force	21,311	21,778	11,018	11,251	10,293	10,527	17,592	17,863	2,938	3,067	1,689	1,755
Percent of population	72.2	72.3	79.4	79.3	65.8	66.1	71.2	71.2	78.0	78.7	79.7	79.6
Employed	20,626	21,129	10,684	10,941	9,943	10,189	17,101	17,388	2,776	2,924	1,622	1,696
Employment-population ratio	69.9	70.2	77.0	77.1	63.6	64.0	69.2	69.3	73.7	75.1	76.5	76.9
Unemployed	684	648	335	310	350	338	491	475	162	143	68	60
Unemployment rate	3.2	3.0	3.0	2.8	3.4	3.2	2.8	2.7	5.5	4.7	4.0	3.4
Associate degree												
Civilian noninstitutional population	12,735	13,247	5,604	5,806	7,131	7,441	10,928	11,272	1,273	1,423	814	844
Civilian labor force	10,101	10,337	4,842	4,961	5,259	5,376	8,619	8,758	1,061	1,152	683	682
Percent of population	79.3	78.0	86.4	85.4	73.7	72.2	78.9	77.7	83.4	81.0	84.0	80.8
Employed	9,850	10,079	4,731	4,838	5,119	5,242	8,426	8,556	1,020	1,108	660	660
Employment-population ratio	77.3	76.1	84.4	83.3	71.8	70.4	77.1	75.9	80.1	77.9	81.1	78.3
Unemployed	251	258	111	123	140	134	193	202	42	44	23	21
Unemployment rate	2.5	2.5	2.3	2.5	2.7	2.5	2.2	2.3	3.9	3.8	3.4	3.1
College graduates												
Civilian noninstitutional population	42,822	44,492	22,312	23,113	20,510	21,379	36,991	38,249	2,973	3,188	1,766	1,840
Civilian labor force	34,342	35,548	18,963	19,558	15,379	15,990	29,537	30,444	2,520	2,693	1,474	1,530
Percent of population	80.2	79.9	85.0	84.6	75.0	74.8	79.8	79.6	84.7	84.5	83.4	83.2
Employed	33,730	34,905	18,656	19,208	15,074	15,697	29,044	29,925	2,446	2,621	1,427	1,491
Employment-population ratio	78.8	78.5	83.6	83.1	73.5	73.4	78.5	78.2	82.3	82.2	80.8	81.0
Unemployed	612	643	307	350	305	293	493	519	74	73	47	39
Unemployment rate	1.8	1.8	1.6	1.8	2.0	1.8	1.7	1.7	2.9	2.7	3.2	2.6

[1] Includes the categories, some college, no degree, and associate degree.

NOTE: Detail for the above race and Hispanic-origin groups will not sum to totals because data for the "other races" group are not presented and Hispanics are included in both the white and black population groups. Beginning in January 1999, data reflect revised population controls used in the household survey.

SOURCE: *Employment and Earnings.* Bureau of Labor Statistics, Jan. 2000

TABLE 1.5

Employment and Unemployment in Families by Race and Hispanic Origin, 1997–1998 Annual Averages

(Numbers in thousands)

Characteristic	1997	1998
Total		
Total families	69,714	70,218
With employed member(s)	57,289	57,986
As percent of total families	82.2	82.6
Some usually work full time[1]	53,226	53,945
With no employed member	12,425	12,232
As percent of total families	17.8	17.4
With unemployed member(s)	4,913	4,503
As percent of total families	7.0	6.4
Some member(s) employed	3,445	3,177
As percent of families with unemployed member(s)	70.1	70.6
Some usually work full time[1]	3,070	2,830
As percent of families with unemployed member(s)	62.5	62.8
White		
Total families	58,514	58,930
With employed member(s)	48,378	48,850
As percent of total families	82.7	82.9
Some usually work full time[1]	45,069	45,567
With no employed member	10,135	10,080
As percent of total families	17.3	17.1
With unemployed member(s)	3,566	3,299
As percent of total families	6.1	5.6
Some member(s) employed	2,632	2,463
As percent of families with unemployed member(s)	73.8	74.7
Some usually work full time[1]	2,353	2,204
As percent of families with unemployed member(s)	66.0	66.8
Black		
Total families	8,308	8,317
With employed member(s)	6,409	6,554
As percent of total families	77.1	78.8
Some usually work full time[1]	5,810	5,953
With no employed member	1,899	1,763
As percent of total families	22.9	21.2
With unemployed member(s)	1,104	984
As percent of total families	13.3	11.8
Some member(s) employed	631	555
As percent of families with unemployed member(s)	57.2	56.4
Some usually work full time[1]	553	485
As percent of families with unemployed member(s)	50.1	49.3
Hispanic origin		
Total families	6,779	7,025
With employed member(s)	5,701	5,947
As percent of total families	84.1	84.7
Some usually work full time[1]	5,285	5,545
With no employed member	1,078	1,078
As percent of total families	15.9	15.3
With unemployed member(s)	789	744
As percent of total families	11.6	10.6
Some member(s) employed	532	522
As percent of families with unemployed member(s)	67.4	70.2
Some usually work full time[1]	473	467
As percent of families with unemployed member(s)	59.9	62.8

TABLE 1.5

Employment and Unemployment in Families by Race and Hispanic Origin, 1997–1998 Annual Averages [CONTINUED]

(Numbers in thousands)

[1] Usually work 35 hours or more a week at all jobs.

Note: Detail for the above race and Hispanic-origin groups will not sum to totals because data for the "other races" group are not presented and Hispanics are included in both the white and black population groups. Data for 1998 are not strictly comparable with data for 1997 and earlier years because of the introduction of new composite estimation procedures and revised population controls in the household survey in January 1998. Detail may not sum to totals due to rounding.

SOURCE: *Employment Characteristics of Families*. Bureau of Labor Statistics, May 1999

for black workers than for white workers at all education levels. (See Table 1.13.)

The poverty rate for black women workers with less than a high school diploma was 30 percent, compared to 19.3 percent for black men. Among high school graduates, the poverty rate for black women (17.6 percent) was more than twice that of black men (7.8 percent). Among black college graduates, however, poverty rates decreased, though black women still had a poverty rate of almost twice (3.1 percent) that of black men (1.6 percent). Poverty rates of white men and women were fairly similar at all education levels. (See Table 1.13.)

Occupations

During 1997 nearly three-fourths (73 percent) of the working poor were employed in one of the following occupational groups: service, technical, sales, and administrative support; or were operators, fabricators, and laborers. Not surprisingly, persons working in managerial and professional specialty occupations have the lowest probability of being poor. In all occupational groups, women were more likely than men to be poor, and blacks were more likely to be below the poverty level than whites. (See Table 1.14.)

About 12.1 percent of those employed in service occupations were living in poverty. Female service workers (14.2 percent) had a higher poverty rate than did their male counterparts (9.2 percent). Household service workers (housekeepers, child-care workers, and cooks), almost all of whom were women, had a poverty rate of 22.4 percent. Protective service providers, such as firefighters, policemen, and guards, 84 percent of whom were men, reported a poverty rate of only 3.1 percent. The overall poverty rate for black service providers (17.3 percent) was considerably higher than that for whites (10.9 percent). (See Table 1.14.)

The poverty rates for women and men employed in administrative support occupations were 3.5 percent and 2.4 percent respectively. Poverty rates for working

Education

Among all persons in the labor force for at least half of 1997, those with less than a high school diploma had a higher poverty rate (15.8 percent) than high school graduates (6.5 percent). Workers with an associate degree (3.1 percent) or college graduates (1.5 percent) reported the lowest poverty rates. Poverty rates generally were higher

TABLE 1.6

Families by Presence and Relationship of Employed Members and Family Type, 1997–1998 Annual Averages

(Numbers in thousands)

Characteristic	Number 1997	Number 1998	Percent distribution 1997	Percent distribution 1998
Married-Couple Families				
Total	53,248	53,689	100.0	100.0
Member(s) employed, total	44,641	45,061	83.8	83.9
Husband only	9,959	10,285	18.7	19.2
Wife only	2,839	2,843	5.3	5.3
Husband and wife	28,422	28,531	53.4	53.1
Other employment combinations	3,421	3,402	6.4	6.3
No member(s) employed	8,607	8,628	16.2	16.1
Familes Maintained By Women[1]				
Total	12,524	12,447	100.0	100.0
Members(s) employed, total	9,263	9,417	74.0	75.7
Householder only	5,282	5,322	42.2	42.8
Householder and other member(s)	2,484	2,582	19.8	20.7
Other member(s), not householder	1,497	1,513	12.0	12.2
No member(s) employed	3,261	3,029	26.0	24.3
Families Maintained By Men[1]				
Total	3,942	4,083	100.0	100.0
Members(s) employed, total	3,385	3,509	85.9	85.9
Householder only	1,703	1,746	43.2	42.8
Householder and other member(s)	1,228	1,283	31.2	31.4
Other member(s), not householder	455	480	11.5	11.8
No member(s) employed	557	574	14.1	14.1

[1] No spouse present.

Note: Data for 1998 are not strictly comparable with data for 1997 and earlier years because of the introduction of new composite estimation procedures and revised population controls in the household survey in January 1998. Detail may not sum to totals due to rounding.

SOURCE: *Employment Characteristics of Families.* Bureau of Labor Statistics, May 1999

TABLE 1.7

Unemployment in Families by Presence and Relationship of Employed Members and Family Type, 1997–1998 Annual Averages

(Numbers in thousands)

Characteristic	Number 1997	Number 1998	Percent distribution 1997	Percent distribution 1998
Married-Couple Families				
With unemployed member(s), total	3,056	2,815	100.0	100.0
No member employed	530	471	17.3	16.7
Some member(s) employed	2,526	2,343	82.7	83.2
Husband unemployed	1,048	948	34.3	33.7
Wife employed	651	594	21.3	21.1
Wife unemployed	906	844	29.6	30.0
Husband employed	787	745	25.8	26.5
Other family member unemployed	1,102	1,023	36.1	36.3
Families Maintained By Women[1]				
With unemployed member(s), total	1,456	1,301	100.0	100.0
No member employed	782	696	53.7	53.5
Some member(s) employed	674	605	46.3	46.5
Householder unemployed	694	612	47.7	47.0
Other member(s) employed	122	99	8.4	7.6
Other member(s) unemployed	572	512	39.3	39.4
Families Maintained By Men[1]				
With unemployed member(s), total	400	388	100.0	100.0
No member employed	156	158	39.0	40.7
Some member(s) employed	244	229	61.0	59.0
Householder unemployed	197	186	49.2	47.9
Other member(s) employed	77	69	19.2	17.8
Other member(s) unemployed	204	202	51.0	52.1

[1] No spouse present.

Note: Data for 1998 are not strictly comparable with data for 1997 and earlier years because of the introduction of new composite estimation procedures and revised population controls in the household survey in January 1998. Detail may not sum to totals due to rounding.

SOURCE: *Employment Characteristics of Families.* Bureau of Labor Statistics, May 1999

women (1.5 percent) and men (1.6 percent) in technical occupations were similar. However, the poverty rate for women (9.5 percent) employed in sales occupations was more than two times that of their male counterparts (3.6 percent), largely because women tend to hold very different types of sales jobs than men. (See Table 1.14.) In fact, the earnings difference between men and women in sales is larger than it is in any other major occupational group. Generally, women are more likely to work in lower paying retail sales positions, while men are more likely to work in higher paying wholesale sales positions. (See Chapter 6 for information on earnings.)

Family Structure

In 1997 nearly 4.1 million families lived below the poverty level despite having at least one member in the labor market for 27 weeks or more. Of these, nearly half were families maintained by women (1.8 million). The poverty rate for families (the ratio of poor families with workers to all families with workers) was 6.9 percent. Not surprisingly, the poverty rate for families with just one member in the labor force (14.4 percent) was over seven times more than that of families with two or more members in the workforce (1.9 percent). Families maintained by women with only one member in the labor force (with a poverty rate of 25.8 percent) were nearly two times more likely to be poor than similar families maintained by men (13.6 percent). Married-couple families with two or more members in the labor force had the lowest poverty rate (1.5 percent). (See Table 1.15.)

EMPLOYMENT BY INDUSTRY

In 1999 four times as many people worked in the service-producing industry (103.4 million) than in the goods-producing industry (25.2 million). Almost 19 million of those in the goods-producing industry worked in manufacturing. More than half (59 percent) of those produced durable goods, while 41 percent produced nondurable goods. In the service-producing industry sector, more than one-third (37.8 percent) were in service industry jobs. Retail trade accounted for another 22 percent of service-producing industry workers. (See Table 1.16.) It is important to understand the difference between a service industry and a service occupation. A service industry provides a service to the economy but employs more than

TABLE 1.8

Families with Own Children—Employment Status of Parents by Age of Youngest Child and Family Type, 1997–1998 Annual Averages

(Numbers in thousands)

Characteristic	Number		Percent distribution	
	1997	1998	1997	1998
With Own Children Under 18 Years				
Total	34,129	34,232	100.0	100.0
Parent(s) employed	30,761	31,100	90.1	90.9
No parent employed	3,369	3,130	9.9	9.1
Married-couple families	24,762	24,820	100.0	100.0
Parent(s) employed	23,987	24,088	96.9	97.1
Mother employed	17,013	16,911	68.7	68.1
Both parents employed	15,964	15,906	64.5	64.1
Mother employed, not father	1,049	1,005	4.2	4.0
Father employed, not mother	6,974	7,178	28.2	28.9
Neither parent employed	775	731	3.1	2.9
Families maintained by women[1]	7,623	7,573	100.0	100.0
Mother employed	5,276	5,440	69.2	71.8
Mother not employed	2,347	2,133	30.8	28.2
Families maintained by men[1]	1,745	1,839	100.0	100.0
Father employed	1,498	1,572	85.8	85.5
Father not employed	247	266	14.2	14.5
With Own Children 6 to 17 Years, None Younger				
Total	18,989	19,209	100.0	100.0
Parent(s) employed	17,274	17,551	91.0	91.4
No parent employed	1,714	1,658	9.0	8.6
Married-couple families	13,442	13,496	100.0	100.0
Parent(s) employed	13,000	13,065	96.7	96.8
Mother employed	10,061	9,991	74.8	74.0
Both parents employed	9,379	9,338	69.8	69.2
Mother employed, not father	682	653	5.1	4.8
Father employed, not mother	2,939	3,074	21.9	22.8
Neither parent employed	442	431	3.3	3.2
Families maintained by women[1]	4,531	4,638	100.0	100.0
Mother employed	3,393	3,573	74.9	77.0
Mother not employed	1,138	1,065	25.1	23.0
Families maintained by men[1]	1,015	1,075	100.0	100.0
Father employed	881	913	86.8	84.9
Father not employed	134	162	13.2	15.1
With Children Under 6 Years				
Total	15,141	15,023	100.0	100.0
Parent(s) employed	13,487	13,550	89.1	90.2
No parent employed	1,654	1,473	10.9	9.8
Married-couple families	11,320	11,324	100.0	100.0
Parent(s) employed	10,988	11,023	97.1	97.3
Mother employed	6,952	6,920	61.4	61.1
Both parents employed	6,585	6,567	58.2	58.0
Mother employed, not father	368	352	3.3	3.1
Father employed, not mother	4,034	4,103	35.6	36.2
Neither parent employed	333	301	2.9	2.7
Families maintained by women[1]	3,092	2,936	100.0	100.0
Mother employed	1,882	1,867	60.9	63.6
Mother not employed	1,209	1,068	39.1	36.4
Families maintained by men[1]	729	763	100.0	100.0
Father employed	617	660	84.6	86.5
Father not employed	112	104	15.4	13.6

[1] No spouse present.

NOTE: Own children include sons, daughters, step-children and adopted children. Not included are nieces, nephews, grandchildren, and other related and unrelated children. Data for 1998 are not strictly comparable with data for 1997 and earlier years because of the introduction of new composite estimation procedures and revised population controls in the household survey in January 1998. Detail may not sum to totals due to rounding.

SOURCE: *Employment Characteristics of Families*. Bureau of Labor Statistics, May 1999

service workers. For example, a restaurant is a service industry. It may employ workers involved in service, such as waiters, but also employs secretaries, managers, and accountants, whose occupations are not considered service occupations.

EMPLOYMENT BY OCCUPATION

In 1997 white-collar employment accounted for 58.7 percent of the total U.S. workforce; blue-collar for 25.1 percent; service jobs for 13.5 percent; and farming, fishing, and forestry for 2.7 percent. Professional, administrative, and managerial workers each accounted for one-quarter of the white-collar work force. (See Figure 1.2.)

In 1999 a nearly equal proportion of workers was employed in managerial or professional jobs (30.3 percent) and in technical, sales, or administration fields (29.2 percent). Other leading occupational categories were operators, fabricators, and laborers (13.6 percent); service occupations (13.4 percent); and precision production, craft, and repair (10.9 percent). (See Table 1.17.)

Women were far more likely than men to work in administrative support, including clerical, and in service occupations. Men dominated such categories as precision production, craft, and repair; fabrication and labor; and farming, forestry, and fishing. (See Table 1.17.)

Blacks were less likely than whites to work in managerial and professional specialties, sales, and precision production positions. Blacks were more likely than whites to work as operators, fabricators, and laborers and in service occupations. Black women were more likely to be in managerial and professional specialties, sales positions, administrative support positions, and service jobs than black men. (See Table 1.17.)

Almost one-quarter (24 percent) of Hispanic-origin workers were in the technical, sales, and administrative support field, with more than half working in administrative support, including clerical. Operators, fabricators, and laborers accounted for another 22 percent, while one-fifth (20 percent) labored in service occupations. (See Table 1.18.) (Hispanic refers to an ethnic group, not a racial category. Here, black and white statistics include Hispanics.)

Hispanic-origin employees (15 percent) were less likely than blacks (21 percent) and whites (31 percent) to be in the managerial and professional specialty occupations. Although only 5.8 percent of Hispanics worked in farming, forestry, and fishing, they were more likely to do so than whites (2.8 percent) and blacks (1.1 percent). (See Tables 1.17 and 1.18.)

EMPLOYEE TENURE

Data on tenure (how long a person has worked for his/her current employer) are often used to gauge employ-

TABLE 1.9

Employment Status of the Population by Sex, Marital Status, and Presence and Age of Own Children Under 18, 1997–1998 Annual Averages
(Numbers in thousands)

Characteristic	1997			1998		
	Total	Men	Women	Total	Men	Women
With Own Children Under 18 Years						
Civilian noninstitutional population	62,787	27,349	35,438	62,912	27,489	35,423
Civilian labor force	51,343	25,877	25,466	51,462	26,018	25,443
Participation rate	81.8	94.6	71.9	81.8	94.6	71.8
Employed	49,178	25,111	24,067	49,480	25,333	24,147
Employment-population ratio	78.3	91.8	67.9	78.6	92.2	68.2
Full-time workers[1]	41,934	24,306	17,628	42,372	24,562	17,811
Part-time workers[2]	7,244	806	6,439	7,108	771	6,337
Unemployed	2,165	766	1,399	1,981	686	1,296
Unemployment rate	4.2	3.0	5.5	3.8	2.6	5.1
Married, spouse present						
Civilian noninstitutional population	50,995	25,292	25,704	51,061	25,325	25,737
Civilian labor force	42,192	24,027	18,165	42,088	24,080	18,009
Participation rate	82.7	95.0	70.7	82.4	95.1	70.0
Employed	40,918	23,383	17,535	40,914	23,506	17,408
Employment-population ratio	80.2	92.5	68.2	80.1	92.8	67.6
Full-time workers[1]	35,042	22,685	12,357	35,197	22,839	12,357
Part-time workers[2]	5,877	698	5,179	5,718	667	5,051
Unemployed	1,273	644	630	1,174	573	601
Unemployment rate	3.0	2.7	3.5	2.8	2.4	3.3
Other marital status[3]						
Civilian noninstitutional population	11,791	2,057	9,734	11,851	2,166	9,686
Civilian labor force	9,151	1,850	7,301	9,374	1,939	7,434
Participation rate	77.6	89.9	75.0	79.1	89.5	76.7
Employed	8,259	1,728	6,531	8,565	1,826	6,739
Employment-population ratio	70.0	84.0	67.1	72.3	84.3	69.6
Full-time workers[1]	6,893	1,621	5,272	7,177	1,724	5,453
Part-time workers[2]	1,367	107	1,261	1,391	104	1,286
Unemployed	891	123	770	807	113	695
Unemployment rate	9.7	6.6	10.5	8.6	5.8	9.3
With Own Children 6 to 17 Years, None Younger						
Civilian noninstitutional population	33,997	14,822	19,175	34,329	14,947	19,383
Civilian labor force	28,812	13,877	14,935	29,003	13,969	15,033
Participation rate	84.7	93.6	77.9	84.5	93.5	77.6
Employed	27,752	13,480	14,273	28,046	13,629	14,417
Employment-population ratio	81.6	90.9	74.4	81.7	91.2	74.4
Full-time workers[1]	23,885	13,071	10,814	24,286	13,238	11,048
Part-time workers[2]	3,868	409	3,459	3,760	391	3,369
Unemployed	1,060	397	662	957	340	617
Unemployment rate	3.7	2.9	4.4	3.3	2.4	4.1
With Children Under 6 Years						
Civilian noninstitutional population	28,789	12,526	16,263	28,583	12,543	16,040
Civilian labor force	22,530	12,000	10,531	22,459	12,049	10,410
Participation rate	78.3	95.8	64.8	78.6	96.1	64.9
Employed	21,426	11,632	9,794	21,434	11,703	9,731
Employment-population ratio	74.4	92.9	60.2	75.0	93.3	60.7
Full-time workers[1]	18,049	11,235	6,814	18,086	11,323	6,763
Part-time workers[2]	3,376	397	2,980	3,348	380	2,968
Unemployed	1,105	368	737	1,025	346	679
Unemployment rate	4.9	3.1	7.0	4.6	2.9	6.5
With No Children Under 18 Years						
Civilian noninstitutional population	138,365	68,385	69,980	140,436	69,396	71,040
Civilian labor force	83,524	45,847	37,677	84,735	46,464	38,271
Participation rate	60.4	67.0	53.8	60.3	67.0	53.9
Employed	78,917	43,045	35,873	80,545	43,922	36,623
Employment-population ratio	57.0	62.9	51.3	57.4	63.3	51.6
Full-time workers[1]	62,902	36,452	26,449	64,429	37,226	27,203
Part-time workers[2]	16,016	6,592	9,424	16,116	6,696	9,420
Unemployed	4,606	2,802	1,804	4,190	2,542	1,648
Unemployment rate	5.5	6.1	4.8	4.9	5.5	4.3

[1] Usually work 35 hours or more a week at all jobs.
[2] Usually work less than 35 hours a week at all jobs.
[3] Includes never-married, divorced, separated and widowed persons.

SOURCE: *Employment Characteristics of Families.* Bureau of Labor Statistics, May 1999

TABLE 1.10

Employment Status of Mothers with Own Children Under 3 Years Old by Single Year of Age of Youngest Child, and Marital Status, 1997–1998 Annual Averages

(Numbers in thousands)

| | | Civilian labor force | | | | | | | |
| | Civilian noninsti-tutional population | | | | | Employed | | Unemployed | |
Characteristic		Total	Percent of population	Total	Percent of population	Full-time workers[1]	Part-time workers[2]	Number	Percent of labor force
1997									
TOTAL MOTHERS									
With children under 3 years old	9,347	5,738	61.4	5,306	56.8	3,560	1,746	432	7.5
2 years	2,871	1,890	65.8	1,763	61.4	1,208	555	127	6.7
1 year	3,306	2,012	60.9	1,851	56.0	1,205	646	161	8.0
Under 1 year	3,170	1,836	57.9	1,692	53.4	1,147	545	144	7.8
Married, spouse present									
With children under 3 years old	7,049	4,296	60.9	4,105	58.2	2,718	1,387	191	4.4
2 years	2,142	1,380	64.4	1,327	62.0	883	444	53	3.8
1 year	2,459	1,468	59.7	1,399	56.9	890	509	69	4.7
Under 1 year	2,448	1,448	59.2	1,379	56.3	945	434	69	4.8
Other marital status[3]									
With children under 3 years old	2,297	1,445	62.9	1,201	52.3	842	361	241	16.7
2 years	729	511	70.1	436	59.8	325	112	74	14.5
1 year	847	545	64.3	452	53.4	315	138	92	16.9
Under 1 year	721	389	54.0	313	43.4	202	111	75	19.3
1998									
TOTAL MOTHERS									
With children under 3 years old	9,333	5,779	61.9	5,384	57.7	3,626	1,758	395	6.8
2 years	2,772	1,786	64.4	1,673	60.4	1,149	524	113	6.3
1 year	3,213	2,055	64.0	1,917	59.7	1,281	636	138	6.7
Under 1 year	3,348	1,938	57.9	1,794	53.6	1,196	598	144	7.4
Married, spouse present									
With children under 3 years old	7,110	4,316	60.7	4,145	58.3	2,765	1,380	171	4.0
2 years	2,073	1,291	62.3	1,244	60.0	831	413	47	3.6
1 year	2,493	1,560	62.6	1,497	60.0	989	508	63	4.0
Under 1 year	2,544	1,465	57.6	1,404	55.2	945	459	61	4.2
Other marital status[3]									
With children under 3 years old	2,225	1,463	65.8	1,238	55.6	860	379	223	15.2
2 years	700	495	70.7	429	61.3	318	111	65	13.1
1 year	721	495	68.7	420	58.3	292	129	75	15.2
Under 1 year	804	473	58.8	389	48.4	250	139	83	17.5

[1]Usually work 35 hours or more a week at all jobs.
[2]Usually work less than 35 hours a week at all jobs.
[3]Includes never-married, divorced, separated and widowed persons.

SOURCE: *Employment Characteristics of Families.* Bureau of Labor Statistics, May 1999

ment security. Some observers regard increases in tenure as a sign of improving security and decreases in tenure as a sign of deteriorating security. There are shortcomings associated with this formulation. For example, during recessions or other periods of declining job security, median tenure and the proportion of workers with long tenure could rise because less-senior workers are more likely to lose their jobs than are workers with longer tenure.

During periods of economic growth, median tenure and the proportion of workers with long tenure could fall because more job opportunities are available for new job entrants, and experienced workers have more opportunities to change employers and take better jobs. Tenure also could rise under improving economic conditions, however, as fewer layoffs occur and good job matches develop between workers and employers.

In February 1998 median male tenure (the point at which half the workers had more tenure and half had less) was 3.8 years, slightly less than the figures obtained in January of 1987, 1991, and 1996. (See Table 1.19.) Since 1983 nearly every age group of men experienced a decline in median tenure, with particularly sharp drops occurring among men ages 65 and over. For men in the 35- to 64-year category, median years of tenure increased between 1996 and 1998 from 10.5 to 11.2 years—the first time the data showed an increase for this age group since 1983.

During this period, the age of the workforce generally shifted upward to older workers, who generally have longer tenure with their current employers. For example, median tenure for 25- to 34-year-old men was 2.8 years in February 1998, compared with 5.5 years for 35- to 44-

year-olds and 11.2 years for 55- to 64-year-olds. (See Table 1.19.) This shift in the age distribution would, by itself, have raised median tenure. This age shift, however, was counterbalanced by the decline in median tenure for men in most age groups, leaving the overall median tenure for men essentially unchanged.

Among women, overall median tenure rose somewhat between 1983 and 1996, with nearly all of the gain taking place from 1991 to 1996. (See Table 1.19.) In 1998 women's median tenure dropped slightly to 3.4 years, down from 1996. The growth between 1991 and 1996 was partly due to increases in median tenure among 35- to 44-year-olds and 45- to 54-year-olds. These increases, even if small, were just the opposite of what was happening with the men. In addition, as with men, the proportion of employed women in the older, longer-tenured age groups rose.

In addition to trends in median tenure, the Bureau of Labor Statistics examined trends in the proportion of workers with relatively long tenure of ten years or more. During the 1983–98 period, the proportion of men who had worked for their current employer ten years or longer fell from 37.7 percent to 32.7 percent, while the proportion of women with such long tenure rose from 24.9 percent to 28.4 percent.

Table 1.20 provides more detailed information on the length of time workers had been with their current employers in February 1998. About one-quarter (27.8 percent) of wage and salary workers had worked for their current employer 12 months or less. These included workers who had recently entered the workforce, as well as workers who had changed employers in the previous year. More than three-quarters of 16- to 19-year-olds had such short tenure, as did over half of workers aged 20 to 24. By comparison, among 55- to 64-year-olds, 11.6 percent had 12 months or less of tenure, while 28.9 percent had worked for their current employer 20 years or more.

Among women and men in nearly every age group, workers who did not have a high school diploma had lower median tenure than those with more education. There appears to be little relationship between tenure and educational attainment for workers who have a high school diploma or higher level of education.

INDUSTRY

In February 1998 workers in mining had the highest median tenure (5.6 years) of any major private-sector industry. The median for mining rose from 3.4 years in January 1983 to a peak of 6.1 years in 1996. (See Table 1.21.) The number of workers in mining in the late 1990s is only half of its peak of the early 1980s. Little hiring has occurred in the industry over the past five to ten years,

TABLE 1.11

People in the Labor Force—Poverty Status and Work Experience by Weeks in the Labor Force, 1997

(Numbers in thousands)

Poverty status and work experience	Total in the labor force	27 weeks or more in the labor force	
		Total	50 to 52 weeks
TOTAL			
Total in labor force	145,323	130,047	115,757
Did not work during the year	2,129	903	740
Worked during the year	143,193	129,144	115,017
Usual full-time workers	113,128	107,169	99,066
Usual part-time workers	30,066	21,975	15,951
Involuntary part-time workers	4,927	3,926	3,064
Voluntary part-time workers	25,139	18,049	12,887
At or above poverty level			
Total in labor force	134,905	122,594	110,083
Did not work during the year	1,135	394	315
Worked during the year	133,771	122,200	109,768
Usual full-time workers	107,738	102,842	95,670
Usual part-time workers	26,033	19,358	14,098
Involuntary part-time workers	3,654	2,984	2,332
Voluntary part-time workers	22,379	16,374	11,765
Below poverty level			
Total in labor force	10,417	7,453	5,675
Did not work during the year	994	509	425
Worked during the year	9,423	6,944	5,249
Usual full-time workers	5,390	4,327	3,396
Usual part-time workers	4,033	2,618	1,853
Involuntary part-time workers	1,273	942	732
Voluntary part-time workers	2,760	1,675	1,121
Poverty rate[1]			
Total in labor force	7.2	5.7	4.9
Did not work during the year	46.7	56.4	57.5
Worked during the year	6.6	5.4	4.6
Usual full-time workers	4.8	4.0	3.4
Usual part-time workers	13.4	11.9	11.6
Involuntary part-time workers	25.8	24.0	23.9
Voluntary part-time workers	11.0	9.3	8.7

[1]Number below the poverty level as a percent of the total in the labor force.
NOTE: Data refer to persons 16 years and over.

SOURCE: *A Profile of the Working Poor.* Bureau of Labor Statistics, 1997

and many lower-tenured workers have lost their jobs, resulting in a large increase in median tenure.

In February 1998 median tenure in manufacturing was 4.9 years, its lowest value since 1991. Some industries within manufacturing have experienced sizable movements in median tenure. For example, workers in motor vehicles and equipment had far less tenure with their employers in 1998 (6.4 years) than in 1983 (13.0 years). In aircraft and parts manufacturing, the median rose from 6.4 years in 1983 to 9.6 years in 1998. (See Table 1.21.)

The median length of time that workers in finance, insurance, and real estate had been with their current employer rose from 3.2 years in 1983 to 3.5 years in 1998. The services industry also experienced an increase in median tenure, from 2.5 years in 1983 to 2.9 years in 1998. Within services, private households, social services, hospitals, other health services, and

TABLE 1.12

People in the Labor Force for 27 Weeks or More—Poverty Status by Age, Sex, Race, and Hispanic Origin, 1997

(Numbers in thousands)

Age and sex	Total	White	Black	Hispanic origin	Below poverty level Total	Below poverty level White	Below poverty level Black	Below poverty level Hispanic origin	Poverty rate[1] Total	Poverty rate[1] White	Poverty rate[1] Black	Poverty rate[1] Hispanic origin
Total, 16 years and older	130,047	109,198	14,848	12,901	7,453	5,381	1,709	1,609	5.7	4.9	11.5	12.5
16 to 19 years	4,855	4,186	532	532	566	422	124	107	11.6	10.1	23.2	20.1
20 to 24 years	12,152	10,033	1,623	1,723	1,394	967	372	232	11.5	9.6	22.9	13.5
25 to 34 years	31,812	25,916	4,189	4,096	2,150	1,532	507	535	6.8	5.9	12.1	13.1
35 to 44 years	36,420	30,385	4,248	3,482	1,874	1,303	462	473	5.1	4.3	10.9	13.6
45 to 54 years	27,679	23,697	2,784	2,001	894	696	155	180	3.2	2.9	5.6	9.0
55 to 64 years	13,296	11,569	1,194	885	474	381	74	76	3.6	3.3	6.2	8.6
65 years and older	3,834	3,412	278	183	102	81	16	6	2.7	2.4	5.7	3.5
Men, 16 years and older	70,310	60,108	6,887	7,835	3,468	2,697	547	970	4.9	4.5	7.9	12.4
16 to 19 years	2,397	2,107	220	303	254	201	46	58	10.6	9.5	20.7	19.1
20 to 24 years	6,465	5,428	763	1,110	603	449	133	148	9.3	8.3	17.4	13.4
25 to 34 years	17,536	14,561	1,993	2,628	1,005	781	144	345	5.7	5.4	7.2	13.1
35 to 44 years	19,722	16,790	1,952	2,042	830	625	129	266	4.2	3.7	6.6	13.0
45 to 54 years	14,764	12,869	1,281	1,127	476	400	54	103	3.2	3.1	4.2	9.1
55 to 64 years	7,269	6,415	549	514	239	196	30	44	3.3	3.1	5.5	8.6
65 years and older	2,156	1,939	129	111	60	44	11	5	2.8	2.3	8.5	4.9
Women, 16 years and older	59,738	49,090	7,961	5,066	3,985	2,684	1,162	639	6.7	5.5	14.6	12.6
16 to 19 years	2,458	2,079	312	229	312	221	78	49	12.7	10.6	25.0	21.3
20 to 24 years	5,687	4,605	860	613	791	518	239	84	13.9	11.2	27.8	13.6
25 to 34 years	14,276	11,355	2,196	1,467	1,144	750	363	190	8.0	6.6	16.5	12.9
35 to 44 years	16,698	13,595	2,296	1,441	1,043	678	333	207	6.2	5.0	14.5	14.3
45 to 54 years	12,915	10,828	1,503	873	418	295	101	77	3.2	2.7	6.7	8.8
55 to 64 years	6,027	5,155	645	371	235	185	44	32	3.9	3.6	6.8	8.6
65 years and older	1,677	1,474	149	72	42	37	5	1	2.5	2.5	3.2	([2])

[1]Number below the poverty level as a percent of the total in the labor force for 27 weeks or more.

[2]Data not shown where base is less than 75,000.

NOTE: Detail for race and Hispanic-origin groups will not sum to totals because data for the "other races" group are not presented and Hispanics are included in both the white and black population groups.

SOURCE: *A Profile of the Working Poor.* Bureau of Labor Statistics, 1997

business services all showed substantial increases from 1983 to 1998.

In transportation and public utilities, median tenure was 4.8 years in February 1998, about a year lower than the median in 1983, 1987, and 1991. Wholesale and retail trade workers showed little change in their median tenure, with retail trade continuing to have the lowest median (1.8 years) among the major private-sector industry groups. The median length of time government employees had worked for their current employer rose from 5.8 years in 1983 to 7.3 years in 1998. (See Table 1.21.)

NUMBER OF JOBS HELD

The average person in the United States held 9.2 different jobs from ages 18 through 34. Men held 9.6 jobs and women held 8.8 jobs from the ages of 18 through 34. Those men and women who eventually obtained a college degree usually held more jobs between the ages of 18 and 24 than did those who graduated from high school but did not attend college. The relatively larger number of jobs among those who attended college may be due to the fact that college students hold summer jobs and part-time jobs while attending school. At older ages, the number of jobs

did not vary much by education, suggesting that people tend to settle into more stable jobs at older ages.

From age 18 to 34, whites held more jobs than either blacks or Hispanics. The differences were more pronounced at younger ages. Between the ages of 18 to 24, whites held 5.8 jobs, compared with 4.7 for blacks and 5 for Hispanics. These racial differences nearly disappeared at older ages, and the number of jobs held by blacks, whites, and Hispanics was nearly identical between ages 30 to 34. (See Table 1.22.)

LOOKING FOR WORK WHILE EMPLOYED

About 6 million persons, 5.6 percent of wage and salary workers, actively looked for a new job in the three months prior to February 1995. Until the late 1990s, very little was known about such job searches among those who already were employed.

Age Made a Difference

Among adult workers, the job search rate (the proportion of wage and salary workers who are actively searching for jobs) decreases with age. (See Figure 1.3 and Table 1.23.) Young adults often hold a series of short-term or part-

TABLE 1.13

People in the Labor Force for 27 Weeks or More—Poverty Status by Educational Attainment, Race, and Sex, 1997
(Numbers in thousands)

Educational attainment and race	Total	Men	Women	Below poverty level			Poverty rate[1]		
				Total	Men	Women	Total	Men	Women
Total, 16 years and older	**130,047**	**70,310**	**59,738**	**7,453**	**3,468**	**3,985**	**5.7**	**4.9**	**6.7**
Less than a high school diploma	16,351	10,145	6,206	2,587	1,461	1,125	15.8	14.4	18.1
Less than 1 year of high school	4,631	3,093	1,537	870	583	287	18.8	18.9	18.7
1–3 years of high school	10,069	6,029	4,040	1,550	779	771	15.4	12.9	19.1
4 years of high school, no diploma	1,652	1,023	629	167	99	67	10.1	9.7	10.7
High school graduates, no college	42,629	22,891	19,738	2,755	1,170	1,585	6.5	5.1	8.0
Some college, no degree	25,922	13,326	12,596	1,258	458	800	4.9	3.4	6.3
Associate degree	10,861	5,227	5,634	337	122	215	3.1	2.3	3.8
College graduates	34,285	18,720	15,564	517	257	261	1.5	1.4	1.7
White, 16 years and older	109,198	60,108	49,090	5,381	2,697	2,684	4.9	4.5	5.5
Less than a high school diploma	13,279	8,506	4,773	1,894	1,147	747	14.3	13.5	15.7
Less than 1 year of high school	3,980	2,731	1,249	772	521	251	19.4	19.1	20.1
1–3 years of high school	8,077	4,976	3,101	1,026	570	457	12.7	11.4	14.7
4 years of high school, no diploma	1,222	798	423	96	56	40	7.9	7.0	9.4
High school graduates, no college	35,572	19,359	16,213	1,913	887	1,026	5.4	4.6	6.3
Some college, no degree	21,490	11,300	10,190	910	370	540	4.2	3.3	5.3
Associate degree	9,341	4,601	4,740	265	96	169	2.8	2.1	3.6
College graduates	29,517	16,342	13,175	399	197	202	1.4	1.2	1.5
Black, 16 years and older	14,848	6,887	7,961	1,709	547	1,162	11.5	7.9	14.6
Less than a high school diploma	2,367	1,265	1,102	575	244	331	24.3	19.3	30.0
Less than 1 year of high school	394	230	164	61	32	29	15.5	13.9	17.7
1–3 years of high school	1,657	867	790	458	176	282	27.6	20.3	35.6
4 years of high school, no diploma	315	168	148	56	36	20	17.8	21.3	13.8
High school graduates, no college	5,568	2,694	2,874	716	210	505	12.9	7.8	17.6
Some college, no degree	3,432	1,498	1,934	298	60	238	8.7	4.0	12.3
Associate degree	1,069	394	675	61	16	45	5.7	4.0	6.7
College graduates	2,412	1,035	1,377	60	17	43	2.5	1.6	3.1

[1]Number below the poverty level as a percent of the total in the labor force for 27 weeks or more.

SOURCE: *A Profile of the Working Poor.* Bureau of Labor Statistics, 1997

time jobs if they are attending school. Once they have completed their schooling, they are more apt to try different kinds of jobs early in their careers to learn which ones best suit their interests and abilities. As workers age, many find suitable job matches and become less likely to seek other employment opportunities. Also, older workers may become more reluctant to change jobs because doing so could jeopardize earnings and benefits, such as pensions and paid vacations (premiums gained through service with the company) that could be lost with a change in employers.

Among teenagers, school enrollment appears to limit the likelihood of searching for another job. Wage and salary workers ages 16 to 19 who were not enrolled in school were twice as likely as those attending school to seek jobs. The difference was smaller among 20- to 24-year-olds. Regardless of age, men are more likely than women to search for another job while employed.

Education and Job Mismatches

In almost all occupational categories, employed persons at higher levels of educational attainment had the highest job-search rates. In some occupations these may be workers who had still not found the job they believed equal to their level of education. For example, the job

search rates for service and sales workers with a bachelor's degree were 12.5 and 7.6 percent, respectively, compared to 5.1 and 5.4 percent, respectively, for those with a high school diploma.

Among the major occupational groups, handlers, equipment cleaners, helpers, and laborers had the highest job-search rate, followed closely by workers in sales occupations. Workers in precision production, craft, and repair occupations had the lowest job search rate, while rates for workers in executive, administrative, and managerial positions; professional specialties; and technical occupations were slightly below the overall average. (See Table 1.23.)

UNIONS

In 1999 the proportion of workers who were union members continued to decline from 1996, but stayed the same as 1998. Union members accounted for 13.9 percent of wage and salary workers in 1998 and 1999. It should be noted that a worker may be represented by a union, but may not be a dues-paying member. In a "right-to-work" state, a worker may join a unionized company, but may not be forced to join the union. Nonetheless, by law, the nonunion worker, working in a union company,

TABLE 1.14

People in the Labor Force for 27 Weeks or More Who Worked During the Year—Poverty Status by Occupation of the Longest Job Held, Race, and Sex, 1997

(Numbers in thousands)

Occupation and race	Total	Men	Women	Below poverty level			Poverty rate[1]		
				Total	Men	Women	Total	Men	Women
Total, 16 years and older[2]	129,144	69,846	59,298	6,944	3,239	3,705	5.4	4.6	6.2
Managerial and professional specialty	37,767	19,253	18,514	691	312	379	1.8	1.6	2.0
Executive, administrative, and managerial	18,526	10,139	8,387	323	176	147	1.7	1.7	1.8
Professional specialty	19,241	9,114	10,127	368	136	232	1.9	1.5	2.3
Technical, sales, and administrative support	38,133	13,631	24,502	1,663	402	1,261	4.4	2.9	5.1
Technicians and related support	4,363	1,943	2,420	66	30	36	1.5	1.6	1.5
Sales occupations	15,408	7,863	7,545	994	281	713	6.5	3.6	9.5
Administrative support, including clerical	18,362	3,825	14,537	603	91	512	3.3	2.4	3.5
Service occupations	17,209	7,186	10,023	2,084	663	1,421	12.1	9.2	14.2
Private household	763	33	730	170	7	163	22.3	(3)	22.4
Protective service	2,286	1,911	374	70	47	23	3.1	2.5	6.2
Service, except private household and protective	14,161	5,242	8,919	1,844	609	1,235	13.0	11.6	13.8
Precision production, craft, and repair	14,612	13,396	1,216	676	596	81	4.6	4.4	6.6
Operators, fabricators, and laborers	18,177	13,719	4,458	1,335	855	480	7.3	6.2	10.8
Machine operators, assemblers, and inspectors	7,979	4,963	3,016	544	243	302	6.8	4.9	10.0
Transportation and material moving occupations	5,415	4,883	532	337	277	60	6.2	5.7	11.3
Handlers, equipment cleaners, helpers, and laborers	4,783	3,872	910	454	336	118	9.5	8.7	13.0
Farming, forestry, and fishing	3,089	2,539	550	495	412	82	16.0	16.2	15.0
White, 16 years and older[2]	108,705	59,814	48,890	5,154	2,557	2,597	4.7	4.3	5.3
Managerial and professional specialty	33,068	17,105	15,963	556	259	298	1.7	1.5	1.9
Executive, administrative, and managerial	16,543	9,236	7,307	284	159	124	1.7	1.7	1.7
Professional specialty	16,525	7,869	8,656	273	99	173	1.6	1.3	2.0
Technical, sales, and administrative support	32,014	11,641	20,373	1,151	290	860	3.6	2.5	4.2
Technicians and related support	3,669	1,655	2,013	55	27	28	1.5	1.6	1.4
Sales occupations	13,327	6,950	6,377	709	194	515	5.3	2.8	8.1
Administrative support, including clerical	15,019	3,036	11,983	387	69	318	2.6	2.3	2.7
Service occupations	13,378	5,660	7,718	1,464	469	996	10.9	8.3	12.9
Private household	614	26	589	132	7	125	21.5	(3)	21.3
Protective service	1,779	1,552	226	47	35	12	2.6	2.3	5.1
Service, except private household and protective	10,984	4,082	6,903	1,286	427	859	11.7	10.5	12.4
Precision production, craft, and repair	12,891	11,990	902	572	521	51	4.4	4.3	5.6
Operators, fabricators, and laborers	14,370	10,964	3,406	962	645	317	6.7	5.9	9.3
Machine operators, assemblers, and inspectors	6,232	3,993	2,239	380	183	196	6.1	4.6	8.8
Transportation and material moving occupations	4,367	3,950	417	242	203	39	5.5	5.1	9.3
Handlers, equipment cleaners, helpers, and laborers	3,771	3,021	750	340	258	82	9.0	8.6	10.9
Farming, forestry, and fishing	2,866	2,360	506	449	373	76	15.7	15.8	15.0
Black, 16 years and older[2]	14,489	6,750	7,739	1,462	481	982	10.1	7.1	12.7
Managerial and professional specialty	2,835	1,105	1,730	101	33	68	3.6	3.0	3.9
Executive, administrative, and managerial	1,183	481	703	19	6	13	1.6	1.3	1.9
Professional specialty	1,652	624	1,028	82	27	55	4.9	4.3	5.3
Technical, sales, and administrative support	4,354	1,250	3,104	424	64	360	9.7	5.1	11.6
Technicians and related support	446	162	283	3	–	3	0.6	–	0.9
Sales occupations	1,365	531	834	230	51	179	16.9	9.7	21.4
Administrative support, including clerical	2,543	557	1,986	191	13	178	7.5	2.3	9.0
Service occupations	2,942	1,082	1,859	510	135	375	17.3	12.5	20.1
Private household	120	4	116	34	–	34	28.5	–	29.5
Protective service	432	297	135	23	11	12	5.3	3.8	8.5
Service, except private household and protective	2,390	781	1,608	453	124	329	19.0	15.9	20.5
Precision production, craft, and repair	1,178	979	199	75	52	23	6.4	5.3	11.4
Operators, fabricators, and laborers	3,038	2,222	816	327	177	150	10.8	8.0	18.4
Machine operators, assemblers, and inspectors	1,310	727	583	146	50	96	11.2	6.9	16.5
Transportation and material moving occupations	877	774	103	86	64	21	9.8	8.3	20.7
Handlers, equipment cleaners, helpers, and laborers	851	721	130	95	62	33	11.2	8.6	25.4
Farming, forestry, and fishing	113	95	19	26	19	6	22.6	20.4	(3)

[1] Number below the poverty level as a percent of the total in the labor force for 27 weeks or more who worked during the year.

[2] Includes a small number of persons whose last job was in the Armed Forces.

[3] Data not shown where base is less than 75,000.

NOTE: Dash represents or rounds to zero.

SOURCE: *A Profile of the Working Poor.* Bureau of Labor Statistics, 1997

TABLE 1.15

Primary Families—Poverty Status, Presence of Related Children, and Work Experience of Family Members in the Labor Force for 27 Weeks or More, 1997

(Numbers in thousands)

Characteristic	Total families	At or above poverty level	Below poverty level	Poverty rate[1]
Total primary families	58,815	54,747	4,068	6.9
With related children under 18	34,140	30,610	3,531	10.3
Without children	24,674	24,137	537	2.2
With one member in the labor force	23,637	20,234	3,402	14.4
With two or more members in the labor force	35,178	34,512	666	1.9
With two members	29,452	28,843	609	2.1
With three or more members	5,726	5,669	57	1.0
Married-couple families:				
With related children under 18	25,536	24,086	1,450	5.7
Without children	20,155	19,810	345	1.7
With one member in the labor force	14,585	13,256	1,330	9.1
Husband	11,004	9,934	1,070	9.7
Wife	2,918	2,697	221	7.6
Relative	663	624	39	5.9
With two or more members in the labor force	31,105	30,641	464	1.5
With two members	26,142	25,709	432	1.7
With three or more members	4,964	4,931	32	0.7
Families maintained by women:				
With related children under 18	6,655	4,856	1,800	27.0
Without children	3,030	2,883	147	4.9
With one member in the labor force	6,904	5,123	1,781	25.8
Householder	5,667	4,103	1,565	27.6
Relative	1,237	1,021	216	17.5
With two or more members in the labor force	2,782	2,615	166	6.0
Families maintained by men:				
With related children under 18	1,949	1,668	281	14.4
Without children	1,489	1,444	45	3.0
With one member in the labor force	2,147	1,856	292	13.6
Householder	1,826	1,581	245	13.4
Relative	321	274	47	14.6
With two or more members in the labor force	1,291	1,256	35	2.7

[1] Number below the poverty level as a percent of the total in the labor force for 27 weeks or more.

NOTE: Data relate to primary families with at least one member in the labor force for 27 weeks or more.

SOURCE: *A Profile of the Working Poor.* Bureau of Labor Statistics, 1997

must benefit from any union contact. A total of 15.3 percent of workers was represented by unions, down from 15.4 percent the year before. (See Table 1.24.) Almost one-half (42.1 percent) of workers represented by unions in 1999 were employed by the government. (See Table 1.25.) Union membership fell steadily from 20.1 percent in 1983, the first year for which comparable data were available, to 13.9 percent for all workers in 1999. The recession of the early 1980s, the movement of jobs overseas, the decline in traditionally unionized heavy industry, management's desire to eliminate union power, the threat of job loss, and unimaginative union leadership all contributed to the decline in union membership.

Instead of demanding better hours, more pay, and improved working conditions—the traditional union demands—most unions agreed to "give backs" (surrendering existing benefits) and lower salaries in exchange for job guarantees during the 1980s. Nonetheless, many companies continued to develop factories overseas or to purchase heavily from foreign producers, which resulted in fewer jobs for American workers and more plant shutdowns.

In the mid- to late 1990s, concerned about their declining membership, many unions became more aggressive in recruiting members. They attempted to gain new members in different types of occupations, such as bookstore clerks, limousine drivers, Catholic schoolteachers, and fashion models. In the New York area, during the late 1990s, unions organized 2,200 asbestos-removal workers, 1,500 demolition workers, 1,400 podiatrists, 300 Red Cross workers, and 300 workers at Sony movie theaters. In Miami unions were trying to organize nursing-home workers. In Las Vegas, unions recruited hotel, hospital, and construction workers.

Although concerned about eroding benefits, wages, and jobs, many workers are still wary of unions. The reputation of some union leaders, both past and present, disturbs them, and many workers fear losing their jobs if they become involved in union activities.

The 1997 UPS strike led to a more positive public view of unions. In addition, Phil Wheeler, director of the United Automobile Workers in New York and New England, claims that workers have reached the point where they are fed up. He notes that while CEOs are making astronomical amounts of money, the workers under them are getting less and less. Wheeler feels that workers can correct the situation by organizing.

Industry and Occupation

About 56 percent of the 16.4 million union members in 1999 were in private nonagricultural industries, where they made up 9.5 percent of wage and salary employment. About 7.1 million union members worked in government (federal, state, and local), accounting for 37.3 percent of government employment. (See Table 1.25.)

Among the private nonagricultural industries, transportation and public utilities had the highest unionization rate (25.5 percent), followed by construction (19.1 percent). Manufacturing (15.6 percent) and mining (10.6 percent) also had above-average unionization rate. On the other hand, just over 2 percent of agricultural workers and those in finance, insurance, and real estate were unionized. (See Table 1.25.)

Among the occupational groups, the unionization rate was highest among those working in protective service jobs (38.2 percent), which include many government workers, such as police officers, firefighters, and teachers. Union membership rates also were high in precision production, craft, and repair (22.4 percent); operators, fabricators, and laborers (20.7 percent); and professional specialty (19.7 percent). Rates were lowest in sales (4.1 percent) and in farming, forestry, and fishing occupations (5.8 percent). (See Table 1.25.)

Characteristics of Union Members

In 1999 union membership was higher among men (16.1 percent) than women (11.4 percent) and higher among blacks (17.2 percent) than either whites (13.5 percent) or Hispanics (11.9 percent). Within these groups, black men continued to have the highest union membership rate (20.5 percent), while white and Hispanic women had the lowest rates (both under 11 percent). Blacks were more likely to be working in blue-collar manufacturing positions, which tend to be more heavily unionized. Workers ages 35 to 64 were more likely to be members of unions than either their younger or older counterparts. Full-time workers were more than twice as likely as part-timers to be union members. (See Table 1.24.)

In 1999 earnings, union members earned a median weekly salary of $672, compared with $516 for wage and salary employees not represented by unions. The union-nonunion earnings ratio was greater for women than for men and for blacks and Hispanics than for whites. (See Table 1.26.)

OCCUPATIONS AND INDUSTRIES. No matter what the occupation, people represented by unions earned more than those who were not. The differences were small among managerial and professional specialties and much larger among operators, fabricators, and laborers; farming, forestry, and fishing; and service occupations. In all industries, except finance, insurance, and real estate; mining; wholesale trade; and federal government work, union-represented workers earned more than nonunion workers. The differences in construction, transportation, and local government were particularly large. (See Table 1.27.)

WORK STOPPAGES (STRIKES)

The number of work stoppages (strikes) has decreased dramatically over the past several decades. In 1974, 424 work stoppages resulted in 31.8 million days idle. (This figure is calculated by multiplying the number of workers times the number of days they were on strike.) For most of the remainder of the 1970s, there were about 200 to 300 work stoppages a year.

This changed dramatically during the 1980s. The number fell from 187 in 1980 to only 40 in 1988, rising slightly to 44 in 1990, with just 5.9 million days idle. In 1995 the number of strikes again tumbled to 31, involving 5.87 million idle days. In 1996 the number of stoppages rose to 37, involving 4.9 million days. By October 1997, 27 strikes had begun, with 4.37 million days idle. The UPS strike in August 1997 accounted for more than 2 million days. By 1998, 34 strikes had begun, with 5.11 million days idle, and affected 387 thousand workers.

OCCUPATIONAL INJURIES, ILLNESSES, AND FATALITIES

The annual rate of occupational injury and illness in full-time workers fluctuates. There were 8.3 cases per 100 workers in 1987, increasing to a high of 8.9 in 1992, and then dropping to 8.5 in 1993, 8.1 in 1995, and to a low of 6.7 in 1998. (See Table 1.28.) Transportation equipment (14.6), primary metal industries (14), and fabricated metal products (13.9) had the most cases per 100 workers in 1998. Finance, insurance, and real estate (1.9); petroleum and coal products (3.9); and instruments and related products (4) had the lowest number of cases per 100 workers in 1998.

In 1987 there were 69.9 lost workdays per 100 workers, and in 1992 there were 93.8 lost workdays per 100 workers. (See Table 1.28.) The number of workdays lost varied by the type of industry and occupation. In 1992 the food and kindred products industry lost 211.9 days per

TABLE 1.16

Employment of Workers on Nonfarm Payrolls by Industry, 1998–1999 Annual Average

[In thousands]

Industry	Annual average 1998	Annual average 1999ᵖ
TOTAL	**125,826**	**128,616**
PRIVATE SECTOR	106,007	108,455
GOODS-PRODUCING	25,347	25,240
Mining	590	53
Metal mining	50	49
Oil and gas extraction	339	293
Nonmetallic minerals, except fuels	109	109
Construction	5,985	6,273
General building contractors	1,372	1,434
Heavy construction, except building	838	862
Special trades contractors	3,744	3,978
Manufacturing	18,772	18,431
Production workers	12,930	12,661
Durable goods	11,170	10,985
Production workers	7,643	7,510
Lumber and wood products	813	826
Furniture and fixtures	530	540
Stone, clay, and glass products	563	569
Primary metal industries	712	690
Fabricated metal products	1,501	1,489
Industrial machinery and equipment	2,203	2,129
Computer and office equipment	379	360
Electronic and other electrical equipment	1,704	1,661
Electronic components and accessories	660	639
Transportation equipment	1,884	1,855
Motor vehicles and equipment	990	1,000
Aircraft and parts	524	490
Instruments and related products	868	839
Miscellaneous manufacturing industries	393	387
Nondurable goods	7,602	7,446
Production workers	5,287	5,151
Food and kindred products	1,686	1,685
Tobacco products	41	39
Textile mill products	598	562
Apparel and other textile products	763	684
Paper and allied products	675	659
Printing and publishing	1,565	1,553
Chemicals and allied products	1,043	1,035
Petroleum and coal products	140	137
Rubber and miscellaneous plastics products	1,009	1,019
Leather and leather products	83	74
SERVICE-PRODUCING	100,480	103,376
Transportation and public utilities	6,600	6,792
Transportation	4,276	4,426
Railroad transportation	231	230
Local and interurban passenger transit	468	482
Trucking and warehousing	1,745	1,813
Water transportation	180	181
Transportation by air	1,183	1,238
Pipelines, except natural gas	14	13
Transportation services	455	469
Communications and public utilities	2,324	2,366
Communications	1,469	1,522
Electric, gas, and sanitary services	855	844
Wholesale trade	6,831	7,004
Retail trade	22,296	22,788
Building materials and garden supplies	948	987
General merchandise stores	2,730	2,775
Department stores	2,426	2,472

TABLE 1.16

Employment of Workers on Nonfarm Payrolls by Industry, 1998–1999 Annual Average [CONTINUED]

[In thousands]

Industry	Annual average 1998	Annual average 1999ᵖ
Retail trade (continued)	22,296	22,788
Food stores	3,482	3,483
Automotive dealers and service stations	2,341	2,406
New and used car dealers	1,048	1,081
Apparel and accessory stores	1,143	1,181
Furniture and home furnishings stores	1,026	1,085
Eating and drinking places	7,760	7,903
Miscellaneous retail establishments	2,867	2,968
Finance, insurance, and real estate	7,407	7,632
Finance	3,593	3,706
Depository institutions.	2,042	2,047
Commercial banks	1,468	1,465
Savings institutions	258	256
Nondepository institutions	658	714
Security and commodity brokers	645	679
Holding and other investment offices	248	266
Insurance	2,344	2,402
Insurance carriers	1,598	1,635
Insurance agents, brokers, and service	746	767
Real estate	1,471	1,525
Services¹	37,526	39,000
Agricultural services	706	759
Hotels and other lodging places	1,776	1,799
Personal services	1,195	1,206
Business services	8,584	9,123
Services to buildings	950	988
Personnel supply services	3,230	3,405
Help supply services	2,872	3,017
Computer and data processing services	1,599	1,780
Auto repair services and parking	1,144	1,184
Miscellaneous repair services	382	397
Motion pictures	573	600
Amusement and recreation services	1,601	1,696
Health services	9,846	9,973
Offices and clinics of medical doctors	1,803	1,865
Nursing and personal care facilities	1,762	1,755
Hospitals	3,926	3,970
Home health care services	672	655
Legal services	973	1,002
Educational services	2,177	2,269
Social services	2,644	2,782
Child day care services	605	632
Residential care	747	781
Museums and botanical and zoological gardens	93	94
Membership organizations	2,361	2,402
Engineering and management services	3,185	3,420
Engineering and architectural services	905	944
Management and public relations	1,034	1,158
Government	19,819	20,161
Federal	2,686	2,668
Federal, except Postal Service	1,819	1,796
State	4,612	4,696
Education	1,916	1,953
Other State government	2,695	2,743
Local	12,521	12,797
Education	7,082	7,265
Other local government	5,440	5,531

¹ Includes other industries not shown separately.

ᵖ = preliminary.

SOURCE: *Monthly Labor Review.* Bureau of Labor Statistics, March 2000

FIGURE 1.2

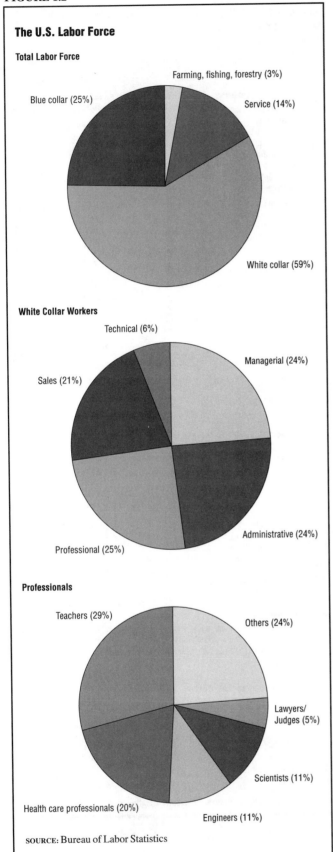

The U.S. Labor Force

Total Labor Force

Farming, fishing, forestry (3%)

Blue collar (25%)

Service (14%)

White collar (59%)

White Collar Workers

Technical (6%)

Sales (21%)

Managerial (24%)

Professional (25%)

Administrative (24%)

Professionals

Teachers (29%)

Others (24%)

Lawyers/Judges (5%)

Scientists (11%)

Health care professionals (20%)

Engineers (11%)

SOURCE: Bureau of Labor Statistics

100 full-time workers, while finance, insurance, and real estate occupations lost only 32.9 days.

Fatalities

According to the *Census of Fatal Occupational Injuries* (Bureau of Labor Statistics), approximately 6,000 workers died each year between 1993 and 1997. (See Table 1.29.) On average, about 17 workers were fatally injured each day during 1999.

Highway traffic incidents and homicides caused most fatal work injuries. These two events totaled over a third of the work injury deaths that occurred in 1998. Work-related highway deaths accounted for 24 percent of the 6,026 total work injuries. Almost half of the highway fatality victims (49 percent) died as a result of vehicle collision. Off-road transport-related incidents (such as tractors or forklifts overturning) and workers being struck by vehicles each accounted for between 4 to 7 percent of total worker fatalities. (See Table 1.29.)

Homicide accounted for 12 percent of fatal work injuries in 1998. Of all occupational homicides, 80 percent were caused by shooting, with between 6 and 7 percent each caused by stabbing and other methods (including bombing). (See Table 1.29.)

Falls accounted for another 12 percent of fatal work injuries. Nine percent of the fatally injured workers were struck by various objects, such as falling trees, machinery, or vehicles that had slipped into gear, or building materials. (See Table 1.29.)

Occupations with large numbers of fatal injuries included truck drivers, construction trades, farm occupations, and sales occupations. The specific events or exposures responsible for workers' deaths varied considerably among occupations. Highway crashes and jackknifings together accounted for about two-thirds of the truck drivers' deaths, while homicides accounted for about one-half of the fatalities among workers in sales occupations. Slightly over one-third of the deaths in farm occupations occurred in tractor-related events. (See Figure 1.4.)

The construction industry accounted for one out of every six fatal work injuries (19 percent) that occurred during 1998. Industries with large numbers of fatalities relative to their employment include agriculture, forestry, and fishing; construction; transportation and public utilities; and manufacturing. (See Table 1.30.)

Men accounted for 54 percent of the fatalities. Whites composed 84 percent of the workplace fatalities; blacks, 11 percent; and other races less than 0.5 percent. Those 25 to 34 years old made up 24 percent; those 35 to 44, 28 percent; and those 45 to 54, 21 percent of the fatalities.

TABLE 1.17

Employed Persons by Occupation, Race, and Sex
(Percent distribution)

Occupation and race	Total		Men		Women	
	1998	1999	1998	1999	1998	1999
TOTAL						
Total, 16 years and over (thousands)	131,463	133,488	70,693	71,446	60,771	62,042
Percent	100.0	100.0	100.0	100.0	100.0	100.0
Managerial and professional specialty	29.6	30.3	28.1	28.6	31.4	32.3
Executive, administrative, and managerial	14.5	14.7	15.0	15.0	13.9	14.2
Professional specialty	15.1	15.6	13.1	13.6	17.4	18.0
Technical, sales, and administrative support	29.3	29.2	19.5	19.7	40.7	40.0
Technicians and related support	3.2	3.3	2.8	2.9	3.8	3.6
Sales occupations	12.1	12.1	11.1	11.3	13.1	13.0
Administrative support, including clerical	14.0	13.8	5.6	5.5	23.8	23.4
Service occupations	13.6	13.4	10.2	9.9	17.5	17.4
Private household	.6	.6	.1	.1	1.3	1.3
Protective service	1.8	1.8	2.8	2.8	.7	.7
Service, except private household and protective	11.1	11.0	7.3	7.1	15.4	15.4
Precision production, craft, and repair	11.0	10.9	18.7	18.6	2.0	2.1
Operators, fabricators, and laborers	13.9	13.6	19.5	19.3	7.4	7.0
Machine operators, assemblers, and inspectors	5.9	5.5	6.9	6.5	4.8	4.4
Transportation and material moving occupations	4.1	4.1	6.8	7.0	.9	.9
Handlers, equipment cleaners, helpers, and laborers	3.9	3.9	5.8	5.9	1.7	1.7
Farming, forestry, and fishing	2.7	2.6	4.0	3.8	1.1	1.1
White						
Total, 16 years and over (thousands)	110,931	112,235	60,604	61,139	50,327	51,096
Percent	100.0	100.0	100.0	100.0	100.0	100.0
Managerial and professional specialty	30.7	31.3	29.1	29.5	32.6	33.4
Executive, administrative, and managerial	15.2	15.4	15.8	15.9	14.6	14.7
Professional specialty	15.5	15.9	13.3	13.6	18.1	18.7
Technical, sales, and administrative support	29.3	29.2	19.5	19.7	41.1	40.6
Technicians and related support	3.2	3.2	2.7	2.9	3.8	3.6
Sales occupations	12.4	12.4	11.5	11.7	13.4	13.3
Administrative support, including clerical	13.7	13.5	5.2	5.1	24.0	23.6
Service occupations	12.4	12.2	9.2	8.9	16.3	16.2
Private household	.6	.6	.1	(1)	1.3	1.3
Protective service	1.7	1.7	2.6	2.6	.6	.6
Service, except private household and protective	10.1	10.0	6.5	6.3	14.4	14.3
Precision production, craft, and repair	11.5	11.5	19.4	19.4	1.9	2.1
Operators, fabricators, and laborers	13.2	13.0	18.5	18.3	6.8	6.5
Machine operators, assemblers, and inspectors	5.5	5.2	6.6	6.2	4.3	4.0
Transportation and material moving occupations	3.9	4.0	6.5	6.6	.8	.8
Handlers, equipment cleaners, helpers, and laborers	3.7	3.8	5.4	5.5	1.6	1.7
Farming, forestry, and fishing	2.9	2.8	4.3	4.1	1.2	1.2
Black						
Total, 16 years and over (thousands)	14,556	15,056	6,871	7,027	7,685	8,029
Percent	100.0	100.0	100.0	100.0	100.0	100.0
Managerial and professional specialty	20.2	21.5	17.0	18.0	23.2	24.5
Executive, administrative, and managerial	9.4	9.9	8.6	8.5	10.1	11.1
Professional specialty	10.8	11.6	8.4	9.5	13.0	13.5
Technical, sales, and administrative support	29.3	28.9	18.3	18.4	39.1	38.2
Technicians and related support	3.0	3.1	2.5	2.7	3.5	3.5
Sales occupations	9.7	9.3	7.8	7.6	11.4	10.8
Administrative support, including clerical	16.5	16.5	8.0	8.1	24.2	23.9
Service occupations	21.6	21.8	17.8	17.4	25.0	25.6
Private household	.8	.8	.1	.1	1.5	1.5
Protective service	3.2	3.2	4.8	4.9	1.7	1.8
Service, except private household and protective	17.6	17.7	12.9	12.4	21.9	22.4
Precision production, craft, and repair	8.0	7.8	14.6	14.3	2.0	2.1
Operators, fabricators, and laborers	19.7	18.9	30.1	29.8	10.4	9.4
Machine operators, assemblers, and inspectors	8.2	7.6	9.7	9.3	7.0	6.1
Transportation and material moving occupations	6.0	5.8	11.1	11.0	1.4	1.3
Handlers, equipment cleaners, helpers, and laborers	5.5	5.5	9.3	9.5	2.0	2.0
Farming, forestry, and fishing	1.2	1.1	2.2	2.2	.3	.2

[1] Less than 0.05 percent.

NOTE: Beginning in January 1999, data reflect revised population controls used in the household survey.

SOURCE: *Employment and Earnings.* Bureau of Labor Statistics, May 1999

TABLE 1.18

Employed White, Black, and Hispanic Origin Workers by Sex, Occupation, Class of Worker, and Full- or Part-Time Status

(In thousands)

Category	Total		White		Black		Hispanic origin	
	1998	1999	1998	1999	1998	1999	1998	1999
SEX								
Total (all civilian workers)	131,463	133,488	110,931	112,235	14,556	15,056	13,291	13,720
Men	70,693	71,446	60,604	61,139	6,871	7,027	8,018	8,067
Women	60,771	62,042	50,327	51,096	7,685	8,029	5,273	5,653
OCCUPATION								
Managerial and professional specialty	38,937	40,467	34,063	35,125	2,947	3,233	1,933	2,040
Executive, administrative, and managerial	19,054	19,584	16,903	17,235	1,368	1,484	1,028	1,097
Professional specialty	19,883	20,883	17,160	17,890	1,579	1,749	905	943
Technical, sales, and administrative support	38,521	38,921	32,490	32,779	4,264	4,356	3,186	3,286
Technicians and related support	4,261	4,355	3,557	3,622	441	467	283	279
Sales occupations	15,850	16,118	13,704	13,956	1,415	1,405	1,245	1,267
Administrative support, including clerical	18,410	18,448	15,229	15,201	2,408	2,484	1,657	1,740
Service occupations	17,836	17,915	13,807	13,725	3,148	3,275	2,670	2,716
Private household	847	831	704	670	116	126	262	244
Protective service	2,417	2,440	1,892	1,886	463	484	204	200
Service, except private household and protective	14,572	14,644	11,211	11,168	2,569	2,666	2,204	2,271
Precision production, craft, and repair	14,411	14,593	12,729	12,908	1,158	1,174	1,793	1,871
Mechanics and repairers	4,786	4,868	4,233	4,284	379	397	496	485
Construction trades	5,594	5,801	5,054	5,275	398	405	785	869
Other precision production, craft, and repair	4,031	3,923	3,441	3,348	381	371	512	517
Operators, fabricators, and laborers	18,256	18,167	14,609	14,535	2,866	2,847	2,917	3,014
Machine operators, assemblers, and inspectors	7,791	7,386	6,146	5,824	1,200	1,143	1,340	1,364
Transportation and material moving occupations	5,363	5,516	4,351	4,488	872	879	640	659
Handlers, equipment cleaners, helpers, and laborers	5,102	5,265	4,112	4,223	795	825	938	992
Construction laborers	821	920	705	787	97	103	193	233
Other handlers, equipment cleaners, helpers, and laborers	4,282	4,346	3,407	3,436	698	722	745	759
Farming, forestry, and fishing	3,502	3,426	3,233	3,165	172	172	792	793
CLASS OF WORKER								
Agriculture:								
Wage and salary workers	2,000	1,944	1,843	1,802	102	87	670	654
Self-employed workers	1,341	1,297	1,280	1,243	36	30	71	79
Unpaid family workers	38	40	37	38	–	–	2	1
Nonagricultural industries:								
Wage and salary workers	119,019	121,323	99,657	101,229	13,917	14,416	11,949	12,327
Government	18,383	18,903	14,686	15,141	2,877	2,937	1,355	1,426
Private industries	100,637	102,420	84,970	86,088	11,040	11,479	10,594	10,901
Private households	962	933	785	741	146	149	281	257
Other industries	99,674	101,487	84,185	85,347	10,894	11,330	10,312	10,644
Self-employed workers	8,962	8,790	8,030	7,846	497	520	590	651
Unpaid family workers	103	95	84	77	4	3	10	7
FULL- OR PART-TIME STATUS								
Full-time workers	108,202	110,302	90,759	92,173	12,429	12,904	11,303	11,767
Part-time workers	23,261	23,186	20,172	20,062	2,126	2,152	1,988	1,953

NOTE: Detail for the above race and Hispanic-origin groups will not sum to totals because data for the "other races" group are not presented and Hispanics are included in both the white and black population groups. Beginning in January 1999, data reflect revised population controls used in the household survey.

SOURCE: *Employment and Earnings.* **Bureau of Labor Statistics, May 1999**

WORKPLACE VIOLENCE

In April 1996 the Society of Human Resource Management surveyed its members on issues of workplace violence. Approximately half (48 percent) of those who responded said they had had a violent occurrence at their workplace since January 1, 1994. An earlier 1992 survey had reported only 33 percent of the respondents had a violent event between 1988 and 1993. Incidents of assaults and shootings were relatively rare. In 1996 four of ten (39 percent) reported that verbal threats were the most common form of violence, followed by pushing and shoving (22 percent) and fistfights (13 percent). (See Figure 1.5.)

By 1999 the Society of Human Resource Management found that workplace violence had increased since 1996 for its members. Fifty-six percent of human resource professionals that were surveyed reported workplace violence incidences between 1996 and 1999. As with earlier surveys, shootings and stabbings accounted for a very low proportion of workplace violence that human resource professionals reported. Verbal threats were most prominent (41 percent), followed by pushing and shoving (19 percent). The most common motivator of workplace violence reported in this survey was personality conflict, though marital issues and work-related stress also played a role. The survey found that employers were responding to rising workplace violence with increased security and related training and prevention.

According to the Bureau of Justice Statistics, from 1992 to 1996, U.S. residents experienced more than 2 million violent victimizations annually while they were working or on duty. The most common type of workplace violent crime was simple assault, with an estimated average of 1.5 million victimizations occurring each year. While at work, U.S residents also suffered 396,000 aggravated assaults, 51,000 rapes and sexual assaults, 84,000 robberies, and 1,000 homicides. (See Table 1.31.) Of the occupations examined, law enforcement had the highest rates of workplace violence, while teaching had the lowest. Police officers experienced 306 victimizations for every 1,000 officers. College or university teaching was the occupation with lowest rate of violence at work—2.5 victimizations per 1,000 teachers. (See Table 1.32.)

In 1998 the Occupational Safety and Health Administration (OSHA) reported that homicide remained the second leading cause of job-related deaths in the United States. Almost 1,000 workers were murdered annually, accounting for 12 percent of fatal work injuries in 1998. (See Table 1.29.) Of all occupational homicides in 1998, 80 percent (down from 82 percent in 1997) were caused by shooting, with between 6 and 7 percent (down from 8 and 9 percent in 1997) each caused by stabbing and other methods (including bombing).

The National Institute for Occupational Safety and Health identified a number of workplace circumstances that put an employee at risk to be the victim of violence. These include public contact, money exchange, delivery jobs, working alone or late at night, and working in areas with high crime.

TABLE 1.19

Median Years of Tenure with Current Employer for Employed Wage and Salary Workers by Age and Sex, Selected Years 1983–1998

Age and sex	January 1983	January 1987	January 1991	February 1996	February 1998
TOTAL					
16 years and over	3.5	3.4	3.6	3.8	3.6
16 to 17 years	.7	.6	.7	.7	.6
18 to 19 years	.8	.7	.8	.7	.7
20 to 24 years	1.5	1.3	1.3	1.2	1.1
25 years and over	5.0	5.0	4.8	5.0	4.7
25 to 34 years	3.0	2.9	2.9	2.8	2.7
35 to 44 years	5.2	5.5	5.4	5.3	5.0
45 to 54 years	9.5	8.8	8.9	8.3	8.1
55 to 64 years	12.2	11.6	11.1	10.2	10.1
65 years and over	9.6	9.5	8.1	8.4	7.8
Men					
16 years and over	4.1	4.0	4.1	4.0	3.8
16 to 17 years	.7	.6	.7	.6	.6
18 to 19 years	.8	.7	.8	.7	.7
20 to 24 years	1.5	1.3	1.4	1.2	1.2
25 years and over	5.9	5.7	5.4	5.3	4.9
25 to 34 years	3.2	3.1	3.1	3.0	2.8
35 to 44 years	7.3	7.0	6.5	6.1	5.5
45 to 54 years	12.8	11.8	11.2	10.1	9.4
55 to 64 years	15.3	14.5	13.4	10.5	11.2
65 years and over	8.3	8.3	7.0	8.3	7.1
Women					
16 years and over	3.1	3.0	3.2	3.5	3.4
16 to 17 years	.7	.6	.7	.7	.7
18 to 19 years	.8	.7	.8	.7	.7
20 to 24 years	1.5	1.3	1.3	1.2	1.1
25 years and over	4.2	4.3	4.3	4.7	4.4
25 to 34 years	2.8	2.6	2.7	2.7	2.5
35 to 44 years	4.1	4.4	4.5	4.8	4.5
45 to 54 years	6.3	6.8	6.7	7.0	7.2
55 to 64 years	9.8	9.7	9.9	10.0	9.6
65 years and over	10.1	9.9	9.5	8.4	8.7

NOTE: Data for 1996 and 1998 are not strictly comparable with data for 1991 and earlier years because population controls from the 1990 census, adjusted for the estimated undercount, are used beginning in 1996. Figures for the 1983-91 period are based on population controls from the 1980 census. Also, beginning in 1996, the figures incorporate the effects of the redesign of the Current Population Survey introduced in January 1994. Data exclude the incorporated and unincorporated self-employed.

SOURCE: *Current Population Survey.* Bureau of Labor Statistics, September 1998

TABLE 1.20

Distribution of Employed Wage and Salary Workers by Tenure with Current Employer, Age, Sex, Race, and Hispanic Origin, February 1998

Age, sex, race, and Hispanic origin	Number employed (in thousands)	Total	Percent distribution by tenure with current employer							
			12 months or less	13 to 23 months	2 years	3 to 4 years	5 to 9 years	10 to 14 years	15 to 19 years	20 years or more
TOTAL										
16 years and over	115,892	100.0	27.8	7.9	4.9	15.8	17.9	10.7	6.1	9.0
16 to 19 years	6,461	100.0	77.9	10.2	6.1	5.5	.3	-	-	-
20 years and over	109,431	100.0	24.8	7.7	4.8	16.4	8.9	11.3	6.5	9.5
20 to 24 years	11,967	100.0	53.5	3.1	9.1	18.4	5.9	(1)	-	-
25 to 34 years	29,291	100.0	31.3	10.4	6.0	21.9	21.5	8.0	.9	-
35 to 44 years	31,684	100.0	20.5	6.7	4.0	15.6	22.0	15.9	9.7	5.6
45 to 54 years	23,482	100.0	14.7	5.2	3.4	12.5	18.7	13.6	10.2	21.7
55 to 64 years	10,377	100.0	11.6	4.0	2.6	11.0	17.3	14.2	10.4	28.9
65 years and over	2,631	100.0	16.1	3.5	3.6	13.1	18.6	13.9	9.5	21.7
Men										
16 years and over.	60,113	100.0	26.9	7.5	4.7	15.9	17.4	10.5	6.2	10.9
16 to 19 years	3,143	100.0	78.3	10.4	5.0	5.9	.4			
20 years and over	56,970	100.0	24.1	7.3	4.7	16.4	18.3	11.1	6.6	11.5
20 to 24 years	6,270	100.0	52.1	12.1	10.3	19.4	6.0	(1)	-	-
25 to 34 years	15,637	100.0	30.6	9.6	5.7	22.6	22.2	8.4	1.0	-
35 to 44 years	16,568	100.0	19.2	6.5	3.5	14.7	21.8	16.7	10.8	6.8
45 to 54 years	11,866	100.0	14.3	4.6	3.1	12.2	16.2	11.5	10.7	27.5
55 to 64 years	5,333	100.0	11.3	3.9	2.6	10.1	15.9	12.2	8.3	35.8
65 years and over	1,297	100.0	16.5	4.9	4.3	14.2	17.7	15.1	6.3	20.9
Women										
16 years and over.	55,779	100.0	28.7	8.3	5.1	15.8	18.3	10.9	6.0	6.9
16 to 19 years	3,318	100.0	77.4	10.0	7.2	5.2	.2	-	-	-
20 years and over	2,461	100.0	25.6	8.2	5.0	16.4	19.5	11.6	6.3	7.4
20 to 24 years	5,697	100.0	55.0	14.2	7.7	17.3	5.7	(1)	-	-
25 to 34 years	13,654	100.0	32.2	11.3	6.4	21.2	20.8	7.4	.7	-
35 to 44 years	15,116	100.0	21.9	6.8	4.5	16.6	22.3	15.0	8.6	4.2
45 to 54 years	11,616	100.0	15.2	5.8	3.8	12.8	21.3	15.7	9.7	15.8
55 to 64 years	5,044	100.0	11.9	4.2	2.6	11.9	18.9	16.3	12.6	21.6
65 years and over	1,334	100.0	15.7	2.1	3.0	12.0	19.6	12.6	12.6	22.4
White										
16 years and over	97,341	100.0	27.5	8.0	4.8	15.7	18.0	10.8	6.2	9.2
Men	51,234	100.0	26.6	7.5	4.6	15.7	17.3	10.7	6.4	11.2
Women	46,108	100.0	28.4	8.6	5.0	15.6	18.7	11.0	5.9	6.9
Black										
16 years and over	13,298	100.0	29.1	6.3	5.4	16.6	16.8	10.0	6.4	9.4
Men	6,123	100.0	28.7	6.1	5.2	16.5	17.3	9.2	6.0	11.1
Women	7,175	100.0	29.5	6.5	5.6	16.6	16.3	10.7	6.7	8.0
Hispanic origin										
16 years and over	12,695	100.0	31.4	8.4	6.5	19.6	17.4	8.6	3.6	4.4
Men	7,468	100.0	30.7	7.9	6.1	19.9	18.1	8.1	4.0	5.2
Women	5,227	100.0	32.5	9.1	7.0	19.0	16.5	9.3	3.2	3.3

[1]Less than 0.05 percent.

NOTE: Detail for the above race and Hispanic-origin groups will not sum to totals because data for the "other races" groups are not presented and Hispanics are included in both the white and black population groups. Detail may not sum to totals because of rounding. Data exclude the incorporated and unincorporated self-employed. Dash represents zero.

SOURCE: *Current Population Survey.* Bureau of Labor Statistics, September 1998

TABLE 1.21

Median Years of Tenure with Current Employer for Employed Wage and Salary Workers by Industry, Selected Years 1983–1998

Industry	January 1983	January 1987	January 1991	February 1996	February 1998
Total, 16 years and over	3.5	3.4	3.6	3.8	3.6
Agriculture	2.2	2.4	2.6	3.4	2.9
Nonagricultural industries	3.6	3.4	3.6	3.8	3.6
Government	5.8	6.5	6.5	6.9	7.3
Private industries	3.2	3.0	3.2	3.3	3.2
Mining	3.4	6.1	5.8	6.1	5.6
Construction	2.0	2.0	2.6	2.9	2.7
Manufacturing	5.4	5.5	5.2	5.4	4.9
Durable goods[1]	5.6	6.0	5.8	5.3	4.9
Lumber and wood products	4.0	3.2	3.6	3.3	3.8
Furniture and fixtures	4.2	3.2	4.0	4.2	3.9
Stone, clay, and glass products	7.0	6.8	6.3	5.1	6.1
Primary metal industries	10.0	10.2	9.7	8.1	8.0
Fabricated metal products	5.7	5.5	5.5	5.1	4.0
Machinery and computing	5.8	6.7	5.9	5.2	4.4
Electrical machinery, equipment, and supplies	4.7	4.8	5.5	4.9	5.0
Transportation equipment[1]	8.8	8.0	7.6	8.3	7.8
Motor vehicles and equipment	13.0	11.2	11.7	7.8	6.4
Aircraft and parts	6.4	6.8	6.3	9.8	9.6
Professional and photographic equipment and watches	4.7	5.9	5.1	5.1	5.5
Toys, amusements, and sporting goods	3.6	5.8	3.2	2.7	3.6
Nondurable goods[1]	5.1	4.9	4.7	5.4	4.9
Food and kindred products	5.2	4.4	4.2	5.1	5.1
Textile mill products	7.0	7.0	5.6	5.4	6.7
Apparel and other finished textile products	3.8	3.2	3.8	3.8	3.8
Paper and allied products	7.6	8.6	7.6	8.4	7.5
Printing and publishing	3.2	3.2	3.5	4.3	4.0
Chemicals and allied products	7.0	7.2	5.7	6.9	5.4
Petroleum and coal products	6.0	11.7	8.4	10.3	9.4
Rubber and miscellaneous plastics products	5.4	4.4	4.7	4.7	4.6
Transportation and public utilities	5.8	5.7	5.8	5.2	4.8
Transportation	4.6	3.9	4.2	4.1	3.8
Communications and other public utilities	8.3	8.4	9.9	8.2	8.2
Wholesale trade	3.8	3.7	3.4	3.9	4.1
Retail trade	1.9	1.8	1.9	1.9	1.8
Finance, insurance, and real estate	3.2	3.0	3.4	4.1	3.5
Banking and other finance	3.3	3.1	3.6	3.9	3.7
Insurance and real estate	3.0	2.9	3.2	4.2	3.4
Services[1]	2.5	2.5	2.7	3.0	2.9
Private households	1.8	1.7	1.9	2.3	2.3
Services, except private households	2.5	2.5	2.7	3.0	2.9
Business services	1.5	1.6	1.8	2.0	1.9
Automobile and repair services	2.3	2.0	2.2	2.9	2.4
Personal services, except private households	2.0	2.0	2.1	2.3	2.3
Entertainment and recreation services	1.8	1.8	2.3	1.9	1.9
Hospitals	3.5	4.6	4.2	5.2	5.2
Health services, except hospitals	2.5	2.4	2.7	2.9	2.9
Educational services	2.7	3.1	3.5	3.8	3.5
Social services	2.2	2.3	2.3	2.8	2.7
Other professional services	2.9	2.8	3.3	3.5	3.3

[1]Includes other industries, not shown separately.

NOTE: Data for 1996 and 1998 are not strictly comparable with data for 1991 and earlier years because population controls from the 1990 census, adjusted for the estimated undercount, are used beginning in 1996. Figures for the 1983-91 period are based on population controls from the 1980 census. Also, beginning in 1996, the figures incorporate the effects of the redesign of the Current Population Survey introduced in January 1994. Data exclude the incorporated and unincorporated self-employed.

SOURCE: *Current Population Survey.* Bureau of Labor Statistics, September 1998

TABLE 1.22

Number of Jobs Held by Individuals from Age 18 to 34 in 1978–98 by Educational Attainment, Sex, Race, Hispanic Origin, and Age

Characteristic	Average number of jobs for persons age 18 to 34 in 1978-98			
	Total[1]	Age 18-24	Age 25-29	Age 30-34
Total	**9.2**	**5.6**	**3.0**	**2.4**
Less than a high school diploma	9.3	5.2	3.0	2.4
High school grad., no college	8.7	5.2	2.8	2.4
Less than a bachelor's degree	9.6	5.8	3.2	2.5
Bachelor's degree or more	9.7	6.3	3.0	2.4
Men	9.6	5.8	3.2	2.6
Less than a high school diploma	10.7	6.1	3.5	2.8
High school grad., no college	9.1	5.5	3.1	2.5
Less than a bachelor's degree	10.0	6.0	3.4	2.6
Bachelor's degree or more	9.3	6.0	2.9	2.4
Women	8.8	5.4	2.8	2.3
Less than a high school diploma	7.4	4.0	2.2	2.0
High school grad., no college	8.2	4.8	2.5	2.3
Less than a bachelor's degree	9.2	5.6	3.0	2.4
Bachelor's degree or more	10.1	6.6	3.1	2.3
White	9.4	5.8	3.0	2.4
Less than a high school diploma	9.8	5.6	3.1	2.6
High school grad., no college	8.7	5.3	2.8	2.4
Less than a bachelor's degree	9.9	6.0	3.2	2.5
Bachelor's degree or more	9.8	6.4	3.0	2.3
Black	8.5	4.7	2.9	2.5
Less than a high school diploma	8.0	3.9	2.7	2.2
High school grad., no college	8.4	4.5	2.9	2.5
Less than a bachelor's degree	8.5	5.0	2.9	2.4
Bachelor's degree or more	9.4	6.0	3.1	2.7
Hispanic origin	8.7	5.0	2.9	2.4
Less than a high school diploma	8.8	4.9	2.8	2.2
High school grad., no college	8.6	5.0	2.8	2.4
Less than a bachelor's degree	8.6	5.1	3.0	2.3
Bachelor's degree or more	8.9	5.3	2.7	2.6

[1] Jobs that were held in more than one of the age categories were counted in each appropriate column, but only once in the total column.

NOTE: The first two columns exclude individuals who turned age 18 before Jan. 1, 1978. The first and last columns exclude individuals who had not yet turned age 35 when interviewed in 1998.

The National Longitudinal Survey of Youth 1979 consists of men and women who were born in the years 1957-64 and were age 14 to 22 when first interviewed in 1979. These individuals were age 33 to 41 in 1998. Educational attainment is defined as of the 1998 survey. Race and Hispanic-origin groups are mutually exclusive. Totals include American Indians, Alaskan Natives, and Asian and Pacific Islanders, not shown separately.

SOURCE: *Number of Jobs, Labor Market Experience, and Earnings.* Bureau of Labor Statistics, June 1998

FIGURE 1.3

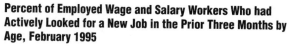

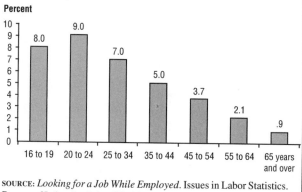

Percent of Employed Wage and Salary Workers Who had Actively Looked for a New Job in the Prior Three Months by Age, February 1995

SOURCE: *Looking for a Job While Employed.* Issues in Labor Statistics. Bureau of Labor Statistics: Washington, D.C.

TABLE 1.23

Employed Wage and Salary Workers Who had Actively Searched for a New Job in the Prior Three Months by Age, Sex, Occupation, and Educational Attainment, February 1995

(Numbers in thousands)

Characteristic	Total	Actively searched for a new job	Job search rate
Age			
Total, 16 years and over	108,876	6,044	5.6
16 to 19 years	5,424	435	8.0
20 to 24 years	12,103	1,091	9.0
25 to 34 years	29,620	2,067	7.0
35 to 44 years	29,806	1,492	5.0
45 to 54 years	20,271	743	3.7
55 to 64 years	9,277	195	2.1
65 years and over	2,375	22	.9
Sex			
Men	56,883	3,343	5.9
Women	51,993	2,701	5.2
Occupation			
Executive, administrative, and managerial	13,773	727	5.3
Professional specialty	16,428	876	5.3
Technicians and related support	3,829	203	5.3
Sales occupations	12,042	804	6.7
Administrative support, including clerical	17,764	971	5.5
Private households	846	55	6.6
Protective service	2,169	126	5.8
Service, except private household and protective	12,393	774	6.2
Precision production, craft, and repair	11,229	502	4.5
Machine operators, assemblers, and inspectors	7,558	352	4.7
Transportation and material moving occupations	4,620	229	5.0
Handlers, equipment cleaners, helpers, and laborers	4,676	328	7.0
Farming, forestry, and fishing	1,549	98	6.3
Educational attainment			
Less than a high school diploma	13,714	578	4.2
High school graduates, no college	34,959	1,555	4.4
Less than a bachelor's degree	32,705	2,093	6.4
College graduates	27,499	1,818	6.6
Bachelor's degree	18,453	1,203	6.5
Advanced degree	9,046	615	6.8

SOURCE: *Looking for a Job While Employed.* Issues in Labor Statistics. Bureau of Labor Statistics: Washington, D.C.

TABLE 1.24

Union Affiliation of Employed Wage and Salary Workers by Selected Characteristics

(Numbers in thousands)

Characteristic	1998					1999				
	Total employed	Members of unions[1]		Represented by unions[2]		Total employed	Members of unions[1]		Represented by unions[2]	
		Total	Percent of employed	Total	Percent of employed		Total	Percent of employed	Total	Percent of employed
SEX AND AGE										
Total, 16 years and over	116,730	16,211	13.9	17,918	15.4	118,963	16,477	13.9	18,182	15.3
16 to 24 years	19,164	1,014	5.3	1,151	6.0	19,606	1,110	5.7	1,239	6.3
25 years and over	97,566	15,198	15.6	16,767	17.2	99,358	15,367	15.5	16,943	17.1
25 to 34 years	29,121	3,332	11.4	3,711	12.7	28,657	3,415	11.9	3,785	13.2
35 to 44 years	31,865	5,013	15.7	5,511	17.3	32,438	4,918	15.2	5,428	16.7
45 to 54 years	23,579	4,737	20.1	5,220	22.1	24,665	4,881	19.8	5,377	21.8
55 to 64 years	10,427	1,923	18.4	2,110	20.2	10,880	1,932	17.8	2,107	19.4
65 years and over	2,574	193	7.5	214	8.3	2,718	221	8.1	247	9.1
Men, 16 years and over	60,973	9,850	16.2	10,638	17.4	61,914	9,949	16.1	10,758	17.4
16 to 24 years	9,927	637	6.4	719	7.2	10,116	716	7.1	781	7.7
25 years and over	51,046	9,213	18.0	9,919	19.4	51,797	9,232	17.8	9,977	19.3
25 to 34 years	15,656	2,112	13.5	2,301	14.7	15,330	2,142	14.0	2,325	15.2
35 to 44 years	16,768	3,055	18.2	3,264	19.5	17,020	2,993	17.6	3,241	19.0
45 to 54 years	11,874	2,771	23.3	2,982	25.1	12,395	2,800	22.6	3,026	24.4
55 to 64 years	5,404	1,177	21.8	1,265	23.4	5,622	1,186	21.1	1,267	22.5
65 years and over	1,343	98	7.3	108	8.0	1,431	111	7.7	118	8.2
Women, 16 years and over	55,757	6,362	11.4	7,280	13.1	57,050	6,528	11.4	7,425	13.0
16 to 24 years	9,237	377	4.1	432	4.7	9,489	393	4.1	458	4.8
25 years and over	46,520	5,985	12.9	6,848	14.7	47,560	6,135	12.9	6,966	14.6
25 to 34 years	13,464	1,219	9.1	1,410	10.5	13,327	1,273	9.6	1,460	11.0
35 to 44 years	15,097	1,958	13.0	2,248	14.9	15,418	1,924	12.5	2,187	14.2
45 to 54 years	11,705	1,967	16.8	2,238	19.1	12,270	2,081	17.0	2,351	19.2
55 to 64 years	5,023	746	14.9	845	16.8	5,258	746	14.2	839	16.0
65 years and over	1,231	95	7.7	106	8.6	1,287	110	8.5	129	10.0
RACE, HISPANIC ORIGIN, AND SEX										
White, 16 years and over	97,531	13,118	13.5	14,460	14.8	99,147	13,349	13.5	14,668	14.8
Men	51,700	8,166	15.8	8,788	17.0	52,492	8,246	15.7	8,896	16.9
Women	45,831	4,952	10.8	5,673	12.4	46,655	5,103	10.9	5,771	12.4
Black, 16 years and over	13,894	2,460	17.7	2,739	19.7	14,346	2,463	17.2	2,757	19.2
Men	6,452	1,337	20.7	1,458	22.6	6,585	1,348	20.5	1,464	22.2
Women	7,443	1,123	15.1	1,282	17.2	7,760	1,116	14.4	1,293	16.7
Hispanic origin, 16 years and over	12,374	1,471	11.9	1,634	13.2	12,810	1,525	11.9	1,684	13.1
Men	7,360	937	12.7	1,017	13.8	7,457	966	13.0	1,052	14.1
Women	5,015	534	10.6	617	12.3	5,353	559	10.4	632	11.8
FULL- OR PART-TIME STATUS[3]										
Full-time workers	95,595	14,825	15.5	16,323	17.1	97,626	14,974	15.3	16,501	16.9
Part-time workers	20,862	1,354	6.5	1,559	7.5	21,065	1,459	6.9	1,634	7.8

[1] Data refer to members of a labor union or an employee association similar to a union.

[2] Data refer to members of a labor union or an employee association similar to a union as well as workers who report no union affiliation but whose jobs are covered by a union or an employee association contract.

[3] The distinction between full- and part-time workers is based on hours usually worked. Beginning in 1994, these data will not sum to totals because full- or part-time status on the principal job is not identifiable for a small number of multiple jobholders.

NOTE: Data refer to the sole or principal job of full- and part-time workers. Excluded are all self-employed workers regardless of whether or not their businesses are incorporated. Detail for the above race and Hispanic-origin groups will not sum to totals because data for the "other races" group are not presented and Hispanics are included in both the white and black population groups. Beginning in January 1999, data reflect revised population controls used in the household survey.

SOURCE: *Employment and Earnings*. Bureau of Labor Statistics, May 1999

TABLE 1.25

Union Affiliation of Employed Wage and Salary Workers by Occupation and Industry

(Numbers in thousands)

Occupation and industry	1998 Total employed	1998 Members of unions[1] Total	1998 Members of unions[1] Percent of employed	1998 Represented by unions[2] Total	1998 Represented by unions[2] Percent of employed	1999 Total employed	1999 Members of unions[1] Total	1999 Members of unions[1] Percent of employed	1999 Represented by unions[2] Total	1999 Represented by unions[2] Percent of employed
OCCUPATION										
Managerial and professional specialty	33,102	4,252	12.8	5,015	15.2	34,693	4,594	13.2	5,352	15.4
Executive, administrative, and managerial	15,473	812	5.2	1,017	6.6	16,000	903	5.6	1,138	7.1
Professional specialty	17,629	3,440	19.5	3,998	22.7	18,693	3,691	19.7	4,215	22.5
Technical, sales, and administrative support	35,379	3,239	9.2	3,677	10.4	35,514	3,191	9.0	3,609	10.2
Technicians and related support	4,150	433	10.4	498	12.0	4,188	461	11.0	523	12.5
Sales occupations	13,378	544	4.1	620	4.6	13,451	549	4.1	613	4.6
Administrative support, including clerical	17,851	2,262	12.7	2,558	14.3	17,874	2,182	12.2	2,474	13.8
Service occupations	16,594	2,209	13.3	2,398	14.5	16,829	2,151	12.8	2,336	13.9
Protective service	2,399	991	41.3	1,048	43.7	2,427	927	38.2	991	40.8
Service, except protective service	14,195	1,218	8.6	1,350	9.5	14,403	1,224	8.5	1,346	9.3
Precision production, craft, and repair	12,274	2,708	22.1	2,834	23.1	12,474	2,800	22.4	2,929	23.5
Operators, fabricators, and laborers	17,443	3,713	21.3	3,894	22.3	17,514	3,627	20.7	3,830	21.9
Machine operators, assemblers, and inspectors	7,498	1,603	21.4	1,672	22.3	7,255	1,490	20.5	1,572	21.7
Transportation and material moving occupations	4,935	1,204	24.4	1,267	25.7	5,041	1,148	22.8	1,216	24.1
Handlers, equipment cleaners, helpers, and laborers	5,010	906	18.1	956	19.1	5,218	989	18.9	1,042	20.0
Farming, forestry, and fishing	1,938	90	4.6	100	5.2	1,940	113	5.8	125	6.4
INDUSTRY										
Private wage and salary workers	98,329	9,306	9.5	10,104	10.3	100,025	9,419	9.4	10,216	10.2
Agriculture	1,739	26	1.5	31	1.8	1,721	43	2.5	48	2.8
Nonagricultural industries	96,590	9,280	9.6	10,073	10.4	98,304	9,376	9.5	10,168	10.3
Mining	589	72	12.2	79	13.4	531	57	10.6	60	11.4
Construction	5,946	1,056	17.8	1,093	18.4	6,230	1,187	19.1	1,224	19.6
Manufacturing	19,763	3,127	15.8	3,315	16.8	19,323	3,024	15.6	3,209	16.6
Durable goods	11,999	1,990	16.6	2,097	17.5	11,824	1,941	16.4	2,063	17.5
Nondurable goods	7,763	1,138	14.7	1,218	15.7	7,499	1,083	14.4	1,146	15.3
Transportation and public utilities	7,147	1,843	25.8	1,931	27.0	7,317	1,865	25.5	1,956	26.7
Transportation	4,316	1,108	25.7	1,156	26.8	4,450	1,136	25.5	1,186	26.7
Communications and public utilities	2,831	735	26.0	775	27.4	2,866	729	25.4	770	26.9
Wholesale and retail trade	24,230	1,283	5.3	1,387	5.7	24,671	1,278	5.2	1,406	5.7
Wholesale trade	4,425	259	5.9	275	6.2	4,573	248	5.4	281	6.1
Retail trade	19,805	1,024	5.2	1,113	5.6	20,098	1,030	5.1	1,126	5.6
Finance, insurance, and real estate	7,420	150	2.0	195	2.6	7,588	156	2.1	191	2.5
Services	31,493	1,750	5.6	2,073	6.6	32,645	1,809	5.5	2,121	6.5
Government workers	18,401	6,905	37.5	7,815	42.5	18,938	7,058	37.3	7,966	42.1
Federal	3,269	1,105	33.8	1,299	39.7	3,264	1,047	32.1	1,275	39.0
State	5,150	1,431	27.8	1,667	32.4	5,233	1,527	29.2	1,781	34.0
Local	9,982	4,370	43.8	4,849	48.6	10,440	4,484	42.9	4,911	47.0

[1] Data refer to members of a labor union or an employee association similar to a union.

[2] Data refer to members of a labor union or an employee association similar to a union as well as workers who report no union affiliation but whose jobs are covered by a union or an employee association contract.

NOTE: Data refer to the sole or principal job of full- and part-time workers. Excluded are all self-employed workers regardless of whether or not their businesses are incorporated. Beginning in January 1999, data reflect revised population controls used in the household survey.

SOURCE: *Employment and Earnings.* Bureau of Labor Statistics, May 1999

TABLE 1.26

Median Weekly Earnings of Full-Time Wage and Salary Workers by Union Affiliation and Selected Characteristics

Characteristic	1998				1999			
	Total	Members of unions[1]	Represented by unions[2]	Non-union	Total	Members of unions[1]	Represented by unions[2]	Non-union
SEX AND AGE								
Total, 16 years and over	$523	$659	$653	$499	$549	$672	$667	$516
16 to 24 years	319	415	410	315	341	437	433	335
25 years and over	572	673	667	537	592	688	683	569
25 to 34 years	502	595	591	489	518	604	601	506
35 to 44 years	597	683	678	576	611	691	687	594
45 to 54 years	620	716	712	592	652	750	745	617
55 to 64 years	592	697	692	560	604	696	697	582
65 years and over	405	610	597	383	404	616	623	381
Men, 16 years and over	598	699	696	573	618	711	708	599
16 to 24 years	334	430	424	326	356	449	443	348
25 years and over	639	712	709	617	668	727	726	648
25 to 34 years	544	618	615	524	577	627	623	560
35 to 44 years	677	722	719	660	702	735	734	691
45 to 54 years	732	755	755	719	763	789	787	751
55 to 64 years	699	738	737	674	725	735	737	718
65 years and over	482	657	659	445	470	666	665	421
Women, 16 years and over	456	596	593	430	473	608	606	449
16 to 24 years	305	389	382	301	324	418	416	321
25 years and over	485	605	602	463	497	618	616	477
25 to 34 years	451	542	542	439	470	557	555	457
35 to 44 years	498	605	605	479	503	612	611	486
45 to 54 years	516	651	645	488	534	686	679	502
55 to 64 years	476	602	596	448	492	623	621	467
65 years and over	350	(3)	522	329	370	567	596	329
RACE, HISPANIC ORIGIN, AND SEX								
White, 16 years and over	545	683	678	513	573	692	689	534
Men	615	719	716	591	638	731	730	615
Women	468	610	607	443	483	619	618	461
Black, 16 years and over	426	578	572	398	445	575	575	415
Men	468	597	592	424	488	588	589	459
Women	400	537	533	376	409	548	545	388
Hispanic origin, 16 years and over	370	540	541	350	385	561	559	363
Men	390	585	584	367	406	604	597	384
Women	337	478	481	322	348	490	490	329

[1] Data refer to members of a labor union or an employee association similar to a union.

[2] Data refer to members of a labor union or an employee association similar to a union as well as workers who report no union affiliation but whose jobs are covered by a union or an employee association contract.

[3] Data not shown where base is less than 50,000.

NOTE: Data refer to the sole or principal job of full-time workers. Excluded are all self-employed workers regardless of whether or not their businesses are incorporated. Detail for the above race and Hispanic-origin groups will not sum to totals because data for the "other races" group are not presented and Hispanics are included in both the white and black population groups. Beginning in January 1999, data reflect revised population controls used in the household survey.

SOURCE: *Employment and Earnings.* Bureau of Labor Statistics, May 1999

TABLE 1.27

Median Weekly Earnings of Full-Time Wage and Salary Workers by Union Affiliation, Occupation, and Industry

Occupation and industry	1998				1999			
	Total	of unions[1]	Represented by unions[2]	Non-union	Total	Members of unions[1]	Represented by unions[2]	Non-union
Occupation								
Managerial and professional specialty	$759	$789	$774	$756	$797	$826	$819	$792
Executive, administrative, and managerial	755	801	789	753	792	823	829	789
Professional specialty	763	787	772	759	800	826	817	794
Technical, sales, and administrative support	477	575	569	463	488	583	580	477
Technicians and related support	599	708	688	590	618	714	711	608
Sales occupations	502	496	492	502	523	513	519	523
Administrative support, including clerical	438	563	558	418	447	574	564	429
Service occupations	327	557	542	305	336	536	529	314
Protective service	598	736	732	450	592	737	728	477
Service, except protective service	305	403	402	295	311	412	409	303
Precision production, craft, and repair	572	753	747	514	594	755	747	546
Operators, fabricators, and laborers	415	585	580	381	429	591	584	398
Machine operators, assemblers, and inspectors	406	559	556	375	423	572	566	394
Transportation and material moving occupations	510	655	644	468	513	668	657	478
Handlers, equipment cleaners, helpers, and laborers	351	514	514	326	363	507	499	340
Farming, forestry, and fishing	302	471	462	299	331	512	514	322
Industry								
Private wage and salary workers	505	625	619	493	521	633	627	510
Agriculture	315	(³)	(³)	314	340	(³)	(³)	337
Nonagricultural industries	509	626	620	496	525	634	628	513
Mining	684	733	723	673	734	710	731	735
Construction	534	790	783	496	552	778	772	509
Manufacturing	551	606	603	532	576	614	611	561
Durable goods	581	629	625	566	594	628	625	584
Nondurable goods	507	565	562	495	529	584	579	518
Transportation and public utilities	624	731	724	586	651	748	742	613
Transportation	570	704	695	519	596	727	718	551
Communications and public utilities	727	763	760	699	751	773	770	738
Wholesale and retail trade	410	480	476	405	421	499	492	418
Wholesale trade	562	611	604	557	573	584	570	573
Retail trade	373	442	439	369	391	472	463	387
Finance, insurance, and real estate	577	545	554	578	598	582	587	599
Services	498	540	548	494	517	554	563	515
Government workers	620	694	688	558	641	714	709	585
Federal	694	690	693	696	729	721	723	737
State	596	646	638	563	615	683	677	578
Local	612	712	702	501	623	726	720	525

[1] Data refer to members of a labor union or an employee association similar to a union.

[2] Data refer to members of a labor union or an employee association similar to a union as well as workers who report no union affiliation but whose jobs are covered by a union or an employee association contract.

[3] Data not shown where base is less than 50,000.

NOTE: Data refer to the sole or principal job of full-time workers. Excluded are all self-employed workers regardless of whether or not their businesses are incorporated. Beginning in January 1999, data reflect revised population controls used in the household survey.

SOURCE: *Employment and Earnings*. Bureau of Labor Statistics, May 1999

TABLE 1.28

Occupational Injury and Illness Rates, Private Sector, 1987–1998

Industry and type of case[2]	Incidence rates per 100 full-time workers[3]											
	1987	1988	1989[1]	1990	1991	1992	1993[4]	1994[4]	1995[4]	1996[4]	1997[4]	1998[4]
Private Sector[5]												
Total cases	8.3	8.6	8.6	8.8	8.4	8.9	8.5	8.4	8.1	7.4	7.1	6.7
Lost workday cases	3.8	4.0	4.0	4.1	3.9	3.9	3.8	3.8	3.6	3.4	3.3	3.1
Lost workdays	69.9	76.1	78.7	84.0	86.5	93.8						
Agriculture, forestry, and fishing[5]												
Total cases	11.2	10.9	10.9	11.6	10.8	11.6	11.2	10.0	9.7	8.7	8.4	7.9
Lost workday cases	5.7	5.6	5.7	5.9	5.4	5.4	5.0	4.7	4.3	3.9	4.1	3.9
Lost workdays	94.1	101.8	100.9	112.2	108.3	126.9						
Mining												
Total cases	8.5	8.8	8.5	8.3	7.4	7.3	6.8	6.3	6.2	5.4	5.9	4.9
Lost workday cases	4.9	5.1	4.8	5.0	4.5	4.1	3.9	3.9	3.9	3.2	3.7	2.9
Lost workdays	144.0	152.1	137.2	119.5	129.6	204.7						
Construction												
Total cases	14.7	14.6	14.3	14.2	13.0	13.1	12.2	11.8	10.6	9.9	9.5	8.8
Lost workday cases	6.8	6.8	6.8	6.7	6.1	5.8	5.5	5.5	4.9	4.5	4.4	4.0
Lost workdays	135.8	142.2	143.3	147.9	148.1	161.9						
General building contractors:												
Total cases	14.2	14.0	13.9	13.4	12.0	12.2	11.5	10.9	9.8	9.0	8.5	8.4
Lost workday cases	6.5	6.4	6.5	6.4	5.5	5.4	5.1	5.1	4.4	4.0	3.7	3.9
Lost workdays	134.0	132.2	137.3	137.6	132.0	142.7						
Heavy construction, except building:												
Total cases	14.5	15.1	13.8	13.8	12.8	12.1	11.1	10.2	9.9	9.0	8.7	8.2
Lost workday cases	6.4	7.0	6.5	6.3	6.0	5.4	5.1	5.0	4.8	4.3	4.3	4.1
Lost workdays	139.1	162.3	147.1	144.6	160.1	165.8						
Special trades contractors:												
Total cases	15.0	14.7	14.6	14.7	13.5	13.8	12.8	12.5	11.1	10.4	10.0	9.1
Lost workday cases	7.1	7.0	6.9	6.9	6.3	6.1	5.8	5.8	5.0	4.8	4.7	4.1
Lost workdays	135.7	141.1	144.9	153.1	151.3	168.3						
Manufacturing												
Total cases	11.9	13.1	13.1	13.2	12.7	12.5	12.1	12.2	11.6	10.6	10.3	9.7
Lost workday cases	5.3	5.7	5.8	5.8	5.6	5.4	5.3	5.5	5.3	4.9	4.8	4.7
Lost workdays	95.5	107.4	113.0	120.7	121.5	124.6						
Durable goods:												
Total cases	12.5	14.2	14.1	14.2	13.6	13.4	13.1	13.5	12.8	11.6	11.3	10.7
Lost workday cases	5.4	5.9	6.0	6.0	5.7	5.5	5.4	5.7	5.6	5.1	5.1	5.0
Lost workdays	96.8	111.1	116.5	123.3	122.9	126.7						
Lumber and wood products:												
Total cases	18.9	19.5	18.4	18.1	16.8	16.3	15.9	15.7	14.9	14.2	13.5	13.2
Lost workday cases	9.6	10.0	9.4	8.8	8.3	7.6	7.6	7.7	7.0	6.8	6.5	6.8
Lost workdays	176.5	189.1	177.5	172.5	172.0	165.8						
Furniture and fixtures:												
Total cases	15.4	16.6	16.1	16.9	15.9	14.8	14.6	15.0	13.9	12.2	12.0	11.4
Lost workday cases	6.7	7.3	7.2	7.8	7.2	6.6	6.5	7.0	6.4	5.4	5.8	5.7
Lost workdays	103.6	115.7				128.4						
Stone, clay, and glass products:												
Total cases	14.9	16.0	15.5	15.4	14.8	13.6	13.8	13.2	12.3	12.4	11.8	11.8
Lost workday cases	7.1	7.5	7.4	7.3	6.8	6.1	6.3	6.5	5.7	6.0	5.7	6.0
Lost workdays	135.8	141.0	149.8	160.5	156.0	152.2						
Primary metal industries:												
Total cases	17.0	19.4	18.7	19.0	17.7	17.5	17.0	16.8	16.5	15.0	15.0	14.0
Lost workday cases	7.4	8.2	8.1	8.1	7.4	7.1	7.3	7.2	7.2	6.8	7.2	7.0
Lost workdays	145.8	161.3	168.3	180.2	169.1	175.5						
Fabricated metal products:												
Total cases	17.0	18.8	18.5	18.7	17.4	16.8	16.2	16.4	15.8	14.4	14.2	13.9
Lost workday cases	7.2	8.0	7.9	7.9	7.1	6.6	6.7	6.7	6.9	6.2	6.4	6.5
Lost workdays	121.9	138.8	147.6	155.7	146.6	144.0						
Industrial machinery and equipment:												
Total cases	11.3	12.1	12.1	12.0	11.2	11.1	11.1	11.6	11.2	9.9	10.0	9.5
Lost workday cases	4.4	4.7	4.8	4.7	4.4	4.2	4.2	4.4	4.4	4.0	4.1	4.0
Lost workdays	72.7	82.8	86.8	88.9	86.6	87.7						
Electronic and other electrical equipment:												
Total cases	7.2	8.0	9.1	9.1	8.6	8.4	8.3	8.3	7.6	6.8	6.6	5.9
Lost workday cases	3.1	3.3	3.9	3.8	3.7	3.6	3.5	3.6	3.3	3.1	3.1	2.8
Lost workdays	55.9	64.6	77.5	79.4	83.0	81.2						
Transportation equipment:												
Total cases	13.5	17.7	17.7	17.8	18.3	18.7	18.5	19.6	18.6	16.3	15.4	14.6
Lost workday cases	5.7	6.6	6.8	6.9	7.0	7.1	7.1	7.8	7.9	7.0	6.6	6.6
Lost workdays	105.7	134.2	138.6	153.7	166.1	186.6						

TABLE 1.28

Occupational Injury and Illness Rates, Private Sector, 1987–1998 [CONTINUED]

Industry and type of case[2]	Incidence rates per 100 full-time workers[3]											
	1987	1988	1989[1]	1990	1991	1992	1993[4]	1994[4]	1995[4]	1996[4]	1997[4]	1998[4]
Finance, insurance, and real estate												
Total cases	2.0	2.0	2.0	2.4	2.4	2.9	2.9	2.7	2.6	2.4	2.2	1.9
Lost workday cases	.9	.9	.9	1.1	1.1	1.2	1.2	1.1	1.0	.9	0.9	0.7
Lost workdays	14.3	17.2	17.6	27.3	24.1	32.9						
Services												
Total cases	5.5	5.4	5.5	6.0	6.2	7.1	6.7	6.5	6.4	6.0	5.6	5.2
Lost workday cases	2.7	2.6	2.7	2.8	2.8	3.0	2.8	2.8	2.8	2.6	2.5	2.4
Lost workdays	45.8	47.7	51.2	56.4	60.0	68.6						

[1] Data for 1989 and subsequent years are based on the *Standard Industrial Classification Manual*, 1987 Edition. For this reason, they are not strictly comparable with data for the years 1985-88, which were based on the *Standard Industrial Classification Manual*, 1972 Edition, 1977 Supplement.

[2] Beginning with the 1992 survey, the annual survey measures only nonfatal injuries and illnesses, while past surveys covered both fatal and nonfatal incidents. To better address fatalities, a basic element of workplace safety, BLS implemented the Census of Fatal Occupational Injuries.

[3] The incidencerates represent the number of injuries and illnesses or lost workdays per 100 full-time workers and were calculated as (N/EH) X 200,000, where:

N = number of injuries and illnesses or lost workdays;

EH = total hours worked by all employees during the calendar year; and 200,000 = base for 100 full-time equivalent workers (working 40 hours per week, 50 weeks per year).

[4] Beginning with the 1993 survey, lost workday estimates will not be generated. As of 1992, BLS began generating percent distributions and the median number of days away from work by industry and for groups of workers sustaining similar work disabilities.

[5] Excludes farms with fewer than 11 employees since 1976.

Data not available.

SOURCE: *Monthly Labor Review*. Bureau of Labor Statistics, March 2000

TABLE 1.29

Fatal Occupational Injuries by Event or Exposure, 1993–1998

Event or exposure[1]	Fatalities			
	1993-97 average	1997[2] Number	1998 Number	1998 Percent
Total	6,335	6,238	6,026	100
Transportation incidents	2,611	2,605	2,630	44
Highway	1,334	1,393	1,431	24
Collision between vehicles, mobile equipment	652	640	701	12
Moving in same direction	109	103	118	2
Moving in opposite directions, oncoming	234	230	271	4
Moving in intersection	132	142	142	2
Vehicle struck stationary object or equipment	249	282	306	5
Noncollision	360	387	373	6
Jackknifed or overturned— no collision	267	298	300	5
Nonhighway (farm, industrial premises)	388	377	384	6
Overturned	214	216	216	4
Aircraft	315	261	223	4
Worker struck by a vehicle	373	367	413	7
Water vehicle	106	109	112	2
Railway	83	93	60	1
Assaults and violent acts	1,241	1,111	960	16
Homicides	995	860	709	12
Shooting	810	708	569	9
Stabbing	75	73	61	1
Other, including bombing	110	79	79	1
Self-inflicted injuries	215	216	223	4
Contact with objects and equipment	1,005	1,035	941	16
Struck by object	573	579	517	9
Struck by falling object	369	384	317	5
Struck by flying object	65	54	58	1
Caught in or compressed by equipment or objects	290	320	266	4
Caught in running equipment or machinery	153	189	129	2
Caught in or crushed in collapsing materials	124	118	140	2
Falls	668	716	702	12
Fall to lower level	591	653	623	10
Fall from ladder	94	116	111	2
Fall from roof	139	154	156	3
Fall from scaffold	83	87	97	2
Fall on same level	52	44	51	1
Exposure to harmful substances or environments	586	554	572	9
Contact with electric current	320	298	334	6
Contact with overhead powerlines	128	138	153	3
Contact with temperature extremes	43	40	46	1
Exposure to caustic, noxious, or allergenic substances	120	123	104	2
Inhalation of substance	70	59	48	1
Oxygen deficiency	101	90	87	1
Drowning, submersion	80	72	75	1
Fires and explosions	199	196	205	3
Other events or exposures[3]	26	21	16	-

[1] Based on the 1992 BLS Occupational Injury and Illness Classification Structure.

[2] The BLS news release issued Aug. 12, 1998, reported a total of 6,218 fatal work injuries for calendar year 1997. Since then, an additional 20 job-related fatalities were identified, bringing the total job-related fatality count for 1997 to 6,238.

[3] Includes the category "Bodily reaction and exertion."

NOTE: Totals for major categories may include subcategories not shown separately. Percentages may not add to totals because of rounding. Dashes indicate less than 0.5 percent or data that are not available or that do not meet publication criteria.

SOURCE: *National Census of Occupational Injuries, 1998.* Bureau of Labor Statistics, August 1999

FIGURE 1.4

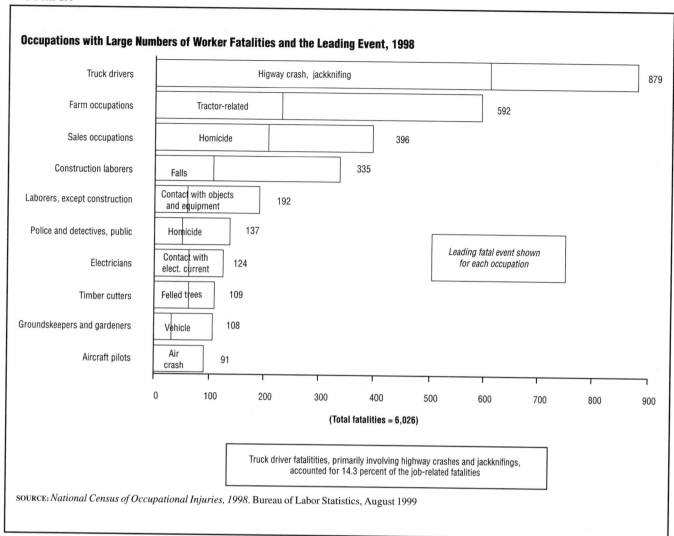

Occupations with Large Numbers of Worker Fatalities and the Leading Event, 1998

Occupation	Leading Event	Fatalities
Truck drivers	Higway crash, jackknifing	879
Farm occupations	Tractor-related	592
Sales occupations	Homicide	396
Construction laborers	Falls	335
Laborers, except construction	Contact with objects and equipment	192
Police and detectives, public	Homicide	137
Electricians	Contact with elect. current	124
Timber cutters	Felled trees	109
Groundskeepers and gardeners	Vehicle	108
Aircraft pilots	Air crash	91

Leading fatal event shown for each occupation

(Total fatalities = 6,026)

Truck driver fatalitities, primarily involving highway crashes and jackknifings, accounted for 14.3 percent of the job-related fatalities

SOURCE: *National Census of Occupational Injuries, 1998.* Bureau of Labor Statistics, August 1999

TABLE 1.30

Fatal Occupational Injuries and Employment by Industry, 1998

Industry	SIC code[1]	Fatalities				Employment[2] (in thousands)	
		1993–97 average Number	1997 (revised) Number	1998 Number	1998 Percent	Number	Percent
Total		6,335	6,238	6,026	100	132,684	100
Private industry		5,662	5,616	5,428	90	113,066	85
Agriculture, forestry, and fishing		831	833	831	14	3,450	3
Agricultural production – crops	01	383	373	378	6	1,012	1
Agricultural production – livestock	02	178	183	174	3	1,092	1
Agricultural services	07	165	178	167	3	1,259	1
Mining		164	158	146	2	618	–
Coal mining	12	39	32	30	–	82	–
Oil and gas extraction	13	88	85	76	1	373	–
Construction		1,034	1,107	1,171	19	8,044	6
General building contractors	15	180	194	212	4	–	–
Heavy construction, except building	16	249	252	271	4	–	–
Special trades contractors	17	597	648	679	11	–	–
Manufacturing		747	744	694	12	20,665	16
Food and kindred products	20	78	78	72	1	1,654	1
Lumber and wood products	24	198	199	170	3	861	1
Transportation and public utilities		944	1,008	909	15	7,713	6
Local and interurban passenger transportation	41	109	106	85	1	552	–
Trucking and warehousing	42	509	573	562	9	2,578	2
Transportation by air	45	91	83	74	1	832	1
Electric, gas, and sanitary services	49	86	89	83	1	1,060	1
Wholesale trade		258	241	228	4	5,077	4
Retail trade		728	670	569	9	22,010	17
Food stores	54	205	192	135	2	3,602	3
Automotive dealers and service stations	55	120	115	119	2	2,221	2
Eating and drinking places	58	174	151	107	2	6,723	5
Finance, insurance, and real estate		114	97	92	2	8,399	6
Services		776	727	757	13	37,090	28
Business services	73	202	183	194	3	6,403	5
Automotive repair, services, and parking	75	108	110	132	2	1,532	1
Government[3]		674	622	598	10	19,618	15
Federal (including resident armed forces)		209	162	164	3	4,468	3
State		129	125	135	2	5,160	4
Local		329	331	295	5	9,990	8
Police protection	9,221	101	114	101	2	–	–

[1] Standard Industrial Classification Manual, 1987 Edition.

[2] Employment is an annual average of employed civilians 16 years of age and older, plus resident armed forces, from the Current Population Survey, 1998.

[3] Includes fatalities to workers employed by government organizations regardless of industry.

NOTE: Totals for major categories may include subcategories not shown separately. Percentages may not add to totals because of rounding. There were 31 fatalities for which there was insufficient information to determine a specific industry classification, though a distinction between private sector and government was made for each. Dashes indicate less than 0.5 percent or data that are not available or that do not meet publication criteria.

SOURCE: *National Census of Occupational Injuries, 1998*. Bureau of Labor Statistics, August 1999

FIGURE 1.5

Violent Incidents in the Workplace

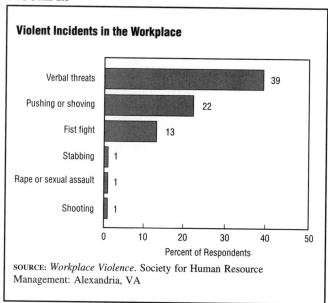

SOURCE: *Workplace Violence*. Society for Human Resource Management: Alexandria, VA

TABLE 1.31

Victims of Violence in the Workplace, 1992–1996

	Victimization in the workplace		All victimizations	
	Annual average	Percent	Annual average	Percent
Total	**2,010,800**	**100.0%**	**10,868,900**	**100.0%**
Homicide[1]	1,023	0.05	22,568	0.2
Rape and sexual assault	50,500	2.5	466,900	4.3
Robbery	83,700	4.2	1,274,500	11.7
Aggravated assault	395,500	19.7	2,364,600	21.7
Simple assault	1,480,000	73.6	6,740,300	62.0

[1]Homicide data from the FBI's UCR include murder and nonnegligent manslaughter.

SOURCE: Greg Warchol. *Workplace Violence, 1992–96*. Bureau of Justice Statistics: Washington, D.C.

TABLE 1.32

Occupations of Victims of Nonfatal Workplace Violence, 1992–1996

	Victims of workplace nonfatal violence	
Occupation	Annual average	Number per 1,000 workers
Total[a]	**2,009,400**	**14.8**
Medical		
Physicians	10,000	15.7
Nurses	69,500	24.8
Technician	24,500	21.4
Other	56,800	10.7
Mental health		
Professional	50,300	79.5
Custodial	8,700	63.3
Other	43,500	64.0
Teaching		
Preschool[b]	2,400	3.6
Elementary	35,400	16.0
Junior high	47,300	57.4
High school	33,300	28.9
College/university	6,600	2.5
Technical/industrial[b]	400	4.4
Special education	9,000	40.7
Other	14,400	10.1
Law enforcement		
Police	234,200	306.0
Private security	58,300	217.8
Prison guard	71,100	117.3
Other	67,600	61.5
Retail sales		
Convenience/liquor store	61,500	68.4
Gas station	15,500	79.1
Bar	26,400	91.3
Other	228,200	17.5
Transportation		
Taxi driver	16,100	183.8
Bus driver	17,200	45.0
Other	43,200	10.0
Other/unspecified	758,000	8.2

Note: Rates are calculated using population estimates from the NCVS for occupation, 1992-96. Detail may not add to total because of rounding.

[a] The total for specified occupations was 1,251,400, with 29.4 victims of workplace violence per 1,000 workers.

[b] Fewer than 10 sample cases.

SOURCE: Greg Warchol. *Workplace Violence, 1992–96*. Bureau of Justice Statistics: Washington, D.C.

CHAPTER 2
THE CHANGING AMERICAN WORKFORCE

A WORKPLACE IN TRANSITION

Throughout most of the 1990s, the rapid increase in the labor force (those working part- or full-time or unemployed but actively looking for a job) put a severe strain on the economic system to produce more jobs. At the same time, multinational companies shifted many tasks overseas, worldwide competition became more intense, and significant economic activity became international. American companies responded to these changes in many ways:

• Greater use of technologically advanced machinery designed to replace human workers;

• Greater pressure on workers to limit wage and benefit demands (especially for new entrants into the job market), or to "give back" already existing benefits;

• Management programs designed to accomplish more per worker so that the economy could remain competitive with international economies (which often have considerably lower standards of living);

• Employee reductions through layoffs or early retirement; and

• Increased attempts to become part of an international economy.

Downsizing the labor force to become more competitive in the international market became the management style of many companies in the late 1980s and early 1990s. Many companies laid off older workers to cut expenses. (See Chapter 1 for information on older workers and Chapter 3 for unemployment statistics of older workers.)

Many of these laid-off workers, however, returned to their firms as contract workers. An estimated one-fifth of contract workers, more than 1 million persons, are working for their old companies after having been laid off or forced to take early retirement. Some are working for less money than they had earned when they were employees. Even if the firm is paying the contract worker at the same rate, the companies do not have to pay for health or retirement benefits.

In 1997 and 1998 a booming economy led to the creation of hundreds of thousands of new jobs. This led to a tight labor market in which there was a demand for workers. Earlier in the decade, workers worried about losing their jobs and tended not to ask for raises. The changing economy, with many areas having a shortage of workers, has changed some workers' outlooks on job possibilities and wage increases. College graduates at the end of the 1990s were finding jobs more easily than in the past, and many received signing bonuses.

At the same time the economy was producing many thousands of jobs, the U.S. Conference of Mayors, in its survey of 13 cities, feared a shortage of low-skill jobs. For example, in 1997, Detroit officials estimated that more than 93,000 people, including welfare recipients participating in workfare, would compete for a projected 18,447 jobs. In a *New York Times* interview, Robert Lehrman, an economics professor at American University, commented that the economy produces 2 million jobs annually and that job seekers, including those leaving welfare, total 1.7 million. The problem, however, is that the majority (87 percent) of the low-skilled jobs are in the suburbs, and the people in need of low-skilled jobs are in the inner cities. Public transportation between the two places is not always available.

SERVICE ECONOMY

The American economy has moved away from producing goods to providing services. From about 1970 to 2000, the service-producing sector has accounted for an increasing proportion of workers. In 1960, for every goods-producing worker, there were about 1.7 service-producing workers. By 1970 the ratio was 1 to 2, and by 1999, it was slightly over 1 in 4. (See Table 2.1.)

TABLE 2.1

Employees on Nonfarm Payrolls by Major Industry, 1948–2000

(In thousands)

Year and Month	Total	Total private	Goods-producing			
			Total	Mining	Construction	Manufacturing
Annual averages						
1948	44,866	39,216	18,774	994	2,198	15,582
1949	43,754	37,897	17,565	930	2,194	14,441
1950	45,197	39,170	18,506	901	2,364	15,241
1951	47,819	41,430	19,959	929	2,637	16,393
1952	48,793	42,185	20,198	898	2,668	16,632
1953	50,202	43,556	21,074	866	2,659	17,549
1954	48,990	42,238	19,751	791	2,646	16,314
1955	50,641	43,727	20,513	792	2,839	16,882
1956	52,369	45,091	21,104	822	3,039	17,243
1957	52,855	45,239	20,967	828	2,962	17,176
1958	51,322	43,483	19,513	751	2,817	15,945
1959[2]	53,270	45,186	20,411	732	3,004	16,675
1960	54,189	45,836	20,434	712	2,926	16,796
1961	53,999	45,404	19,857	672	2,859	16,326
1962	55,549	46,660	20,451	650	2,948	16,853
1963	56,653	47,429	20,640	635	3,010	16,995
1964	58,283	48,686	21,005	634	3,097	17,274
1965	60,763	50,689	21,926	632	3,232	18,062
1966	63,901	53,116	23,158	627	3,317	19,214
1967	65,803	54,413	23,308	613	3,248	19,447
1968	67,897	56,058	23,737	606	3,350	19,781
1969	70,384	58,189	24,361	619	3,575	20,167
1970	70,880	58,325	23,578	623	3,588	19,367
1971	71,211	58,331	22,935	609	3,704	18,623
1972	73,675	60,341	23,668	628	3,889	19,151
1973	76,790	63,058	24,893	642	4,097	20,154
1974	78,265	64,095	24,794	697	4,020	20,077
1975	76,945	62,259	22,600	752	3,525	18,323
1976	79,382	64,511	23,352	779	3,576	18,997
1977	82,471	67,344	24,346	813	3,851	19,682
1978	86,697	71,026	25,585	851	4,229	20,505
1979	89,823	73,876	26,461	958	4,463	21,040
1980	90,406	74,166	25,658	1,027	4,346	20,285
1981	91,152	75,121	25,497	1,139	4,188	20,170
1982	89,544	73,707	23,812	1,128	3,904	18,780
1983	90,152	74,282	23,330	952	3,946	18,432
1984	94,408	78,384	24,718	966	4,380	19,372
1985	97,387	80,992	24,842	927	4,668	19,248
1986	99,344	82,651	24,533	777	4,810	18,947
1987	101,958	84,948	24,674	717	4,958	18,999
1988	105,209	87,823	25,125	713	5,098	19,314
1989	107,884	90,105	25,254	692	5,171	19,391
1990	109,403	91,098	24,905	709	5,120	19,076
1991	108,249	89,847	23,745	689	4,650	18,406
1992	108,601	89,956	23,231	635	4,492	18,104
1993	110,713	91,872	23,352	610	4,668	18,075
1994	114,163	95,036	23,908	601	4,986	18,321
1995	117,191	97,885	24,265	581	5,160	18,524
1996	119,608	100,189	24,493	580	5,418	18,495
1997	122,690	103,133	24,962	596	5,691	18,675
1998	125,826	106,007	25,347	590	5,985	18,772
1999	128,615	108,455	25,240	535	6,273	18,432

From 1990 to 2000 only the construction industry in the goods-producing area has employed more workers, while the numbers working in mining have fallen significantly. The number of workers in manufacturing has stayed somewhat level from 1970 to 2000, but the proportion of manufacturing jobs fell from 35 percent of all jobs in 1947 to just 14 percent in 1999.

Indeed, in 1945 at the conclusion of World War II, the services industry accounted for 10 percent of nonfarm employment, compared with 38 percent for manufacturing. (See Figure 2.1.) In 1982 services surpassed manufacturing as the largest employer among major industry groups. By 1996 the services industry accounted for 29 percent of nonfarm employment, and manufacturing, at 15 percent, was actually somewhat smaller than retail trade.

Service-producing industries include jobs in transportation, wholesale and retail trade, services, and finance, etc. Within the service-producing industry, ser-

TABLE 2.1

Employees on Nonfarm Payrolls by Major Industry, 1948–2000 [CONTINUED]

(In thousands)

Year and Month	Total	Transportation and public utilities	Wholesale trade	Retail trade	Finance, insurance, and real estate	Government Services	Federal	State	Local
					Service-producing				
					Annual averages				
1948	26,092	4,189	2,612	6,659	1,800	5,181	1,863	(1)	(1)
1949	26,189	4,001	2,610	6,654	1,828	5,239	1,908	(1)	(1)
1950	26,691	4,034	2,643	6,743	1,888	5,356	1,928	(1)	(1)
1951	27,860	4,226	2,735	7,007	1,956	5,547	2,302	(1)	(1)
1952	28,595	4,248	2,821	7,184	2,035	5,699	2,420	(1)	(1)
1953	29,128	4,290	2,862	7,385	2,111	5,835	2,305	(1)	(1)
1954	29,239	4,084	2,875	7,360	2,200	5,969	2,188	(1)	(1)
1955	30,128	4,141	2,934	7,601	2,298	6,240	2,187	1,168	3,558
1956	31,264	4,244	3,027	7,831	2,389	6,497	2,209	1,250	3,819
1957	31,889	4,241	3,037	7,848	2,438	6,708	2,217	1,328	4,071
1958	31,811	3,976	2,989	7,761	2,481	6,765	2,191	1,415	4,232
1959[2]	32,857	4,011	3,092	8,035	2,549	7,087	2,233	1,484	4,366
1960	33,755	4,004	3,153	8,238	2,628	7,378	2,270	1,536	4,547
1961	34,142	3,903	3,142	8,195	2,688	7,619	2,279	1,607	4,708
1962	35,098	3,906	3,207	8,359	2,754	7,982	2,340	1,668	4,881
1963	36,013	3,903	3,258	8,520	2,830	8,277	2,358	1,747	5,121
1964	37,278	3,951	3,347	8,812	2,911	8,660	2,348	1,856	5,392
1965	38,839	4,036	3,477	9,239	2,977	9,036	2,378	1,996	5,700
1966	40,743	4,158	3,608	9,637	3,058	9,498	2,564	2,141	6,080
1967	42,495	4,268	3,700	9,906	3,185	10,045	2,719	2,302	6,371
1968	44,158	4,318	3,791	10,308	3,337	10,567	2,737	2,442	6,660
1969	46,023	4,442	3,919	10,785	3,512	11,169	2,758	2,533	6,904
1970	47,302	4,515	4,006	11,034	3,645	11,548	2,731	2,664	7,158
1971	48,276	4,476	4,014	11,338	3,772	11,797	2,696	2,747	7,437
1972	50,007	4,541	4,127	11,822	3,908	12,276	2,684	2,859	7,790
1973	51,897	4,656	4,291	12,315	4,046	12,857	2,663	2,923	8,146
1974	53,471	4,725	4,447	12,539	4,148	13,441	2,724	3,039	8,407
1975	54,345	4,542	4,430	12,630	4,165	13,892	2,748	3,179	8,758
1976	56,030	4,582	4,562	13,193	4,271	14,551	2,733	3,273	8,865
1977	58,125	4,713	4,723	13,792	4,467	15,302	2,727	3,377	9,023
1978	61,113	4,923	4,985	14,556	4,724	16,252	2,753	3,474	9,446
1979	63,363	5,136	5,221	14,972	4,975	17,112	2,773	3,541	9,633
1980	64,748	5,146	5,292	15,018	5,160	17,890	2,866	3,610	9,765
1981	65,655	5,165	5,375	15,171	5,298	18,615	2,772	3,640	9,619
1982	65,732	5,081	5,295	15,158	5,340	19,021	2,739	3,640	9,458
1983	66,821	4,952	5,283	15,587	5,466	19,664	2,774	3,662	9,434
1984	69,690	5,156	5,568	16,512	5,684	20,746	2,807	3,734	9,482
1985	72,544	5,233	5,727	17,315	5,948	21,927	2,875	3,832	9,687
1986	74,811	5,247	5,761	17,880	6,273	22,957	2,899	3,893	9,901
1987	77,284	5,362	5,848	18,422	6,533	24,110	2,943	3,967	10,100
1988	80,084	5,512	6,030	19,023	6,630	25,504	2,971	4,076	10,339
1989	82,630	5,614	6,187	19,475	6,668	26,907	2,988	4,182	10,609
1990	84,497	5,777	6,173	19,601	6,709	27,934	3,085	4,305	10,914
1991	84,504	5,755	6,081	19,284	6,646	28,336	2,966	4,355	11,081
1992	85,370	5,718	5,997	19,356	6,602	29,052	2,969	4,408	11,267
1993	87,361	5,811	5,981	19,773	6,757	30,197	2,915	4,488	11,438
1994	90,256	5,984	6,162	20,507	6,896	31,579	2,870	4,576	11,682
1995	92,925	6,132	6,378	21,187	6,806	33,117	2,822	4,635	11,849
1996	95,115	6,253	6,482	21,597	6,911	34,454	2,757	4,606	12,056
1997	97,727	6,408	6,648	21,966	7,109	36,040	2,699	4,582	12,276
1998	100,480	6,600	6,831	22,296	7,407	37,526	2,686	4,612	12,521
1999	103,375	6,792	7,004	22,787	7,632	39,000	2,669	4,695	12,796

[2] Data include Alaska and Hawaii beginning in 1959. This inclusion resulted in an increase of 212,000 (0.4 percent) in the nonfarm total for the March 1959 benchmark month.

NOTE: Establishment survey estimates are currently projected from March 1998 benchmark levels. When more recent benchmark data are introduced, all unadjusted data (beginning April 1998) and all seasonally adjusted data (beginning January 1995) are subject to revision.

SOURCE: *Employment and Earnings.* Bureau of Labor Statistics

vice industry jobs include legal services, hotels, health services, educational services, and social services, among others. However, all jobs within the service industry are not necessarily service occupations. For example, while hotels are part of the services industry within the service-producing sector, they employ workers who are not only in service occupations, but also secretaries, managers, and accountants whose occupations are not considered service occupations.

About 20.2 million persons (20 percent of the non-farm working population) worked for the government in

FIGURE 2.1

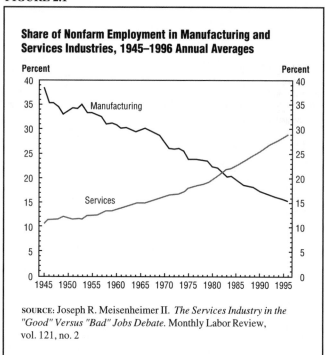

Share of Nonfarm Employment in Manufacturing and Services Industries, 1945–1996 Annual Averages

SOURCE: Joseph R. Meisenheimer II. *The Services Industry in the "Good" Versus "Bad" Jobs Debate.* Monthly Labor Review, vol. 121, no. 2

1999. Between 1990 and 1999, the federal government lost 13.5 percent of its workers, while state and local governments increased their workforce by 8 percent and 15 percent, respectively. (See Table 2.1.)

Because average wages are higher in manufacturing than in services, some observers view employment shifts to services as a change from "good" to "bad" jobs. In "The Services Industry in the 'Good' Versus 'Bad' Jobs Debate" (*Monthly Labor Review*, February 1998), Joseph R. Meisenheimer II found that many service industries equal or exceed manufacturing and other industries on measures of job quality, while some services industries could be viewed as less desirable by these measures.

Meisenheimer stresses the importance of examining more than just average pay when assessing the quality of jobs in each industry. Within each industry, there are jobs at a variety of different quality levels. The quality of services-industry jobs is especially diverse, encompassing many of the "best" jobs in the economy and a substantial share of the "worst." Thus, employment shifts away from manufacturing and toward services do not necessarily signal deterioration in overall job quality in the United States, although, in many cases, it certainly can.

HOW LONG DO AMERICANS WORK?

Between 1990 and 1995 America stood out among all nations as a nation with an advanced economy that had the longest work year. Japan's average work year, on the other hand, declined during that time period. The United States has a long work year due in part to a lack of legally mandated, employer-paid vacation time. Such paid vacation time is common in many countries in Europe.

In 1999 about 76 percent of nonfarm American workers were working full-time (35 hours or more), while the remaining 24 percent were working part-time (less than 35 hours). The average worker labored 39.5 hours per week (average hours of part-time and full-time), while the average full-time employee worked 43.3 hours per week. Women (32 percent) were more likely to work part-time than men (17 percent). As a result, men worked an average of 42.4 hours per week, and women worked an average of 36.2 hours per week. (See Table 2.2.) Almost 20 percent of all nonfarm workers spent more than 49 hours a week on the job. Almost one-third (32 percent) of agricultural workers labored more than 49 hours per week. (See Table 2.3.)

Some occupations required more time than others. Transportation and material-moving workers worked 43.3 hours per week (45.9 hours for workers on full-time schedules). Executive, administrative, and managerial people averaged about 43.9 hours (45.7 hours a week for full-time). On the other hand, private household workers averaged only 28.5 hours a week (41.5 hours for full-time). (See Table 2.2.)

According to the Bureau of Labor Statistics (BLS), the average number of hours worked each week has changed little since the mid-1970s, but the proportion of persons working very long workweeks has risen. Figure 2.2 shows that the proportion of nonagricultural wage and salary workers who worked exactly 40 hours per week declined between 1976 and 1993, while the share working 49 hours or more rose. The proportions working fewer than 40 hours and 41 to 48 hours remained fairly stable.

From 1976 to 1993 average hours at work increased only 1 hour for men and 2 hours for women. (See Table 2.4.) Part of these increases can be attributed to the changing age profile of the American workforce. By 1993 baby-boomers—those born between 1946 and 1964—had all moved into the middle working ages of 25 to 54. Meanwhile, younger and older workers made up a declining share of employment. Workweeks typically are longer for workers age 25 to 54, and part-time employment is more common among younger and older workers.

Table 2.5 shows the calculation as if the age distribution of those at work had remained unchanged since 1976. After removing the effect of age, the workweek for men was virtually unchanged, and women's weekly hours rose by only a single hour.

Many employees are working longer hours by skipping or shortening their lunch breaks. In 1996 the National Restaurant Association reported that 40 percent of the

TABLE 2.2

Persons at Work in Nonfarm Occupations by Sex and Usual Full- or Part-Time Status
(Numbers in thousands)

Occupation and Sex	Total at work	1999 Worked 1 to 34 hours — Total	For economic reasons	For noneconomic reasons — Usually work full time	Usually work part time	Worked 35 hours or more	Average hours — Total at work	Persons who usually work full time
Total, 16 years and over[1]	124,812	29,988	3,182	8,593	18,214	94,824	39.5	43.3
Managerial and professional specialty	38,571	7,246	466	2,919	3,861	31,326	42.0	44.7
Executive, administrative, and managerial	18,951	2,746	154	1,335	1,257	16,205	43.9	45.7
Professional specialty	19,620	4,500	312	1,584	2,603	15,120	40.2	43.7
Technical, sales, and administrative support	37,460	10,597	849	2,564	7,184	26,864	37.7	42.3
Technicians and related support	4,201	912	55	328	529	3,289	39.4	42.2
Sales occupations	15,528	4,613	463	765	3,384	10,915	38.7	44.6
Administrative support, including clerical	17,731	5,071	331	1,470	3,270	12,660	36.4	40.4
Service occupations	17,181	6,678	847	955	4,876	10,503	34.9	42.1
Private household	799	462	63	42	358	336	28.5	41.5
Protective service	2,331	382	36	146	200	1,949	42.4	44.9
Service, except private household and protective	14,051	5,833	748	767	4,319	8,218	34.0	41.4
Precision production, craft, and repair	14,089	1,963	380	1,031	552	12,126	42.2	43.3
Operators, fabricators, and laborers	17,510	3,505	640	1,125	1,740	14,005	40.4	43.1
Machine operators, assemblers, and inspectors	7,127	1,045	209	478	358	6,082	40.9	42.2
Transportation and material moving occupations	5,284	924	150	308	466	4,360	43.3	45.9
Handlers, equipment cleaners, helpers, and laborers	5,100	1,537	281	339	917	3,563	36.8	41.4
Men, 16 years and over[1]	66,484	11,162	1,494	4,062	5,606	55,322	42.4	44.9
Managerial and professional specialty	19,760	2,526	208	1,246	1,072	17,234	45.1	46.7
Executive, administrative, and managerial	10,440	1,089	79	601	409	9,351	46.4	47.7
Professional specialty	9,320	1,437	129	645	664	7,882	43.5	45.7
Technical, sales, and administrative support	13,676	2,549	224	748	1,578	11,127	41.8	45.0
Technicians and related support	2,031	310	21	149	140	1,721	41.9	43.6
Sales occupations	7,827	1,457	135	333	989	6,371	43.0	46.7
Administrative support, including clerical	3,818	782	68	266	449	3,035	39.3	42.3
Service occupations	6,861	1,973	280	338	1,355	4,888	38.0	43.4
Private household	39	24	4	3	16	15	27.7	42.7
Protective service	1,896	260	23	113	123	1,636	43.6	45.5
Service, except private household and protective	4,926	1,689	252	221	1,215	3,237	35.9	42.4
Precision production, craft, and repair	12,842	1,705	340	933	432	11,137	42.4	43.4
Operators, fabricators, and laborers	13,344	2,409	442	797	1,169	10,935	41.4	43.9
Machine operators, assemblers, and inspectors	4,505	515	101	267	148	3,990	42.1	43.0
Transportation and material moving occupations	4,774	727	125	267	335	4,047	44.1	46.2
Handlers, equipment cleaners, helpers, and laborers	4,065	1,166	217	264	686	2,899	37.3	41.7
Women, 16 years and over[1]	58,328	18,826	1,688	4,531	12,607	39,502	36.2	41.2
Managerial and professional specialty	18,811	4,719	258	1,673	2,788	14,092	38.8	42.4
Executive, administrative, and managerial	8,511	1,657	75	733	849	6,854	40.7	43.1
Professional specialty	10,300	3,063	183	939	1,940	7,238	37.3	41.7
Technical, sales, and administrative support	23,784	8,047	625	1,816	5,606	15,737	35.3	40.5
Technicians and related support	2,170	602	34	179	389	1,568	37.0	40.5
Sales occupations	7,701	3,156	328	432	2,396	4,544	34.2	41.7
Administrative support, including clerical	13,913	4,289	263	1,204	2,821	9,624	35.6	39.9
Service occupations	10,320	4,705	567	617	3,521	5,615	32.8	40.9
Private household	760	438	58	38	342	321	28.5	41.4
Protective service	435	122	13	33	77	313	37.2	42.0
Service, except private household and protective	9,125	4,144	495	546	3,103	4,981	33.0	40.8
Precision production, craft, and repair	1,248	259	40	98	120	989	39.3	41.7
Operators, fabricators, and laborers	4,166	1,096	198	327	571	3,070	37.5	40.6
Machine operators, assemblers, and inspectors	2,621	529	109	211	210	2,092	38.8	40.7
Transportation and material moving occupations	510	197	25	40	131	313	35.7	41.8
Handlers, equipment cleaners, helpers, and laborers	1,035	370	64	76	231	665	34.9	40.0

[1] Excludes farming, forestry, and fishing occupations.

NOTE: Beginning in January 1999, data reflect revised population controls used in the household survey.

SOURCE: *Employment and Earnings*. Bureau of Labor Statistics, January 2000

---

surveyed workers said they did not leave the office for a lunch break. Forty-five percent reported they had less time for lunch than they ever had. In a *New York Times* interview, John Ragna, a Winter Park, Florida, workplace consultant, commented that people are feeling more pres-sure to get more things done at work, sometimes at the cost of working through lunch. Many workers say they stay on the jobs to get things done because they fear being downsized. Fewer workers often mean the remaining ones have to do more.

TABLE 2.3

Persons at Work in Agriculture and Nonagricultural Activities by Hours of Work

Hours of work	1999					
	Thousands of persons			Percent distribution		
	All industries	Agriculture	Nonagricultural industries	All industries	Agriculture	Nonagricultural industries
Total, 16 years and over	128,081	3,132	124,948	100.0	100.0	100.0
1 to 34 hours	30,913	913	30,000	24.1	29.2	24.0
1 to 4 hours	1,230	67	1,164	1.0	2.1	.9
5 to 14 hours	4,844	197	4,647	3.8	6.3	3.7
15 to 29 hours	15,339	436	14,903	12.0	13.9	11.9
30 to 34 hours	9,500	213	9,286	7.4	6.8	7.4
35 hours and over	97,167	2,219	94,948	75.9	70.8	76.0
35 to 39 hours	8,670	160	8,510	6.8	5.1	6.8
40 hours	47,955	826	47,129	37.4	26.4	37.7
41 hours and over	40,542	1,234	39,309	31.7	39.4	31.5
41 to 48 hours	14,722	231	14,491	11.5	7.4	11.6
49 to 59 hours	14,986	366	14,620	11.7	11.7	11.7
60 hours and over	10,834	637	10,198	8.5	20.3	8.2
Average hours, total at work	39.6	41.9	39.5	–	–	–
Average hours, persons who usually work full time	43.4	48.1	43.3	–	–	–

NOTE: Detail on persons at work may not sum to the totals shown because of minor editing problems associated with the redesigned survey. Beginning in January 1999, data reflect revised population controls used in the household survey.

SOURCE: *Employment and Earnings.* Bureau of Labor Statistics, January 2000

FIGURE 2.2

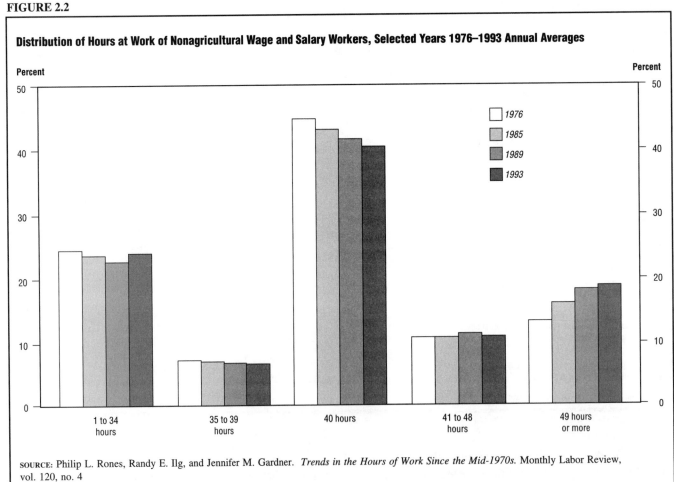

Distribution of Hours at Work of Nonagricultural Wage and Salary Workers, Selected Years 1976–1993 Annual Averages

SOURCE: Philip L. Rones, Randy E. Ilg, and Jennifer M. Gardner. *Trends in the Hours of Work Since the Mid-1970s.* Monthly Labor Review, vol. 120, no. 4

TABLE 2.4

Percent Distribution of Nonagricultural Wage and Salary Workers at Work and Their Average Weekly Hours by Age and Sex, 1976 and 1993 Annual Averages

Characteristics	Total at work		Average hours	
	1976	1993	1976	1993
Total (thousands)	73,276	102,615	38.1	39.2
16 to 24 years	24.0	16.7	33.6	32.5
25 to 54 years	62.2	72.6	40.1	41.1
55 years and over	13.8	10.7	37.2	36.8
Men (thousands)	42,994	54,573	41.0	42.0
16 to 24 years	21.8	16.2	35.4	34.2
25 to 54 years	64.3	73.1	43.1	44.1
55 years and over	14.0	10.7	39.7	39.6
Women (thousands)	30,282	48,042	34.0	36.0
16 to 24 years	27.1	17.2	31.5	30.7
25 to 54 years	59.2	72.1	35.3	37.7
55 years and over	13.6	10.7	33.4	33.6

SOURCE: *How Long Is the Workweek?* Issues in Labor Statistics. Bureau of Labor Statistics: Washington, D.C.

Who Is Working the Longer Workweeks?

The growth in the share of workers reporting very long workweeks is often attributed to a shift in employment towards high-hour occupations, such as managers, professionals, and certain sales workers. (See Figure 2.3.) This may reflect the considerable responsibilities associated with many of these types of jobs. In addition, employers are often not required by law to pay overtime premiums to workers in these occupations, as they must do for most hourly paid workers. These salaried workers tend to be better paid.

On the other hand, sales and transportation workers who also work long workweeks are not, on average, highly paid. In these cases, a large proportion of workers may work 49 hours or more per week due to the direct relationship of hours and earnings (the more they work, the more they earn). Indeed, full-time sales workers employed by motor vehicle and boat dealerships averaged nearly 50 hours per week in 1995. However, full-time sales workers in apparel stores, occupations in which significant commissions are a less common form of pay, averaged less than 39 hours.

For specific segments of the population, the workweek showed a tendency to increase at the end of the twentieth century. According to the Bureau of Labor Statistics, women who had children worked more hours each week in 1998 than they did in 1969. The increase was most pronounced in women with children between the ages of 6 and 17. Between 1969 and 1998 hours worked per week for these women increased by 2.5 hours. Women with children between 3 and 5 years of age increased their workweek by 1.4 hours between 1969 and 1998. Men with children, on the other hand, decreased the length of their work week between 1969 and 1998; men with children under 3 years worked 0.8 hours less, and men with children between 3 and 5 years worked 0.3 hours less.

TABLE 2.5

Average Workweek

	Average hours		Age-adjusted hours
	1976	1993	1993
Men, 16 years and older	41.0	42.0	41.2
Women, 16 years and older	34.0	36.0	35.0

SOURCE: *How Long Is the Workweek?* Issues in Labor Statistics. Bureau of Labor Statistics: Washington, D.C.

Another study by the Bureau of Labor Statistics looked at welfare recipients who were able to obtain jobs. The study showed that this population segment usually worked a relatively high number of hours per week—usually over 30 hours—for relatively low pay. Such jobs usually paid between $8,000 to $10,000 per year.

Increases in average hours worked per week can have peripheral effects. A study by the insurance industry estimated that for each 1 percent increase in average hours worked per week, a 3.4 percent increase can be expected in injury and illness rates. Increases in work hours per week can also lead to job-related tiredness and stress, which can in turn result in injury and illness.

In 1997 many trade organizations reported that their members were working a lot of overtime because of the economic expansion. The Professional Secretaries International (Kansas City, Missouri) found that the proportion of its 27,000 members putting in 40 to 44 hours per week rose from 64.7 percent in 1992 to 68.4 percent in 1997. According to the National Restaurant Association, its members increased their average hours from 51.2 in 1992 to 56 hours in 1997. The BLS reported that the weekly hours for temporaries rose from 27.1 in 1982 to 32.3 in 1997. Manufacturing jobs reached an average of 4.8 hours per week overtime in May 1997, "quite a high level," according to William Goodman, a research analyst with the BLS. Goodman did not think that manufacturing overtime had "been this high since World War II."

The Work Year

The *Current Population Survey* shows that, from 1976 to 1993, U.S. workers, particularly women, have increasingly been working year round. More dramatic than the shift toward either full- or part-time work has been the trend toward year-round employment. (See Table 2.6 and Figure 2.4.)

Part-Time Work

People work part-time for various reasons. In 1999, 33 percent of part-time employees usually worked full-time. Eleven percent of part-time workers took part-time work due to economic conditions. These economic rea-

FIGURE 2.3

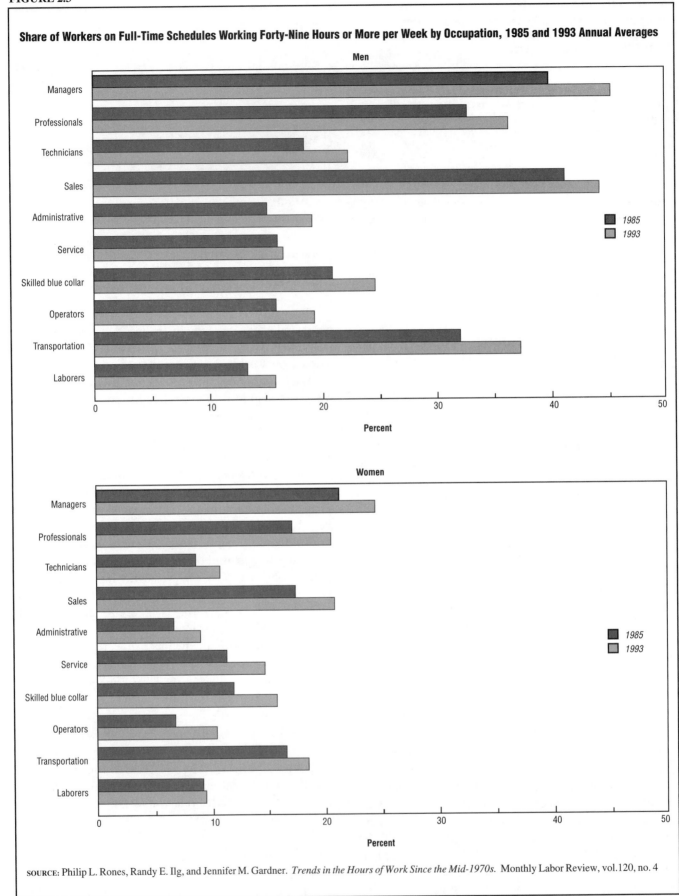

Share of Workers on Full-Time Schedules Working Forty-Nine Hours or More per Week by Occupation, 1985 and 1993 Annual Averages

SOURCE: Philip L. Rones, Randy E. Ilg, and Jennifer M. Gardner. *Trends in the Hours of Work Since the Mid-1970s.* Monthly Labor Review, vol.120, no. 4

TABLE 2.6

Average Annual Hours

	Men	Women
	(In thousands)	
Average annual work hours:		
1976	1,805	1,293
1993	1,905	1,526
1976-93 change	+l00	+233
Age-adjusted change	+62	+193

SOURCE: Philip L. Rones, Randy E. Ilg, and Jennifer M. Gardner. *Trends in the Hours of Work Since the Mid-1970s.* Monthly Labor Review, vol. 120, no. 4

FIGURE 2.4

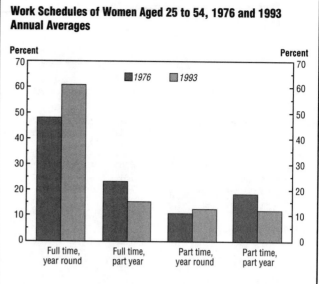

Work Schedules of Women Aged 25 to 54, 1976 and 1993 Annual Averages

SOURCE: Philip L. Rones, Randy E. Ilg, and Jennifer M. Gardner. *Trends in the Hours of Work Since the Mid-1970s.* Monthly Labor Review, vol.120, no. 4

TABLE 2.7

Persons at Work 1 to 34 Hours in All and Nonagricultural Industries by Reason for Working Less than 35 Hours and Usual Full- or Part-Time Status
(Numbers in thousands)

Reason for working less than 35 hours	1999					
	All industries			Nonagricultural industries		
	Total	Usually work full time	Usually work part time	Total	Usually work full time	Usually work part time
Total, 16 years and over	30,913	10,079	20,834	30,000	9,807	20,193
Economic reasons	3,357	1,281	2,076	3,189	1,193	1,996
Slack work or business conditions	1,968	1,021	947	1,861	962	899
Could only find part-time work	1,079	–	1,079	1,056	–	1,056
Seasonal work	147	97	50	115	74	41
Job started or ended during week	162	162	–	157	157	–
Noneconomic reasons	27,556	8,798	18,758	26,811	8,614	18,197
Child-care problems	856	86	770	843	84	759
Other family or personal obligations	5,629	746	4,882	5,476	727	4,749
Health or medical limitations	712	–	712	674	–	674
In school or training	6,463	100	6,363	6,320	97	6,223
Retired or Social Security limit on earnings	1,984	–	1,984	1,863	–	1,863
Vacation or personal day	3,239	3,239	–	3,188	3,188	–
Holiday, legal or religious	966	966	–	956	956	–
Weather-related curtailment	824	824	–	781	781	–
All other reasons	6,884	2,837	4,047	6,710	2,781	3,929
Average hours:						
Economic reasons	23.1	24.0	22.5	23.2	24.1	22.6
Noneconomic reasons	21.5	25.7	19.6	21.6	25.8	19.6

NOTE: Beginning in January 1999, data reflect revised population controls used in the household survey.

SOURCE: *Employment and Earnings.* Bureau of Labor Statistics, January 2000

TABLE 2.8

Multiple Jobholders by Selected Demographic and Economic Characteristics
(Numbers in thousands)

Characteristic	Both sexes Number 1998	Both sexes Number 1999	Both sexes Rate[1] 1998	Both sexes Rate[1] 1999	Men Number 1998	Men Number 1999	Men Rate[1] 1998	Men Rate[1] 1999	Women Number 1998	Women Number 1999	Women Rate[1] 1998	Women Rate[1] 1999
AGE												
Total, 16 years and over[2]	7,926	7,802	6.0	5.8	4,178	4,104	5.9	5.7	3,748	3,698	6.2	6.0
16 to 19 years	335	343	4.8	4.8	138	153	3.9	4.1	198	190	5.7	5.5
20 years and over	7,590	7,460	6.1	5.9	4,040	3,952	6.0	5.8	3,550	3,508	6.2	6.0
20 to 24 years	788	751	6.3	5.8	363	341	5.5	5.1	425	410	7.2	6.7
25 years and over	6,802	6,708	6.1	5.9	3,677	3,610	6.1	5.9	3,126	3,098	6.1	5.9
25 to 54 years	6,011	5,886	6.3	6.1	3,228	3,146	6.3	6.1	2,783	2,740	6.3	6.1
55 years and over	791	822	4.8	4.8	449	464	4.9	4.9	342	358	4.6	4.7
55 to 64 years	682	701	5.3	5.3	378	387	5.4	5.3	303	314	5.2	5.2
65 years and over	109	122	2.9	3.1	71	77	3.3	3.4	39	45	2.5	2.7
RACE AND HISPANIC ORIGIN												
White	6,832	6,674	6.2	5.9	3,622	3,514	6.0	5.7	3,210	3,159	6.4	6.2
Black	802	831	5.5	5.5	406	442	5.9	6.3	396	389	5.2	4.8
Hispanic origin	503	490	3.8	3.6	299	280	3.7	3.5	204	210	3.9	3.7
MARITAL STATUS												
Married, spouse present	4,414	4,309	5.8	5.6	2,664	2,566	6.2	5.9	1,750	1,744	5.3	5.2
Widowed, divorced, or separated	1,385	1,356	6.7	6.5	498	490	5.8	5.8	887	866	7.3	7.0
Single (never married)	2,127	2,137	6.1	5.9	1,016	1,048	5.3	5.3	1,110	1,089	7.0	6.7
FULL- OR PART-TIME STATUS												
Primary job full time, secondary job part time	4,478	4,293	–	–	2,608	2,497	–	–	1,870	1,796	–	–
Primary and secondary jobs both part time	1,635	1,657	–	–	512	519	–	–	1,124	1,138	–	–
Primary and secondary jobs both full time	266	298	–	–	188	204	–	–	78	94	–	–
Hours vary on primary or secondary job	1,504	1,513	–	–	848	861	–	–	656	652	–	–

[1]Multiple jobholders as a percent of all employed persons in specified group.

[2]Includes a small number of persons who work part time on their primary job and full time on their secondary jobs(s), not shown separately.

NOTE: Detail for the above race and Hispanic-origin groups will not sum to totals because data for the "other races" group are not presented and Hispanics are included in both the white and black population groups. Beginning in January 1999, data reflect revised population controls used in the household survey.

SOURCE: *Employment and Earnings.* Bureau of Labor Statistics, January 2000

TABLE 2.9

Distribution by Occupation of Employed Contingent and Noncontingent Workers, and Contingency Rates by Occupation, February 1995

Occupation	Contingent workers Estimate 1	Contingent workers Estimate 2	Contingent workers Estimate 3	Non-contingent workers
Total, 16 years and older (thousands)	2,739	3,422	6,034	117,174
Percent distribution	100.0	100.0	100.0	100.0
Executive, administrative, and managerial	4.9	5.5	7.6	14.0
Professional specialty	17.2	16.6	20.6	14.6
Technicians and related support	1.8	2.2	2.7	3.2
Sales occupations	6.2	6.9	6.4	12.2
Administrative support, including clerical	20.9	18.7	17.7	15.0
Service occupations	17.9	19.8	16.0	13.4
Precision production, craft, and repair	11.0	11.3	10.0	10.8
Operators, fabricators, and laborers	17.4	16.1	15.8	14.2
Farming, forestry and fishing	2.6	3.0	3.0	2.6
Contingency rates				
Total	2.2	2.8	4.9	. . . .
Executive, administrative, and managerial	.8	1.1	2.7	. . . .
Professional specialty	2.6	3.1	6.8	. . . .
Technicians and related support	1.3	1.9	4.2	. . . .
Sales occupations	1.2	1.6	2.6	. . . .
Administrative support, including clerical	3.1	3.4	5.8	. . . .
Service occupations	3.0	4.1	5.8	. . . .
Precision production, craft, and repair	2.3	2.9	4.6	. . . .
Operators, fabricators, and laborers	2.7	3.1	5.4	. . . .
Farming, forestry and fishing	2.2	3.2	5.6	. . . .

SOURCE: Anne E. Polivka. *A Profile of Contingent Workers.* Monthly Labor Review, vol. 119, no. 10

sons, usually caused by employers' circumstances, included slack work, material shortages, or the availability of only part-time work. Most (89 percent) workers who usually worked part-time did so for noneconomic reasons. They did not want to work full-time or were unavailable, perhaps because they were going to school, were taking care of children, or had other family or personal obligations. (See Table 2.7.)

MULTIPLE JOBS

In 1999, 5.8 percent of workers held multiple jobs. The multiple job-holding rate among men declined slightly from 7 percent in 1970 to 5.7 in 1999. On the other hand, the proportion of women holding more than one job increased significantly from 2 percent in 1970 to 6.0 percent in 1999. Single women (6.7 percent) and widowed, divorced, and separated women (7.0 percent) were most likely to have more than one job. Married women (5.2 percent) and single men (5.3 percent) were the least likely. (See Table 2.8.)

CONTINGENT WORKERS AND ALTERNATIVE WORK ARRANGEMENTS

According to the BLS, even though most studies have found no change in workers' overall job tenure (see Chapter 1), reports of corporate downsizing, production streamlining, and the increasing use of temporary workers have caused many workers to question employers' commitment to long-term, stable employment relationships. There is also a growing sense that employers, in their attempts to reduce costs, have increased their use of "employment intermediaries," such as temporary help services and contract companies, and are relying more on alternative staffing arrangements, such as on-call workers and independent contractors. Permanent workers sometimes fear they will be replaced by these alternatives.

Workers may take employment in a nonstandard arrangement, such as working for a temporary agency, for a number of reasons, including inability to find a permanent job, wanting to work fewer hours when they have a young child at home, or wanting to learn about a number of different jobs or fields. In addition, some nonstandard work arrangements, such as consulting or contracting, may provide workers with relatively more flexible and lucrative employment opportunities. To find out more about these types of workers, the BLS analyzed data from a special supplement to the *Current Population Survey* (see below).

Contingent Workers

The BLS defines contingent work as any job in which an individual does not have an explicit or implicit contract for long-term employment. This includes independent contractors, on-call workers, and those working for tem-

porary help services. The February *1995 Current Population Survey* estimated that between 2.7 and 6 million workers (2.2 to 4.9 percent of total employment) were in contingent positions. By 1999 a temporary employment agency in Milwaukee estimated that 2.5 percent of the U.S. workforce consisted of contingent workers.

The reason the estimates ran from 2.7 to 6 million is due to alternative definitions. Estimate 1, the narrowest estimate, included wage and salary workers who held their jobs for 1 year or less and expected to be employed for an additional year or less. Estimate 2, the middle estimate, added the self-employed and independent contractors. Estimate 3, the broadest estimate, dropped the time limit on wage and salary workers and included any worker who believed his or her job was temporary. (See Tables 2.9 and 2.10.)

Contingent workers were more likely to be in professional specialties; administrative support; service; and operators, fabricators, and labor occupations, and less likely to be in executive, administrative, and managerial; technical; or sales occupations. (See Table 2.9.) It might seem surprising that contingent workers were overrepresented in professional specialty occupations. However, this category includes teachers, who had an above average rate of contingency. In fact, according to Estimate 3, teachers accounted for more than 10 percent of all contingent workers.

Colleges and universities use many adjunct or temporary teachers with short-term contracts. It could also be, however, that the growing uncertainties of the tenure process play an important role in how college and university teachers look at their jobs. Teachers at the college and university level had rates ranging from 10 percent under the narrowest estimate to 25.9 percent under the broadest level. Others in the professional category, including editors, reporters, photographers, actors, directors, and athletes, accounted for 5.1 percent of all contingent workers, according to Estimate 1. These figures indicate that many contingent workers are highly skilled.

The highest rate of contingent workers in the administrative support occupation (3.1 percent) comes closer to the stereotypical notion that contingent workers hold jobs that require relatively little formal training. Service occupations also had a high rate (3 percent) of contingent workers. The subcategory within service occupations with the highest rate of contingency workers was food service occupations, which include waitresses and waiters, cooks, and bartenders.

Although contingent workers labor in every industry, they were much more likely to be concentrated in the services industry than were noncontingent workers. About 54 percent of contingent workers were employed in the services industry, compared with only 34.5 percent of

TABLE 2.10

Distribution by Industry of Employed Contingent and Noncontingent Workers, and Contigency Rates by Industry, February 1995

Industry, sex, and race	Contingent workers			Non-contingent workers
	Estimate 1	Estimate 2	Estimate 3	
Total, 16 years and older (thousands)	2,739	3,422	6,034	117,174
Percent distribution	100.0	100.0	100.0	100.0
Agriculture	2.8	3.0	2.6	2.6
Mining	.2	.2	.3	.6
Construction	11.5	11.8	9.8	5.5
Manufacturing	10.0	9.5	10.8	17.1
Transportation and public utilities	3.8	3.2	4.3	7.2
Wholesale trade	1.3	1.4	1.8	3.9
Retail trade	12.1	11.9	10.3	17.0
Finance, insurance, and real estate	2.0	1.9	2.6	6.7
Services	53.5	54.8	54.0	34.5
Public administration	2.7	2.2	3.6	5.0
Contingency rates				
Total, 16 years and older	2.2	2.8	4.9	....
Agriculture	2.5	3.3	5.0	....
Mining	1.0	1.0	2.7	....
Construction	4.5	5.8	8.4	....
Manufacturing	1.3	1.6	3.1	....
Transportation and public utilities	1.2	1.3	3.0	....
Wholesale trade	.7	1.0	2.3	....
Retail trade	1.6	2.0	3.0	....
Finance, insurance, and real estate	.7	.8	2.0	....
Services	3.4	4.3	7.5	....
Public administration	1.2	1.2	3.6	....

SOURCE: Anne E. Polivka. *A Profile of Contingent Workers.* Monthly Labor Review, vol. 119, no. 10

noncontingent workers. (See Table 2.10.) However, it is important to recognize that, although those in the services industry make up a large proportion of contingent workers, most workers (an estimated 92 to 96 percent) in this industry were not contingent.

CONTINGENCY WORKER CHARACTERISTICS. Black and Hispanic workers were somewhat more likely than whites to be contingency workers. (See Table 2.11.) Contingent workers were more than twice as likely as noncontingent workers to be between the ages of 16 and 24. Contingent workers were also 3 to 4 times more likely to be enrolled in school than noncontingent workers. Among those not enrolled in school, a larger proportion of contingent (17.2 percent) than noncontingent workers (10.5 percent) did not have a high school diploma. (See Table 2.11.)

Alternative Work Arrangements

Employees in alternative work arrangements are individuals whose place, time, and quantity of work are potentially unpredictable or individuals whose employment is arranged through an employment intermediary. By 1997 these included workers such as independent contractors (6.7 percent of total employed), on-call workers (1.6 percent), workers paid by temporary help firms (1.0 percent), and workers whose services are provided through contract firms (0.6 percent). (See Table 2.12.)

Interest in workers in alternative arrangements is relatively recent, and there has been a dearth of data to analyze the number of workers in these arrangements. Nonetheless, some of these alternative arrangements have been in existence for decades. The ranks of independent contractors include construction workers and farmhands working in arrangements that evolved little in the twentieth century. On-call workers include substitute teachers, registered nurses, and performance artists, three other relatively old professions in which the manner of obtaining work has changed little. On the other hand, temporary help agencies only trace their widespread existence in the United States to shortly after World War II. There also is evidence that providing employees to fulfill the administrative or business needs of other companies is a spreading phenomenon.

By 1997 the BLS found that approximately 12.6 million persons, or 11 percent of the work force, fell into at least 1 of the 4 categories. The largest category was independent contractors, with 8.5 million, followed by on-call workers (almost 2 million), temporary help agency workers (1.3 million), and contract company employees (809,000). (See Tables 2.13 and 2.14 for selected characteristics of workers in alternative work arrangements.)

TEMPORARY WORKFORCE. In its 1997 survey, the National Association of Temporary and Staffing Services

(NATSS) found that many of those who enter the workforce for the first time see temporary work as an "entry level transitional form of employment." One-fifth (21 percent) of those who became temporary employees had been students prior to their employment.

The survey asked the respondents why they became temporary workers. Three-quarters (74 percent) saw working as a temporary employee as "a way to get full-time work," and 73 percent wanted additional income. Two-thirds (64 percent) wanted to improve skills and have flexible work time. Only one-fifth (19 percent) worked at temporary jobs because they could not work full-time. (See Table 2.15.)

NATSS projects an increase in hiring temporary workers in industrial, construction, technical, and professional worker categories as businesses reduce staff. According to the Census Bureau (*Service Annual Survey: 1997*, Washington, D.C., 1999), in 1993, office support temporary workers accounted for 37 percent ($10.7 billion) of total receipts for temporary help agencies. By 1997 receipts were 35 percent ($18.0 billion) of the total revenue, the biggest proportion of the receipts to the temporary agencies. Industrial and construction temporary employees brought in 19 percent ($8.0 billion) of the total revenue in 1993; by 1997 they were 24 percent ($12.3 billion). The temporary employment of technical and professional workers increased. Total revenues more than doubled from $6.7 billion in 1993 to $15.5 billion in 1997.

AT-HOME WORK

Steady Work

Between 1960 and 1980 the number of Americans working at home steadily declined, largely reflecting a drop in the number of family farmers who gave up farming. In addition, many professionals, such as doctors and lawyers, left their home offices and joined group practices or larger firms in office buildings. This trend was reversed in the 1990 census, which showed a dramatic increase in the number of people who worked at home, up 56 percent from 1980 to 3.4 million people in 1990. (See Figure 2.5.)

In 1990 more than half the workers who worked in their homes (54 percent) were self-employed. Only 36 percent of those who worked at home were employed by private sector companies (Figure 2.6). According to the Census Bureau, the proportion of women who worked at home (52 percent) was greater than for those who worked away from home (45 percent). Those who worked at home were also older on average that those who did not. Forty-four percent of the at-home workers were 45 years old or older, compared with only 29 percent over this age among people who worked away from home.

Almost half of the workers whose workplace was home (46 percent) worked in the service industries,

TABLE 2.11

Employed Contingent and Noncontingent Workers, by Sex, Race, Hispanic Origin, Age, and Educational Attainment, February, 1995

(Percent distribution)

Characteristic	Contingent workers			Non-contingent workers[1]
	Estimate 1	Estimate 2	Estimate 3	
Total, 16 years and older	100.0	100.0	100.0	100.0
Sex				
Men	49.3	49.4	49.6	54.0
Women	50.7	50.7	50.4	46.0
Race and Hispanic origin				
White	80.1	80.1	80.9	85.7
Black	14.0	13.6	13.3	10.5
Hispanic origin	13.6	12.9	11.3	8.3
Age (in years)				
Total	100.0	100.0	100.0	100.0
16 to 19	16.7	15.2	10.7	4.3
20 to 24	25.0	22.1	19.8	9.6
25 to 34	26.0	27.5	26.3	26.1
35 to 44	18.5	19.8	21.0	28.0
45 to 54	8.2	9.5	12.6	19.8
55 to 64	3.8	3.7	5.9	9.4
65 and older	1.8	2.1	3.7	2.8
Men	100.0	100.0	100.0	100.0
16 to 19	14.6	13.9	9.7	4.0
20 to 24	24.4	21.7	19.6	9.6
25 to 34	26.2	27.5	27.8	26.4
35 to 44	20.3	20.9	20.5	28.0
45 to 54	6.7	8.6	11.4	19.5
55 to 64	5.3	4.9	7.2	9.4
65 and older	2.4	2.6	3.9	3.1
Women	100.0	100.0	100.0	100.0
16 to 19	18.7	16.6	11.7	4.6
20 to 24	25.7	22.6	20.1	9.6
25 to 34	25.8	27.4	24.8	25.7
35 to 44	16.8	18.8	21.4	28.1
45 to 54	9.6	10.5	13.8	20.2
55 to 64	2.3	2.6	4.6	9.4
65 and older	1.2	1.7	3.6	2.5
Educational attainment (those not enrolled in school)				
Total	100.0	100.0	100.0	100.0
Less than a high school diploma	17.2	16.9	14.6	10.5
High school graduate, no college	28.7	28.4	29.4	33.6
Less than a bachelor's degree	28.7	28.8	25.8	28.7
College graduates	17.8	17.8	17.5	18.2
Advanced degree	7.6	8.2	12.7	9.1

[1]Noncontingent workers are those who do not fall into any estimate of "contingent" workers.

NOTE: Detail for the above race and Hispanic-origin groups will not sum to totals because data for the "other races" group are not presented and Hispanics are included in both the white and black population groups. Detail for other characteristics may not sum to totals due to rounding.

SOURCE: Anne E. Polivka. *A Profile of Contingent Workers.* Monthly Labor Review, vol. 119, no. 10

which include businesses and repair services, personal services, entertainment and recreation services, and other professional and related services.

Work As Part of Primary Job

In May 1997 the Bureau of Labor Statistics reported that more than 21 million persons did some work at home

TABLE 2.12

Workers in Alternative Arrangements as a Percent of Total Employment, Feburary 1995 and 1997

Type of alternative arrangement	Percent of total employed, February 1995	Percent of total employed, February 1997
Independent contractors Workers identified as independent contractors, independent consultants, or freelance workers, whether they were self-employed or wage and salary workers	6.7	6.7
On-call workers Workers called to work only as needed, although they can be scheduled to work for several days or weeks in a row	1.6	1.6
Temporary help agency workers Workers paid by a temporary help agency, whether or not their job actually was temporary	1.0	1.0
Workers provided by contract firms Workers employed by a company that provides them or their services to others under contract and who are usually assigned to only one customer and usually work at the customer's worksite	.5	.6

SOURCE: Sharon R. Cohany. *Workers in Alternative Employment Arrangements: A Second Look.* Monthly Labor Review, Vol. 121, No. 11

as part of their primary job. While the number of persons reporting they worked at home grew by only 1.5 million since 1991, there was a sharp increase in the number of persons who were paid for working at home. In 1997, 3.6 million wage and salary workers—about 3.3 percent of all wage and salary workers—were paid for the work they did at home. In 1991 only 1.9 million wage and salary workers—1.9 percent of the total—were doing work at home for pay.

More than half (51.5 percent) of those working at home were wage and salary workers who were not paid expressly for their time. About 17 percent, however, were wage and salary workers who were paid for the hours they put in at home. Virtually all the remainder were self-employed workers, nearly two-thirds of whom had home-based businesses. (See Table 2.16.)

Of the 3.6 million wage and salary workers doing paid work at home, 88 percent were in "white-collar" occupations. Nearly a million of these workers were in professional specialty occupations, while 867,000 were executives and managers. A large number of paid home workers were in sales and administrative occupations. Almost half (44 percent) of those doing paid work at home were in the services industry. More than half a million in manufacturing were paid for work at home. (See Table 2.17.)

The Bureau of Labor Statistics went on to report that about 11.1 million workers were simply "taking work home from the office" (wage and salary workers who were not being officially compensated for the work they did at home). As with those who were paid, persons not paid for the work they did at home were overwhelmingly employed in white-collar occupations. Teachers were

especially likely to do unpaid work at home: 2.8 million teachers reported doing so in 1997.

From an industry perspective, half (51.5 percent) of the unpaid home workers worked in services (6.1 million), followed by manufacturing (1.5 million). About 6.5 million of self-employed persons did some work at home in May 1997, more than half of all the self-employed who were at work during the survey reference week. More than 4.1 million of the self-employed indicated that they were working in home-based businesses. See Chapter 9 for more information on home-based businesses.

FLEXIBLE SCHEDULES

In May 1997 about 28 percent of full-time wage and salary workers had flexible work schedules that allowed them to vary the time they began or ended work. The increase in flexible work schedules was widespread across demographic groups, occupations, and industries. Whites (28.7 percent) were more likely to work flexible schedules than blacks (20.1 percent) or Hispanics (18.4 percent). (See Table 2.18.) Parents (29.9 percent) were more likely than workers with no children under 18 (26.8 percent) to work a flexible schedule.

About 42.4 percent of executives, administrators, and managers and 41 percent of sales workers were able to vary their work hours. On the other hand, fewer than one-quarter of those employed in administrative support roles or as service workers had such flexibility. Operators, fabricators, and laborers, as well as workers in precision production, craft, and repair, were also less likely to have flexible work schedules. (See Table 2.19.)

Among private-sector employees, the proportion of workers with flexible schedules was much higher in service-

TABLE 2.13

Employed Persons with Alternative and Traditional Work Arrangements, by Selected Characteristics, February 1997

[Percent distribution]

Characteristic	Workers with alternative arrangements				Workers with traditional arrangements
	Independent contractors	On-call workers	Temporary help agency workers	Workers provided by contract firms	
Age and sex					
Total, 16 years and older (thousands)	8,456	1,996	1,300	809	114,199
Percent	100.0	100.0	100.0	100.0	100.0
16 to 19 years	8	9.7	6.1	2.0	5.0
20 to 24 years	2.4	11.9	16.5	8.2	9.8
25 to 34 years	18.3	22.4	30.3	34.2	25.4
35 to 44 years	31.1	25.4	21.5	31.1	27.7
45 to 54 years	26.5	14.4	16.2	14.2	20.4
55 to 64 years	13.9	9.7	6.7	7.7	9.2
65 years and older	7.0	6.5	2.8	2.7	2.5
Men, 16 years and older	66.6	49.0	44.7	69.8	52.7
16 to 19 years	3	5.3	2.8	1.1	2.5
20 to 24 years	1.5	6.4	9.6	7.7	5.1
25 to 34 years	11.4	11.8	15.2	24.0	13.7
35 to 44 years	20.7	12.1	6.9	22.0	14.6
45 to 54 years.	17.7	6.9	6.2	9.1	10.5
55 to 64 years	9.9	3.9	2.2	5.1	4.9
65 years and older	5.1	2.6	1.8	.9	1.4
Women, 16 years and older.	33.4	51.0	55.3	30.2	47.3
16 to 19 years	5	4.3	3.2	.7	2.4
20 to 24 years	9	5.5	6.9	.5	4.7
25 to 34 years	7.0	10.6	15.2	10.3	11.7
35 to 44 years	10.4	13.4	14.5	9.1	13.1
45 to 54 years	8.8	7.5	10.0	5.1	9.9
55 to 64 years	4.0	5.8	4.5	2.6	4.3
65 years and older	1.9	3.9	1.1	1.9	1.1
Race and Hispanic origin					
White	90.7	89.3	75.1	81.6	84.8
Black	5.3	7.8	21.3	12.9	10.9
Hispanic origin	7.3	13.3	12.3	6.3	9.6

NOTE: Workers with traditional arrangements are those who do not fall into any of the "alternative arrangements" categories. Details for the above race and Hispanic-origin groups will not sum to totals because data for the "other races" group are not presented and Hispanics are included in both the white and black population groups. Details for other characteristics may not sum to totals because of rounding.

SOURCE: Sharon R. Cohany. *Workers in Alternative Employment Arrangements: A Second Look.* Monthly Labor Review, Vol. 121, No. 11

producing industries (31.7 percent) than in goods-producing industries (23.3 percent). In the public sector, flexible schedules were more common among federal government employees (34.5 percent) than workers in state (29.4 percent) or local (13.1 percent) government, which includes public elementary and secondary schools. (See Table 2.19.)

SHIFT SCHEDULES

In May 1997 among full-time wage and salary workers, 82.9 percent were on regular daytime schedules; alternate schedules worked included evening shifts (4.6 percent), employer-arranged irregular schedules (3.9 percent), night shifts (3.5 percent), and rotating shifts (2.9 percent). Men (19.1 percent) were more likely than women (13.7 percent) to work an alternate shift. (See Table 2.18.)

Shift work was most common among workers in service-oriented occupations, such as protective service (55.1

percent—which includes police, firefighters, and guards) and food service (42.0 percent), and among those employed as operators, fabricators, and laborers (27.0 percent). It was lowest for managers and professionals (9.4 percent) and those in administrative support occupations (8.8 percent).

In private sector industries, the percent of workers on alternative shifts was highest in eating and drinking places (47.2 percent) and lowest in construction (3.7 percent). Although shift work was generally less common in the public sector, nearly half the local government workers employed in "justice, public order, and safety," the category that includes police and fire departments, were shift workers.

WORKER DISPLACEMENT

Displaced workers are persons 20 years and older who lost or left jobs because their plant or company closed or

TABLE 2.14

Employed Persons with Alternative and Traditional Work Arrangements, by Educational Attainment and Sex, February 1997
[Percent distribution]

Educational attainment and sex	Workers with alternative arrangements				Workers with traditional arrangements
	Independent contractors	On-call workers	Temporary help agency workers	Workers provided by contract firms	
Total, 25 to 64 years (thousands)	7,590	1,437	970	705	94,424
Percent	100.0	100.0	100.0	100.0	100.0
Less than a high school diploma	8.7	13.4	11.1	7.1	9.7
High school graduate, no college	30.3	28.7	30.7	36.9	32.8
Less than a bachelor's degree	26.8	32.0	36.3	23.3	28.0
College graduate	34.1	25.9	21.9	32.7	29.5
Men, 25 to 64 years old (thousands)	5,047	692	397	486	49,873
Percent	100.0	100.0	100.0	100.0	100.0
Less than a high school diploma	9.9	18.6	13.9	6.4	11.3
High school graduate, no college	31.3	33.4	27.5	35.6	31.9
Less than a bachelor's degree	25.2	30.3	35.1	24.9	26.4
College graduate	33.5	17.6	23.5	33.1	30.4
Women, 25 to 64 years old (thousands)	2,543	745	573	219	44,551
Percent	100.0	100.0	100.0	100.0	100.0
Less than a high school diploma	6.2	8.6	9.2	9.1	7.9
High school graduate, no college	28.4	24.3	33.0	39.5	33.8
Less than a bachelor's degree	30.0	33.6	37.2	20.0	29.8
College graduate	35.3	33.6	20.6	31.4	28.5

NOTE: Workers with traditional arrangements are those who do not fall into any of the "alternative arrangements" categories. Details may not sum to totals due to rounding.

SOURCE: Sharon R. Cohany. *Workers in Alternative Employment Arrangements: A Second Look.* Monthly Labor Review, Vol. 121, No. 11

moved, there was insufficient work for them to do, or their position or shift was abolished. A total of 3.6 million workers were displaced between January 1995 and December 1997 from jobs they had held for at least 3 years.

Of the 3.6 million displaced workers, 75.9 percent were reemployed and 10 percent were unemployed when surveyed in February 1998. (See Table 2.20.) The February 1998 survey found the reemployment rate highest for workers 25 to 54, with 81.5 percent working again. The reemployment rates for older workers ages 55 to 64 and 65 and over were 59.6 percent and 34.7 percent, respectively. Seventy-eight percent of men were working in a new job, compared with 72.6 percent of women. Among those not reemployed at the time of the survey, men were slightly more likely (12 percent) than women (7.8 percent) to be unemployed. The proportion of displaced women who left the labor force (19.5 percent), however, was over twice that of men (9.3 percent). (See Table 2.20.)

Industry and Occupation

Manufacturing continued to account for the largest proportion of displacements (27 percent). Approximately 53 percent of this decline occurred among workers in the durable goods manufacturing industries. These industries tend to be among those most affected by cyclical changes in economic conditions.

About 7 of 10 workers displaced from manufacturing were reemployed at the time of the survey. This compared

with 80 percent of the workers displaced from the services industries and over four-fifths (83.7 percent) of the workers displaced from construction. (See Table 2.21.)

Managerial and professional specialty employees (26 percent) and technical, sales, and administrative support (35 percent) accounted for 61 percent of the displaced workers by occupation. More than three-fourths (80.1 percent) of the managerial and professional specialty group and 76.6 percent of the technical, sales, and administrative support were employed at the time of the survey. On the other hand, only 55.9 percent of the machine operators, assemblers, and inspectors were working again. In fact 23 percent of this occupation had left the labor force. (See Table 2.22.)

Earnings

Of the 2.4 million reemployed displaced workers who had lost full-time wage and salary jobs, 2.0 million were again working in such jobs in February 1998. The remainder was holding part-time wage and salary jobs, was self-employed, or working as unpaid workers in family businesses. More than one-half of those reemployed in full-time wage and salary jobs were earning as much or more than they did prior to their job loss. About one-fourth, however, suffered earnings losses of 20 percent or more.

SECURITY

The Society for Human Resource Management (SHRM, *1996 Job Security and Layoffs Survey,* Alexan-

TABLE 2.15

How Important Were Each of the Following Factors in Your Decision to Become a Temporary Employee?
(Percentage represents those answering very and somewhat important)

	1994	1997
A way to get full time work	76 %	74 %
Additional income	78	73
Improve skills	67	64
Flexible work time	63	64
Between full time jobs	59	55
Less stress	45	46
Need time for family	44	43
New to area	33	30
Can't work full-time	21	19

SOURCE: Bruce Steinberg. *Profile of the Temporary Work Force*. Contemporary Times, Spring 1998. National Association of Temporary and Staffing Services: Alexandria, VA

FIGURE 2.5

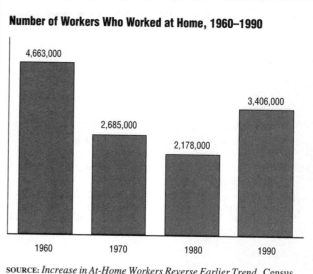

Number of Workers Who Worked at Home, 1960–1990

SOURCE: *Increase in At-Home Workers Reverse Earlier Trend*. Census Brief. U.S. Census Bureau: Washington, D.C.

dria, Virginia, August 1996), surveyed its members on the issue of layoffs and job security. About 65 percent of the businesses responding reported that their employees felt very secure, secure, or somewhat secure. (See Figure 2.7.) Smaller firms were more likely to report secure employees than were larger firms.

Firms that had not had layoffs since 1994 were also more likely to report that their employees felt secure (86 percent) than did firms who had laid off workers (47 percent). Companies planning future layoffs reported that 61 percent of their employees felt very insecure, insecure, or somewhat insecure, while only 9 percent of firms who did not plan layoffs reported such insecurity among their workforce. The SHRM concluded that the majority of their survey respondents thought their employees were secure in their jobs. About one-third believed their employees felt insecure and agreed that the employees' views were justified.

Almost half of all the responding companies (49 percent) reported that employees felt more insecure since January 1, 1994; 14 percent, more secure; and 37 percent, no change. Again larger firms reported more feelings of insecurity than did smaller companies.

According to a Gallup Poll, more people surveyed in 1998 (60 percent) felt that they were "not at all likely" to lose their job than they did in 1996 (51 percent). Twelve percent indicated they were very likely or fairly likely to lose their jobs in 1998, compared to 16 percent in July 1982. (See Figure 2.8.)

On the other hand, in February 1997, Alan Greenspan, chairman of the Federal Reserve (the central bank of the United States), thought that downsizing and job insecurity must have been rising because workers in a booming economy were not pressing for wage increases.

FIGURE 2.6

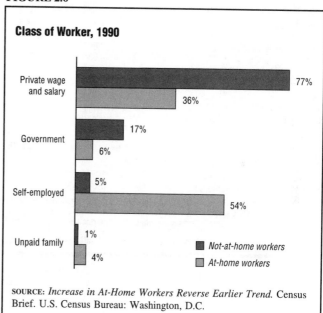

Class of Worker, 1990

Private wage and salary — 77% Not-at-home workers, 36% At-home workers
Government — 17% Not-at-home workers, 6% At-home workers
Self-employed — 5% Not-at-home workers, 54% At-home workers
Unpaid family — 1% Not-at-home workers, 4% At-home workers

■ Not-at-home workers
▨ At-home workers

SOURCE: *Increase in At-Home Workers Reverse Earlier Trend*. Census Brief. U.S. Census Bureau: Washington, D.C.

He believes that changing technology makes workers feel insecure. Citing a survey taken of 444 large companies by the International Survey Research Corporation in Chicago, Greenspan observed that between 1979 and 1990, no more than 24 percent of respondents felt insecure. In the 1990s the proportion increased, reaching 46 percent in 1995 and 1996. Other economists disagreed. For example, Henry Farber at Princeton University commented that there was no direct evidence that workers had a higher sense of job insecurity.

TABLE 2.16

Job-Related Work at Home on Primary Job—All Workers by Sex, Occupation, Industry, and Pay Status, May 1997

(Numbers in thousands)

Characteristic	Total	Rate[1]	Worked at home			
			Percent distribution by class of worker[2]			
			Wage and salary		Self-employed[3]	
			Paid	Unpaid	Total	Home-based business
Total, 16 years and over	21,478	17.8	17.0	51.5	30.1	19.2
Men	11,202	17.3	15.0	50.1	33.8	19.3
Women	10,275	18.3	19.1	53.1	26.2	19.2
Occupation						
Managerial and professional specialty	13,120	36.7	14.0	61.7	23.5	13.1
Executive, administrative, and managerial	5,940	34.0	14.6	54.8	29.8	17.1
Professional specialty	7,180	39.2	13.5	67.5	18.2	9.7
Technical, sales, and administrative support	5,457	15.0	25.0	40.7	32.0	18.6
Technicians and related support	417	10.6	26.9	60.3	11.3	8.6
Sales occupations	3,356	22.4	19.1	39.1	40.4	21.5
Administrative support, including clerical	1,684	9.7	36.3	39.0	20.5	15.4
Service occupations	1,250	7.2	20.4	23.0	54.0	49.3
Precision production, craft, and repair	1,145	8.2	10.1	26.5	62.0	49.2
Operators, fabricators, and laborers	506	2.9	14.4	31.2	51.1	42.5
Industry						
Mining	73	12.3	(4)	(4)	(4)	(4)
Construction	1,330	16.2	10.3	20.0	66.8	54.6
Manufacturing	2,318	11.5	22.3	62.7	14.2	8.3
Transportation and public utilities	963	10.9	21.2	56.2	21.0	13.7
Wholesale trade	1,202	24.4	28.5	42.8	27.7	15.4
Retail trade	1,964	9.2	14.7	36.9	47.3	27.1
Finance, insurance, and real estate	2,008	25.7	16.4	48.6	33.1	14.5
Services	10,954	25.1	14.8	55.6	28.3	18.8
Public administration	666	12.3	29.5	69.2	—	—
Race and Hispanic origin						
White	19,646	19.2	17.0	50.7	30.9	19.7
Black	1,117	8.5	16.6	64.8	16.2	12.1
Hispanic origin	830	7.2	17.5	53.9	27.8	18.8

[1] Refers to the number of persons working at home as a percent of the total at work. The calculation excludes those persons who did not respond to the questions on work at home.

[2] Excludes unpaid family workers, not shown separately.

[3] Includes both the incorporated and unincorporated self-employed.

[4] Data not shown where the base is less than 75,000.

NOTE: Data refer to employed persons in nonagricultural industries who reported work at home during the survey reference week as part of their primary job. Detail for the above race and Hispanic-origin groups will not sum to totals because data for the "other races" group are not presented and Hispanics are included in both the white and black population groups. Data reflect revised population controls used in the Current Population Survey effective with January 1997 estimates. Dash represents zero.

SOURCE: *Work at Home in 1997*. BLS News. Bureau of Labor Statistics: Washington, D.C.

TABLE 2.17

Paid Job-Related Work at Home on Primary Job—Wage and Salary Workers by Selected Characteristics, May 1997

(Numbers in thousands)

| Characteristic | Worked at home[1] | Percent distribution by hours worked at home | | | Mean hours | |
| | | Less than 8 hours | 8 hours or more | | Worked at home | Total at work on primary job |
			Total	35 hours or more		
Total, 16 years and over	**3,644**	**47.7**	**52.3**	**16.0**	**14.9**	**40.8**
Men	1,683	42.2	57.8	19.5	17.0	46.6
Women	1,960	52.3	47.7	12.9	13.1	35.9
Occupation						
Managerial and professiona specialty	1,836	48.8	51.2	15.3	14.5	42.2
Executive, administrative, and managerial	867	51.9	48.1	16.7	14.6	43.8
Professional specialty	969	46.0	54.0	14.1	14.3	40.7
Technical, sates, and administrative support	1,363	47.4	52.6	13.8	14.1	39.2
Technicians and related support	112	45.3	54.7	18.4	16.2	44.4
Sales occupations	640	39.3	60.7	16.8	16.6	42.8
Administrative support, including clerical	611	56.0	44.0	9.8	11.2	34.5
Service occupations	256	36.3	63.7	31.7	24.4	38.5
Precision production, craft, and repair	116	56.5	43.5	12.4	11.3	42.0
Operators, fabricators, and laborers	73	(2)	(2)	(2)	(2)	(2)
Industry						
Construction	136	39.4	60.6	21.2	17.1	37.1
Manufacturing	517	43.5	56.5	18.4	15.2	43.3
Transportation and public utilities	205	58.2	41.8	16.8	13.4	43.4
Wholesale trade	343	35.9	64.1	13.5	16.2	43.9
Retail trade	289	59.8	40.2	11.3	10.9	37.1
Finance, insurance, and real estate	330	49.6	56.4	17.3	15.8	41.9
Services	1,616	46.9	53.1	15.6	15.2	39.8
Public administration	196	58.7	41.3	17.4	13.8	39.9
Race and Hispanic origin						
White	3,345	47.8	52.2	15.4	14.7	40.7
Black	185	43.5	56.5	19.3	17.0	43.9
Hispanic origin	145	36.4	63.6	21.1	18.2	38.8

[1] Includes persons who worked at home but did not report the number of hours worked. Persons who did not report the number of hours worked are excluded from the because data for the distribution.

[2] Data not shown where the base is less than 75,000.

NOTE: Data refer to employed persons in nonagricultural industries who reported work at home during the survey reference week as part of their primary job. Detail for the above race and Hispanic-origin groups will not sum to totals because data for the "other races" group are not presented and Hispanics are included in both the white and black population groups. Data reflect revised population controls used in the Current Population Survey effective with January 1997 estimates.

SOURCE: *Work at Home in 1997.* BLS News. Bureau of Labor Statistics: Washington, D.C.

TABLE 2.18

Flexible Schedules and Shift Work of Full-Time Wage and Salary Workers by Sex, Race, and Hispanic Origin, May, Selected Years 1985–1997

Characteristic	Percent with flexible schedules			Percent with alternate shifts		
	May 1985	May 1991	May 1997	May 1985	May 1991	May 1997
Sex						
Total, 16 years and over	12.4	15.1	27.6	15.9	17.8	16.8
Men	13.1	15.5	28.7	17.8	20.1	19.1
Women	11.3	14.5	26.2	13.0	14.6	13.7
Race and Hispanic origin						
White	12.8	15.5	28.7	15.3	17.1	16.1
Black	9.1	12.1	20.1	19.9	23.3	20.9
Hispanic origin	8.9	10.6	18.4	15.5	19.1	16.0

NOTE: Data for May 1997 are not strictly comparable with data for earlier years because the 1997 data incorporate 1990 census-based population controls and the effects of a major redesign of the Current Population Survey introduced in January 1994. Data exclude the incorporated and unincorporated self-employed.

SOURCE: *Workers on Flexible and Shift Schedules in 1997*. BLS News. Bureau of Labor Statistics: Washington, D.C.

TABLE 2.19

Flexible Schedules—Full-Time and Salary Workers by Occupation and Industry, May 1997

(Numbers in thousands)

Occupation and industry	Both sexes Total[1]	With flexible schedules Number	With flexible schedules Percent of total	Men Total[1]	With flexible schedules Number	With flexible schedules Percent of total	Women Total[1]	With flexible schedules Number	With flexible schedules Percent of total
Occupation									
Managerial and professional specialty	27,384	10,651	38.9	13,882	6,407	46.2	13,502	4,245	31.4
Executive, administrative, and managerial	13,469	5,705	42.4	7213	3,251	45.1	6,255	2,454	39.2
Professional specialty	13,915	4,947	35.5	6,668	3,156	47.3	7,247	1,791	24.7
Mathematical and computer scientists	1,308	772	59.0	887	549	61.9	421	223	53.0
Natural scientists	507	327	64.5	353	240	68.0	154	87	56.2
Teachers, college and university	494	320	64.7	330	224	68.0	164	95	58.2
Technical, sales, and administrative support	25,779	7,828	30.4	9,992	3,613	36.2	15,787	4,215	26.7
Technicians and related support	3,376	1,040	30.8	1,724	611	35.4	1,651	429	26.0
Sales occupations	9,001	3,687	41.0	5,106	2,315	45.3	3,895	1,372	35.2
Sales workers, retail and personal services	3,165	951	30.0	1,428	464	32.5	1,737	487	28.0
Administrative support, including clerical	13,402	3,101	23.1	3,162	687	21.7	10,240	2,414	23.6
Service occupations	11,055	2,373	21.5	6,306	1,256	19.9	4,749	1,116	23.5
Private household	308	125	40.5	21	16	(2)	287	109	37.8
Protective service	1,891	314	16.6	1,619	254	15.7	272	60	22.2
Service, except private household and protective	8,855	1,934	21.8	4,665	986	21.1	4,190	947	22.6
Food service	2,777	630	22.7	1,441	263	18.3	1,336	366	27.4
Health service	1,466	258	17.6	205	26	12.9	1,261	232	18.4
Cleaning and building service	2,000	326	16.3	1,252	208	16.6	749	117	15.7
Personal service	871	254	29.1	216	63	29.0	655	191	29.2
Precision production, craft, and repair	11,519	2,623	17.6	10,506	1,861	17.7	1,013	162	16.0
Mechanics and repairers	3,863	708	18.3	3,672	658	17.9	192	50	26.3
Construction trades	4,069	718	17.7	3,996	707	17.7	74	12	(2)
Other precision production, craft, and repair	3,587	596	16.6	2,839	497	17.5	748	99	13.3
Operators, fabricators, and laborers	14,812	2,156	14.6	11,388	1,815	15.9	3,424	342	10.0
Machine operators, assemblers, and inspectors	6,813	702	10.3	4,359	521	12.0	2,454	181	7.4
Transportation and material moving	4,351	961	22.1	4,064	914	22.5	287	47	16.3
Handlers, equipment cleaners, helpers, and laborers	3,648	494	13.5	2,965	379	12.8	683	114	16.7
Industry									
Private sector	75,612	21,795	28.8	45,023	13284	29.5	30,589	8,511	27.8
Goods-producing industries	25,925	6,033	23.3	19,458	4,640	23.8	6,466	1,393	21.5
Agriculture	1,492	448	30.0	1,265	373	29.5	227	74	32.8
Mining	541	122	22.6	473	106	22.4	68	16	(2)
Construction	5,389	1,218	22.6	4,974	1,086	21.8	415	132	31.8
Manufacturing	18,503	4,245	22.9	12,747	3,074	24.1	5,756	1,170	20.3
Durable goods	11,179	2,572	23.0	8,148	1,944	23.9	3,031	629	20.7
Nondurable goods	7,324	1,673	22.8	4,599	1,131	24.6	2,725	542	19.9
Service producing industries	49,687	15,763	31.7	25,565	8,644	33.8	24,122	7,118	29.5
Transportation and public utilities	6,088	1,669	27.4	4,518	1215	26.9	1,570	454	28.9
Wholesale trade	3,969	1,281	32.3	2,854	979	34.3	1,115	302	27.1
Retail trade	12,111	3,745	30.9	6,812	1,988	29.2	5,299	1,757	33.2
Eating and drinking places	3,135	987	31.5	1,758	497	28.2	1,377	490	35.6
Finance, insurance, and real estate	5,857	2,096	35.8	2,288	1,028	44.9	3,569	1,068	29.9
Services	21,662	6,971	32.2	9,094	3,434	37.8	12,568	3,537	28.1
Private households	391	148	37.7	42	27	(2)	350	120	34.4
Business, automobile, and repair	5,060	1,607	31.8	3,319	1,118	33.7	1,740	489	28.1
Personal, except private household	1,627	522	32.1	749	227	30.3	878	295	33.7
Entertainment and recreation	1,051	397	37.8	619	231	37.3	432	167	38.5
Professional services	13,497	4,286	31.8	4,336	1,820	42.0	9,161	2,465	26.9
Forestry and fisheries	36	11	(2)	29	11	(2)	7	–	–
Government	14,937	3,236	21.7	7,050	1,668	23.7	7,887	1,568	19.9
Federal	2,828	977	34.5	1,621	535	33.0	1,208	442	36.6
State	4,125	1,214	29.4	1,856	606	32.7	2,270	608	26.8
Local	7,983	1,046	13.1	3,573	527	14.8	4,410	519	11.8

[1]Includes persons who did not provide information on flexible schedules

[2]Percent not shown where base is less than 75,000.

NOTE: Data relate to the sole or principal job of full-time wage and salary workers who were at work during the survey reference week and exclude all self-employed persons, regardless of whether or not their businesses were incorporated. Data reflect revised population controls used in the Current Population Survey effective with the January 1997 estimates. Dash represents or rounds to zero.

SOURCE: *Workers on Flexible and Shift Schedules in 1997*. BLS News. Bureau of Labor Statistics: Washington, D.C.

TABLE 2.20

Displaced Workers by Age, Sex, Race, Hispanic Origin, and Employment Status in February 1998

Age, sex, race, and Hispanic origin	Total (thousands)	Percent distribution by employment status			
		Total	Employed	Unemployed	Not in the labor force
TOTAL					
Total, 20 years and over	3,578	100.0	75.9	10.0	14.1
20 to 24 years	108	100.0	61.2	11.8	27.0
25 to 54 years	2,835	100.0	81.5	9.9	8.5
55 to 64 years	471	100.0	59.6	9.9	30.4
65 years and over	163	100.0	34.7	10.6	54.8
Men					
Total, 20 years and over	1,898	100.0	78.8	12.0	9.3
20 to 24 years	49	100.0	(2)	(2)	(2)
25 to 54 years	1,488	100.0	84.3	11.3	4.4
55 to 64 years	280	100.0	61.9	12.6	25.4
65 years and over	81	100.0	42.0	16.8	41.3
Women					
Total, 20 years and over	1,680	100.0	72.6	7.8	19.5
20 to 24 years	59	100.0	(2)	(2)	(2)
25 to 54 years	1,347	100.0	78.4	8.5	13.1
55 to 64 years	191	100.0	56.2	6.0	37.8
65 years and over	82	100.0	27.4	4.3	68.2
White					
Total, 20 years and over	3,063	100.0	76.0	9.4	14.6
Men	1,653	100.0	78.7	11.9	9.4
Women	1,410	100.0	72.7	6.6	20.7
Black					
Total, 20 years and over	366	100.0	73.1	16.3	10.6
Men	160	100.0	76.6	16.7	6.7
Women	206	100.0	70.4	16.0	13.6
Hispanic origin					
Total, 20 years and over	354	100.0	71.6	15.4	13.0
Men	188	100.0	78.4	16.6	5.0
Women	166	100.0	63.7	14.1	22.1

[1]Data refer to persons who had 3 or more years of tenure on a job they had lost or left between January 1995 and December 1997 because of plant or company closings or moves, insufficient work, or the abolishment of their positions or shifts.

[2] Data not shown where base is less than 75,000.

NOTE: Detail for the above race and Hispanic-origin groups will not sum to totals because data for the "other races" group are not presented and Hispanics are included in both the white and black population groups.

SOURCE: *Worker Displacement.* Bureau of Labor Statistics, Aug. 1998

TABLE 2.21

Displaced Workers by Industry and Class of Worker of Lost Job and Employment Status in February 1998

Industry and class of worker of lost job	Total (thousands)	Percent distribution by employment status			
		Total	Employed	Unemployed	Not in the labor force
Total, 20 years and over(2)	3,578	100.0	75.9	10.0	14.1
Agricultural wage and salary workers	45	100.0	(3)	(3)	(3)
Nonagricultural wage and salary workers	3,490	100.0	75.7	10.0	4.3
Private wage and salary workers	3,218	100.0	75.5	10.3	14.2
Mining	20	100.0	(3)	(3)	(3)
Construction	176	100.0	83.7	14.1	2.2
Manufacturing	972	100.0	71.3	12.8	15.9
Durable goods	520	100.0	76.7	11.4	1.9
Lumber and wood products	22	100.0	(3)	(3)	(3)
Furniture and fixtures	35	100.0	(3)	(3)	(3)
Stone, clay, and glass products	15	100.0	(3)	(3)	(3)
Primary metal industries	21	100.0	(3)	(3)	(3)
Fabricated metal products	66	100.0	(3)	(3)	(3)
Machinery, except electrical	121	100.0	67.3	16.3	16.4
Electrical machinery	73	100.0	(3)	(3)	(3)
Transportation equipment	95	100.0	64.4	20.6	15.0
Automobiles	37	100.0	(3)	(3)	(3)
Other transportation equipment	58	100.0	(3)	(3)	(3)
Professional and photographic equipment	46	100.0	(3)	(3)	(3)
Other durable goods industries	27	100.0	(3)	(3)	(3)
Nondurable goods	452	100.0	65.0	14.5	20.4
Food and kindred products	86	100.0	60.7	19.6	19.7
Textile mill products	44	100.0	(3)	(3)	(3)
Apparel and other finished textile products	109	100.0	43.2	17.9	39.0
Paper and allied products	32	100.0	(3)	(3)	(3)
Printing and publishing	81	100.0	79.7	10.7	9.6
Chemical and allied products	44	100.0	(3)	(3)	(3)
Rubber and miscellaneous plastics products	39	100.0	59.8	28.5	11.7
Other nondurable goods industries	18	100.0	(3)	(3)	(3)
Transportation and public utilities	277	100.0	74.6	8.0	17.4
Transportation	157	100.0	74.6	11.3	14.1
Communications and other public utilities	120	100.0	74.6	3.7	21.7
Wholesale and retail trade	777	100.0	75.0	7.8	17.2
Wholesale trade	163	100.0	74.7	13.1	12.2
Retail trade	614	100.0	75.1	6.4	18.5
Finance, insurance, and real estate	288	100.0	75.0	13.1	11.8
Services	708	100.0	80.0	8.3	11.7
Professional services	403	100.0	81.6	6.0	12.4
Other service industries	305	100.0	77.8	11.3	10.8
Government workers	272	100.0	78.7	6.2	15.1

[1] Data refer to persons who had 3 or more years of tenure on a job they had lost or left between January 1995 and December 1997 because of plant or company closings or moves, insufficient work, or the abolishment of their positions or shifts.

[2] Total includes a small number of unpaid family workers and persons who did not report industry or class of worker.

[3] Data not shown where base is less than 75,000.

SOURCE: *Worker Displacement.* Bureau of Labor Statistics, Aug. 1998

TABLE 2.22

Displaced Workers by Occupation of Lost Job and Employment Status in February 1998

Occupation of lost job	Total (thousands)	Total	Employed	Unemployed	Not in the labor force
Total, 20 years and over(2)	3,578	100.0	75.9	10.0	14.1
Managerial and professional specialty	947	100.0	80.1	9.2	10.6
Executive, administrative, and managerial	554	100.0	78.0	11.3	10.7
Professional specialty	393	100.0	83.1	6.4	10.5
Technical, sales, and administrative support	1,259	100.0	76.6	7.3	16.1
Technicians and related support	138	100.0	87.1	5.2	7.7
Sales occupations	527	100.0	72.7	10.8	16.5
Administrative support, including clerical	594	100.0	77.5	4.7	17.8
Service occupations	285	100.0	69.8	10.2	20.0
Precision production, craft, and repair	391	100.0	88.3	5.3	6.5
Mechanics and repairers	132	100.0	86.5	5.6	7.9
Construction trades	103	100.0	87.4	4.5	8.1
Other precision production, craft, and repair	155	100.0	90.3	5.5	4.2
Operators, fabricators, and laborers	606	100.0	60.9	20.3	18.8
Machine operators, assemblers, and inspectors	343	100.0	55.9	21.0	23.0
Transportation and material moving occupations	137	100.0	68.6	19.6	11.8
Handlers, equipment cleaners, helpers, and laborers	125	100.0	65.9	19.0	15.1
Farming, forestry, and fishing	58	100.0	(3)	(3)	(3)

[1]Data refer to persons who had 3 or more years of tenure on a job they had lost or left between January 1995 and December 1997 because of plant or company closings or moves, insufficient work, or the abolishment of their positions or shifts.

[2]Total includes a small number who did not report occupation.

[3]Data not shown where base is less than 75,000.

SOURCE: *Worker Displacement.* Bureau of Labor Statistics, Aug. 1998

FIGURE 2.7

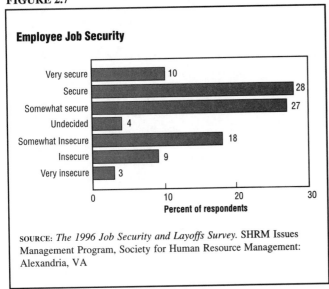

SOURCE: *The 1996 Job Security and Layoffs Survey.* SHRM Issues Management Program, Society for Human Resource Management: Alexandria, VA

FIGURE 2.8

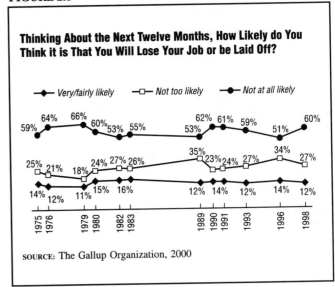

SOURCE: The Gallup Organization, 2000

CHAPTER 3

UNEMPLOYMENT

The United States unemployment rate reached a post-World War II high of 9.7 percent in 1982. It remained high at 9.6 percent in 1983 as a result of the most severe economic recession since the Great Depression of the 1930s. The unemployment rate then dropped, approaching 5 percent in 1989, but again began increasing, reaching 7 percent in 1991 and rising almost to 8 percent in 1992. As the economy improved, the rate fell to 6.9 percent in 1993. By 1998 the U.S. unemployment rate had dropped to 4.5 percent, and in 1999, reached a low of 4.2 percent. (See Table 1.1 in Chapter 1.) By April 2000 unemployment had declined to 3.9 percent, the lowest level in 3 decades. (See Figure 3.1.)

However, some previously laid-off workers, especially those over 55 years old, had stopped looking for work and were not counted in the unemployment rate. In addition, by midyear 1999, about 1.86 million people, many of whom would likely be unemployed, were in prisons and jails.

INTERNATIONAL UNEMPLOYMENT

In the fourth quarter of 1998 the United States and Japan each had the lowest unemployment rates (4.4 percent). This is already much higher than Japan's 1991 rate of 2.1 percent. France (11.5 percent), Italy (12.4 percent), Canada (8.0 percent), and Australia (7.7 percent) had particularly high rates. (See Table 3.1.)

BY STATES

Unemployment rates in the United States vary from state to state. In July 1998 West Virginia (6.8 percent), New Mexico (6.4 percent), Alaska (6.2 percent), and Louisiana (5.9 percent) had the highest unemployment rates. Nebraska (2.1 percent), North Dakota (2.2 percent), and Minnesota (2.3 percent) had the lowest rates. (See Table 3.2.)

FIGURE 3.1

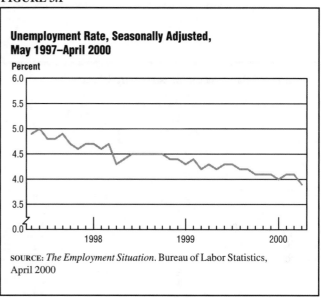

Unemployment Rate, Seasonally Adjusted, May 1997–April 2000

SOURCE: *The Employment Situation.* Bureau of Labor Statistics, April 2000

AGE

Unemployment does not occur evenly in all occupations or sectors of society. Younger workers under 25 years of age are far more likely to be unemployed than older workers are. Their jobs are often more marginal, and younger workers leave their jobs more often than older ones. They also have less seniority to protect themselves against layoffs.

While the average unemployment rate was 4.2 percent in 1999, those 16 to 24 years experienced a rate of 9.9 percent. Young adults 20 to 24 years old (7.5 percent) had more than double the unemployment rate of workers 25 to 54 years old (3.2 percent). (See Table 3.3.)

RACE, GENDER, AND MARITAL STATUS

In 1999 blacks (8 percent unemployment rate) and Hispanics (6.4 percent) were considerably more likely to

TABLE 3.1

nemployment Rates, Approximating U.S. Concepts, in Nine Countries, Quarterly Data, Seasonally Adjusted

Country	Annual average		1997				1998			
	1997	1998	I	II	III	IV	I	II	III	IV
nited States	4.9	4.5	5.2	5.0	4.9	4.7	4.6	4.4	4.5	4.4
anada	9.2	8.3	9.6	9.4	9.0	8.9	8.6	8.4	8.3	8.0
ustralia	8.6	8.0	8.7	8.7	8.6	8.3	8.1	8.1	8.2	7.7
apan	3.4	4.1	3.3	3.4	3.4	3.5	3.7	4.2	4.3	4.4
ance	12.4	11.8	12.4	12.5	12.5	12.3	12.0	11.8	11.7	11.5
ermany	7.8	7.5	7.7	7.8	7.8	7.8	7.7	7.6	7.4	7.3
aly[1]	12.3	12.3	12.3	12.3	12.2	12.3	12.2	12.3	12.4	12.4
weden	10.1	8.4	10.9	10.6	9.7	9.1	8.7	8.6	8.4	7.6
nited Kingdom	7.0	6.3	7.4	7.2	6.9	6.6	6.4	6.2	6.3	6.2

Quarterly rates are for the first month of the quarter.

Data not available.

OTE: Quarterly figures for France, Germany, and the United Kingdom are calculated by applying annual adjustment factors to current published data, and therefore should be viewed as less precise indicators of unemployment under U.S. concepts than the annual figures. For further qualifications and historical data, see *Comparative Labor Force Statistics, 10 Countries* (Bureau of Labor Statistics, August 1996).

ɔURCE: Bureau of Labor Statistics, August 1999

TABLE 3.2

Unemployment Rates by State, Seasonally Adjusted

State	July 1997	June 1998	July 1998ᵖ	State	July 1997	June 1998	July 1998ᵖ
Alabama	5.3	3.8	3.6	Missouri	4.1	4.2	4.2
Alaska	8.0	6.4	6.2	Montana	5.4	5.4	5.1
Arizona	4.5	4.0	3.7	Nebraska	2.6	1.7	2.1
Arkansas	5.4	4.8	4.7	Nevada	4.0	4.4	4.2
California	6.2	5.8	5.6	New Hampshire	3.1	2.7	2.4
Colorado	3.2	3.4	3.3	New Jersey	5.1	4.8	4.8
Connecticut	5.1	3.8	3.4	New Mexico	6.0	6.7	6.4
Delaware	4.0	4.0	4.1	New York	6.5	5.5	5.5
District of Columbia	7.9	8.2	8.3	North Carolina	3.6	3.1	3.2
Florida	4.7	4.5	4.3	North Dakota	2.5	2.2	2.2
Georgia	4.6	4.1	4.0	Ohio	4.4	4.5	4.6
Hawaii	6.5	6.0	5.8	Oklahoma	4.2	4.0	4.4
Idaho	5.3	5.0	4.9	Oregon	5.8	5.4	5.4
Illinois	4.6	4.5	4.4	Pennsylvania	5.3	4.4	4.5
Indiana	3.5	2.8	2.6	Rhode Island	5.4	4.1	4.4
Iowa	3.1	2.5	2.5	South Carolina	4.4	3.2	3.8
Kansas	3.7	3.5	3.7	South Dakota	3.0	2.7	2.8
Kentucky	5.4	4.4	4.2	Tennessee	5.7	3.9	3.8
Louisiana	6.2	5.2	5.9	Texas	5.4	5.0	4.9
Maine	5.4	4.0	4.5	Utah	3.1	3.2	3.5
Maryland	5.2	4.5	4.7	Vermont	3.9	3.5	3.5
Massachusetts	4.0	3.4	3.1	Virginia	4.0	3.1	3.0
Michigan	4.3	3.6	4.2	Washington	4.7	4.7	4.7
Minnesota	3.2	2.6	2.3	West Virginia	6.9	6.9	6.8
Mississippi	5.7	4.6	4.9	Wisconsin	3.8	3.0	3.4
				Wyoming	5.1	4.7	4.6

ᵖ = preliminary

SOURCE: *Current Labor Statistics.* Bureau of Labor Statistics, 2000

---

be out of work than whites (3.7 percent). Many blacks work in occupations that have suffered as the American economy has changed from an industrial to a service economy. (See Chapter 2.) In 1999 black teenagers experienced an unemployment rate of 27.9 percent, compared to 12 percent for white teenagers. Black male teenagers (30.9 percent) were more likely to be unemployed than black female teenagers (25.1 percent). (See Table 3.4.) In 1999 men (4.1 percent) and women (4.3 percent) 16 years and over had similar unemployment rates. (See Table 3.5.)

TABLE 3.3

Unemployment rates by sex and age, monthly data seasonally adjusted
[Civilian workers]

Sex and age	Annual average		1999												2000
	1998	1999	Jan.	Feb.	Mar.	Apr.	May	June	July	Aug.	Sept.	Oct.	Nov.	Dec.	Jan.
Total, 16 years and over	4.5	4.2	4.3	4.4	4.2	4.3	4.2	4.3	4.3	4.2	4.2	4.1	4.1	4.1	4.0
16 to 24 years	10.4	9.9	10.1	10.2	10.0	10.0	9.6	9.8	9.7	9.6	10.0	10.0	10.0	9.8	9.3
16 to 19 years	14.6	13.9	15.1	14.2	14.2	14.1	13.1	13.6	13.2	13.5	14.6	13.9	14.0	13.8	12.6
16 to 17 years	17.2	16.3	17.9	15.8	16.6	16.6	16.1	16.3	15.4	15.9	16.1	15.9	16.5	16.5	14.0
18 to 19 years	12.8	12.4	12.9	13.0	12.7	12.4	11.2	11.8	11.7	12.1	13.8	12.4	12.3	12.1	11.4
20 to 24 years	7.9	7.5	7.1	7.7	7.4	7.5	7.5	7.6	7.6	7.3	7.2	7.7	7.7	7.4	7.4
25 years and over	3.4	3.1	3.2	3.3	3.1	3.3	3.2	3.2	3.2	3.2	3.1	3.0	3.0	3.0	3.0
25 to 54 years	3.5	3.2	3.3	3.4	3.2	3.3	3.2	3.3	3.3	3.2	3.2	3.1	3.1	3.0	3.0
55 years and over	2.7	2.8	2.9	2.9	2.8	2.9	2.7	3.0	2.9	2.7	2.6	2.7	2.6	2.7	2.8
Men, 16 years and over	4.4	4.1	4.2	4.3	4.0	4.1	4.2	4.1	4.1	4.1	4.0	4.1	4.0	4.0	3.9
16 to 24 years	11.1	10.3	10.7	10.3	10.1	10.5	10.2	10.5	10.2	9.9	9.9	10.4	10.2	10.6	9.7
16 to 19 years	16.2	14.7	16.4	14.9	15.0	14.8	13.9	14.3	13.8	13.9	14.6	14.2	14.9	15.2	14.0
16 to 17 years	19.1	17.0	19.3	16.0	17.3	18.3	17.6	16.8	16.1	16.2	16.6	15.5	16.9	17.7	14.3
18 to 19 years	14.1	13.1	14.3	13.9	13.5	12.6	11.5	12.7	12.2	12.6	13.2	13.2	13.6	13.5	13.7
20 to 24 years	8.1	7.7	7.3	7.6	7.2	7.9	8.0	8.3	8.1	7.6	7.2	8.2	7.5	7.8	7.2
25 years and over	3.2	3.0	3.0	3.2	2.8	3.0	3.1	3.0	3.0	3.1	3.0	2.9	2.8	2.8	2.8
25 to 54 years	3.3	3.0	3.1	3.2	2.9	3.0	3.1	3.0	3.0	3.1	3.0	3.0	2.9	2.9	2.9
55 years and over	2.8	2.8	2.8	2.9	2.6	2.7	2.8	2.7	3.0	2.9	2.9	2.8	2.6	2.5	2.5
Women, 16 years and over	4.6	4.3	4.4	4.4	4.5	4.6	4.2	4.4	4.4	4.3	4.3	4.2	4.2	4.1	4.2
16 to 24 years	9.8	9.5	9.5	10.0	9.9	9.5	8.9	9.1	9.1	9.3	10.0	9.6	9.8	8.9	8.9
16 to 19 years	12.9	13.2	13.7	13.4	13.4	13.4	12.2	13.0	12.6	13.2	14.7	13.4	13.0	12.2	11.1
16 to 17 years	15.1	15.5	16.3	15.5	15.9	14.8	14.5	15.7	14.7	15.6	15.6	16.3	16.1	15.1	13.7
18 to 19 years	11.5	11.6	11.5	12.0	11.7	12.1	10.9	10.9	11.2	11.6	14.5	11.4	10.8	10.5	8.9
20 to 24 years	7.8	7.2	7.0	7.9	7.7	7.1	6.9	6.8	7.1	7.0	7.2	7.2	7.9	7.0	7.6
25 years and over	3.6	3.3	3.4	3.4	3.4	3.6	3.3	3.5	3.5	3.3	3.2	3.1	3.1	3.2	3.2
25 to 54 years	3.8	3.4	3.5	3.5	3.5	3.7	3.4	3.5	3.6	3.4	3.4	3.2	3.3	3.2	3.3
55 years and over	2.6	2.8	3.0	2.8	3.1	3.1	2.6	3.3	2.9	2.4	2.1	2.5	2.6	2.9	3.1

SOURCE: *Monthly Labor Review.* Bureau of Labor Statistics, March 2000.

A married person was much less likely to be unemployed than a single, widowed, or divorced individual. This observation held true across all races. In 1999 single, never married males (7.8 percent) had more than triple the unemployment rate of married males (2.2 percent). Widowed, divorced, or separated males (4.6 percent) had over 2 times the rate of married men (2.2 percent). While only 2.1 percent of white married men were unemployed, 6.7 percent of single whites and 4.3 percent of widowed, divorced, or separated white males were out of work. Among blacks, 3.8 percent of married men, 16 years and over were unemployed, compared to 6.3 percent of widowed, divorced, or separated and 14 percent of singles. (See Table 3.5.)

The same situation held true for married, single, divorced, widowed, and separated women. While 7.4 percent of single females over 16 years of age were unemployed, only 2.7 percent of married women and 4.5 percent of widowed, divorced, or separated women were unemployed. Single white women over the age of 16 (6.3 percent) were twice as likely to be out of work as married women (2.5 percent) were. Single black women (11.7 percent) were almost 3 times as likely to be unemployed as married black women (4.2 percent). (See Table 3.5.)

EDUCATIONAL ATTAINMENT

The more education an individual has, the less likely he or she will be unemployed. (See Chapter 4.) In 1999,

while 6.7 percent of those with less then a high school diploma were unemployed, only 1.8 percent of college graduates were. High school graduates with no college had an unemployment rate of 3.5 percent, while those with some college, but no degree, faced a 2.8 percent unemployment rate. (See Table 3.4.)

OCCUPATIONS AND INDUSTRIES

Some occupations are more susceptible to unemployment than others. In 1999 people employed in managerial and professional specialties (1.9 percent) were much less likely to find themselves unemployed than those working as operators, fabricators, and laborers (6.2 percent). Within each occupational grouping, differences exist. While the overall technical, sales, and administrative support field had 3.7 percent unemployed, those in sales occupations were more likely to be unemployed (4.2 percent) than technicians (2.3 percent) and administrative support, including clerical (3.5 percent). (See Table 3.6.)

Gender also plays a role. Women in sales occupations had an unemployment rate of 5.4 percent, compared to 3 percent for men. While women and men had similar unemployment rates in managerial and professional specialty fields, more female operators, fabricators, and laborers were out of work than males. (See Table 3.6.)

TABLE 3.4

Selected unemployment indicators, monthly data seasonally adjusted

[Unemployment rates]

Selected categories	Annual average		1999												2000
	1998	1999	Jan.	Feb.	Mar.	Apr.	May	June	July	Aug.	Sept.	Oct.	Nov.	Dec.	Jan.
Characteristic															
Total, all workers	4.5	4.2	4.3	4.4	4.2	4.3	4.2	4.3	4.3	4.2	4.2	4.1	4.1	4.1	4.0
Both sexes, 16 to 19 years	14.6	13.9	15.1	14.2	14.2	14.1	13.1	13.6	13.2	13.5	14.6	13.8	14.0	13.8	12.6
Men, 20 years and over	3.7	3.5	3.5	3.7	3.3	3.5	3.6	3.5	3.5	3.5	3.4	3.5	3.3	3.3	3.3
Women, 20 years and over	4.1	3.8	3.8	3.8	3.9	4.0	3.7	3.8	3.9	3.7	3.7	3.5	3.6	3.6	3.7
White, total	3.9	3.7	3.8	3.8	3.6	3.8	3.7	3.8	3.7	3.7	3.6	3.5	3.5	3.5	3.4
Both sexes, 16 to 19 years	12.6	12.0	12.7	12.0	12.0	12.1	11.4	12.0	11.4	11.7	12.3	11.8	12.0	12.2	10.8
Men, 16 to 19 years	14.1	12.6	13.8	12.6	12.8	12.6	12.2	12.0	11.7	12.3	12.7	11.9	12.8	13.3	12.4
Women, 16 to 19 years	10.9	11.3	11.5	11.4	11.2	11.6	10.6	12.0	11.1	11.0	11.9	11.7	11.2	10.9	9.1
Men, 20 years and over	3.2	3.0	3.1	3.3	2.9	3.0	3.1	3.2	3.1	3.2	2.9	2.9	2.8	2.8	2.8
Women, 20 years and over	3.4	3.3	3.3	3.3	3.3	3.6	3.3	3.4	3.3	3.2	3.2	3.1	3.1	3.0	3.1
Black, total	8.9	8.0	7.8	8.2	8.0	7.8	7.6	7.6	8.6	7.8	8.3	8.3	8.0	7.9	8.2
Both sexes, 16 to 19 years	27.6	27.9	28.9	28.1	30.0	27.8	25.2	24.8	26.9	28.1	30.8	30.8	28.4	25.3	23.9
Men, 16 to 19 years	30.1	30.9	33.3	31.2	32.4	32.0	27.9	28.8	30.7	29.6	30.3	35.3	31.0	27.5	24.0
Women, 16 to 19 years	25.3	25.1	24.5	25.0	27.6	23.8	22.5	21.2	23.4	26.7	31.4	26.1	25.9	23.0	23.8
Men, 20 years and over	7.4	6.7	6.1	6.7	6.0	6.3	6.6	6.4	7.2	6.3	7.1	7.7	7.0	7.0	7.4
Women, 20 years and over	7.9	6.8	6.7	7.0	7.1	6.9	6.5	6.7	7.7	6.9	6.7	6.1	6.6	6.7	7.2
Hispanic origin, total	7.2	6.4	6.7	6.8	6.0	6.8	6.7	6.6	6.3	6.5	6.6	6.3	6.1	5.9	5.6
Married men, spouse present	2.4	2.2	2.3	2.4	2.1	2.3	2.3	2.2	2.3	2.3	2.2	2.2	2.1	2.2	2.0
Married women, spouse present	2.9	2.7	2.8	2.8	2.7	2.9	2.6	2.7	2.8	2.7	2.6	2.5	2.5	2.5	2.6
Women who maintain families	7.2	6.4	6.3	6.5	6.6	7.1	6.0	6.5	6.4	6.3	6.4	6.0	6.0	6.2	6.2
Full-time workers	4.3	4.1	4.1	4.3	4.0	4.2	4.0	4.0	4.1	4.1	4.0	4.0	3.9	3.9	3.9
Part-time workers	5.3	5.0	5.2	4.9	5.0	5.0	5.2	5.3	4.9	4.6	5.0	4.7	4.9	4.9	4.6
Industry															
Nonagricultural wage and salary workers	4.6	4.3	4.3	4.4	4.3	4.4	4.3	4.4	4.4	4.2	4.3	4.2	4.2	4.1	4.2
Mining	3.2	5.7	6.3	7.1	5.5	8.4	5.9	4.8	6.0	4.2	6.7	5.0	4.6	4.1	2.6
Construction	7.5	7.0	7.3	7.4	7.0	7.3	7.2	7.3	6.9	7.6	6.9	6.7	5.7	6.6	6.4
Manufacturing	3.9	3.6	3.5	3.7	3.5	3.4	3.5	3.7	3.5	3.8	3.9	3.7	3.7	3.6	3.2
Durable goods	3.4	3.5	3.3	3.3	3.1	3.2	3.4	3.5	3.7	3.7	4.0	3.5	3.7	3.6	2.8
Nondurable goods	4.7	3.9	3.9	4.3	4.2	3.9	3.8	4.0	3.1	4.1	3.9	4.0	3.7	3.5	3.9
Transportation and public utilities	3.4	3.0	2.6	3.1	2.9	2.9	3.2	2.9	3.4	3.0	2.8	3.1	3.3	3.0	3.7
Wholesale and retail trade	5.5	5.2	5.3	5.2	5.4	5.4	5.3	5.3	5.2	4.8	5.2	4.9	5.3	5.2	5.1
Finance, insurance, and real estate	2.5	2.3	2.4	2.4	2.0	3.2	2.2	2.4	2.4	2.4	2.3	2.3	2.3	2.1	2.5
Services	4.5	4.1	4.2	4.1	4.2	4.1	4.0	4.2	4.4	4.0	4.1	4.0	3.9	3.8	4.2
Government workers	2.3	2.2	2.2	2.3	2.1	2.4	2.5	2.3	2.2	2.1	2.0	2.1	2.0	2.1	2.1
Agricultural wage and salary workers	8.3	8.9	9.1	10.8	9.4	9.5	10.1	9.3	9.0	9.6	5.7	7.7	8.3	7.1	5.0
Educational attainment[1]															
Less than a high school diploma	7.1	6.7	7.2	7.4	6.3	6.8	6.8	6.8	6.8	7.0	6.8	6.6	6.5	6.0	6.6
High school graduates, no college	4.0	3.5	3.5	3.5	3.5	3.6	3.6	3.8	3.6	3.5	3.5	3.3	3.3	3.5	3.5
Some college, less than a bachelor's degree	3.0	2.8	2.9	3.1	2.8	2.9	2.8	2.6	3.0	3.1	2.7	2.7	2.7	2.5	2.6
College graduates	1.8	1.8	1.8	1.9	1.9	2.0	1.8	2.0	1.8	1.6	1.7	1.7	1.7	1.8	1.8

[1] Data refer to persons 25 years and over.

SOURCE: *Monthly Labor Review.* Bureau of Labor Statistics, March 2000.

In 1999 those working in construction, apparel, retail trade, and agriculture industries were most likely to find themselves without jobs. Those in government and certain segments of the manufacturing industry (including chemicals and allied products) were the least likely to be unemployed. (See Table 3.7.)

HOW LONG DOES UNEMPLOYMENT LAST?

In 1999 the average length of unemployment was 13.4 weeks, down from the 15.8 weeks in 1997 and 16.7 weeks in 1996. The median duration of unemployment (half were unemployed more and half less) was 6.4 weeks. Almost one half (44 percent) of the unemployed had been unemployed for less than 5 weeks, and a little less than one-third (31 percent) had been out of work for 5 to 14 weeks. About 13 percent were out of work 15 to 26 weeks and 12 percent for 27 weeks and over. (See Table 3.8.)

Gender and Age

Men (an average of 14 weeks) tended to stay unemployed somewhat longer than women (12.7 weeks). Generally, the older the job seeker, the longer it took to find work. Young adults 16 to 19 years old were unemployed an average of 8.7 weeks, compared to almost 18 weeks for those 55 to 64 years old. (See Table 3.8.)

Because better-paying jobs usually take longer to find, men 45 years and older, who were more likely to be seeking higher-paying employment than either women or younger people, remained unemployed longer.

TABLE 3.5

Unemployed Persons by Marital Status, Race, Age, and Gender

Marital status, race, and age	Men				Women			
	Thousands of persons		Unemployment rates		Thousands of persons		Unemployment rates	
	1998	1999	1998	1999	1998	1999	1998	1999
Total, 16 years and over	3,266	3,066	4.4	4.1	2,944	2,814	4.6	4.3
Married, spouse present	1,034	990	2.4	2.2	985	921	2.9	2.7
Widowed, divorced, or separated	435	411	4.8	4.6	628	585	4.9	4.5
Single (never married)	1,798	1,665	8.5	7.8	1,332	1,308	7.8	7.4
White, 16 years and over	2,431	2,274	3.9	3.6	2,053	1,999	3.9	3.8
Married, spouse present	836	797	2.2	2.1	808	749	2.7	2.5
Widowed, divorced, or separated	334	320	4.5	4.3	449	427	4.4	4.2
Single (never married)	1,261	1,157	7.4	6.7	797	823	6.3	6
Black, 16 years and over	671	626	8.9	8.2	756	684	9.0	7.8
Married, spouse present	133	130	3.9	3.8	120	119	4.5	4.2
Widowed, divorced, or separated	84	77	6.9	6.3	156	134	7.0	6.1
Single (never married)	455	419	15.4	14.0	480	430	13.5	11.7
Total, 25 years and over	1,998	1,870	3.2	3.0	1,926	1,805	3.6	3.3
Married, spouse present	980	925	2.3	2.1	878	828	2.7	2.5
Widowed, divorced, or separated	415	393	4.8	4.5	590	544	4.8	4.3
Single (never married)	602	553	5.5	4.9	458	433	5.4	4.9
White, 25 years and over	1,516	1,415	2.8	2.6	1,361	1,294	3.1	2.9
Married, spouse present	790	744	2.1	2.0	717	671	2.5	2.4
Widowed, divorced, or separated	318	305	4.4	4.3	418	396	4.3	4.0
Single (never married)	407	366	4.7	4.2	226	227	3.8	3.8
Black, 25 years and over	373	345	6.0	5.4	471	423	6.8	5.9
Married, spouse present	126	120	3.8	3.6	109	107	4.3	4.0
Widowed, divorced, or separated	81	74	6.8	6.2	151	127	6.9	5.9
Single (never married)	166	152	9.5	8.4	211	188	9.5	8.1

NOTE: Beginning in January 1999, data reflect revised population controls used in the household survey.

SOURCE: *Employment and Earnings.* Bureau of Labor Statistics, January 2000

Race and Ethnic Groups

Blacks (17.2 weeks) were out of work longer than whites (12.2 weeks). Workers of Hispanic origin were unemployed for an average of 12.5 weeks. (See Table 3.8.)

Marital Status

Widowed, divorced, or separated women (15 weeks) were unemployed somewhat longer than those who had never been married (11.8 weeks) or those who were still living with their spouses (12.6 weeks). Married men living with their wives (15.3 weeks) and widowed, divorced, or separated (16 weeks) were out of work longer than never married men (12.7 weeks). (See Table 3.8.)

Occupations

In 1999 almost half (45 percent) of those unemployed in service occupations were out of work less than 5 weeks, and 25 percent were still looking for work after 15 weeks. More than one-third (41 percent) of those seeking managerial and professional positions were unemployed less than 5 weeks, and another 28 percent still lacked jobs after 15 weeks. (See Table 3.9.)

Managerial and professional specialties (14.4 weeks) had the longest average duration of unemployment. Many of these had experienced the downsizing of staff in major companies. They were often older workers looking for higher-paying jobs. Operators, fabricators, and laborers had an average duration of 14 weeks, and service occupations endured unemployment for an average of 13.8 weeks. (See Table 3.9.)

Industry

Forty-three percent of construction workers (as well as transportation and utilities workers and finance, insurance, and real estate workers) found work within 5 weeks. Almost one-quarter (24 percent) of construction workers still needed jobs after 15 weeks. Construction workers were out of work an average of 12.8 weeks. Public administration workers had the longest average duration of unemployment (19.8 weeks). The manufacturing labor force took an average of 15 weeks to find a job. More than one-third (40.2 percent) were unemployed for less than 5 weeks, and another 30 percent were unemployed more than 15 weeks. (See Table 3.9.)

REASONS FOR UNEMPLOYMENT

In 1999 most of those classified as unemployed had lost their jobs or had completed temporary jobs (44.6 percent). Approximately one-third (34.1 percent) had left the labor force (see below) and were returning. Only 8 per-

TABLE 3.6

Unemployed Persons by Occupation and Gender

	Thousands of persons Total		Unemployment rates					
			Total		Men		Women	
Occupation	1998	1999	1998	1999	1998	1999	1998	1999
Total, 16 years and over[1]	6,210	5,880	4.5	4.2	4.4	4.1	4.6	4.3
Managerial and professional specialty	722	770	1.8	1.9	1.7	1.8	2.0	1.9
Executive, administrative, and managerial	343	376	1.8	1.9	1.6	1.7	2.0	2.0
Professional specialty	380	394	1.9	1.9	1.8	1.8	2.0	1.9
Technical, sales, and administrative support	1,550	1,477	3.9	3.7	3.3	3.2	4.2	3.9
Technicians and related support	96	101	2.2	2.3	2.3	2.6	2.1	1.9
Sales occupations	745	714	4.5	4.2	3.3	3.0	5.6	5.4
Administrative support, including clerical	710	662	3.7	3.5	4.0	3.7	3.6	3.4
Service occupations	1,216	1,081	6.4	5.7	6.3	5.5	6.4	5.8
Private household	74	67	8.0	7.4	8.7	6.0	8.0	7.5
Protective service	85	72	3.4	2.9	3.1	2.4	5.0	4.9
Service, except private household and protective	1,057	943	6.8	6.0	7.5	6.7	6.3	5.7
Precision production, craft, and repair	630	607	4.2	4.0	4.1	3.9	4.8	5.2
Mechanics and repairers	149	136	3.0	2.7	3.1	2.6	2.3	4.8
Construction trades	338	330	5.7	5.4	5.6	5.3	10.4	8.8
Other precision production, craft, and repair	143	142	3.4	3.5	3.1	3.1	4.6	4.7
Operators, fabricators, and laborers	1,304	1,207	6.7	6.2	6.3	5.9	7.7	7.3
Machine operators, assemblers, and inspectors	494	440	6.0	5.6	5.0	4.7	7.6	7.2
Transportation and material moving occupations	279	235	4.9	4.1	4.8	4.0	6.3	5.3
Handlers, equipment cleaners, helpers, and laborers	531	532	9.4	9.2	9.6	9.4	8.8	8.4
Construction laborers	136	140	14.2	13.2	14.2	13.0	16.0	18.2
Other handlers, equipment cleaners, helpers, and laborers	395	392	8.4	8.3	8.4	8.4	8.5	8.0
Farming, forestry, and fishing	244	249	6.5	6.8	6.1	6.2	8.0	9.0
No previous work experience	520	469	–	–	–	–	–	–
16 to 19 years	361	328	–	–	–	–	–	–
20 to 24 years	80	67	–	–	–	–	–	–
25 years and over	80	74	–	–	–	–	–	–

[1]Includes a small number of persons whose last job was in the Armed Forces.

NOTE: Beginning in January 1999, data reflect revised population controls used in the household survey.

SOURCE: *Employment and Earnings*. Bureau of Labor Statistics, January 2000

cent were new entrants to the labor force. About 28 percent of the men and 21 percent of the women had been laid off permanently. (See Table 3.10.)

Duration by Reason of Unemployment

More than 2 of 5 (43.7 percent) workers who had lost their jobs or who had completed temporary jobs were unemployed less than 5 weeks. Over one-fourth (25.2 percent) were unemployed 15 weeks or more. Nearly 3 of 5 (55.5 percent) of those who were on temporary layoff were out of work for 5 weeks or less. More than one-third (35.6 percent) of those who were permanently laid off found work in 5 weeks or less. (See Table 3.11.)

Younger job losers and temporary workers tended to find work more quickly than older workers. Nearly two-thirds (65 percent) of 16- to 19-year-old workers who had lost their jobs or who had completed temporary jobs had found work in 5 weeks or less. (See Table 3.11.)

JOB SEARCH

Unemployed workers use different methods to find new jobs. In 1999 most tried an average of 1.78 different

techniques. In 1999 almost two-thirds (65.4 percent) approached the employer directly. About one-half (49.4 percent) sent out resumes or filled out applications. Approximately 1 in 7 (14 percent) sought the help of friends and relatives. Almost 18 percent went to public employment agencies, and 7 percent visited private employment agencies. (See Table 3.12.)

New entrants to the job market (62.5 percent) were less likely to seek out employers directly than those who had lost their jobs or who had completed temporary jobs (68.5 percent). They were also less likely to use employment agencies than job losers. (See Table 3.12.)

WITHDRAWN FROM THE LABOR FORCE

The labor force includes those working and those unemployed who are still looking for work. In 1999 more than half (55 percent) of those people who were not in the labor force were ages 55 or older. More than 6 of 10 (63 percent) were women. (See Table 3.13.)

Reasons for Not Working

In 1996, 15.8 million people between the ages of 25 and 54 neither worked nor looked for work at any time

TABLE 3.7

Unemployed Persons by Industry and Sex

Occupation	Thousands of persons Total		Unemployment rates					
			Total		Men		Women	
	1998	1999	1998	1999	1998	1999	1998	1999
Total, 16 years and over	6,210	5,880	4.5	4.2	4.4	4.1	4.6	4.3
Nonagricultural private wage and salary workers	4,873	4,590	4.6	4.3	4.5	4.1	4.8	4.5
Mining	20	33	3.2	5.7	3.4	5.8	1.8	5.4
Construction	532	520	7.5	7.0	7.7	7.1	5.9	5.8
Manufacturing	816	739	3.9	3.6	3.3	3.1	5.2	4.7
Durable goods	426	434	3.4	3.5	3.0	3.2	4.2	4.3
Lumber and wood products	43	41	5.2	5.2	5.3	5.4	4.8	4.4
Funiture and fixtures	26	26	3.8	4.0	3.5	3.2	4.6	5.7
Stone, clay, and glass products	18	19	3.1	2.9	2.4	2.8	5.4	3.5
Primary metal industries	27	20	3.6	2.5	3.4	2.7	4.8	1.5
Fabricated metal products	49	53	3.5	4.0	3.4	3.8	3.7	4.8
Machinery, except electrical	78	77	3.1	3.1	2.9	3.1	3.8	3.1
Electrical machinery, equipment, and supplies	54	65	2.7	3.3	2.4	2.7	3.3	4.3
Transportation equipment	72	69	3.0	2.9	2.6	2.4	4.4	4.5
Automobiles	47	39	3.4	2.9	3.0	2.1	4.9	5.2
Other transportation equipment	25	30	2.4	3.0	2.1	2.9	3.5	3.5
Professional and photographic equipment	20	24	2.5	3.2	2.0	2.8	3.4	3.7
Other durable goods industries	38	40	5.6	5.6	4.2	5.3	7.5	6.4
Nondurable goods	390	305	4.7	3.9	3.7	3.0	6.2	5.2
Food and kindred products	111	74	6.4	4.4	5.2	3.2	8.6	6.6
Textile mill products	29	26	4.7	4.8	3.7	3.6	5.9	6.4
Apparel and other textile products	76	66	8.8	8.6	6.0	6.7	10.1	9.5
Paper and allied products	18	18	2.6	2.8	2.4	2.8	3.3	2.6
Printing and publishing	67	48	3.8	2.8	3.5	2.9	4.2	2.6
Chemicals and allied products	34	28	2.5	2.2	2.1	1.7	3.3	3.1
Rubber and miscellaneous plastics products	38	33	3.8	3.6	3.1	2.8	5.5	5.3
Other nondurable goods industries	16	12	4.6	3.7	4.0	2.5	5.9	6.6
Transportation and public utilities	254	235	3.4	3.0	3.3	3.0	3.5	3.2
Transportation	185	164	4.0	3.4	4.0	3.5	4.0	3.3
Communications and other public utilities	69	71	2.4	2.4	2.1	2.0	2.9	3.1
Wholesale and retail trade	1,493	1,422	5.5	5.2	5.1	4.5	6.0	6.0
Wholesale trade	185	156	3.7	3.1	3.4	2.6	4.6	4.1
Retail trade	1,308	1,266	6.0	5.7	5.7	5.1	6.2	6.2
Finance, insurance, and real estate	197	191	2.5	2.3	2.3	2.4	2.6	2.3
Service industries	1,562	1,450	4.5	4.1	4.7	4.2	4.4	4.0
Professional services	593	546	2.9	2.6	2.5	2.3	3.1	2.7
Other service industries	968	903	6.9	6.2	6.5	5.7	7.3	6.8
Agricultural wage and salary workers	180	189	8.3	8.9	7.9	8.6	9.3	9.6
Government, self-employed, and unpaid famiy workers	636	631	2.2	2.1	2.0	2.1	2.3	2.1
No previous work experience	520	469	–	–	–	–	–	–

NOTE: Beginning in January 1999, data reflect revised population controls used in the household survey.

SOURCE: *Employment and Earnings.* Bureau of Labor Statistics, January 2000

during the prior year. Women accounted for about 3 out of 4 of these persons. The reasons they were not in the labor market differed markedly from those reported by men. The large majority, 69 percent, were taking care of home or family, 20 percent were either ill or disabled, and a little over 5 percent were in school. In contrast, among the 4 million men of these ages who neither worked nor looked for work, 8 percent were taking care of family or home, and 63 percent were either ill or disabled. (See Table 3.14.)

Income and Education

Women who neither worked nor looked for work tended to be somewhat better off economically than their male counterparts. As of March 1997 about 38 per-cent of the women had family or personal income of less than $20,000, compared with 60 percent of the men. On the other hand, 21 percent of the women, but only 7 percent of the men, had incomes of $60,000 or more. (See Table 3.14.)

About 25 percent of women nonworkers were high school dropouts, compared with 33 percent of men. At the upper educational level, 16 percent of the women versus 12 percent of the men were college graduates.

Still Wanted a Job

In 1999 only 7 percent of those who were no longer part of the labor force still wanted a job, and 40 percent of those who wanted a job had looked for work during the

TABLE 3.8

Unemployed Persons by Selected Demographic Characteristics and Duration of Unemployment

Characteristic	1999						Weeks	
	Thousands of persons							
				15 weeks and over			Average (mean) duration	Median duration
	Total	Less than 5 weeks	5 to 14 weeks	Total	15 to 26 weeks	27 weeks and over		
TOTAL								
Total, 16 years and over	**5,880**	**2,568**	**1,832**	**1,480**	**755**	**725**	**13.4**	**6.4**
16 to 19 years	1,162	617	374	170	98	72	8.7	4.2
20 to 24 years	1,042	515	324	203	113	89	10.9	4.7
25 to 34 years	1,278	539	402	337	179	159	13.5	6.9
35 to 44 years	1,154	449	353	352	176	177	15.9	7.9
45 to 54 years	753	271	234	248	116	132	16.7	8.5
55 to 64 years	367	129	109	128	58	70	17.8	8.9
65 years and over	124	47	36	41	15	26	19.5	8.2
Men, 16 years and over	3,066	1,309	957	800	401	399	14.0	6.7
16 to 19 years	633	332	207	94	55	39	8.7	4.3
20 to 24 years	562	274	171	117	65	53	11.4	4.9
25 to 34 years	624	257	195	172	90	82	14.1	7.2
35 to 44 years	571	213	180	178	90	88	16.6	8.2
45 to 54 years	403	141	125	137	62	75	17.3	9.0
55 to 64 years	203	67	60	77	31	45	19.8	9.7
65 years and over	70	24	20	26	8	17	22.8	9.6
Women, 16 years and over	2,814	1,259	875	680	354	326	12.7	6.1
16 to 19 years	529	285	167	76	43	33	8.8	4.2
20 to 24 years	480	241	153	86	49	37	10.3	4.5
25 to 34 years	654	282	207	166	89	77	13.0	6.6
35 to 44 years	584	236	174	174	86	88	15.2	7.5
45 to 54 years	350	130	109	111	54	57	16.0	8.1
55 to 64 years	163	63	49	51	26	25	15.3	7.9
65 years and over	54	22	16	16	7	9	15.2	6.4
Race and Hispanic origin								
White, 16 years and over	4,273	1,977	1,323	972	520	452	12.2	5.6
Men	2,274	1,021	712	540	283	257	12.7	6.0
Women	1,999	956	611	432	237	195	11.5	5.1
Black, 16 years and over	1,309	468	412	429	195	235	17.2	8.8
Men	626	219	193	214	96	118	18.0	9.0
Women	684	249	219	216	99	117	16.5	8.6
Hispanic origin, 16 years and over	945	426	296	223	120	103	12.5	6.1
Men	480	221	149	110	60	50	12.1	5.7
Women	466	205	147	113	60	53	12.9	6.5
Marital status								
Men, 16 years and over								
Married, spouse present	990	386	310	294	149	145	15.3	7.8
Widowed, divorced, or separated	411	157	128	126	60	66	16.0	8.1
Single (never married)	1,665	766	519	380	193	187	12.7	5.6
Women, 16 years and over								
Married, spouse present	921	412	278	231	123	108	12.6	5.9
Widowed, divorced, or separated	585	233	183	169	81	88	15.0	7.5
Single (never married)	1,308	614	414	280	150	130	11.8	5.5

NOTE: Detail for the above race and Hispanic-origin groups will not sum to totals because data for the "other races" group are not presented and Hispanics are included in both the white and black population groups. Beginning in January 1999, data reflect revised population controls used in the household survey.

SOURCE: *Employment and Earnings.* Bureau of Labor Statistics, January 2000

previous year. Some of the reasons those who were available for work gave for not currently looking were discouragement over job prospects (23 percent), family responsibilities (11 percent), in school or training (18 percent), and ill health or disability (8 percent). (See Table 3.13.)

TABLE 3.9

Unemployed Persons by Occupation, Industry, and Duration of Unemployment

| Characteristic | 1999 Thousands of persons | | | | | | Weeks | |
| | Total | Less than 5 weeks | 5 to 14 weeks | 15 weeks and over | | | Average (mean) duration | Median duration |
				Total	15 to 26 weeks	27 weeks and over		
OCCUPATION								
Managerial and professional specialty	770	316	240	214	107	107	14.4	7.1
Technical, sales, and administrative support	1,477	672	457	347	190	157	12.2	5.9
Service occupations	1,081	490	320	271	123	148	13.8	5.9
Precision production, craft, and repair	607	271	189	147	81	66	12.7	6.0
Operators, fabricators, and laborers	1,207	511	374	322	166	156	14.0	7.0
Farming, forestry, and fishing	249	100	92	57	30	26	11.9	6.8
INDUSTRY[1]								
Agriculture	189	75	72	41	25	17	11.2	7.1
Construction	527	225	174	127	72	55	12.8	6.8
Manufacturing	743	299	223	221	113	108	15.0	7.6
Durable goods	437	178	123	137	70	67	15.5	7.7
Nondurable goods	306	121	100	84	43	41	14.3	7.6
Transportation and public utilities	267	108	85	74	36	38	14.8	7.1
Wholesale and retail trade	1,430	676	436	318	167	151	12.0	5.2
Finance, insurance, and real estate	195	79	55	61	33	28	13.9	7.4
Services	1,675	754	522	399	198	201	13.1	6.0
Public administration	123	40	39	45	21	24	19.8	9.6
No previous work experience	469	199	152	118	55	63	14.4	6.4

[1]Includes wage and salary workers only.

NOTE: Beginning in January 1999, data reflect revised population controls used in the household survey.

SOURCE: *Employment and Earnings.* Bureau of Labor Statistics, January 2000

TABLE 3.10

Unemployed Persons by Reason for Unemployment, Sex, and Age
(Numbers in thousands)

| Reason | Total, 16 years and over | | Men, 20 years and over | | Women, 20 years and over | | Both sexes, 16 to 19 years | |
	1998	1999	1998	1999	1998	1999	1998	1999
NUMBER OF UNEMPLOYED								
Total unemployed	6,210	5,880	2,580	2,433	2,424	2,285	1,205	1,162
Job losers and persons who completed temporary jobs	2,822	2,622	1,588	1,459	1,053	990	181	173
On temporary layoff	866	848	483	475	322	310	61	63
Not on temporary layoff	1,957	1,774	1,105	984	731	680	120	110
Permanent job losers	1,353	1,225	763	685	527	481	64	59
Persons who completed temporary jobs	603	549	343	299	204	199	56	51
Job leavers	734	783	318	336	330	333	86	114
Reentrants	2,132	2,005	611	592	944	866	577	547
New entrants	520	469	63	46	97	96	361	328
PERCENT DISTRIBUTION								
Job losers and persons who completed temporary jobs	45.5	44.6	61.5	60.0	43.4	43.3	15.0	14.9
On temporary layoff	13.9	14.4	18.7	19.5	13.3	13.6	5.1	5.4
Not on temporary layoff	31.5	30.2	42.8	40.4	30.2	29.7	10.0	9.5
Job leavers	11.8	13.3	12.3	13.8	13.6	14.6	7.2	9.8
Reentrants	34.3	34.1	23.7	24.3	39.0	37.9	47.9	47.1
New entrants	8.4	8.0	2.4	1.9	4.0	4.2	30.0	28.2
UNEMPLOYED AS A PERCENT OF THE CIVILIAN LABOR FORCE								
Job losers and persons who completed temporary jobs	2.1	1.9	2.3	2.1	1.8	1.6	2.2	2.1
Job leavers	.5	.6	.5	.5	.6	.5	1.0	1.4
Reentrants	1.5	1.4	.9	.8	1.6	1.4	7.0	6.6
New entrants	.4	.3	.1	.1	.2	.2	4.4	3.9

NOTE: Beginning in January 1999, data reflect revised population controls used in the household survey.

SOURCE: *Employment and Earnings.* Bureau of Labor Statistics, January 2000

TABLE 3.11

Unemployed Persons by Reason for Unemployment, Sex, Age, and Duration of Unemployment

(Percent distribution)

Reason, sex, and age	Total unemployed		Less than 5 weeks	5 to 14 weeks	15 weeks and over		
	Thousands of persons	Percent			Total	15 to 26 weeks	27 weeks and over
Total, 16 years and over	5,880	100.0	43.7	31.2	25.2	12.8	12.3
Job losers and persons who completed temporary jobs	2,622	100.0	43.7	31.2	25.1	14.5	10.5
On temporary layoff	848	100.0	55.5	31.6	12.9	9.3	3.7
Not on temporary layoff	1,774	100.0	38.1	31.1	30.8	17.1	13.8
Permanent job losers	1,225	100.0	35.6	31.0	33.4	18.7	14.7
Persons who completed temporary jobs	549	100.0	43.7	31.3	25.1	13.4	11.7
Job leavers	783	100.0	51.1	29.2	19.6	10.3	9.4
Reentrants	2,005	100.0	41.0	31.5	27.5	11.9	15.6
New entrants	469	100.0	42.4	32.3	25.2	11.8	13.5
Men, 20 years and over	2,433	100.0	40.1	30.8	29.0	14.2	14.8
Job losers and persons who completed temporary jobs	1,459	100.0	41.4	32.0	26.6	15.2	11.4
On temporary layoff	475	100.0	51.8	34.3	13.9	10.6	3.3
Not on temporary layoff	984	100.0	36.3	30.9	32.7	17.4	15.4
Permanent job losers	685	100.0	33.8	30.4	35.7	18.9	16.8
Persons who completed temporary jobs	299	100.0	42.0	32.1	25.9	13.8	12.1
Job leavers	336	100.0	48.2	28.7	23.1	11.1	11.9
Reentrants	592	100.0	33.0	29.5	37.5	14.1	23.4
New entrants	46	100.0	33.5	27.1	39.4	9.0	30.4
Women, 20 years and over	2,285	100.0	42.6	31.0	26.4	13.6	12.8
Job losers and persons who completed temporary jobs	990	100.0	43.5	30.7	25.8	15.1	10.7
On temporary layoff	310	100.0	56.9	30.1	13.1	8.2	4.8
Not on temporary layoff	680	100.0	37.3	31.0	31.6	18.2	13.4
Permanent job losers	481	100.0	35.1	31.4	33.5	20.0	13.5
Persons who completed temporary jobs	199	100.0	42.6	30.3	27.1	13.6	13.4
Job leavers	333	100.0	49.2	30.3	20.5	11.4	9.1
Reentrants	866	100.0	40.1	31.6	28.3	12.5	15.8
New entrants	96	100.0	34.1	29.3	36.7	16.1	20.6
Both sexes, 16 to 19 years	1,162	100.0	53.1	32.2	14.7	8.5	6.2
Job losers and persons who completed temporary jobs	173	100.0	65.0	27.4	7.5	6.2	1.4
On temporary layoff	63	100.0	76.2	18.8	4.9	3.8	1.1
Not on temporary layoff	110	100.0	58.7	32.3	9.0	7.5	1.5
Permanent job losers	59	100.0	59.6	34.2	6.1	5.6	.5
Persons who completed temporary jobs	51	100.0	57.5	30.1	12.4	9.7	2.6
Job leavers	114	100.0	65.4	27.5	7.2	4.5	2.7
Reentrants	547	100.0	51.0	33.6	15.3	8.6	6.8
New entrants	328	100.0	46.1	34.0	19.9	10.9	9.0

NOTE: Beginning in January 1999, data reflect revised population controls used in the household survey.

SOURCE: *Employment and Earnings.* Bureau of Labor Statistics, January 2000

TABLE 3.12

Unemployed Jobseekers by Sex, Reason for Unemployment, and Active Jobsearch Methods Used

	Thousands of persons		1999 Methods used as a percent of total jobseekers							
Sex and reason	Total unemployed	Total job-seekers	Employer directly	Sent out resumes or filled out applications	Placed or answered ads	Friends or relatives	Public employment agency	Private employment agency	Other	Average number of methods used
Total, 16 years and over	5,880	5,032	65.4	49.4	14.5	14.0	17.6	7.0	9.7	1.78
Job losers and persons who completed temporary jobs[1]	2,622	1,774	68.5	49.1	17.8	17.4	23.9	9.6	10.9	1.98
Job leavers	783	783	68.6	51.2	17.0	13.6	18.1	7.9	9.6	1.86
Reentrants	2,005	2,005	62.2	48.5	11.7	11.9	13.9	5.5	9.3	1.63
New entrants	469	469	62.5	50.9	9.6	10.4	8.7	2.1	6.6	1.51
Men, 16 years and over	3,066	2,553	66.7	48.2	14.6	15.1	17.6	7.0	10.3	1.80
Job losers and persons who completed temporary jobs[1]	1,563	1,050	69.3	47.7	17.7	18.7	23.3	9.2	11.8	1.98
Job leavers	389	389	71.1	49.6	16.8	14.7	18.9	8.3	9.7	1.89
Reentrants	895	895	62.8	47.6	11.0	12.6	13.1	5.2	10.0	1.63
New entrants	219	219	62.1	50.4	10.0	8.9	6.9	.9	5.8	1.45
Women, 16 years and over	2,814	2,479	64.1	50.6	14.4	12.8	17.5	7.0	9.0	1.76
Job losers and persons who completed temporary jobs[1]	1,059	724	67.2	51.2	18.0	15.5	24.7	10.1	9.5	1.97
Job leavers	394	394	66.2	52.9	17.1	12.4	17.3	7.6	9.5	1.83
Reentrants	1,111	1,111	61.7	49.2	12.2	11.4	14.5	5.8	8.8	1.83
New entrants	250	250	62.9	51.3	9.3	11.7	10.4	3.1	7.3	1.56

[1] Data on the number of jobseekers and the jobsearch methods used exclude persons on temporary layoff.

NOTE: The jobseeker total is less than the total unemployed because it does not include persons on temporary layoff. The percent using each method will always total more than 100 because many jobseekers use more than one method. Beginning in January 1999, data reflect revised population controls used in the household survey.

SOURCE: *Employment and Earnings.* Bureau of Labor Statistics, January 2000

TABLE 3.13

Persons Not in the Labor Force by Desire and Availability for Work, Age, and Sex
(In thousands)

	Total		Age						Sex			
			16 to 24 years		25 to 54 years		55 years and over		Men		Women	
Category	1998	1999	1998	1999	1998	1999	1998	1999	1998	1999	1998	1999
Total not in the labor force	67,547	68,385	11,343	11,740	18,732	18,785	37,472	37,861	24,799	25,210	42,748	43,175
Do not want a job now[1]	62,735	63,818	9,491	9,938	16,580	16,814	36,664	37,066	22,790	23,307	39,945	40,511
Want a job[1]	4,812	4,568	1,852	1,802	2,152	1,971	807	795	2,008	1,903	2,803	2,665
Did not search for work in previous year	2,859	2,723	1,011	981	1,240	1,144	608	599	1,134	1,083	1,725	1,640
Searched for work in previous year[2]	1,953	1,844	841	822	912	827	200	196	875	820	1,078	1,024
Not available to work now	643	644	332	345	275	258	36	41	250	249	392	395
Available to work now	1,310	1,201	509	477	637	569	164	155	624	571	686	629
Reason not currently looking:												
Discouragement over job prospects[3]	331	273	108	86	170	146	53	41	198	161	133	113
Reasons other than discouragement	979	927	401	391	467	423	111	114	427	411	552	517
Family responsibilities	143	132	37	29	93	92	13	11	23	29	120	103
In school or training	206	214	173	176	32	34	1	4	105	110	102	104
Ill health or disability	104	97	14	13	69	57	21	26	52	39	52	58
Other[4]	525	485	177	173	273	239	75	73	247	234	278	251

[1] Includes some persons who are not asked if they want a job.

[2] Persons who had a job in the prior 12 months must have searched since the end of that job.

[3] Includes believes no work available, could not find work, lacks necessary schooling or training, employer thinks too young or old, and other types of discrimination.

[4] Includes those who did not actively look for work in the prior 4 weeks for such reasons as child-care and transportation problems, as well as a small number for which reason for nonparticipation was not ascertained.

NOTE: Beginning in January 1999, data reflect revised population controls used in the household survey.

SOURCE: *Employment and Earnings.* Bureau of Labor Statistics, January 2000

TABLE 3.14

Persons 25 to 54 Years Old Who Did Not Work or Look for Work in 1996 by Reason, Income, and Sex, March 1997

(Numbers in thousands)

	Total nonworkers		Percent distribution by income			
Characteristic	Number	Percent	Under $20,000	$20,000 to $39,999	$40,000 to $59,999	$60,000 or more
Men, 25 to 54 years	4,038	100.0	60.2	22.1	10.9	6.7
Ill or disabled	2,527	62.6	61.9	21.2	11.6	5.4
Retired	188	4.7	33.8	28.5	19.4	18.2
Home responsibilities	341	8.4	54.8	28.8	8.8	7.6
Going to school	398	9.9	60.0	21.7	6.4	11.9
Could not find work	217	5.4	61.6	15.9	17.1	5.4
Other	367	9.1	67.1	22.7	5.5	4.7
Women, 25 to 54 years	11,717	100.0	38.2	24.5	16.0	21.3
Ill or disabled	2,291	19.6	62.1	20.1	8.1	9.7
Retired	371	3.2	29.0	19.8	20.0	31.2
Home responsibilities	8,064	68.8	30.3	26.3	18.6	24.8
Going to school	607	5.2	48.5	23.4	9.9	18.3
Could not find work	114	.7	81.3	7.9	5.1	5.8
Other	269	1.7	44.2	22.1	16.5	17.2

NOTE: Income refers to family income for those who were living with their families or to personal income for those not in families. Income refers to earnings, disability or unemployment benefits, interest income, and other sources. Detail may not sum to totals due to rounding.

SOURCE: *Who's Not Working?* Issues in Labor Statistics. Bureau of Labor Statistics: Washington, D.C.

CHAPTER 4
THE EDUCATION OF AMERICAN WORKERS

Education is an investment in skills, and like all investments, it involves both costs and returns. The cost of finishing high school to the student is quite low. However, the cost to the student of attending college is higher because it includes tuition, books, fees, and the earnings a student gives up either by not working at all during college or by working part-time. It is important to remember that while the returns from a high school or college education can be measured economically, there are invaluable social, emotional, and intellectual returns that cannot be measured in statistics.

While some returns from education accrue for the individual, others benefit society and the nation in general. Returns related to the economy, specifically the labor market, include better job opportunities and jobs that are less sensitive to general economic conditions. Other societal returns often attributed to education include a greater interest and participation in civil affairs.

A BETTER-EDUCATED NATION

American workers are better educated than ever before. Before the end of World War II (1939–1945), with the exception of doctors, lawyers, engineers, teachers, and some other professionals, very few people earned higher degrees for the purpose of preparing for a career or vocation. For the most part, a person who wanted training for a job or occupation went to a vocational high school or became apprenticed (learning on the job from a highly skilled person) in the trades they wanted to learn.

The GI Bill of Rights, introduced after World War II, changed the way Americans looked at higher education. The soldiers, sailors, and airmen returning to civilian life wanted to make better lives for themselves, and the U.S. government was willing to pay to give them the chance. Federal money paid to America's returning veterans opened up and enlarged trade and vocational schools and

filled college classrooms across the nation. Since then, American colleges and universities have been graduating more and more engineers, accountants, scientists, businessmen, technicians, nurses, and others with similar technical careers.

How Well Educated Are Americans?

From approximately 1925 to 2000 the median number of school years completed has risen from 8.4 years in 1930 to 13.0 years. As late as 1930 fewer than 1 in 5 Americans had completed 4 or more years of high school. Since that time the proportion has steadily increased, reaching 82.8 percent of those 25 years and older in 1998. Among young people 25 to 29 years of age, 88.1 percent completed 4 or more years of high school. (See Figure 4.1 and Table 4.1.) By 1998 almost 25 percent of people 25 years and older had completed 4 or more years of college,

FIGURE 4.1

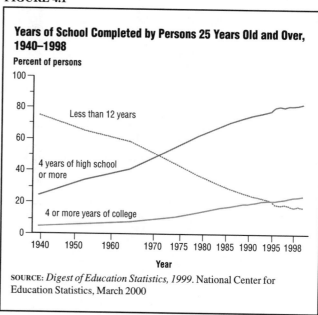

Years of School Completed by Persons 25 Years Old and Over, 1940–1998

SOURCE: *Digest of Education Statistics, 1999.* National Center for Education Statistics, March 2000

TABLE 4.1

Years of School Completed by Persons Age 25 and Over and 25 to 29, by Race/Ethnicity and Sex, 1910–1998

	Percent, by years of school completed											
	All races			White, non-Hispanic[1]			Black, non-Hispanic[1]			Hispanic		
Age and year	Less than 5 years of elementary school	High school completion or higher[2]	4 or more years of college[3]	Less than 5 years of elementary school	High school completion or higher[2]	4 or more years of college[3]	Less than 5 years of elementary school	High school completion or higher[2]	4 or more years of college[3]	Less than 5 years of elementary school	High school completion or higher[2]	4 or more years of college[3]
1	2	3	4	5	6	7	8	9	10	11	12	13
Males and females												
25 and over												
1910[4]	23.8	13.5	2.7	—	—	—	—	—	—	—	—	—
1920[4]	22.0	16.4	3.3	—	—	—	—	—	—	—	—	—
1930[4]	17.5	19.1	3.9	—	—	—	—	—	—	—	—	—
April 1940	13.7	24.5	4.6	10.9	26.1	4.9	41.8	7.7	1.3	—	—	—
April 1950	11.1	34.3	6.2	8.9	36.4	6.6	32.6	13.7	2.2	—	—	—
April 1960	8.3	41.1	7.7	6.7	43.2	8.1	23.5	21.7	3.5	—	—	—
March 1970	5.3	55.2	11.0	4.2	57.4	11.6	14.7	36.1	6.1	15.8	44.5	7.6
March 1980	3.4	68.6	17.0	1.9	71.9	18.4	9.1	51.4	7.9	13.5	47.9	8.5
March 1985	2.7	73.9	19.4	1.4	77.5	20.8	6.1	59.9	11.1	12.9	48.5	8.4
March 1986	2.7	74.7	19.4	1.4	78.2	20.1	5.3	62.5	10.9	11.9	50.9	8.6
March 1987	2.4	75.6	19.9	1.3	79.0	20.5	4.9	63.6	10.8	12.2	51.0	10.0
March 1988	2.5	76.2	20.3	1.2	79.8	21.8	4.8	63.5	11.2	12.2	50.9	9.9
March 1989	2.5	76.9	21.1	1.2	80.7	22.8	5.2	64.7	11.7	12.3	50.8	9.2
March 1990	2.5	77.6	21.3	1.1	81.4	23.1	5.1	66.2	11.3	12.5	51.3	9.7
March 1991	2.4	78.4	21.4	1.1	82.4	23.3	4.7	66.8	11.5	11.8	52.6	9.3
March 1992	2.1	79.4	21.4	0.9	83.4	23.2	3.9	67.7	11.9	11.8	53.1	9.0
March 1993	2.1	80.2	21.9	0.8	84.1	23.8	3.7	70.5	12.2	10.8	53.3	9.1
March 1994	1.9	80.9	22.2	0.8	84.9	24.3	2.7	73.0	12.9	10.6	53.4	9.3
March 1995	1.9	81.7	23.0	0.7	85.9	23.4	2.5	73.8	13.3	10.4	53.1	9.3
March 1996	1.8	81.7	23.6	0.6	86.0	25.9	2.2	74.6	13.8	9.4	54.7	10.3
March 1997	1.7	82.1	23.9	0.6	86.3	26.2	2.0	75.3	13.3	9.3	55.5	11.0
March 1998	1.7	82.8	24.4	0.6	87.1	26.6	1.7	76.4	14.8			
25 to 29												
1920[4]	—	—	—	12.9	22.0	4.5	44.6	6.3	1.2	—	—	—
April 1940	5.9	38.1	5.9	3.4	41.2	6.4	27.0	12.3	1.6	—	—	—
April 1950	4.6	52.8	7.7	3.3	56.3	8.2	16.1	23.6	2.8	—	—	—
April 1960	2.8	60.7	11.0	2.2	63.7	11.8	7.2	38.6	5.4	—	—	—
March 1970	1.1	75.4	16.4	0.9	77.8	17.3	2.2	58.4	10.0	—	—	—
March 1980	0.8	85.4	22.5	0.3	89.2	25.0	0.7	76.7	11.6	6.7	58.0	7.7
March 1985	0.7	86.1	22.2	0.2	89.5	24.4	0.4	80.5	11.6	6.0	60.9	11.1
March 1986	0.9	86.1	22.4	0.4	89.6	25.2	0.5	83.5	11.8	5.6	59.1	9.0
March 1987	0.9	86.0	22.0	0.4	89.4	24.7	0.4	83.5	11.5	4.8	59.8	8.7
March 1988	1.0	85.9	22.7	0.3	89.7	25.1	0.3	80.9	12.0	6.0	62.3	11.3
March 1989	1.0	85.5	23.4	0.3	89.3	26.3	0.5	82.3	12.7	5.4	61.0	10.1
March 1990	1.2	85.7	23.2	0.3	90.1	26.4	1.0	81.7	13.4	7.3	58.2	8.2
March 1991	1.0	85.4	23.2	0.3	89.8	26.7	0.5	81.8	11.0	5.8	56.7	9.2
March 1992	0.9	86.3	23.6	0.3	90.7	27.2	0.8	80.9	11.1	5.2	60.9	9.5
March 1993	0.7	86.7	23.7	0.3	91.2	27.2	0.2	82.7	13.3	4.0	60.9	8.3
March 1994	0.8	86.1	23.3	0.3	91.1	27.1	0.6	84.1	13.6	3.6	60.3	8.0
March 1995	1.0	86.9	24.7	0.3	92.5	28.8	0.2	86.7	15.4	4.9	57.2	8.9
March 1996	0.8	87.3	27.1	0.2	92.6	31.6	0.4	86.0	14.6	4.3	61.1	10.0
March 1997	0.8	87.4	27.8	0.1	92.9	32.6	0.6	86.9	14.2	4.2	61.8	11.0
March 1998	0.7	88.1	27.3	0.1	93.6	32.3	0.4	88.3	15.8	3.7	62.8	10.4
Males												
25 and over												
April 1940	15.1	22.7	5.5	12.0	24.2	5.9	46.2	6.9	1.4	—	—	—
April 1950	12.2	32.6	7.3	9.8	34.6	7.9	36.9	12.6	2.1	—	—	—
April 1960	9.4	39.5	9.7	7.4	41.6	10.3	27.7	20.0	3.5	—	—	—
March 1970	5.9	55.0	14.1	4.5	57.2	15.0	17.9	35.4	6.8	—	—	—
March 1980	3.6	69.2	20.9	2.0	72.4	22.8	11.3	51.2	7.7	16.5	44.9	9.2
March 1990	2.7	77.7	24.4	1.3	81.6	26.7	6.4	65.8	11.9	12.9	50.3	9.8
March 1994	2.1	81.1	25.1	0.8	85.1	27.8	3.9	71.8	12.7	11.4	53.4	9.6
March 1995	2.0	81.7	26.0	0.8	86.0	28.9	3.4	73.5	13.7	10.8	52.9	10.1
March 1996	1.9	81.9	26.0	0.7	86.1	28.8	2.9	74.6	12.5	10.2	53.0	10.3
March 1997	1.8	82.0	26.2	0.6	86.3	29.0	2.9	73.8	12.5	9.2	54.9	10.6
March 1998	1.7	82.8	26.5	0.7	87.1	29.3	2.3	75.4	14.0	9.3	55.7	11.1

TABLE 4.1

Years of School Completed by Persons Age 25 and Over and 25 to 29, by Race/Ethnicity and Sex, 1910–1998 [CONTINUED]

	Percent, by years of school completed												
Age and year	All races			White, non-Hispanic[1]			Black, non-Hispanic[1]			Hispanic		
	Less than 5 years of elementary school	High school completion or higher[2]	4 or more years of college[3]	Less than 5 years of elementary school	High school completion or higher[2]	4 or more years of college[3]	Less than 5 years of elementary school	High school completion or higher[2]	4 or more years of college[3]	Less than 5 years of elementary school	High school completion or higher[2]	4 or more years of college[3]
1	2	3	4	5	6	7	8	9	10	11	12	13
	Females											
25 and over												
April 1940	12.4	26.3	3.8	9.8	28.1	4.0	37.5	8.4	1.2	—	—	—
April 1950	10.0	36.0	5.2	8.1	38.2	5.4	28.6	14.7	2.4	—	—	—
April 1960	7.4	42.5	5.8	6.0	44.7	6.0	19.7	23.1	3.6	—	—	—
March 1970	4.7	55.4	8.2	3.9	57.7	8.6	11.9	36.6	5.6	—	—	—
March 1980	3.2	68.1	13.6	1.8	71.5	14.4	7.4	51.5	8.1	15.3	44.2	6.2
March 1990	2.2	77.5	18.4	1.0	81.3	19.8	4.1	66.5	10.8	11.7	51.3	8.7
March 1994	1.7	80.8	19.6	0.7	84.7	21.1	1.8	73.9	13.1	10.3	53.2	8.6
March 1995	1.7	81.6	20.2	0.6	85.8	22.2	1.8	74.1	13.0	10.4	53.8	8.4
March 1996	1.7	81.6	21.4	0.5	85.9	23.2	1.6	74.6	14.8	10.6	53.3	8.3
March 1997	1.6	82.2	21.7	0.5	86.3	23.7	1.3	76.5	14.0	9.5	54.6	10.1
March 1998	1.6	82.9	22.4	0.6	87.1	24.1	1.2	77.1	15.5	9.2	55.3	10.9

[1] Includes persons of Hispanic origin for years prior to 1980.

[2] Data for years prior to 1993 include all persons with at least 4 years of high school.

[3] Data for 1993 and later years are for persons with a bachelor's degree or higher.

[4] Estimates based on Bureau of the Census retrojection of 1940 Census data on education by age.

—Data not available.

NOTE: Data for 1980 and subsequent years are for the noninstitutional population.

SOURCE: *Digest of Education Statistics, 1999.* National Center for Education Statistics, March 2000

compared to roughly 2 percent in 1940. People 25 years and older who had less than 12 years of education have decreased steadily since 1940, and roughly 15 percent of these people had less than 12 years of education in 1998, compared to almost 80 percent in 1940. (See Figure 4.1.)

More High School Graduates in College

At the end of the 1998–99 school year, 2.8 million students graduated from high school, representing about 70 percent of all 17-year olds. In 1996 about 1.7 million or 65 percent of high school graduates were enrolled in college. In 1960 only 45 percent of high school graduates enrolled in college.

GENDER. Increased female enrollment has contributed to the growth in college enrollment. From 1980 to 1997 male enrollment increased by only 8 percent, while the number of females rose by 29 percent. (See Table 4.2.) Between 1997 and 2009 female enrollment is projected to increase another 17 percent, while male enrollment will rise 9 percent.

OLDER STUDENTS. Between the school years 1990 and 1997 the number of older students attending colleges grew faster than the number of younger students, but this is beginning to change. During that period, enrollment of students under age 25 increased by 2 percent, while enrollment of persons 35 and over increased by 17 per-

cent. (See Table 4.2 and Figure 4.2.) From 1997 to 2000 the National Center for Education and Statistics projects a rise of 6 percent in enrollments of persons 25 and under and an increase of 3 percent in the number 25 and over.

Observers attribute the enrollment of older students to the higher education levels required by many occupations and the growing number of students who leave school to work and return later. The main reasons older students begin or return to degree programs are career transitions and the need for new skills to obtain different jobs.

MINORITY ENROLLMENT. The enrollment of minority students (non-Hispanic blacks, Hispanics, Asians, and American Indians) in higher education has been rising steadily. In 1976 only 16 percent of college students were from minority groups, compared to 26.8 percent in 1997. (See Table 4.3.) Much of the increase can be traced to larger numbers of Hispanic and Asian/Pacific Islander students, who made up 55 percent of minority enrollment in institutions of higher education during 1997.

While white students still comprise the large majority of college students, the trend is toward more racial and ethnic diversity on campuses. In 1976 white students made up 84 percent of higher education enrollment. In 1997 whites accounted for 73.2 percent of those attending college; blacks, 11 percent; Hispanics, 8.6 percent;

TABLE 4.2

Total Fall Enrollment in Institutions of Higher Education, by Gender and Age, 1970–2009

[In thousands]

| Sex and age | 1970 | 1975 | 1980 | 1990 | 1993 | 1994 | 1995 | 1996 | 1997 | Projected | | | |
										1998	1999	2000	2009
1	2	3	4	5	6	7	8	9	10	11	12	13	14
Men and women, total	**8,581**	**11,185**	**12,097**	**13,819**	**14,305**	**14,279**	**14,262**	**14,300**	**14,345**	**14,608**	**14,881**	**15,072**	**16,336**
14 to 17 years old	259	278	247	177	127	138	148	229	208	213	217	223	263
18 and 19 years old	2,600	2,786	2,901	2,950	2,840	2,787	2,894	3,004	3,084	3,192	3,319	3,379	3,903
20 and 21 years old	1,880	2,243	2,424	2,761	2,674	2,724	2,705	2,643	2,670	2,688	2,769	2,896	3,286
22 to 24 years old	1,457	1,753	1,989	2,144	2,570	2,482	2,411	2,316	2,233	2,165	2,204	2,227	2,592
25 to 29 years old	1,074	1,774	1,871	1,982	2,002	1,985	2,120	2,124	2,049	2,036	1,994	1,945	2,184
30 to 34 years old	487	967	1,243	1,322	1,345	1,414	1,236	1,194	1,189	1,224	1,231	1,242	1,259
35 years old and over	823	1,383	1,421	2,484	2,747	2,750	2,747	2,790	2,911	3,090	3,147	3,160	2,849
Men	**5,044**	**6,149**	**5,874**	**6,284**	**6,427**	**6,372**	**6,343**	**6,344**	**6,330**	**6,297**	**6,370**	**6,432**	**6,937**
14 to 17 years old	130	126	99	87	54	62	61	92	91	98	97	100	111
18 and 19 years old	1,349	1,397	1,375	1,421	1,288	1,302	1,338	1,342	1,376	1,402	1,455	1,479	1,692
20 and 21 years old	1,095	1,245	1,259	1,368	1,284	1,264	1,282	1,224	1,249	1,238	1,269	1,323	1,481
22 to 24 years old	964	1,047	1,064	1,107	1,344	1,238	1,153	1,175	1,136	1,077	1,088	1,095	1,253
25 to 29 years old	783	1,122	993	940	903	936	962	993	969	952	930	907	1,010
30 to 34 years old	308	557	576	537	584	601	561	480	490	499	499	501	494
35 years old and over	415	654	507	824	970	969	986	1,039	1,018	1,031	1,032	1,026	896
Women	**3,537**	**5,036**	**6,223**	**7,535**	**7,877**	**7,907**	**7,919**	**7,956**	**8,015**	**8,311**	**8,511**	**8,639**	**9,399**
14 to 17 years old	129	152	148	90	73	75	87	137	117	115	120	123	152
18 and 19 years old	1,250	1,389	1,526	1,529	1,552	1,485	1,557	1,662	1,708	1,790	1,864	1,900	2,211
20 and 21 years old	786	998	1,165	1,392	1,391	1,461	1,424	1,419	1,421	1,449	1,501	1,573	1,805
22 to 24 years old	493	706	925	1,037	1,226	1,243	1,258	1,141	1,097	1,088	1,116	1,132	1,339
25 to 29 years old	291	652	878	1,043	1,098	1,049	1,159	1,131	1,081	1,084	1,064	1,037	1,173
30 to 34 years old	179	410	667	784	761	812	675	714	699	725	733	741	765
35 years old and over	409	729	914	1,659	1,777	1,781	1,760	1,752	1,893	2,059	2,115	2,133	1,954
Full-time	**5,816**	**6,841**	**7,098**	**7,821**	**8,128**	**8,138**	**8,129**	**8,213**	**8,322**	**8,242**	**8,449**	**8,600**	**9,666**
14 to 17 years old	242	253	223	144	92	118	123	164	175	177	186	190	228
18 and 19 years old	2,406	2,619	2,669	2,548	2,370	2,321	2,387	2,516	2,620	2,712	2,837	2,899	3,372
20 and 21 years old	1,647	1,910	2,075	2,151	2,148	2,178	2,109	2,098	2,154	2,154	2,229	2,336	2,661
22 to 24 years old	881	924	1,121	1,350	1,612	1,551	1,517	1,586	1,505	1,403	1,416	1,421	1,640
25 to 29 years old	407	630	577	770	839	869	908	902	868	816	793	767	852
30 to 34 years old	100	264	251	387	424	440	430	379	392	385	386	386	375
35 years old and over	134	241	182	471	643	660	653	568	608	595	602	600	539
Men	**3,505**	**3,927**	**3,689**	**3,808**	**3,891**	**3,855**	**3,807**	**3,816**	**3,839**	**3,738**	**3,801**	**3,852**	**4,262**
14 to 17 years old	124	114	87	71	37	51	54	71	79	79	82	83	93
18 and 19 years old	1,265	1,329	1,270	1,230	1,079	1,081	1,091	1,111	1,155	1,179	1,231	1,257	1,446
20 and 21 years old	990	1,074	1,109	1,055	1,003	1,029	999	961	996	981	1,008	1,053	1,180
22 to 24 years old	650	633	665	742	896	811	789	853	800	731	730	728	821
25 to 29 years old	327	445	360	401	443	457	454	440	427	402	390	378	416
30 to 34 years old	72	181	124	156	180	193	183	143	159	160	160	159	150
35 years old and over	75	149	74	152	253	232	238	237	222	206	200	193	157
Women	**2,311**	**2,915**	**3,409**	**4,013**	**4,237**	**4,283**	**4,321**	**4,398**	**4,483**	**4,503**	**4,649**	**4,748**	**5,404**
14 to 17 years old	117	138	136	73	55	67	69	93	95	98	104	107	135
18 and 19 years old	1,140	1,290	1,399	1,318	1,291	1,240	1,296	1,405	1,465	1,533	1,606	1,642	1,926
20 and 21 years old	657	835	966	1,096	1,145	1,149	1,111	1,137	1,158	1,173	1,221	1,283	1,482
22 to 24 years old	231	291	456	608	716	740	729	734	705	671	686	693	819
25 to 29 years old	80	185	217	369	396	412	455	462	442	414	403	389	436
30 to 34 years old	28	83	127	231	244	247	247	236	233	226	227	227	225
35 years old and over	59	92	108	319	390	428	415	331	385	389	402	407	382

Asian or Pacific Islanders, 6.1 percent; and American Indians and Alaskan Natives, 1 percent.

Between 1976 and 1997 the number of white students grew by 12 percent and the number of black students by 48 percent. Other minority groups increased by even higher proportions: American Indians more than doubled, Hispanics tripled, and Asian/Pacific Islanders quadrupled. Women in general increased enrollment by 54 percent between 1976 and 1997, compared to a 9 percent increase for men. (See Table 4.3.)

Degrees Conferred

TYPES OF DEGREES. Students can earn a variety of vocational certifications and college degrees. Associate degrees are usually awarded by junior colleges or community colleges after about 2 years of course work. Voca-

TABLE 4.2

Total Fall Enrollment in Institutions of Higher Education, by Gender and Age, 1970–2009 [CONTINUED]

[In thousands]

Sex and age	1970	1975	1980	1990	1993	1994	1995	1996	1997	Projected			
										1998	1999	2000	2009
1	2	3	4	5	6	7	8	9	10	11	12	13	14
Part-time	2,765	4,344	4,998	5,998	6,177	6,141	6,133	6,087	6,023	6,366	6,432	6,471	6,670
14 to 17 years old	17	42	38	32	35	19	25	65	33	36	30	33	35
18 and 19 years old	194	340	418	402	470	466	507	488	464	480	482	480	531
20 and 21 years old	233	447	441	610	526	546	596	544	516	534	540	560	624
22 to 24 years old	576	717	844	794	958	930	894	729	728	763	788	805	952
25 to 29 years old	668	1,032	1,209	1,213	1,163	1,116	1,212	1,222	1,181	1,220	1,202	1,178	1,332
30 to 34 years old	388	670	905	935	921	973	805	815	797	839	845	856	884
35 years old and over	689	1,098	1,145	2,012	2,104	2,091	2,093	2,222	2,303	2,495	2,545	2,560	2,311
Men	1,540	2,222	2,185	2,476	2,537	2,517	2,535	2,528	2,491	2,559	2,569	2,581	2,675
14 to 17 years old	5	18	17	16	17	11	7	21	12	18	14	17	18
18 and 19 years old	84	153	202	191	210	220	246	231	221	223	224	222	246
20 and 21 years old	105	219	201	313	281	235	283	263	254	257	261	270	301
22 to 24 years old	314	358	392	365	448	427	365	323	336	346	359	366	433
25 to 29 years old	456	631	594	539	460	479	508	553	542	550	540	529	595
30 to 34 years old	236	361	397	381	404	408	378	337	331	339	339	342	344
35 years old and over	340	486	382	672	717	737	748	801	796	824	832	833	739
Women	1,225	2,121	2,814	3,521	3,640	3,624	3,598	3,558	3,532	3,807	3,863	3,891	3,995
14 to 17 years old	12	24	20	17	18	8	18	45	21	17	16	16	17
18 and 19 years old	110	188	215	211	261	245	261	257	243	256	258	257	285
20 and 21 years old	128	228	240	297	245	311	313	282	262	277	280	290	323
22 to 24 years old	262	359	452	429	510	504	529	407	392	417	430	439	520
25 to 29 years old	212	401	616	674	702	637	704	669	639	670	661	648	737
30 to 34 years old	151	309	507	554	517	565	427	478	466	500	506	514	540
35 years old and over	349	612	762	1,340	1,386	1,354	1,345	1,421	1,508	1,670	1,713	1,727	1,572

NOTE: Distributions by age are estimates based on samples of the civilian non-institutional population. Because of rounding, details may not add to totals. Historical numbers may differ from those in previous editions.

SOURCE: *Digest of Education Statistics, 1999.* National Center for Education Statistics, March 2000

tional degrees are awarded by private institutions, as well as community and junior colleges. These degrees prepare people for specific jobs, such as court reporter, legal assistant, or computer programmer. Bachelor's degrees usually take a minimum of 4 years to complete. Private and public universities also award advanced master's, doctoral, or professional (doctor or lawyer) degrees.

HOW MANY? At the end of the 1996–97 school year about 571,000 associate's degrees, 1.2 million bachelor's, 419,000 master's, 78,700 first-professional, and 45,800 doctoral degrees were awarded. (See Figure 4.3 and Table 4.4.) While more women than men earned associate's, bachelor's, and master's degrees, more men than women earned first-professional and doctor's degrees; this trend was projected to remain similar through 2009. In some cases, the total amount of each type of degree awarded was projected to increase through 2009; 628,000 associate's degrees were expected to be awarded, as well as 1.25 million bachelor's degrees. Other degree types were expected to decrease. (See Table 4.4.)

In 1997, despite the growth in enrollment, non-Hispanic black and Hispanic students were underrepresented in attaining college degrees. While black and Hispanic

FIGURE 4.2

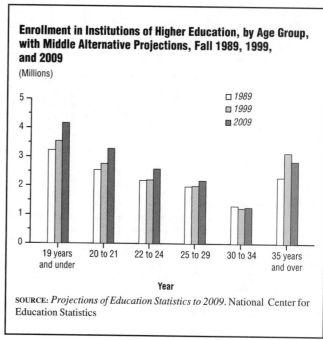

Enrollment in Institutions of Higher Education, by Age Group, with Middle Alternative Projections, Fall 1989, 1999, and 2009

(Millions)

SOURCE: *Projections of Education Statistics to 2009.* National Center for Education Statistics

TABLE 4.3

Total Fall Enrollment in Institutions of Higher Education and Degree-Granting Institutions, by Level of Study, Sex, and Race/Ethnicity of Student, 1976–1997

Level of study, sex, and race/ethnicity of student	Institutions of higher education, in thousands						Degree-granting institutions, in thousands[1]		Percentage distribution of students[2]							
									Institutions of higher education						Degree-granting institutions[1]	
	1976	1980	1990	1995	1996	1997	1996	1997	1976	1980	1990	1995	1996	1997	1996	1997
1	2	3	4	5	6	7	8	9	10	11	12	13	14	15	16	17
All students																
Total	10,985.6	12,086.8	13,818.6	14,261.8	14,300.3	14,345.4	14,367.5	14,502.3	100.0	100.0	100.0	100.0	100.0	100.0	100.0	100.0
White, non-Hispanic	9,076.1	9,833.0	10,722.5	10,311.2	10,226.0	10,160.9	10,263.9	10,266.1	84.3	83.5	79.9	74.7	73.9	73.2	73.8	73.1
Total minority	1,690.8	1,948.8	2,704.7	3,496.2	3,609.3	3,723.2	3,637.4	3,771.2	15.7	16.5	20.1	25.3	26.1	26.8	26.2	26.9
Black, non-Hispanic	1,033.0	1,106.8	1,247.0	1,473.7	1,499.4	1,532.8	1,505.6	1,551.0	9.6	9.4	9.3	10.7	10.8	11.0	10.8	11.0
Hispanic	383.8	471.7	782.4	1,093.8	1,152.2	1,200.1	1,166.1	1,218.5	3.6	4.0	5.8	7.9	8.3	8.6	8.4	8.7
Asian or Pacific Islander	197.9	286.4	572.4	797.4	823.6	851.5	828.2	859.2	1.8	2.4	4.3	5.8	6.0	6.1	6.0	6.1
American Indian/Alaskan Native	76.1	83.9	102.8	131.3	134.0	138.8	137.6	142.5	0.7	0.7	0.8	1.0	1.0	1.0	1.0	1.0
Nonresident alien	218.7	305.0	391.5	454.4	464.9	461.3	466.3	465.0	—	—	—	—	—	—	—	—
Men	5,794.4	5,868.1	6,283.9	6,342.5	6,344.0	6,330.0	6,352.8	6,396.0	100.0	100.0	100.0	100.0	100.0	100.0	100.0	100.0
White, non-Hispanic	4,813.7	4,772.9	4,861.0	4,594.1	4,553.0	4,504.8	4,552.2	4,548.8	85.3	84.4	80.5	75.6	74.9	74.3	74.8	74.2
Total minority	826.6	884.4	1,176.6	1,484.2	1,524.3	1,562.2	1,533.4	1,582.3	14.7	15.6	19.5	24.4	25.1	25.7	25.2	25.8
Black, non-Hispanic	469.9	463.7	484.7	555.9	563.6	572.5	564.1	579.8	8.3	8.2	8.0	9.1	9.3	9.4	9.3	9.5
Hispanic	209.7	231.6	353.9	480.2	501.3	518.1	506.6	525.8	3.7	4.1	5.9	7.9	8.2	8.5	8.3	8.6
Asian or Pacific Islander	108.4	151.3	294.9	393.3	403.6	414.0	405.5	417.7	1.9	2.7	4.9	6.5	6.6	6.8	6.7	6.8
American Indian/Alaskan Native	38.5	37.8	43.1	54.8	55.7	57.6	57.2	59.0	0.7	0.7	0.7	0.9	0.9	0.9	0.9	1.0
Nonresident alien	154.1	210.8	246.3	264.3	266.7	262.9	267.2	264.9	—	—	—	—	—	—	—	—
Women	5,191.2	6,218.7	7,534.7	7,919.2	7,956.3	8,015.5	8,014.7	8,106.3	100.0	100.0	100.0	100.0	100.0	100.0	100.0	100.0
White, non-Hispanic	4,262.4	5,060.1	5,861.5	5,717.2	5,673.1	5,656.1	5,711.7	5,717.4	83.1	82.6	79.3	74.0	73.1	72.4	73.1	72.3
Total minority	864.2	1,064.4	1,528.1	2,012.0	2,085.0	2,161.0	2,104.0	2,188.9	16.9	17.4	20.7	26.0	26.9	27.6	26.9	27.7
Black, non-Hispanic	563.1	643.0	762.3	917.8	935.8	960.2	941.4	971.3	11.0	10.5	10.3	11.9	12.1	12.3	12.0	12.3
Hispanic	174.1	240.1	428.5	613.7	650.9	682.0	659.5	692.7	3.4	3.9	5.8	7.9	8.4	8.7	8.4	8.8
Asian or Pacific Islander	89.4	135.2	277.5	404.1	420.0	437.4	422.6	441.5	1.7	2.2	3.8	5.2	5.4	5.6	5.4	5.6
American Indian/Alaskan Native	37.6	46.1	59.7	76.5	78.2	81.3	80.4	83.4	0.7	0.8	0.8	1.0	1.0	1.0	1.0	1.1
Nonresident alien	64.6	94.2	145.2	190.1	198.2	198.4	199.0	200.1	—	—	—	—	—	—	—	—
Full-time	6,703.6	7,088.9	7,821.0	8,128.8	8,213.5	8,322.4	8,303.0	8,438.1	100.0	100.0	100.0	100.0	100.0	100.0	100.0	100.0
White, non-Hispanic	5,512.6	5,717.0	6,016.5	5,833.8	5,847.5	5,886.7	5,906.1	5,960.1	84.2	83.4	79.9	74.9	74.4	73.9	74.3	73.8
Total minority	1,030.9	1,137.5	1,514.9	1,955.3	2,017.2	2,079.8	2,046.8	2,118.7	15.8	16.6	20.1	25.1	25.6	26.1	25.7	26.2
Black, non-Hispanic	659.2	685.6	718.3	840.4	861.0	880.7	871.9	896.6	10.1	10.0	9.5	10.8	10.9	11.1	11.0	11.1
Hispanic	211.1	247.0	394.7	553.2	577.1	599.6	588.8	614.0	3.2	3.6	5.2	7.1	7.3	7.5	7.4	7.6
Asian or Pacific Islander	117.7	162.0	347.4	488.7	503.9	520.6	508.5	526.6	1.8	2.4	4.6	6.3	6.4	6.5	6.4	6.5
American Indian/Alaskan Native	43.0	43.0	54.4	73.0	75.2	79.0	77.5	81.5	0.7	0.6	0.7	0.9	1.0	1.0	1.0	1.0
Nonresident alien	160.0	234.4	289.6	339.7	348.7	355.9	350.1	359.2	—	—	—	—	—	—	—	—
Part-time	4,282.1	4,997.9	5,997.7	6,133.0	6,086.8	6,023.1	6,064.6	6,064.3	100.0	100.0	100.0	100.0	100.0	100.0	100.0	100.0
White, non-Hispanic	3,563.5	4,116.0	4,706.0	4,477.4	4,378.5	4,274.3	4,357.8	4,306.0	84.4	83.5	79.8	74.4	73.3	72.2	73.3	72.3
Total minority	659.9	811.3	1,189.8	1,540.9	1,592.1	1,643.4	1,590.6	1,652.5	15.6	16.5	20.2	25.6	26.7	27.8	26.7	27.7
Black, non-Hispanic	373.8	421.2	528.7	633.3	638.4	652.1	633.6	654.5	8.9	8.5	9.0	10.5	10.7	11.0	10.7	11.0
Hispanic	172.7	224.8	387.7	540.7	575.1	600.6	577.3	604.5	4.1	4.6	6.6	9.0	9.6	10.1	9.7	10.1
Asian or Pacific Islander	80.2	124.4	225.1	308.6	319.7	330.9	319.6	332.6	1.9	2.5	3.8	5.1	5.4	5.6	5.4	5.6
American Indian/Alaskan Native	33.1	40.9	48.4	58.3	58.8	59.9	60.0	61.0	0.8	0.8	0.8	1.0	1.0	1.0	1.0	1.0
Nonresident alien	58.7	70.6	101.8	114.7	116.2	105.4	116.2	105.8	—	—	—	—	—	—	—	—
Undergraduate																
Total	9,419.0	10,469.1	11,959.1	12,231.7	12,259.4	12,298.3	12,326.9	12,450.6	100.0	100.0	100.0	100.0	100.0	100.0	100.0	100.0
White, non-Hispanic	7,740.5	8,480.7	9,272.6	8,805.6	8,730.9	8,681.8	8,769.5	8,783.9	83.4	82.7	79.0	73.6	72.8	72.1	72.8	72.1
Total minority	1,535.3	1,778.5	2,467.7	3,158.5	3,254.4	3,351.5	3,282.1	3,398.5	16.6	17.3	21.0	26.4	27.2	27.9	27.2	27.9
Black, non-Hispanic	943.4	1,018.8	1,147.2	1,333.6	1,352.6	1,379.9	1,358.6	1,398.1	10.2	9.9	9.8	11.1	11.3	11.5	11.3	11.5
Hispanic	352.9	433.1	724.6	1,012.0	1,065.6	1,107.8	1,079.4	1,125.9	3.8	4.2	6.2	8.5	8.9	9.2	9.0	9.2
Asian or Pacific Islander	169.3	248.7	500.5	692.2	713.2	736.6	717.6	743.7	1.8	2.4	4.3	5.8	6.0	6.1	6.0	6.1
American Indian/Alaskan Native	69.7	77.9	95.5	120.7	122.9	127.2	126.5	130.8	0.8	0.8	0.8	1.0	1.0	1.1	1.0	1.1
Nonresident alien	143.2	209.9	218.7	267.6	274.1	265.0	275.3	268.2	—	—	—	—	—	—	—	—

TABLE 4.3

Total Fall Enrollment in Institutions of Higher Education and Degree-Granting Institutions, by Level of Study, Sex, and Race/Ethnicity of Student, 1976–1997 [CONTINUED]

Level of study, sex, and race/ethnicity of student	Institutions of higher education, in thousands						Degree-granting institutions, in thousands[1]		Percentage distribution of students[2]							
									Institutions of higher education						Degree-granting institutions[1]	
	1976	1980	1990	1995	1996	1997	1996	1997	1976	1980	1990	1995	1996	1997	1996	1997
1	2	3	4	5	6	7	8	9	10	11	12	13	14	15	16	17
Undergraduate																
Men	4,896.8	4,997.4	5,379.8	5,401.1	5,411.1	5,405.4	5,420.7	5,468.5	100.0	100.0	100.0	100.0	100.0	100.0	100.0	100.0
White, non-Hispanic	4,052.2	4,054.9	4,184.4	3,918.1	3,890.7	3,857.3	3,890.8	3,899.3	84.4	83.5	79.6	74.5	73.9	73.3	73.8	73.2
Total minority	748.2	802.7	1,069.3	1,339.3	1,375.0	1,408.4	1,384.1	1,427.9	15.6	16.5	20.4	25.5	26.1	26.7	26.2	26.8
Black, non-Hispanic	430.7	428.2	448.0	506.8	513.1	520.6	513.6	527.7	9.0	8.8	8.5	9.6	9.7	9.9	9.7	9.9
Hispanic	191.7	211.2	326.9	444.2	464.0	479.1	469.2	486.7	4.0	4.3	6.2	8.4	8.8	9.1	8.9	9.1
Asian or Pacific Islander	91.1	128.5	254.5	338.1	346.9	356.1	348.8	359.4	1.9	2.6	4.8	6.4	6.6	6.8	6.6	6.7
American Indian/Alaskan Native	34.8	34.8	39.9	50.2	51.0	52.6	52.4	54.1	0.7	0.7	0.8	1.0	1.0	1.0	1.0	1.0
Nonresident alien	96.4	139.8	126.1	143.8	145.3	139.6	145.8	141.4	—	—	—	—	—	—	—	—
Women	4,522.1	5,471.7	6,579.3	6,830.6	6,848.4	6,892.9	6,906.3	6,982.1	100.0	100.0	100.0	100.0	100.0	100.0	100.0	100.0
White, non-Hispanic	3,688.3	4,425.8	5,088.2	4,887.5	4,840.2	4,824.5	4,878.7	4,884.6	82.4	81.9	78.4	72.9	72.0	71.3	72.0	71.3
Total minority	787.0	975.8	1,398.5	1,819.2	1,879.3	1,943.0	1,898.1	1,970.6	17.6	18.1	21.6	27.1	28.0	28.7	28.0	28.7
Black, non-Hispanic	512.7	590.6	699.2	826.9	839.5	859.3	845.0	870.3	11.5	10.9	10.8	12.3	12.5	12.7	12.5	12.7
Hispanic	161.2	221.8	397.6	567.8	601.6	628.7	610.1	639.3	3.6	4.1	6.1	8.5	9.0	9.3	9.0	9.3
Asian or Pacific Islander	78.2	120.2	246.0	354.1	366.3	380.5	368.8	384.4	1.7	2.2	3.8	5.3	5.5	5.6	5.4	5.6
American Indian/Alaskan Native	34.9	43.1	55.5	70.5	71.9	74.5	74.1	76.7	0.8	0.8	0.9	1.1	1.1	1.1	1.1	1.1
Nonresident alien	46.8	70.1	92.6	123.8	128.8	125.4	129.5	126.8	—	—	—	—	—	—	—	—
Graduate																
Total	1,322.5	1,340.9	1,586.2	1,732.5	1,743.1	1,750.6	1,742.3	1,753.5	100.0	100.0	100.0	100.0	100.0	100.0	100.0	100.0
White, non-Hispanic	1,115.6	1,104.7	1228.4	1,282.3	1,273.9	1,260.2	1,272.6	1,261.8	89.2	88.5	86.6	82.6	81.7	80.7	81.6	80.7
Total minority	134.5	144.0	190.5	270.7	286.0	301.6	286.3	302.3	10.8	11.5	13.4	17.4	18.3	19.3	18.4	19.3
Black, non-Hispanic	78.5	75.1	83.9	118.6	125.5	131.7	125.5	131.6	6.3	6.0	5.9	7.6	8.0	8.4	8.0	8.4
Hispanic	26.4	32.1	47.2	68.0	72.7	78.4	72.8	78.7	2.1	2.6	3.3	4.4	4.7	5.0	4.7	5.0
Asian or Pacific Islander	24.5	31.6	53.2	75.6	79.0	82.1	79.1	82.6	2.0	2.5	3.8	4.9	5.1	5.3	5.1	5.3
American Indian/Alaskan Native	5.1	5.2	6.2	8.5	8.9	9.4	8.9	9.4	0.4	0.4	0.4	0.5	0.6	0.6	0.6	0.6
Nonresident alien	72.4	92.2	167.3	179.5	183.2	188.8	183.3	189.4	—	—	—	—	—	—	—	—
Men	707.9	672.2	737.4	767.5	760.5	756.1	759.4	757.9	100.0	100.0	100.0	100.0	100.0	100.0	100.0	100.0
White, non-Hispanic	589.1	538.5	538.8	541.6	530.2	519.5	529.0	520.4	90.2	89.2	86.8	83.1	82.3	81.5	82.3	81.4
Total minority	63.7	65.0	82.1	110.4	113.9	118.2	114.0	118.8	9.8	10.8	13.2	16.9	17.7	18.5	17.7	18.6
Black, non-Hispanic	32.0	28.2	29.3	39.8	41.2	42.8	41.2	42.8	4.9	4.7	4.7	6.1	6.4	6.7	6.4	6.7
Hispanic	14.6	15.7	20.6	28.2	29.5	31.3	29.6	31.5	2.2	2.6	3.3	4.3	4.6	4.9	4.6	4.9
Asian or Pacific Islander	14.4	18.6	29.7	39.0	39.7	40.4	39.7	40.7	2.2	3.1	4.8	6.0	6.2	6.3	6.2	6.4
American Indian/Alaskan Native	2.7	2.5	2.6	3.4	3.6	3.7	3.6	3.7	0.4	0.4	0.4	0.5	0.6	0.6	0.6	0.6
Nonresident alien	55.1	68.7	116.4	115.6	116.3	118.4	116.4	118.7	—	—	—	—	—	—	—	—
Women	614.6	668.7	848.8	965.0	982.6	994.5	982.8	995.6	100.0	100.0	100.0	100.0	100.0	100.0	100.0	100.0
White, non-Hispanic	526.5	566.2	689.5	740.7	743.7	740.7	743.6	741.4	88.1	87.8	86.4	82.2	81.2	80.2	81.2	80.2
Total minority	70.8	79.0	108.3	160.3	172.1	183.3	172.3	183.5	11.9	12.2	13.6	17.8	18.8	19.8	18.8	19.8
Black, non-Hispanic	46.5	46.9	54.6	78.8	84.3	88.8	84.3	88.8	7.8	7.3	6.8	8.7	9.2	9.6	9.2	9.6
Hispanic	11.8	16.4	26.6	39.9	43.1	47.1	43.2	47.2	2.0	2.5	3.3	4.4	4.7	5.1	4.7	5.1
Asian or Pacific Islander	10.1	13.0	23.6	36.6	39.3	41.7	39.4	41.8	1.7	2.0	3.0	4.1	4.3	4.5	4.3	4.5
American Indian/Alaskan Native	2.4	2.7	3.6	5.0	5.3	5.7	5.3	5.7	0.4	0.4	0.5	0.6	0.6	0.6	0.6	0.6
Nonresident alien	17.3	23.5	50.9	63.9	66.9	70.4	66.9	70.7	—	—	—	—	—	—	—	—
First-professional																
Total	244.1	276.8	273.4	297.6	297.7	296.5	298.3	298.3	100.0	100.0	100.0	100.0	100.0	100.0	100.0	100.0
White, non-Hispanic	220.0	247.7	221.5	223.3	221.2	218.9	221.7	220.4	91.3	90.4	82.6	76.9	76.2	75.7	76.3	75.8
Total minority	21.1	26.3	46.5	67.0	68.9	70.1	69.0	70.4	8.7	9.6	17.4	23.1	23.8	24.3	23.7	24.2
Black, non-Hispanic	11.2	12.8	15.9	21.4	21.4	21.2	21.5	21.4	4.6	4.7	5.9	7.4	7.4	7.3	7.4	7.3
Hispanic	4.5	6.5	10.7	13.8	14.0	13.9	13.9	13.9	1.9	2.4	4.0	4.8	4.8	4.8	4.8	4.8
Asian or Pacific Islander	4.1	6.1	18.7	29.6	31.4	32.8	31.4	32.9	1.7	2.2	7.0	10.2	10.8	11.4	10.8	11.3
American Indian/Alaskan Native	1.3	0.8	1.1	2.1	2.2	2.3	2.2	2.3	0.5	0.3	0.4	0.7	0.7	0.8	0.7	0.8
Nonresident alien	3.1	2.9	5.4	7.3	7.7	7.5	7.6	7.5	—	—	—	—	—	—	—	—

TABLE 4.3

Total Fall Enrollment in Institutions of Higher Education and Degree-Granting Institutions, by Level of Study, Sex, and Race/Ethnicity of Student, 1976–1997 [CONTINUED]

Level of study, sex, and race/ethnicity of student	Institutions of higher education, in thousands						Degree-granting institutions, in thousands[1]		Percentage distribution of students[2]							
									Institutions of higher education						Degree-granting institutions[1]	
	1976	1980	1990	1995	1996	1997	1996	1997	1976	1980	1990	1995	1996	1997	1996	1997
1	2	3	4	5	6	7	8	9	10	11	12	13	14	15	16	17
First-professional																
Men	1,189.6	198.5	166.8	173.9	172.5	168.4	172.7	169.6	100.0	100.0	100.0	100.0	100.0	100.0	100.0	100.0
White, non-Hispanic	172.4	179.5	137.8	134.4	132.0	128.0	132.3	129.1	92.1	91.5	84.5	79.5	78.9	78.3	78.9	78.3
Total minority	14.7	16.7	25.3	34.6	35.3	35.5	35.4	35.7	7.9	8.5	15.5	20.5	21.1	21.7	21.1	21.7
Black, non-Hispanic	7.2	7.4	7.4	9.4	9.4	9.1	9.4	9.2	3.9	3.8	4.5	5.5	5.6	5.6	5.6	5.6
Hispanic	3.5	4.6	6.4	7.8	7.8	7.6	7.7	7.6	1.9	2.4	3.9	4.6	4.6	4.7	4.6	4.6
Asian or Pacific Islander	2.9	4.1	10.8	16.2	17.0	17.6	17.1	17.6	1.6	2.1	6.6	9.6	10.2	10.7	10.2	10.7
American Indian/Alaskan Native	1.0	0.5	0.6	1.2	1.2	1.2	1.2	1.2	0.6	0.3	0.4	0.7	0.7	0.7	0.7	0.7
Nonresident alien	2.5	2.3	3.8	4.9	5.1	4.9	5.1	4.9	—	—	—	—	—	—	—	—
Women	54.5	78.4	106.6	123.7	125.3	128.1	125.6	128.6	100.0	100.0	100.0	100.0	100.0	100.0	100.0	100.0
White, non-Hispanic	47.6	68.1	83.7	88.9	89.1	90.9	89.4	91.3	88.2	87.6	79.7	73.3	72.6	72.4	72.7	72.5
Total minority	6.4	9.6	21.3	32.4	33.6	34.6	33.6	34.7	11.8	12.4	20.3	26.7	27.4	27.6	27.3	27.5
Black, non-Hispanic	3.9	5.5	8.5	12.1	12.0	12.0	12.1	12.1	7.3	7.0	8.1	10.0	9.8	9.6	9.8	9.6
Hispanic	1.0	1.9	4.3	6.0	6.2	6.2	6.2	6.2	1.9	2.4	4.1	5.0	5.1	5.0	5.0	4.9
Asian or Pacific Islander	1.1	2.0	7.9	13.4	14.4	15.3	14.4	15.3	2.1	2.6	7.6	11.0	11.7	12.2	11.7	12.1
American Indian/Alaskan Native	0.2	0.3	0.5	0.9	1.0	1.1	1.0	1.1	0.4	0.3	0.5	0.8	0.8	0.8	0.8	0.8
Nonresident alien	0.5	0.6	1.6	2.4	2.6	2.6	2.6	2.6	—	—	—	—	—	—	—	—

[1] Data are for 4-year and 2-year degree-granting institutions that were eligible to participate in Title IV federal financial aid programs.

[2] Distribution for U.S. citizens only.

—Not applicable.

NOTE: Because of under reporting and nonreporting of racial/ethnic data, some figures are slightly lower than corresponding data in other tables. Trend tabulations of institutions of higher education data are based on institutions that were accredited by an agency or association that was recognized by the U.S. Department of Education. The Department of Education no longer distinguishes between those institutions and other institutions that are eligible to participate in Title IV programs. The new degree-granting classification is very similar to the earlier higher education classification, except that it includes some additional institutions, primarily 2-year colleges, and excludes a few higher education institutions that did not award degrees. Because of rounding, details may not add to totals.

SOURCE: *Digest of Education Statistics, 1999.* National Center for Education Statistics, March 2000

students made up 21 percent of the undergraduate student body, they earned only about 13 percent of all bachelor's degrees in 1997. Similarly, minorities were underrepresented at the master's, doctoral, and first-professional degree levels.

Of the 1.17 million bachelor's degrees conferred in 1996–1997, 19 percent were for business and management, while 11 percent were awarded for social sciences and 9 percent for education. Interest in these latter subjects, however, has been growing in recent years. Computer and information sciences, virtually unknown a generation ago, now account for 2 percent of bachelor's degrees, although interest in this major has been dropping in recent years. (See Table 4.5 for the kinds of associate, master's, and doctoral degrees.)

FIGURE 4.3

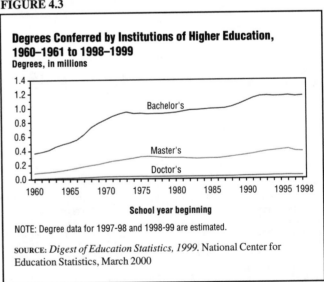

Degrees Conferred by Institutions of Higher Education, 1960–1961 to 1998–1999
Degrees, in millions

NOTE: Degree data for 1997-98 and 1998-99 are estimated.

SOURCE: *Digest of Education Statistics, 1999.* National Center for Education Statistics, March 2000

LABOR FORCE PARTICIPATION

Adults with higher levels of education were more likely to participate in the labor force than those with less education. About 80.2 percent of adults 25 years of age and over with a bachelor's degree participated in the labor force in 1998, compared to 65.1 percent high school graduates and just 42.8 percent of those who had not graduated. The labor force participation rates for blacks age 25 and older with high school diplomas and bache-

TABLE 4.4

Earned Degrees Conferred by Institutions of Higher Education, by Level of Degree and Gender of Student, 1869–1870 to 2008–2009

Year	Associate degrees			Bachelor's degrees			Master's degrees			First-professional degrees			Doctor's degrees		
	Total	Men	Women	Total	Men	Women	Total	Men	Women	Total	Men	Women	Total	Men	Women
1	2	3	4	5	6	7	8	9	10	11	12	13	14	15	16
1869–70	—	—	—	[1]9,371	[1]7,993	[1]1,378	0	0	0	[2]	[2]	[2]	1	1	0
1879–80	—	—	—	[1]12,896	[1]10,411	[1]2,485	879	868	11	[2]	[2]	[2]	54	51	3
1889–90	—	—	—	[1]15,539	[1]12,857	[1]2,682	1,015	821	194	[2]	[2]	[2]	149	147	2
1899–1900	—	—	—	[1]27,410	[1]22,173	[1]5,237	1,583	1,280	303	[2]	[2]	[2]	382	359	23
1909–10	—	—	—	[1]37,199	[1]28,762	[1]8,437	2,113	1,555	558	[2]	[2]	[2]	443	399	44
1919–20	—	—	—	[1]48,622	[1]31,980	[1]16,642	4,279	2,985	1,294	[2]	[2]	[2]	615	522	93
1929–30	—	—	—	[1]122,484	[1]73,615	[1]48,869	14,969	8,925	6,044	[2]	[2]	[2]	2,299	1,946	353
1939–40	—	—	—	[1]186,500	[1]109,546	[1]76,954	26,731	16,508	10,223	[2]	[2]	[2]	3,290	2,861	429
1949–50	—	—	—	[1]432,058	[1]328,841	[1]103,217	58,183	41,220	16,963	[2]	[2]	[2]	6,420	5,804	616
1959–60	—	—	—	[1]392,440	[1]254,063	[1]138,377	74,435	50,898	23,537	[2]	[2]	[2]	9,829	8,801	1,028
1960–61	—	—	—	365,174	224,538	140,636	84,609	57,830	26,779	25,253	24,577	676	10,575	9,463	1,112
1961–62	—	—	—	383,961	230,456	153,505	91,418	62,603	28,815	25,607	24,836	771	11,622	10,377	1,245
1962–63	—	—	—	411,420	241,309	170,111	98,684	67,302	31,382	26,590	25,753	837	12,822	11,448	1,374
1963–64	—	—	—	461,266	265,349	195,917	109,183	73,850	35,333	27,209	26,357	852	14,490	12,955	1,535
1964–65	—	—	—	493,757	282,173	211,584	121,167	81,319	39,848	28,290	27,283	1,007	16,467	14,692	1,775
1965–66	111,607	63,779	47,828	520,115	299,287	220,828	140,602	93,081	47,521	30,124	28,982	1,142	18,237	16,121	2,116
1966–67	139,183	78,356	60,827	558,534	322,711	235,823	157,726	103,109	54,617	31,695	30,401	1,294	20,617	18,163	2,454
1967–68	159,441	90,317	69,124	632,289	357,682	274,607	176,749	113,552	63,197	33,939	32,402	1,537	23,089	20,183	2,906
1968–69	183,279	105,661	77,618	728,845	410,595	318,250	193,756	121,531	72,225	35,114	33,595	1,519	26,158	22,722	3,436
1969–70	206,023	117,432	88,591	792,316	451,097	341,219	208,291	125,624	82,667	34,918	33,077	1,841	29,866	25,890	3,976
1970–71	252,311	144,144	108,167	839,730	475,594	364,136	230,509	138,146	92,363	37,946	35,544	2,402	32,107	27,530	4,577
1971–72	292,014	166,227	125,787	887,273	500,590	386,683	251,633	149,550	102,083	43,411	40,723	2,688	33,363	28,090	5,273
1972–73	316,174	175,413	140,761	922,362	518,191	404,171	263,371	154,468	108,903	50,018	46,489	3,529	34,777	28,571	6,206
1973–74	343,924	188,591	155,333	945,776	527,313	418,463	277,033	157,842	119,191	53,816	48,530	5,286	33,816	27,365	6,451
1974–75	360,171	191,017	169,154	922,933	504,841	418,092	292,450	161,570	130,880	55,916	48,956	6,960	34,083	26,817	7,266
1975–76	391,454	209,996	181,458	925,746	504,925	420,821	311,771	167,248	144,523	62,649	52,892	9,757	34,064	26,267	7,797
1976–77	406,377	210,842	195,535	919,549	495,545	424,004	317,164	167,783	149,381	64,359	52,374	11,985	33,232	25,142	8,090
1977–78	412,246	204,718	207,528	921,204	487,347	433,857	311,620	161,212	150,408	66,581	52,270	14,311	32,131	23,658	8,473
1978–79	402,702	192,091	210,611	921,390	477,344	444,046	301,079	153,370	147,709	68,848	52,652	16,196	32,730	23,541	9,189
1979–80	400,910	183,737	217,173	929,417	473,611	455,806	298,081	150,749	147,332	70,131	52,716	17,415	32,615	22,943	9,672
1980–81	416,377	188,638	227,739	935,140	469,883	465,257	295,739	147,043	148,696	71,956	52,792	19,164	32,958	22,711	10,247
1981–82	434,526	196,944	237,582	952,998	473,364	479,634	295,546	145,532	150,014	72,032	52,223	19,809	32,707	22,224	10,483
1982–83	449,620	203,991	245,629	969,510	479,140	490,370	289,921	144,697	145,224	73,054	51,250	21,804	32,775	21,902	10,873
1983–84	452,240	202,704	249,536	974,309	482,319	491,990	284,263	143,595	140,668	74,468	51,378	23,090	33,209	22,064	11,145
1984–85	454,712	202,932	251,780	979,477	482,528	496,949	286,251	143,390	142,861	75,063	50,455	24,608	32,943	21,700	11,243
1985–86	446,047	196,166	249,881	987,823	485,923	501,900	288,567	143,508	145,059	73,910	49,261	24,649	33,653	21,819	11,834
1986–87	436,304	190,839	245,465	991,264	480,782	510,482	289,349	141,269	148,080	71,617	46,523	25,094	34,041	22,061	11,980
1987–88	435,085	190,047	245,038	994,829	477,203	517,626	299,317	145,163	154,154	70,735	45,484	25,251	34,870	22,615	12,255
1988–89	436,764	186,316	250,448	1,018,755	483,346	535,409	310,621	149,354	161,267	70,856	45,046	25,810	35,720	22,648	13,072
1989–90	455,102	191,195	263,907	1,051,344	491,696	559,648	324,301	153,653	170,648	70,988	43,961	27,027	38,371	24,401	13,970
1990–91	481,720	198,634	283,086	1,094,538	504,045	590,493	337,168	156,482	180,686	71,948	43,846	28,102	39,294	24,756	14,538
1991–92	504,231	207,481	296,750	1,136,553	520,811	615,742	352,838	161,842	190,996	74,146	45,071	29,075	40,659	25,557	15,102
1992–93	514,756	211,964	302,792	1,165,178	532,881	632,297	369,585	169,258	200,327	75,387	45,153	30,234	42,132	26,073	16,059
1993–94	530,632	215,261	315,371	1,169,275	532,422	636,853	387,070	176,085	210,985	75,418	44,707	30,711	43,185	26,552	16,633
1994–95	539,691	218,352	321,339	1,160,134	526,131	634,003	397,629	178,598	219,031	75,800	44,853	30,947	44,446	26,916	17,530
1995–96	555,216	219,514	335,702	1,164,792	522,454	642,338	406,301	179,081	227,220	76,734	44,748	31,986	44,652	26,841	17,811
1996–97	571,226	223,948	347,278	1,172,879	520,515	652,364	419,401	180,947	238,454	78,730	45,564	33,166	45,876	27,146	18,730
1997–98[3]	558,000	224,000	335,000	1,160,000	517,000	643,000	391,000	171,000	221,000	78,100	44,900	33,100	44,600	26,900	17,700
1998–99[3]	563,000	226,000	337,000	1,166,000	518,000	648,000	385,000	165,000	220,000	76,300	44,600	31,700	44,100	26,300	17,700
1999–2000[3]	568,000	227,000	341,000	1,164,000	509,000	655,000	385,000	163,000	222,000	74,200	42,500	31,600	43,900	26,000	17,900
2000–01[3]	581,000	228,000	353,000	1,150,000	505,000	645,000	383,000	161,000	221,000	73,100	41,100	32,000	43,800	25,900	17,900
2001–02[3]	593,000	230,000	363,000	1,174,000	510,000	664,000	380,000	160,000	220,000	72,500	40,500	32,000	43,600	25,800	17,800
2002–03[3]	601,000	231,000	370,000	1,199,000	516,000	684,000	379,000	159,000	220,000	71,800	39,900	31,900	43,400	25,700	17,700
2003–04[3]	605,000	232,000	373,000	1,216,000	519,000	697,000	381,000	160,000	221,000	71,300	39,500	31,700	43,400	25,700	17,700
2004–05[3]	604,000	232,000	372,000	1,222,000	519,000	703,000	384,000	160,000	224,000	71,400	39,400	31,900	43,500	25,800	17,800
2005–06[3]	608,000	233,000	375,000	1,225,000	523,000	702,000	389,000	161,000	227,000	71,900	39,500	32,400	43,800	25,800	17,900
2006–07[3]	614,000	234,000	380,000	1,233,000	525,000	708,000	392,000	162,000	231,000	72,700	39,800	33,000	44,000	25,900	18,100
2007–08[3]	620,000	235,000	385,000	1,244,000	528,000	716,000	397,000	163,000	234,000	73,600	40,100	33,500	44,200	26,000	18,200
2008–09[3]	628,000	236,000	392,000	1,257,000	531,000	725,000	400,000	164,000	236,000	74,300	40,300	34,000	44,300	26,100	18,200

[1] Includes first-professional degrees.

[2] First-professional degrees are included with bachelor's degrees.

[3] Projected.

—Data not available.

NOTE: Some data have been revised from previously published figures. Because of rounding, details may not add to totals.

SOURCE: *Digest of Education Statistics, 1999.* National Center for Education Statistics, March 2000

TABLE 4.5

Degrees Conferred by Institutions of Higher Education, by Control of Institution, Level of Degree, and Discipline Division, 1996–1997

	Public institutions				Private institutions			
Discipline division	Associate degrees	Bachelor's degrees	Master's degrees	Doctor's degrees	Associate degrees	Bachelor's degrees	Master's degrees	Doctor's degrees
1	2	3	4	5	6	7	8	9
Total	465,494	776,677	233,237	29,838	105,732	396,202	186,164	16,038
Agriculture and natural resources[1]	6,104	20,863	3,890	1,193	359	1,739	626	24
Architecture and related programs	256	6,038	2,845	87	60	1,906	1,189	48
Area, ethnic, and cultural studies	72	3,238	923	96	12	2,601	728	86
Biological sciences/life sciences	2,045	41,702	4,505	3,350	71	22,273	1,961	1,462
Business[2]	75,915	134,199	38,792	917	33,484	92,434	58,827	419
Communications	1,436	33,078	2,712	245	594	14,152	2,515	51
Communications technologies	1,604	423	93	0	139	115	281	4
Computer and information sciences	7,271	14,938	5,806	570	3,719	9,830	4,292	287
Construction trades	1,526	28	0	0	402	80	0	0
Education	9,339	77,846	69,244	5,080	1,187	27,387	40,843	1,671
Engineering	1,694	46,460	17,707	4,442	258	14,725	8,080	1,759
Engineering-related technologies	20,732	10,016	892	9	13,078	3,800	148	0
English language and literature/letters	1,374	33,418	5,668	1,190	81	15,927	2,054	385
Foreign languages and literatures	445	8,970	2,314	583	244	4,704	763	332
Health professions and related sciences	81,380	55,554	20,631	1,653	17,541	30,077	15,327	1,019
Home economics and vocational home economics	8,214	14,299	1,596	241	337	2,272	1,292	141
Law and legal studies	5,632	1,168	614	11	3,336	870	2,272	70
Liberal arts and sciences, general studies, and humanities	171,170	21,325	1,118	41	10,171	13,451	1,543	36
Library science	124	43	3,998	45	2	5	984	1
Mathematics	762	8,351	2,886	830	30	4,469	897	344
Mechanics and repairers	9,859	28	0	0	2,321	20	0	0
Multi/interdisciplinary studies	9,088	20,271	1,929	205	94	5,866	890	246
Parks, recreation, leisure, and fitness studies	789	11,864	1,658	97	124	3,537	308	11
Philosophy and religion	44	3,049	436	235	45	4,636	816	358
Physical sciences and science technologies	2,470	12,759	4,207	3,241	56	6,772	1,356	1,233
Precision production trades	6,601	302	0	0	3,767	24	3	0
Protective services	18,890	19,759	1,132	31	999	5,406	713	0
Psychology	1,452	49,421	5,993	1,913	160	24,770	8,360	2,140
Public administration and services	3,917	14,974	15,349	308	353	5,675	9,432	210
R.O.T.C. and military technologies	554	2	136	0	2	2	0	0
Social sciences and history	3,694	82,077	9,423	2,509	362	42,814	5,364	1,480
Theological studies/religious vocations	0	0	0	0	574	5,591	4,975	1,395
Transportation and material moving workers	1,217	1,576	79	0	395	1,971	840	0
Visual and performing arts	6,654	28,638	5,718	716	6,939	21,445	4,909	344
Not classified by field of study	3,170	0	943	0	4,436	4,856	3,576	482

[1]Includes "Agricultural business and production," "Agricultural sciences," and "Conservation and renewable natural resources."

[2]Includes "Business management and administrative services," "Marketing operations/marketing and distribution," and "Consumer and personal services."

SOURCE: *Digest of Education Statistics, 1999.* National Center for Education Statistics, March 2000

lor's degrees were higher than the average for each ethnic group with similar levels of education. (See Table 4.6.)

Persons with lower levels of education were more likely to be unemployed than those with higher levels of education. In 1998 the 7.1 percent of adults (25 years and over) who had not completed high school were unemployed, compared to 4 percent for those with 4 years of high school and 1.8 percent for those with a bachelor's degree or higher. Among whites, blacks, and Hispanics of 25 years or older, blacks in 1998 who had not completed high school had the highest percent of unemployment (11.6 percent). (See Table 4.7 and Figure 4.4.)

Labor Force Participation for Bachelor's Degree Recipients

The U.S. Department of Education conducted a longitudinal study of people who had received bachelor's degrees in 1992–93. By April 1997, 76.3 percent of these people were employed and not enrolled in college. Gender specific percentages were very similar; 78.5 percent of men and 74.4 percent of women were employed and not enrolled in a degree program in 1997. For ethnic groups, blacks had the highest percentage of people employed and not enrolled (79.4 percent), and Asian-Pacific Islanders had the lowest rate (69.7 percent). Of the entire group, the majority received bachelor's degrees in business and management (85.8 percent), and public affairs/social services (80.4 percent). The biological sciences had the least degree recipients from this group (50.7 percent). (See Table 4.8.)

DROPOUTS AND HIGH SCHOOL GRADUATES

In general, high school dropouts and youth find it difficult to enter the job market. Only 43.7 percent of

TABLE 4.6

Labor Force Participation of Persons 16 Years Old and Over, by Age, Sex, Race/Ethnicity, and Highest Level of Education, 1998

	Labor force participation rate[1]						Employment/population ratio[2]					
				College						College		
Age, sex, and race/ethnicity	Total	Less than high school graduate[3]	High school graduate	Some college, no degree	Associate degree	Bachelor's degree or higher	Total	Less than high school graduate[3]	High school graduate	Some college, no degree	Associate degree	Bachelor's degree or higher
1	2	3	4	5	6	7	8	9	10	11	12	13
16 to 19 years old[4]	52.8	46.0	70.6	60.9	([5])	([5])	45.1	38.0	61.8	56.2	([5])	([5])
Men	53.3	47.2	72.5	58.7	([5])	([5])	44.7	38.4	62.7	53.6	([5])	([5])
Women	52.3	44.6	68.8	62.6	([5])	([5])	45.5	37.5	61.0	58.2	([5])	([5])
White[6]	56.0	49.3	73.1	63.7	([5])	([5])	49.0	42.0	66.1	59.3	([5])	([5])
Black[6]	41.6	34.7	62.0	52.3	([5])	([5])	30.1	23.2	48.1	45.0	([5])	([5])
Hispanic[7]	45.7	39.1	69.1	56.8	([5])	([5])	36.0	29.5	57.5	49.7	([5])	([5])
20 to 24 years old[4]	77.5	68.0	82.3	73.6	86.1	84.6	71.4	57.1	74.8	69.3	82.4	81.2
Men	82.0	80.8	89.5	74.2	86.8	84.6	75.4	69.3	81.9	69.6	83.3	80.9
Women	94.5	51.2	74.2	73.1	85.6	84.6	87.2	41.0	67.0	69.0	82.0	81.3
White[6]	79.5	70.8	83.9	75.9	86.5	86.0	74.4	61.8	77.8	72.0	3.1	82.7
Black[6]	70.6	58.3	76.0	67.3	90.2	81.2	58.8	38.9	62.3	60.2	82.6	77.4
Hispanic[7]	76.1	70.2	81.2	76.1	80.2	85.3	68.9	62.0	73.4	70.8	75.5	80.0
25 and older	67.3	42.8	65.1	72.2	79.3	80.2	65.0	39.7	62.5	69.9	77.3	78.8
Men	76.2	55.2	76.2	79.3	86.4	85.0	73.8	51.8	73.2	77.0	84.4	83.6
Women	59.2	31.5	55.9	65.8	73.7	75.0	57.1	28.8	53.6	63.6	71.8	73.5
White[6]	67.1	43.1	64.3	71.2	78.9	79.8	65.1	40.4	62.1	69.2	77.1	78.5
Black[6]	67.9	40.0	70.4	78.0	83.3	84.8	63.6	35.4	65.2	73.7	80.1	82.3
Hispanic[7]	69.6	58.7	74.4	79.7	83.9	83.5	65.8	54.5	70.3	76.5	81.1	80.8

[1] Percent of the civilian population who are employed or seeking employment.

[2] Number of persons employed as a percent of civilian population.

[3] Includes persons reporting no school years completed.

[4] Excludes persons enrolled in school.

[5] Sample size too small for stable estimates.

[6] Includes persons of Hispanic origin.

[7] Hispanics may be of any race.

SOURCE: *Digest of Education Statistics, 1999.* National Center for Education Statistics, March 2000

1997–98 dropouts were in the labor force (employed or looking for work); 17.2 percent were unemployed, and 39 percent were not in the labor force. In contrast, 64.9 percent of high school graduates were employed in 1998 and 35.1 percent were either unemployed or not in the labor force. (See Figure 4.5.)

Penalties of Not Graduating from High School

Without prior job experience or specialized training, dropouts often have difficulty finding jobs. In October 1997, 66.9 percent of recent high school graduates not enrolled in college were employed, compared to 44.9 percent of recent school dropouts. Employment rates vary by gender and race/ethnicity. For example male high school dropouts were more likely to be employed (57.2 percent) than female dropouts (28.1 percent). White high school dropouts were more likely to be employed (approximately 50 percent) than black dropouts (less than 20 percent). Whites who had completed high school but not enrolled in college were more likely to be employed (approximately 78 percent) than blacks (roughly 55 percent). (See Table 4.9 and Figure 4.6.)

The disadvantage of not having a high school diploma persists well into a person's thirties. For example in 1998, 79 percent of males ages 25 to 34 who completed 9 to 11 years of school were working, compared to 84 percent of males in this age group who graduated from high school. Among females ages 25 to 34, less than half (44 percent) of high school dropouts were employed, compared to 70 percent of their female peers with a high school diploma. (See Figure 4.7.)

Of those who were working, there was a clear economic advantage to finishing high school. Among workers ages 25 to 34, those who attended 9 to 11 years of school earned substantially less than those who completed high school. In 1997 for example, the median (half earned more and half earned less) annual salary of males with 9 to 11 years of schooling was only 74 percent of the median salary of high school graduates. The median annual salary of female high school dropouts was only 60 percent of that of female high school graduates. (See Figure 4.8.)

EDUCATIONAL ATTAINMENT AND EARNINGS

Many people decide to attend college because they think a college degree will get them a better job and more earnings. Individuals with a higher level of education are generally more likely to be working. In 1998 male and

TABLE 4.7

Unemployment Rate of Persons 16 Years Old and Over, by Age, Sex, Race/Ethnicity, and Highest Degree Attained, 1996, 1997, and 1998

Sex, race/ethnicity, and highest degree attained	Percent unemployed, 1996 [1]				Percent unemployed, 1997 [1]				Percent unemployed, 1998 [1]			
	16- to 24-year-olds [2]			25 years old and over	16- to 24-year-olds [2]			25 years old and over	16- to 24-year-olds [2]			25 years old and over
	Total	16 to 19 years	20 to 24 years		Total	16 to 19 years	20 to 24 years		Total	16 to 19 years	20 to 24 years	
1	2	3	4	5	6	7	8	9	10	11	12	13
All persons												
All education levels	12.0	16.7	9.3	4.2	11.3	16.0	8.5	3.8	10.4	14.6	7.9	3.4
Less than a high school graduate	19.7	19.7	19.4	8.7	18.4	18.9	17.1	8.1	14.0	13.2	16.1	7.1
High school graduate, no college	12.0	14.9	10.8	4.7	11.0	14.0	9.6	4.3	10.1	12.5	9.1	4.0
Some college, no degree	7.0	8.1	6.7	4.0	7.1	8.5	6.7	3.5	6.3	7.7	5.9	3.2
Associate degree	4.8	—	4.5	3.3	4.5	—	4.3	2.7	4.3	—	4.1	2.5
Bachelor's degree or higher	5.3	—	5.3	2.2	3.7	—	3.7	2.0	4.0	—	4.1	1.8
Men												
All education levels	12.6	18.1	9.5	4.1	11.8	16.9	8.9	3.6	11.1	16.2	8.1	3.2
Less than a high school graduate	19.8	21.2	16.4	7.8	18.3	19.7	15.1	7.2	17.4	18.7	14.2	6.1
High school graduate, no college	11.9	15.1	10.6	4.7	10.8	13.9	9.6	4.2	10.0	13.6	8.5	3.9
Some college, no degree	7.5	9.4	7.1	3.9	7.5	9.2	7.1	3.3	6.7	8.7	6.2	3.0
Associate degree	4.1	—	4.2	3.2	—	—	—	2.6	4.2	—	—	2.3
Bachelor's degree or higher	6.1	—	6.1	2.1	4.2	—	4.3	1.9	4.3	—	4.3	1.6
Women												
All education levels	11.3	15.2	9.0	4.3	10.7	15.0	8.1	3.9	9.8	12.9	7.8	3.6
Less than a high school graduate	19.5	18.1	25.3	10.1	18.6	17.9	21.2	9.6	16.6	15.8	20.0	8.6
High school graduate, no college	12.2	14.7	10.9	4.6	11.2	14.2	9.7	4.3	10.3	11.4	9.8	4.1
Some college, no degree	6.6	7.2	6.4	4.1	6.7	8.0	6.3	3.7	5.9	7.0	5.6	3.4
Associate degree	5.2	—	4.8	3.3	4.8	—	4.5	2.8	4.5	—	4.2	2.7
Bachelor's degree or higher	4.8	—	4.8	2.4	3.2	—	3.3	2.2	3.8	—	3.9	2.0
White [3]												
All education levels	10.2	14.2	7.8	3.7	9.4	13.6	6.9	3.3	8.8	12.6	6.5	3.0
Less than a high school graduate	16.7	17.0	16.0	8.0	15.5	16.2	13.5	7.2	14.3	14.9	12.6	6.3
High school graduate, no college	9.9	12.2	8.9	4.0	9.1	11.6	7.9	3.6	8.4	10.8	7.2	3.4
Some college, no degree	6.0	7.0	5.8	3.5	5.9	7.1	5.6	3.0	5.5	6.9	5.1	2.8
Associate degree	4.2	—	3.9	3.0	3.6	—	3.4	2.5	3.9	—	3.7	2.2
Bachelor's degree or higher	5.1	—	5.1	2.1	3.1	—	3.2	1.8	3.9	—	3.9	1.7
Black [3]												
All education levels	23.9	33.6	18.8	7.7	23.2	32.4	18.3	7.3	20.7	27.6	16.8	6.4
Less than a high school graduate	37.8	37.6	38.2	12.6	36.3	36.4	35.8	13.1	33.1	33.1	33.2	11.6
High school graduate, no college	23.0	31.5	20.0	9.1	20.9	28.1	18.4	8.1	19.5	22.8	18.2	7.4
Some college, no degree	13.7	17.1	13.1	6.7	15.1	21.0	14.0	6.1	11.2	14.0	10.6	5.5
Associate degree	9.7	—	10.0	5.5	—	—	—	—	8.1	—	—	4.0
Bachelor's degree or higher	6.1	—	6.0	3.1	6.5	—	6.4	3.6	4.6	—	4.6	2.9
Hispanic origin [4]												
All education levels	15.5	23.6	11.8	7.1	13.8	21.6	10.3	6.1	13.2	21.3	9.3	5.5
Less than a high school graduate	20.1	26.1	14.6	9.7	18.8	25.7	13.0	8.5	17.9	24.3	11.9	7.2
High school graduate, no college	13.6	20.7	11.5	6.6	11.4	15.7	9.9	5.7	11.6	17.3	9.6	5.5
Some college, no degree	10.5	13.2	9.8	4.9	8.9	11.3	8.4	4.1	7.9	12.4	7.0	4.0
Associate degree	—	—	—	4.9	—	—	—	—	—	—	—	3.4
Bachelor's degree or higher	—	—	—	3.8	—	—	—	3.5	—	—	—	3.2

[1] The unemployment rate is the percent of individuals in the labor force who are not working and who made specific efforts to find employment sometime during the prior 4 weeks. The labor force includes both employed and unemployed persons.

[2] Excludes persons enrolled in school.

[3] Includes persons of Hispanic origin.

[4] Persons of Hispanic origin may be of any race.

—Data not available.

SOURCE: *Digest of Education Statistics, 1999.* National Center for Education Statistics, March 2000

female college graduates ages 25 to 34 were more likely to be employed than male and female high school graduates of the same age (92 and 84 percent and 88 and 70 percent, respectively). (See Figure 4.7.)

The financial returns of attending and graduating from college become even more evident when comparing the median annual earnings of those who attended and graduated from college to the median annual earnings of high school graduates. In 1997 males ages 25 to 34 who had completed a bachelor's degree earned 50 percent more than their male peers who had only a high school diploma. For females in the same age group, the earnings premium was even greater. Females who completed a bachelor's degree earned 91 percent more than females with only a high school diploma. Since 1970 the earnings advantage for 25- to 34-year-olds who attended some college or earned a bachelor's degree was generally greater for females than for males. (See Figure 4.8.) Table 4.10 shows the hourly earnings for the different levels of education for selected years between 1970 and 1994.

Choosing a Field of Study

When most students decide what to study in college, they often consider what type of job they can get with their major and how much they will earn. In 1994 about three-fourths (78 percent) of 1992–93 graduates who were working reported having a job related to their major. A similar proportion (76 percent) believed that their jobs had career potential. Only 60 percent thought that a college degree was required to get their job. (See Table 4.11 and Figure 4.9.)

About two-thirds of the college graduates of the class of 1992–93 had jobs in professional, managerial, and

FIGURE 4.4

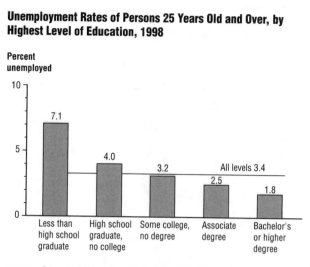

Unemployment Rates of Persons 25 Years Old and Over, by Highest Level of Education, 1998

SOURCE: *Digest of Education Statistics, 1999.* National Center for Education Statistics, March 2000

TABLE 4.8

Percentage Distribution of 1992–1993 Bachelor's Degree Recipients According to Employment and Enrollment Status in April 1997, by Selected Characteristics

Selected student characteristics	Employment and enrollment status in April 1997			
	Employed and not enrolled	Enrolled and employed	Enrolled and not employed	Not employed and not enrolled
Total	76.3	13.0	4.7	6.1
Sex				
Male	78.5	12.1	5.4	4.1
Female	74.4	13.8	4.1	7.7
Race–ethnicity				
White	76.8	13.1	4.3	5.8
Black	79.4	11.3	4.6	4.7
Hispanic	70.5	15.0	6.0	8.5
Asian/Pacific Islander	69.7	11.9	10.0	8.4
American Indian/Alaskan Native	76.4	6.5	6.2	10.9
Marital status in April 1997				
Never married	74.5	14.1	6.6	4.9
Married/cohabit as married	77.6	12.1	3.0	7.3
Divorced/separated/widowed	78.1	13.3	4.3	4.3
Number of children				
No children	76.0	13.8	5.7	4.5
One	79.0	9.6	2.6	8.9
Two or more children	74.6	12.2	1.0	12.2
Baccalaureate degree major				
Professional fields	80.2	12.0	2.4	5.4
Arts and sciences	68.6	15.1	9.1	7.2
Other	79.9	11.9	2.4	5.9
Baccalaureate degree major				
Business and management	85.8	7.4	1.8	4.9
Education	71.0	20.1	2.3	6.7
Engineering	80.0	14.1	3.6	2.3
Health professions	79.2	9.8	4.2	6.8
Public affairs/social services	80.4	12.4	0.7	6.5
Biological sciences	50.7	16.6	25.4	7.3
Mathematics and other sciences	74.5	13.1	7.7	4.7
Social sciences	71.1	16.7	6.1	6.2
History	72.8	11.8	11.1	4.3
Humanities	71.7	13.6	5.2	9.5
Psychology	63.9	18.2	8.4	9.5
Other	79.9	11.9	2.4	5.9

NOTE: Details may not add to 100.0 due to rounding.

SOURCE: *The Condition of Education 1999.* National Center for Education Statistics

FIGURE 4.5

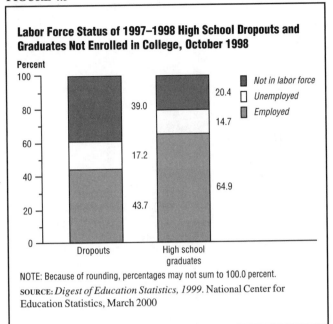

Labor Force Status of 1997–1998 High School Dropouts and Graduates Not Enrolled in College, October 1998

Percent

- Not in labor force
- Unemployed
- Employed

Dropouts: 39.0, 17.2, 43.7

High school graduates: 20.4, 14.7, 64.9

NOTE: Because of rounding, percentages may not sum to 100.0 percent.

SOURCE: *Digest of Education Statistics, 1999*. National Center for Education Statistics, March 2000

technical areas in 1994. The remainder worked in non-professional, nonmanagerial, and nontechnical areas.

Starting Salaries

The median starting salary (in 1997 constant dollars) for 1993 graduates who worked full-time was $24,156.

Graduates who majored in computer sciences and engineering had higher starting salaries than average, while students who majored in education, the humanities, and social and behavioral sciences had the lowest starting salaries. (See Table 4.12.)

The majors that both sexes choose account for some of the salary differences between male and female college graduates. In 1993 females were more likely than males to major in education, and males were more likely to major in computer sciences and engineering. (See Table 4.12.) Nevertheless, among college graduates working full-time, females earned less than males in social and behavioral sciences, natural sciences, and business and management; the latter had the greatest disparity between male and female starting incomes. (See Figure 4.10.)

Median Incomes

There is a long-term difference between the earnings of males and females with the same educational attainment. Among full-time, year-round workers, males earned more than females across all levels of education. In 1997 for instance, the median income for male college graduates (in 1998 constant dollars) was $40,811 compared to $32,529 for female college graduates. Hispanic males and females in 1997 both had higher median annual earnings ($36,250 and $32,087 respectively) than blacks ($31,561 and $30,859 respectively). (See Table 4.13.)

TABLE 4.9

Employment Rates for Recent High School Completers Not Enrolled in College and for Recent High School Dropouts, by Race/Ethnicity, October 1972–1997

October	Recent high school completers not enrolled in college				Recent high school dropouts			
	Total[1]	White	Black	Hispanic[2]	Total[1]	White	Black	Hispanic[2]
1972	70.1	73.5	48.3	([2])	46.8	47.0	42.8	([2])
1974	69.1	72.9	46.0	56.2	49.3	53.9	36.2	49.9
1976	68.8	73.1	38.6	65.3	44.8	49.6	20.9	52.7
1978	74.9	79.0	45.8	67.8	51.2	54.2	22.3	56.1
1980	68.9	74.6	34.7	62.3	44.6	51.2	20.9	52.2
1982	60.4	68.4	29.3	56.6	38.0	44.6	16.2	45.5
1984	64.0	70.7	44.8	55.4	44.0	51.4	24.2	41.0
1986	65.2	71.5	41.1	53.7	48.0	50.4	31.5	41.0
1988	71.9	78.2	55.8	53.6	43.6	47.6	17.6	44.7
1989	71.7	77.6	53.7	54.6	46.7	57.6	26.4	42.1
1990	67.8	75.0	45.2	56.3	46.3	56.3	30.9	39.9
1991	59.6	67.0	32.3	57.9	36.8	38.6	24.7	36.2
1992	62.7	71.9	37.0	53.2	36.2	43.1	—	41.4
1993	64.2	71.8	42.3	47.7	46.9	52.6	27.1	34.5
1994	64.2	73.1	38.0	43.7	42.9	51.7	34.1	41.2
1995	63.1	71.4	51.5	43.0	47.7	51.6	33.5	43.9
1996	59.0	68.5	41.7	45.1	42.3	45.3	21.5	54.5
1997	66.9	73.8	53.3	([2])	44.9	48.8	17.4	([2])

—Too few sample observations for a reliable estimate.

[1]Included in the totals but not shown separately are members of other racial–ethnic groups.

[2]Due to the small sample sizes for the Hispanic category, 3-year averages were calculated. For example, the 3-year average for 1996 is the average percentage of recent high school completers not enrolled in college or recent school dropouts in 1995, 1996, and 1997. Thus, 3-year averages cannot be calculated for 1972 and 1997.

NOTE: Recent high school completers are individuals ages 16–24 who completed high school during the survey year. Recent high school dropouts are individuals ages 16–24 who had not completed high school, were not enrolled during the survey month, and were in school 12 months earlier. In 1994, the survey instrument for the Current Population Survey (CPS) was changed and weights were adjusted.

SOURCE: *The Condition of Education 1999*. National Center for Education Statistics

FIGURE 4.6

Employment Rates for Recent High School Completers Not Enrolled in College and for Recent High School Dropouts, October 1972–1997

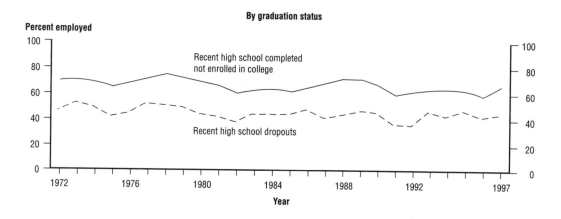

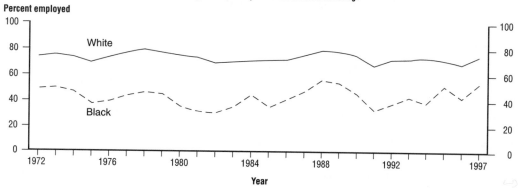

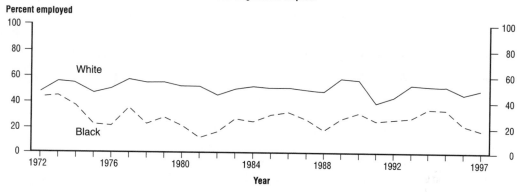

NOTE: Recent high school completers are individuals ages 16–24 who completed high school during the survey years. Recent high school dropouts are individuals ages 16–24 who had not completed high school, were enrolled during the survey months, and were in school 12 months earlier. In 1994, the survey instrument for the CPS was changed and weights were adjusted. In 1992, there were too few sample observations for a reliable estimate of black recent school dropouts. See the supplement note to indicator 51 for further discussion.

SOURCE: *The Condition of Education 1999.* National Center for Education Statistics

FIGURE 4.7

Employment Rate of 25- to 34-Year Olds, by Gender and Educational Attainment, March 1971–1998

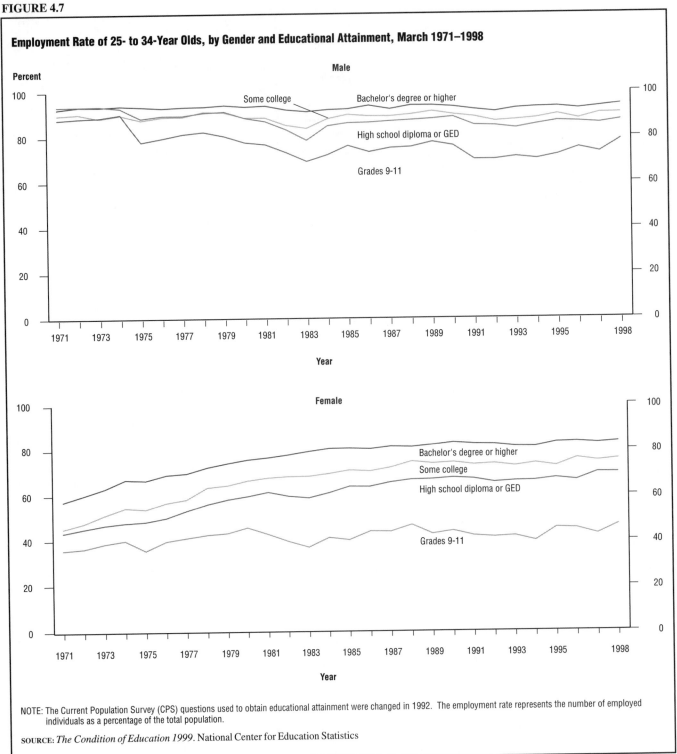

NOTE: The Current Population Survey (CPS) questions used to obtain educational attainment were changed in 1992. The employment rate represents the number of employed individuals as a percentage of the total population.

SOURCE: *The Condition of Education 1999*. National Center for Education Statistics

Between 1989 and 1998 median annual income of male full-time workers, when adjusted for inflation, declined 5 percent, compared to 3 percent increase for female full-time workers. Income of men who were year-round full-time workers with 4 or more years of college decreased by 1 percent, compared to a 13 percent drop for men with 1 to 3 years of high school. Income for men who had completed high school dropped by 10 percent. (See Table 4.14.)

Women's incomes were much lower than men's incomes, even after adjusting for level of education. (See Table 4.14 and Figure 4.11.) Similarly, a far greater percentage of men with a bachelor's degree or more (22.5 percent) earned more than $75,000 annually than did women (5.7 percent). (See Table 4.15.)

Women do better when their major fields are taken into account because women's distribution of employ-

FIGURE 4.8

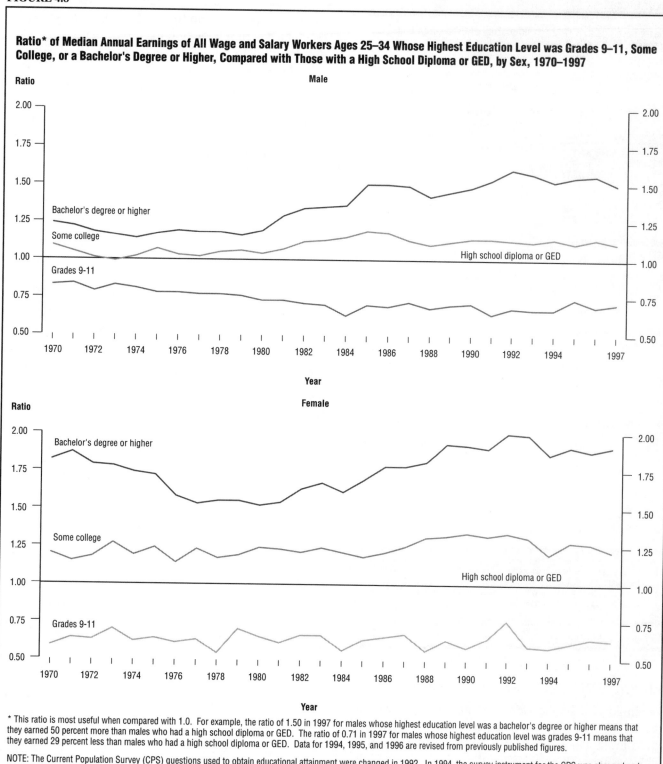

Ratio* of Median Annual Earnings of All Wage and Salary Workers Ages 25–34 Whose Highest Education Level was Grades 9–11, Some College, or a Bachelor's Degree or Higher, Compared with Those with a High School Diploma or GED, by Sex, 1970–1997

* This ratio is most useful when compared with 1.0. For example, the ratio of 1.50 in 1997 for males whose highest education level was a bachelor's degree or higher means that they earned 50 percent more than males who had a high school diploma or GED. The ratio of 0.71 in 1997 for males whose highest education level was grades 9-11 means that they earned 29 percent less than males who had a high school diploma or GED. Data for 1994, 1995, and 1996 are revised from previously published figures.

NOTE: The Current Population Survey (CPS) questions used to obtain educational attainment were changed in 1992. In 1994, the survey instrument for the CPS was changed and weights were adjusted.

SOURCE: *The Condition of Education, 1999.* National Center for Education Statistics

ment by field of study differs significantly from men's. What is highly significant is that almost all of the major fields in which men were concentrated had above-average median earnings, while the majors in which women were concentrated were characterized by below-average medians. Men were more likely to have degrees in engineering, computer science, architecture, mathematics, economics, theology, and business. Women were more likely to have degrees in social work, psychology, nursing, physical therapy, and education.

TABLE 4.10

Hourly Earnings and Years of Education of Prime-Age Workers, 1970–1994

| Educational tier[1] | Total | Highest educational attainment | | | |
		High school dropout	High school diploma only	Some university courses	University degree
1970 average hourly wages (1994 prices)					
Total	$13.33	$10.32	$12.33	$14.85	$20.27
1	10.42	9.72	11.22	12.13	—
2	11.94	10.70	12.28	13.64	15.08
3	14.49	11.63	12.74	15.39	20.55
4	19.78	—	16.24	16.96	20.87
1978 average hourly wages (1994 prices)					
Total	14.38	10.64	12.68	14.10	20.36
1	11.55	10.21	12.12	14.05	—
2	12.58	11.03	12.94	13.20	13.41
3	14.90	11.55	12.72	14.37	19.96
4	20.90	—	14.67	15.19	22.15
1986 average hourly wages (1994 prices)					
Total	14.22	9.49	11.86	13.97	20.13
1	10.66	9.07	11.02	12.37	—
2	11.93	9.93	11.93	12.63	13.78
3	15.32	10.29	12.34	14.67	20.24
4	20.42	—	13.41	15.97	21.69
1994 average hourly wages (1994 prices)					
Total	14.80	9.00	11.30	13.18	22.42
1	10.01	8.37	10.42	11.43	—
2	11.33	9.40	10.89	11.77	14.53
3	16.01	11.36	12.19	14.08	21.94
4	23.00	—	14.44	15.26	25.07

[1]Occupations ranked by average education of practitioners in 1971-72. Tier 1: 10.5 or fewer years; tier 2: 10.6 to 12.0 years; tier 3: 12.1 to 14.5 years; tier 4: 14.6 or more years.

NOTE: The wage data represent average annual hourly earnings (total labor income divided by number of hours worked), deflated by the personal consumption price index in the gross domestic product accounts. The appendix describes in more detail the methods used in calculating the entries in this table. The results for high school dropouts in tier 4 and those with a university degree in tier 1 are not reported because the sample sizes are too small.

SOURCE: Frederic L. Pryor and David Schaffer. *Wages and the University Educated: A Paradox Resolved.* Monthly Labor Review, vol. 120, no. 7

EDUCATIONAL ATTAINMENT AND POVERTY

In general, as individuals attain higher educational levels, the risk of living in poverty falls rapidly. Of all those in the labor force for at least half of 1997, those with less than a high school diploma had a much higher poverty rate (15.8 percent) than high school graduates (6.5 percent). Workers with an associate (3.1 percent) or college degree (1.5 percent) reported the lowest poverty rates. (See Table 4.16.)

Poverty rates are higher for black workers than for white workers at all educational levels except for those with less than 1 year of high school. Poverty rates for white men and women were fairly similar at all education levels. Among black men and women, however, there were marked differences, especially at lower educational levels. The poverty rate for black women workers with less than a high school diploma (30 percent) was higher than for black men (19.3 percent). Moreover, among high school graduates, the poverty rate of black women (17.6 percent) was more than twice that of black men (7.8 percent). Among black college graduates, these differences decreased greatly, but black women were almost twice as likely to be unemployed (3.1 percent) than black men (1.6 percent). (See Table 4.16.)

TABLE 4.11

Percentage of 1992–1993 College Graduates, by Employment and Enrollment Status, Relatedness of Jobs to Education, and Selected Characteristics, April 1994

Selected characteristics	Employment and enrollment status					Relatedness of job to education[1]		
	Employed full time, not enrolled	Employed part time, not enrolled	In labor force, enrolled[2]	Not in labor force, enrolled	Not employed, not enrolled[3]	Job related to field of study	Job required college degree	Job had career potential
Total	**67.1**	**8.7**	**12.4**	**5.5**	**6.3**	**77.6**	**59.9**	**75.7**
Field of study								
Business and management	80.0	5.3	7.9	1.9	4.9	87.1	54.1	79.6
Education	59.9	16.1	14.4	4.8	498	80.4	72.1	78.1
Engineering	69.2	3.4	13.7	7.2	6.5	90.0	83.0	85.8
Health professions	68.6	8.4	12.9	4.5	5.6	94.4	77.4	84.6
Public affairs/social services	70.3	9.0	9.2	5.0	6.5	73.5	53.0	71.6
Biological sciences	44.3	8.4	17.4	18.3	11.5	69.5	54.7	62.1
Mathematics and science	60.8	8.5	14.9	9.9	5.9	87.1	71.0	80.8
Social sciences	66.6	7.0	13.1	6.I	7.2	57.7	48.8	72.3
History	64.9	8.1	16.4	6.6	4.0	40.6	43.4	69.3
Humanities	59.2	12.8	13,5	5.9	8.5	58.2	50.1	69.1
Psychology	56.5	6.9	19.5	8.8	8.3	59.2	54.5	54.1
Other	69.4	9.0	11.4	3.6	6.6	75.2	55.0	70.5
Sex								
Male	69.2	6.8	11.9	6.3	5.7	76.6	59.I	78.0
Female	65.3	10.3	12.8	4.7	6.9	78.4	60.5	73.6
College grade point average								
Less than 3.0	71.7	8.9	11.1	2.2	6.1	73.2	54.6	74.2
3.0 to 3.49	68.2	7.9	12.7	5.0	6.3	78.7	63.0	74.7
35 and higher	61.I	9.3	14.1	9.4	6.0	81.5	61.6	79.2

[1] Includes only those who worked full time and who were not enrolled in postsecondary education.

[2] Includes persons who worked full time or part time or who were unemployed.

[3] Includes persons who were not in the work force or who were unemployed.

SOURCE: *The Condition of Education, 1997.* National Center for Education Statistics: Washington, D.C.

FIGURE 4.9

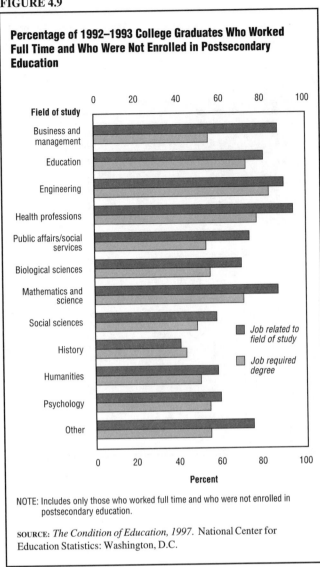

Percentage of 1992–1993 College Graduates Who Worked Full Time and Who Were Not Enrolled in Postsecondary Education

NOTE: Includes only those who worked full time and who were not enrolled in postsecondary education.

SOURCE: *The Condition of Education, 1997.* National Center for Education Statistics: Washington, D.C.

TABLE 4.12

Annual Median Starting Salaries (in 1997 Constant Dollars) of 1993 College Graduates, by Gender and Major Field of Study, and the Percentage Difference Between Male and Female Starting Salaries

Major field of study	All graduates	Male		Female		Female/male percentage difference
		Percentage in field	Median starting salary	Percentage in field	Median starting salary	
Total	$24,156	100	$26,738	100	$22,508	*(15.8)
Humanities	21,469	9	22,307	12	21,100	(5.4)
Social and behavioral sciences	21,984	13	23,885	15	21,061	*(11.8)
Natural sciences	22,347	7	24,798	6	20,991	*(15.3)
Computer sciences and engineering	32,802	16	33,148	3	30,866	(6.9)
Education	20,456	6	21,737	17	20,114	(7.5)
Business and management	26,658	32	28,382	23	24,363	*(14.2)
Other professional or technical	24,959	17	24,938	23	24,974	0.1

*Male starting salaries were greater than female salaries (p< 0.05).

NOTE: Data presented are for bachelor's degree recipients who were working full time and who were not enrolled in postsecondary education 1 year after graduation. Details may not add to totals due to rounding.

SOURCE: *Economic and Other Outcomes of Education.* Digest of Education Statistics, 1999. National Center for Education Statistics

FIGURE 4.10

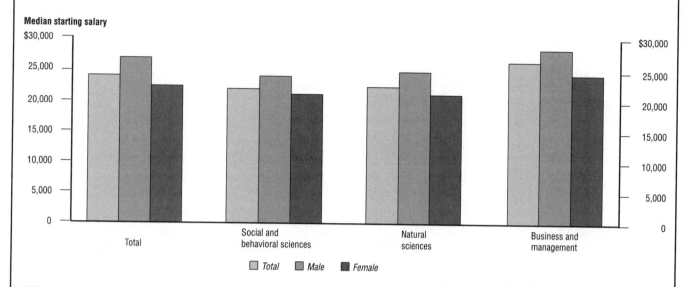

Annual Median Starting Salaries (in 1997 Constant Dollars) of 1993 College Graduates with Significant Starting Salary Differences Between Males and Females, by Major Field of Study and Gender

NOTE: Data presented are for bachelor's degree recipients who were working full time and who were not enrolled in postsecondary education 1 year after graduation.

SOURCE: *Economic and Other Outcomes of Education.* Digest of Education Statistics, 1999. National Center for Education Statistics

TABLE 4.13

Median Annual Earnings (in Constant 1998 Dollars) of Wage and Salary Workers Ages 25–34 Whose Highest Education Level was a Bachelor's Degree or Higher, by Sex and Race/Ethnicity, 1970–1997

Year	Male				Female			
	Total	White	Black	Hispanic	Total	White	Black	Hispanic
All wage and salary workers								
1970	$43,053	$43,596	—	—	$26,178	$25,598	$31,834	—
1971	42,803	43,369	$38,953	—	27,777	27,252	30,430	—
1972	43,604	44,092	40,965	—	27,495	26,800	30,572	—
1973	43,173	43,553	38,339	—	26,883	26,622	28,981	—
1974	40,221	40,926	33,403	—	25,996	25,834	27,641	—
1975	37,947	38,335	33,898	—	25,793	25,340	28,597	—
1976	39,074	39,403	36,504	—	24,772	24,380	28,568	—
1977	38,975	39,362	35,001	—	24,381	23,941	28,380	—
1978	39,209	39,329	37,343	$37,481	24,100	23,880	25,001	—
1979	37,895	38,113	33,207	32,824	24,393	24,380	24,865	—
1980	36,199	36,803	30,261	31,593	23,704	23,556	25,568	—
1981	36,623	37,089	31,013	29,325	23,453	23,285	24,327	$24,444
1982	35,263	35,637	30,519	33,895	24,186	24,004	25,215	23,025
1983	35,789	36,305	28,424	31,964	25,026	24,920	25,806	24,589
1984	36,788	37,939	29,654	31,525	25,276	25,177	26,146	24,874
1985	39,071	39,497	36,072	38,816	26,554	26,553	25,769	26,473
1986	39,385	40,079	30,737	39,667	27,864	27,735	27,534	26,735
1987	39,512	41,203	27,294	36,274	28,553	28,338	29,121	29,346
1988	38,544	40,722	29,163	30,155	28,521	28,746	28,346	26,530
1989	38,483	40,108	28,474	27,851	29,239	29,225	28,088	30,499
1990	36,699	37,607	32,136	33,487	28,873	29,133	28,835	25,947
1991	36,934	37,672	28,166	30,782	27,939	28,529	25,634	23,737
1992	36,983	38,222	31,055	30,833	29,045	29,170	27,679	27,851
1993	35,983	37,032	29,804	30,151	28,629	29,095	25,456	25,461
1994	35,437	37,210	26,524	30,781	28,229	28,644	25,651	25,614
1995	35,547	37,750	30,957	31,268	27,761	28,014	23,997	27,247
1996	36,531	37,058	32,896	30,031	27,394	27,559	26,204	26,312
1997	36,358	37,047	29,105	31,653	29,367	29,527	27,162	28,550
Year-round, full-time wage and salary workers								
1970	$46,911	$47,139	—	—	$33,531	$33,287	—	—
1971	46,416	46,859	—	—	32,712	32,870	$32,225	—
1972	47,176	47,485	$42,772	—	33,375	33,438	32,174	—
1973	47,363	47,973	41,277	—	33,211	33,118	34,158	—
1974	44,646	45,156	38,496	—	31,094	31,347	28,893	—
1975	42,599	42,917	35,872	—	31,047	31,241	29,456	—
1976	43,108	43,193	39,690	—	31,251	31,176	31,663	—
1977	42,715	38,108	31,853	—	30,304	27,741	26,156	—
1978	42,736	42,856	40,476	—	29,579	29,616	27,637	—
1979	41,550	41,538	39,974	—	29,294	29,480	27,146	—
1980	39,961	40,307	32,821	$35,355	29,452	29,600	28,572	—
1981	40,130	40,370	35,640	37,474	29,465	29,652	27,367	—
1982	38,592	39,137	34,299	37,039	29,132	29,398	27,090	—
1983	40,338	40,808	34,695	35,040	29,124	29,448	27,029	$27,480
1984	40,783	41,147	33,197	36,820	30,543	30,696	29,305	30,793
1985	41,635	42,449	38,977	41,827	31,855	32,329	27,690	31,224
1986	43,410	44,294	35,000	43,436	32,642	32,938	29,902	30,189
1987	43,685	44,459	33,680	40,154	32,001	32,528	29,974	31,883
1988	42,764	43,437	30,519	35,325	33,106	33,820	30,134	31,896
1989	42,040	43,476	30,745	34,527	33,957	34,082	31,397	33,711
1990	39,698	40,221	33,857	38,879	33,455	33,720	32,101	30,339
1991	42,095	42,823	32,806	37,938	32,524	32,889	28,141	29,086
1992	41,458	42,316	35,110	33,371	32,778	32,909	31,384	30,901
1993	40,755	41,538	30,993	34,297	33,849	34,281	29,162	29,116
1994	39,777	40,442	28,094	35,280	32,571	33,213	28,248	28,627
1995	40,049	41,548	32,850	36,668	32,177	32,553	27,760	30,431
1996	40,206	40,977	37,394	35,203	31,263	31,533	28,547	30,934
1997	40,811	41,427	31,561	36,250	32,529	32,579	30,859	32,087

— Too few sample observations for a reliable estimate.

NOTE: The Current Population Survey (CPS) questions used to obtain educational attainment were changed in 1992. In 1994, the survey instrument for the CPS was changed and weights were adjusted.

SOURCE: *The Condition of Education 1999*. National Center for Education Statistics

TABLE 4.14

Median Annual Income of Year-Round Full-Time Workers 25 Years Old and Over, by Level of Education Completed and Sex, 1989–1998

Sex and year 1	Total 2	Elementary/secondary			Some college, no degree[3] 6	Associate degree[4] 7	College				
		Less than 9th grade 3	9th to 12th grade, no diploma[1] 4	High school graduate[2] 5			Bachelor's degree or higher[5]				
							Total[5] 8	Bachelor's[6] 9	Master's[7] 10	Professional[7] 11	Doctorate[7] 12
Current dollars											
Men											
1989	$30,465	$17,555	$21,065	$26,609	$31,308	—	$41,892	$38,565	—	—	—
1990	30,733	17,394	20,902	26,653	31,734	—	42,671	39,238	—	—	—
1991	31,613	17,623	21,402	26,779	31,663	$33,817	45,138	40,906	$49,734	$73,996	$57,187
1992	32,057	17,294	21,274	27,280	32,103	33,433	45,802	41,355	49,973	76,220	57,418
1993	32,359	16,863	21,752	27,370	32,077	33,690	47,740	42,757	51,867	80,549	63,149
1994	33,440	17,532	22,048	28,037	32,279	35,794	49,228	43,663	53,500	75,009	61,921
1995	34,551	18,354	22,185	29,510	33,883	35,201	50,481	45,266	55,216	79,667	65,336
1996	35,622	17,962	22,717	30,709	34,845	37,131	51,436	45,846	60,508	85,963	71,227
1997	36,678	19,291	24,726	31,215	35,945	38,022	53,450	48,616	61,690	85,011	76,234
1998	37,906	19,380	23,958	31,477	36,934	40,274	56,524	51,405	62,244	94,737	75,078
Women											
1989	20,570	12,188	13,923	17,528	21,631	—	28,799	26,709	—	—	—
1990	21,372	12,251	14,429	18,319	22,227	—	30,377	28,017	—	—	—
1991	22,043	12,066	14,455	18,836	22,143	25,000	31,310	29,079	34,949	46,742	43,303
1992	23,139	12,958	14,559	19,427	23,157	25,624	32,304	30,326	36,037	46,257	45,790
1993	23,629	12,415	15,386	19,963	23,056	25,883	34,307	31,197	38,612	50,211	47,248
1994	24,399	12,430	15,133	20,373	23,514	25,940	35,378	31,741	39,457	50,615	51,119
1995	24,875	13,577	15,825	20,463	23,997	27,311	35,259	32,051	40,263	50,000	48,141
1996	25,808	14,414	16,953	21,175	25,167	28,083	36,461	33,525	41,901	57,624	56,267
1997	26,974	14,161	16,697	22,067	26,335	28,812	38,038	35,379	44,949	61,051	53,037
1998	27,956	14,467	16,482	22,780	27,420	29,924	39,786	36,559	45,283	57,565	57,796
Constant 1998 dollars											
Men											
1989	$40,047	$23,076	$27,690	$34,978	$41,155	—	$55,068	$50,694	—	—	—
1990	38,328	21,693	26,068	33,240	39,576	—	53,216	48,935	—	—	—
1991	37,833	21,091	25,613	32,048	37,893	$40,471	54,020	48,955	$59,520	$88,556	$68,440
1992	37,244	20,092	24,716	31,694	37,297	38,842	53,213	48,046	58,058	88,552	66,708
1993	36,502	19,022	24,537	30,874	36,184	38,003	53,852	48,231	58,507	90,862	71,234
1994	36,779	19,283	24,250	30,837	35,503	39,369	54,144	48,023	58,843	82,500	68,105
1995	36,954	19,631	23,728	31,563	36,240	37,649	53,992	48,414	59,056	85,208	69,880
1996	37,007	18,660	23,600	31,903	36,200	38,575	53,436	47,628	62,860	89,305	73,996
1997	37,249	19,591	25,111	31,701	36,505	38,614	54,283	49,373	62,651	86,335	77,421
1998	37,906	19,380	23,958	31,477	36,934	40,274	56,524	51,405	62,244	94,737	75,078
Women											
1989	27,040	16,021	18,302	23,041	28,434	—	37,857	35,109	—	—	—
1990	26,654	15,279	17,995	22,846	27,720	—	37,884	34,941	—	—	—
1991	26,380	14,440	17,299	22,542	26,500	29,919	37,471	34,801	41,826	55,939	51,824
1992	26,883	15,055	16,915	22,570	26,904	29,770	37,531	35,233	41,868	53,741	53,199
1993	26,654	14,004	17,356	22,519	26,008	29,197	38,699	35,191	43,555	56,639	53,297
1994	26,836	13,671	16,644	22,408	25,862	28,530	38,911	34,911	43,397	55,670	56,224
1995	26,605	14,521	16,926	21,886	25,666	29,211	37,711	34,280	43,063	53,478	51,489
1996	26,811	14,974	17,612	21,998	26,145	29,175	37,879	34,828	43,530	59,864	58,455
1997	27,394	14,382	16,957	22,411	26,745	29,261	38,630	35,930	45,649	62,002	53,863
1998	27,956	14,467	16,482	22,780	27,420	29,924	39,786	36,559	45,283	57,565	57,796
Number with income (in thousands)											
Men											
1989	44,596	2,425	3,312	16,392	9,028	—	13,439	7,473	—	—	—
1990	44,406	2,250	3,315	16,394	9,113	—	13,334	7,569	—	—	—
1991	44,199	1,807	3,083	15,025	8,034	2,899	13,350	8,456	3,073	1,147	674
1992	44,752	1,815	3,009	14,722	8,067	3,203	13,937	8,719	3,178	1,295	745
1993	45,873	1,790	3,083	14,604	8,493	3,557	14,346	9,178	3,131	1,231	808
1994	47,566	1,895	3,057	15,109	8,783	3,735	14,987	9,636	3,225	1,258	868
1995	48,500	1,946	3,335	15,331	8,908	3,926	15,054	9,597	3,395	1,208	853
1996	49,764	2,041	3,441	15,840	9,173	3,931	15,339	9,898	3,272	1,277	893
1997	50,807	1,914	3,548	16,225	9,170	4,086	15,864	10,349	3,228	1,321	966
1998	52,381	1,870	3,613	16,442	9,375	4,347	16,733	11,058	3,414	1,264	998

TABLE 4.14

Median Annual Income of Year-Round Full-Time Workers 25 Years Old and Over, by Level of Education Completed and Sex, 1989–1998 [CONTINUED]

Sex and year 1	Total 2	Elementary/secondary			College						
		Less than 9th grade 3	9th to 12th grade, no diploma[1] 4	High school graduate[2] 5	Some college, no degree[3] 6	Associate degree[4] 7	Bachelor's degree or higher[6]				
							Total[5] 8	Bachelor's[6] 9	Master's[7] 10	Professional[7] 11	Doctorate[7] 12
Number with income (in thousands) cont.											
Women											
1989	28,056	906	1,830	11,785	6,217	—	7,318	4,465	—	—	—
1990	28,636	847	1,861	11,810	6,462	—	7,655	4,704	—	—	—
1991	29,474	733	1,819	10,959	5,633	2,523	7,807	5,263	2,025	312	206
1992	30,346	734	1,659	11,039	5,904	2,655	8,355	5,604	2,192	334	225
1993	30,683	765	1,576	10,513	6,279	3,067	8,483	5,735	2,166	323	260
1994	31,379	696	1,675	10,785	6,256	3,210	8,756	5,901	2,174	398	283
1995	32,673	774	1,763	11,064	6,329	3,336	9,406	6,434	2,268	421	283
1996	33,549	750	1,751	11,363	6,582	3,468	9,636	6,689	2,213	413	322
1997	34,624	791	1,765	11,475	6,628	3,538	10,427	7,173	2,448	488	318
1998	35,628	814	1,878	11,613	7,070	3,527	10,725	7,288	2,639	468	329

[1] Includes 1 to 3 years high school for 1989 and 1990.

[2] Includes 4 years of high school for 1989 and 1990, and equivalency certificates for the other years.

[3] Includes 1 to 3 years of college and associate degrees for 1989 and 1990.

[4] Not reported separately for 1989 and 1990.

[5] Includes 4 or more years of college for 1989 and 1990.

[6] Includes 4 years of college for 1989 and 1990.

[7] Data not collected in 1989 and 1990.

— Data not available or not applicable.

NOTE: Data for 1992 and later years are based on 1990 Census counts. Because of rounding, details may not add to totals.

SOURCE: *Digest of Education Statistics, 1999*. National Center for Education Statistics, March 2000

FIGURE 4.11

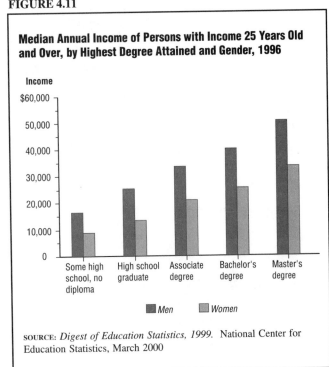

Median Annual Income of Persons with Income 25 Years Old and Over, by Highest Degree Attained and Gender, 1996

SOURCE: *Digest of Education Statistics, 1999.* National Center for Education Statistics, March 2000

TABLE 4.15

Total Annual Money Income and Median Income of Persons 25 Years Old and Over, by Educational Attainment and Sex, 1997

Sex, earnings, and age	Total	Less than 9th grade	Some high school (no diploma)	High school graduate (includes equivalency)	Some college, no degree	Associate degree	College — Bachelor's degree or higher				
							Total	Bachelor's degree	Master's degree	Professional degree	Doctor's degree
1	2	3	4	5	6	7	8	9	10	11	12
Men, 25 years old and over					**Number, in thousands**						
Total	82,378	6,159	8,018	26,575	14,122	5,670	21,832	14,090	4,640	1,749	1,353
With income	64,293	2,993	5,103	20,615	11,540	5,003	19,039	12,338	3,996	1,547	1,158
					Percentage distribution of men with income						
Total	100.0	100.0	100.0	100.0	100.0	100.0	100.0	100.0	100.0	100.0	100.0
$1 to $4,999 or loss	5.4	11.4	10.4	5.8	5.3	3.6	3.4	3.5	3.7	2.5	2.0
$5,000 to $9,999	5.5	15.9	9.2	5.8	4.9	4.9	3.0	3.3	3.0	2.1	1.7
$10,000 to $14,999	8.2	23.4	15.6	9.4	7.8	5.7	3.5	3.9	2.9	2.3	2.3
$15,000 to $24,999	18.0	27.0	27.8	22.5	17.7	18.1	9.4	11.1	7.2	5.1	5.2
$25,000 to $34,999	18.7	11.6	18.3	22.7	21.2	20.0	13.6	16.5	9.1	7.8	5.6
$35,000 to $49,999	19.8	7.5	11.8	20.9	22.2	24.6	20.1	21.3	20.0	15.1	15.2
$50,000 to $74,999	15.0	1.7	5.1	10.1	14.9	17.4	24.6	23.8	29.2	16.5	27.0
$75,000 and over	9.3	1.6	1.8	2.7	6.1	5.6	22.5	16.6	24.9	48.6	41.2
Median income	$31,262	$14,825	$20,314	$27,005	$31,174	$33,218	$46,736	$41,579	$51,813	$71,459	$65,593
Women, 25 years old and over					**Number, in thousands**						
Total	89,835	6,623	8,758	31,599	15,518	7,198	20,142	14,215	4,592	820	515
With income	56,134	1,624	3,574	18,794	10,702	5,502	15,938	11,108	3,726	663	441
					Percentage distribution of women with income						
Total	100.0	100.0	100.0	100.0	100.0	100.0	100.0	100.0	100.0	100.0	100.0
$1 to $4,999 or loss	12.6	25.6	22.8	14.2	13.1	9.3	7.9	8.7	6.6	3.3	5.7
$5,000 to $9,999	11.6	24.4	22.3	14.0	11.0	8.6	6.5	7.1	5.3	3.9	4.3
$10,000 to $14,999	13.6	26.0	22.6	17.1	13.7	11.3	6.7	7.3	5.9	4.5	2.0
$15,000 to $24,999	24.6	18.0	21.5	30.2	28.0	26.9	16.5	19.3	10.1	11.0	8.6
$25,000 to $34,999	17.3	4.2	7.6	15.1	18.3	22.2	20.9	22.5	18.7	13.3	11.8
$35,000 to $49,999	12.3	1.6	2.4	6.9	10.8	15.2	22.1	20.4	27.7	19.5	23.8
$50,000 to $74,999	5.8	0.1	0.6	1.8	4.1	5.3	13.7	10.9	19.8	17.5	27.2
$75,000 and over	2.2	0.1	0.2	0.6	1.1	1.1	5.7	3.9	5.9	27.0	16.6
Median income	$19,891	$10,007	$10,775	$16,225	$19,332	$22,220	$30,882	$26,328	$36,428	$45,650	$45,910

NOTE: Because of rounding, details may not add to totals.

SOURCE: *Digest of Education Statistics, 1999.* National Center for Education Statistics, March 2000

TABLE 4.16

Persons in the Labor Force for 27 Weeks or More—Poverty Status by Educational Attainment, Race, and Gender, 1997

(Numbers in thousands)

Educational attainment and race	Total	Men	Women	Below poverty level			Poverty rate[1]		
				Total	Men	Women	Total	Men	Women
Total, 16 years and older	130,047	70,310	59,738	7,453	3,468	3,985	5.7	4.9	6.7
Less than a high school diploma	16,351	10,145	6,206	2,587	1,461	1,125	15.8	14.4	18.1
Less than 1 year of high school	4,631	3,093	1,537	870	583	287	18.8	18.9	18.7
1-3 years of high school	10,069	6,029	4,040	1,550	779	771	15.4	12.9	19.1
4 years of high school, no diploma	1,652	1,023	629	167	99	67	10.1	9.7	10.7
High school graduates, no college	42,629	22,891	19,738	2,755	1,170	1,585	6.5	5.1	8.0
Some college, no degree	25,922	13,326	12,596	1,258	458	800	4.9	3.4	6.3
Associate degree	10,861	5,227	5,634	337	122	215	3.1	2.3	3.8
College graduates	34,285	18,720	15,564	517	257	261	1.5	1.4	1.7
White, 16 years and older	109,198	60,108	49,090	5,381	2,697	2,684	4.9	4.5	5.5
Less than a high school diploma	13,279	8,506	4,773	1,894	1,147	747	14.3	13.5	15.7
Less than 1 year of high school	3,980	2,731	1,249	772	521	251	19.4	19.1	20.1
1-3 years of high school	8,077	4,976	3,101	1,026	570	457	12.7	11.4	14.7
4 years of high school, no diploma	1,222	798	423	96	56	40	7.9	7.0	9.4
High school graduates, no college	35,572	19,359	16,213	1,913	887	1,026	5.4	4.6	6.3
Some college, no degree	21,490	11,300	10,190	910	370	540	4.2	3.3	5.3
Associate degree	9,341	4,601	4,740	265	96	169	2.8	2.1	3.6
College graduates	29,517	16,342	13,175	399	197	202	1.4	1.2	1.5
Black, 16 years and older	14,848	6,887	7,961	1,709	547	1,162	11.5	7.9	14.6
Less than a high school diploma	2,367	1,265	1,102	575	244	331	24.3	19.3	30.0
Less than 1 year of high school	394	230	164	61	32	29	15.5	13.9	17.7
1-3 years of high school	1,657	867	790	458	176	282	27.6	20.3	35.6
4 years of high school, no diploma	315	168	148	56	36	20	17.8	21.3	13.8
High school graduates, no college	5,568	2,694	2,874	716	210	505	12.9	7.8	17.6
Some college, no degree	3,432	1,498	1,934	298	60	238	8.7	4.0	12.3
Associate degree	1,069	394	675	61	16	45	5.7	4.0	6.7
College graduates	2,412	1,035	1,377	60	17	43	2.5	1.6	3.1

[1] Number below the poverty level as a percent of the total in the labor force for 27 weeks or more.

SOURCE: *A Profile of the Working Poor*. Bureau of Labor Statistics, August 1999

CHAPTER 5

THE WORKFORCE OF TOMORROW

Making informed career decisions requires reliable information about job opportunities in the future. Job opportunities result from the relationships between the population, labor force, and the demand for goods and services. Population ultimately limits the size of the labor force that drives how much can be produced. Demand for various goods and services determines employment in the industries providing them. Occupational employment opportunities, in turn, result from skills needed within specific industries. Opportunities for registered nurses and other health-related specialists, for example, have surged in response to the rapid growth in demand for health services as the population has aged.

Based on population and economic growth, the Bureau of Labor Statistics (BLS) predicts where future job growth is expected by industry and occupation and what the demographic makeup of the workforce is likely to be. The latest predictions released are for the decade 1998 to 2008. These 10-year projections are widely used for studying long-range economic and employment trends, planning education and training programs, and developing career information.

LABOR FORCE

The civilian labor force comprises individuals ages 16 and older who are either working or looking for work. They represent the supply of workers available to fill all the jobs that will be created over the 1998–2008 period. The population and labor force will continue to grow over the 1998–2008 period, although more slowly than during the previous 10-year period. The labor force is projected to increase by 16.9 million (12.3 percent) between 1998 and 2008, reaching 154 million workers in 2008. (See Figure 5.1 and Table 5.1.)

Labor-force growth will slow down because population growth is declining, from 14 percent growth between 1978 and 1988 to

FIGURE 5.1

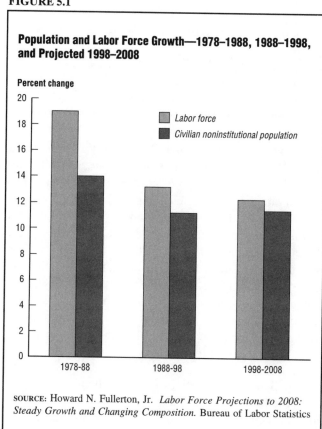

Population and Labor Force Growth—1978–1988, 1988–1998, and Projected 1998–2008

SOURCE: Howard N. Fullerton, Jr. *Labor Force Projections to 2008: Steady Growth and Changing Composition.* Bureau of Labor Statistics

1978 and 1988 to 11.7 percent projected growth over the 1998–2008 period. (See Figure 5.1.) The labor force is actually growing faster than the population because a larger proportion of the population is working or looking for work.

Older Workers

The labor force is getting older as the baby boomers age. According to the Bureau of Labor Statistics, workers between ages 55 to 64 will be the fastest growing portion

TABLE 5.1

Civilian Labor Force, 16 and Older, by Gender, Age, Race, and Hispanic Origin, 1978, 1988, 1998, and Projected 2008
[Numbers in thousands]

Group	Level				Change			Percent change			Percent distribution				Annual growth rate (percent)		
	1978	1988	1998	2008	1978–88	1988–98	1998–2008	1978–88	1988–98	1998–2008	1978	1988	1998	2008	1978–88	1988–98	1998–2008
Total	102,251	121,669	137,673	154,576	19,418	16,004	16,903	19.0	13.2	12.3	100.0	100.0	100.0	100.0	1.8	1.2	1.2
Men	59,620	66,927	73,959	81,132	7,307	7,032	7,173	12.3	10.5	9.7	58.3	55.0	53.7	52.5	1.2	1.0	.9
Women	42,631	54,742	63,714	73,444	12,111	8,972	9,729	28.4	16.4	15.3	41.7	45.0	46.3	47.5	2.5	1.5	1.4
16 to 24	25,022	22,536	21,894	25,210	−2,486	−642	3,316	−9.9	−2.8	15.1	24.5	18.5	15.9	16.3	−1.0	−.3	1.4
25 to 54	62,414	84,041	98,718	104,133	21,627	14,677	5,415	34.7	17.5	5.5	61.0	69.1	71.7	67.4	3.0	1.6	.5
55 and older	14,814	15,092	17,062	25,233	278	1,970	8,171	1.9	13.1	47.9	14.5	12.4	12.4	16.3	.2	1.2	4.0
White	89,634	104,756	115,415	126,665	15,122	10,659	11,251	16.9	10.2	9.7	87.7	86.1	83.8	81.9	1.6	1.0	.9
Black	10,432	13,205	15,982	19,101	2,773	2,777	3,119	26.6	21.0	19.5	10.2	10.9	11.6	12.4	2.4	1.9	1.8
Asian and other[1]	2,185	3,708	6,278	8,809	1,523	2,570	2,531	69.7	69.3	40.3	2.1	3.0	4.6	5.7	5.4	5.4	3.4
Hispanic origin[2]	...	8,982	14,317	19,585	...	5,335	5,268	...	59.4	36.8	...	7.4	10.4	12.7	...	4.8	3.2
Other than Hispanic origin[2]	...	112,687	123,356	134,991	...	10,669	11,635	...	9.5	9.4	...	92.6	89.6	87.3	...	.9	.9
White non-Hispanic[2]	...	96,141	101,767	109,216	...	5,626	7,449	...	5.9	7.3	...	79.0	73.9	70.7	...	.6	.7

[1]The "Asian and other" group includes (1) Asians and Pacific Islanders and (2) American Indians and Alaska Natives. The historical data are derived by subtracting "black" from the "black and other" group; projections are made directly, not by subtraction.

[2]Data by Hispanic origin are not available before 1980.

SOURCE: Howard N. Fullerton, Jr. *Labor Force Projections to 2008: Steady Growth and Changing Composition.* Bureau of Labor Statistics

of the workforce between 1996 and 2006. The median age of U.S. workers will increase to 41 years in 2006, up from 38 years in 1996. This, coupled with a population growth rate that is expected to lag behind the job growth rate, is predicted to create a situation where employers will need to rely on older workers to fill or keep jobs. Baby boomers seem willing to stay in their jobs; a 1998 poll presented at an annual American Association of Retired Persons (AARP) conference showed that 80 percent of baby boomers intended to keep working at least part-time after retirement age. Reasons for continuing to work ranged from job enjoyment, to the desire to start a business, to the need for income.

The labor force participation rate changes with age. Participation is low for young persons because of school and child care, rises during the prime working ages of 25 to 54, and then declines after age 55 as workers retire. In 1998 for example, the labor force participation rate for those ages 16 to 24 was 15.9 percent, and for those ages 25 to 54, it was 71.7 percent. For persons ages 55 and older, the participation rate was 12.4 percent. (See Table 5.1.)

The number of workers in the two age groups with large numbers of baby boomers (born between 1946 and 1964)—people aged 45 to 54 and those ages 55 to 64—will grow by 30 percent by 2008. Only the trailing edge of the baby boomers, those born between 1962 and 1964, will be younger than age 45 in 2008. (See Figure 5.2.)

Over the 1998–2008 period many baby boomers will move from an age group having a very high labor force participation rate into one with a much lower rate. The 55- to 64-year old labor force is projected to grow by 56 percent by 2008.

Gender

From 1988 to 2008 women will continue to make up a growing proportion of the labor force, rising from 45 to 48 percent. (See Figure 5.3.) The labor force participation rate for women rose from 57 percent in 1988 to 60 percent in 1998 and is projected to increase to 62 percent by 2008. On the other hand, men's labor force participation rates have declined steadily over the 1988–2008 period, from 76 percent in 1988 to 75 percent in 1998. The rate is projected to be 74 percent in 2008. (See Figure 5.4.)

Race and Ethnic Groups

Due to the effects of immigration, the labor force growth of Hispanics, Asians, and others will be much faster than that of blacks and white non-Hispanics. Hispanics are projected to be the fastest growing group over the 1998–2008 period, increasing more than three times as fast as the overall labor force, followed closely by the "Asian and other" group. As a result, by 2008, more Hispanics will be in the labor force than blacks. Despite relatively slow growth, white non-Hispanics will have the largest growth in the number of workers between 1998 and 2008. (See Table 5.1 and Figure 5.5.)

FIGURE 5.2

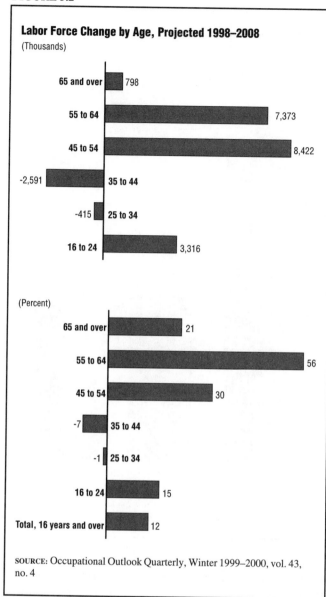

Labor Force Change by Age, Projected 1998–2008
(Thousands)

65 and over — 798
55 to 64 — 7,373
45 to 54 — 8,422
35 to 44 — -2,591
25 to 34 — -415
16 to 24 — 3,316

(Percent)

65 and over — 21
55 to 64 — 56
45 to 54 — 30
35 to 44 — -7
25 to 34 — -1
16 to 24 — 15
Total, 16 years and over — 12

SOURCE: Occupational Outlook Quarterly, Winter 1999–2000, vol. 43, no. 4

ECONOMIC GROWTH

The economy's need for workers stems from the demand for goods and services, which is measured by the gross domestic product (GDP). The GDP is projected to grow at a rate of 2.1 percent per year over the 1996–2006 period and to reach approximately $9.5 trillion by 2008. By comparison, the GDP grew at an average annual rate of 2.3 percent during the 1986–1996 period. (See Figure 5.6.)

The slowdown in GDP growth reflects slower labor force growth, from an average annual rate of 1.5 percent over the 1986–96 period to 1.1 percent between 1996 and 2006. In the face of the projected slowing of labor force growth, the projection calls for rising productivity (more output per worker) in order to meet the ever-growing demand for goods and services. (See Figure 5.6.) Faster, more powerful machines and new equipment will enable workers to produce more efficiently, increasing output

FIGURE 5.3

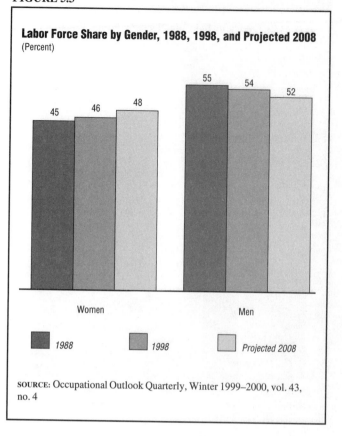

Labor Force Share by Gender, 1988, 1998, and Projected 2008
(Percent)

Women — 45, 46, 48
Men — 55, 54, 52

1988 | 1998 | Projected 2008

SOURCE: Occupational Outlook Quarterly, Winter 1999–2000, vol. 43, no. 4

FIGURE 5.4

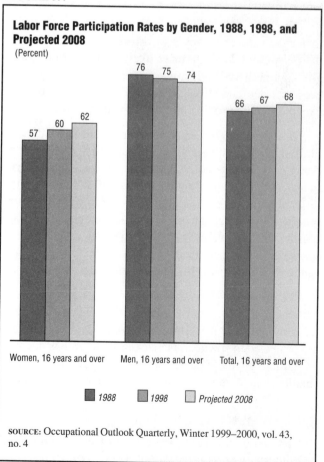

Labor Force Participation Rates by Gender, 1988, 1998, and Projected 2008
(Percent)

Women, 16 years and over — 57, 60, 62
Men, 16 years and over — 76, 75, 74
Total, 16 years and over — 66, 67, 68

1988 | 1998 | Projected 2008

SOURCE: Occupational Outlook Quarterly, Winter 1999–2000, vol. 43, no. 4

FIGURE 5.5

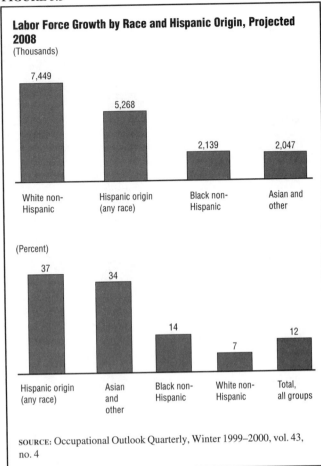

Labor Force Growth by Race and Hispanic Origin, Projected 2008
(Thousands)

SOURCE: Occupational Outlook Quarterly, Winter 1999–2000, vol. 43, no. 4

FIGURE 5.6

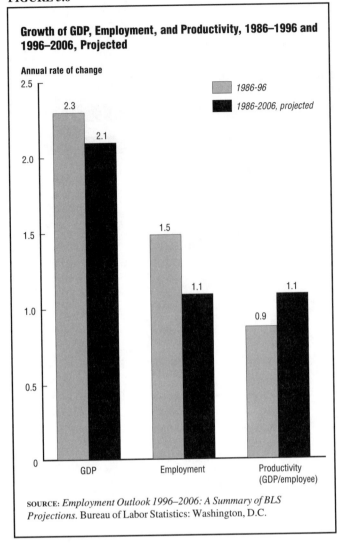

Growth of GDP, Employment, and Productivity, 1986–1996 and 1996–2006, Projected

SOURCE: *Employment Outlook 1996–2006: A Summary of BLS Projections.* Bureau of Labor Statistics: Washington, D.C.

faster than the company's workforce grows. High-productivity companies are more likely to prosper in a globally competitive environment, increasing their output even further and either hiring additional workers or expecting more production from existing workers.

Domestic and foreign consumers, including individuals, businesses, and governments, purchase thousands of American products. Shifts in consumer tastes and government priorities can affect the growth of and demand for different kinds of goods and services. Technical changes in products also affect demand. For example, the use of more plastics instead of steel in automobiles increases demand for plastics and decreases demand for steel. Such changes can have a significant effect on industry employment.

Traditionally, households have spent most of their income on housing, transportation, and medical care. This trend should continue. However, through 2008, consumers are projected to spend an increasing share of their income on durable goods, such as computers and furniture, and a smaller share on nondurable goods, such as food and fuel.

EMPLOYMENT BY INDUSTRY

The BLS develops projections of employment for 262 industries or industry groups that make up the econo-

my as a whole. Because of expected shifts in spending, employment growth rates will vary significantly among industries. As a consequence, the structure of industry employment will change over the 1998–2008 period.

Changes in demand for an industry's products constitute the most important cause of differences in employment growth rates among industries. Technological change is another factor affecting industry employment. For example, automated equipment in manufacturing plants enables fewer workers to produce more goods, and its use is a major reason for declining employment in manufacturing. This decline in generally better-paying blue-collar jobs in manufacturing is a major reason that the earnings of the less educated have fallen behind from 1980 to 2000.

Changes in business practices also have an impact on employment. When businesses use contractors or temporary help services, they reduce their total employment. At the same time, employment rises for contractors and the temporary help supply services industry. This often means a loss of better-paying jobs and a gain in lower-paying jobs.

FIGURE 5.7

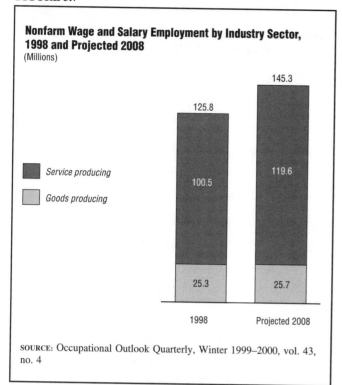

Nonfarm Wage and Salary Employment by Industry Sector, 1998 and Projected 2008
(Millions)

■ Service producing
▨ Goods producing

125.8 (1998): Service producing 100.5, Goods producing 25.3
145.3 (Projected 2008): Service producing 119.6, Goods producing 25.7

SOURCE: Occupational Outlook Quarterly, Winter 1999–2000, vol. 43, no. 4

FIGURE 5.8

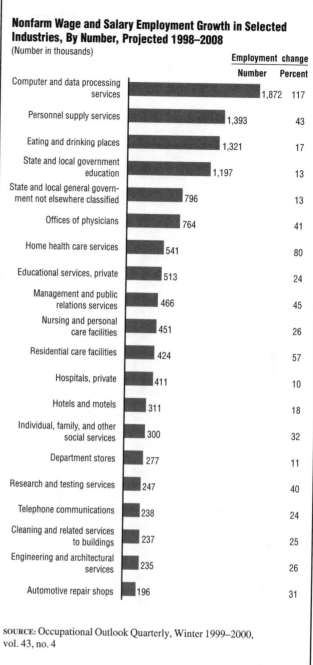

Nonfarm Wage and Salary Employment Growth in Selected Industries, By Number, Projected 1998–2008
(Number in thousands)

Industry	Employment change Number	Percent
Computer and data processing services	1,872	117
Personnel supply services	1,393	43
Eating and drinking places	1,321	17
State and local government education	1,197	13
State and local general government not elsewhere classified	796	13
Offices of physicians	764	41
Home health care services	541	80
Educational services, private	513	24
Management and public relations services	466	45
Nursing and personal care facilities	451	26
Residential care facilities	424	57
Hospitals, private	411	10
Hotels and motels	311	18
Individual, family, and other social services	300	32
Department stores	277	11
Research and testing services	247	40
Telephone communications	238	24
Cleaning and related services to buildings	237	25
Engineering and architectural services	235	26
Automotive repair shops	196	31

SOURCE: Occupational Outlook Quarterly, Winter 1999–2000, vol. 43, no. 4

For analytical purposes, industries fall into the goods-producing sector and the services-producing sector. The divisions within the goods-producing sector are agriculture production, forestry, and fishing; mining; construction; and manufacturing. In the services-producing sector, the divisions are transportation, communications, and utilities; wholesale trade; retail trade; finance, insurance, and real estate; services (see below); and government. Within each division, industries are combined into groups. For example, within the retail trade division, food stores is an industry group that comprises the industry's grocery stores, meat and fish markets, and retail bakeries.

Growth

Job growth can be measured both by percentage and numerical change. The fastest growing occupations do not necessarily provide the largest number of jobs. A larger occupation with slower growth may produce more openings than a smaller occupation with faster growth.

Services-producing industries are projected to account for all the growth of wage and salary employment over the 1998–2008 period, just as they did between 1988 and 1998. Almost all wage and salary employment growth will be in the service-producing sector, which is projected to increase 19 percent by 2008. Wage and salary employment in the services-producing sector rose 3.9 million, from 96.6 million to 100.5 million between 1996 and 1998. Over the 1998–2008 period, it is projected to increase another 19.1 million. Goods-producing employment is projected to grow slightly over the same

period. (See Figure 5.7.) Figures 5.8 and 5.9 show industries with the largest projected wage and salary employment growth and decline in the number of workers. Computer and data processing services are expected to have the largest wage and salary employment growth by 2008. Apparel manufacturing will have the greatest decline in wage and salary employment by 2008, followed by the general federal government industry. Figure 5.10 shows the industries with the fastest-growing wage and salary employment by percent of change. Again, the computer and data processing service industry is projected to have a 117 percent increase in wage and salary employment growth by 2008.

FIGURE 5.9

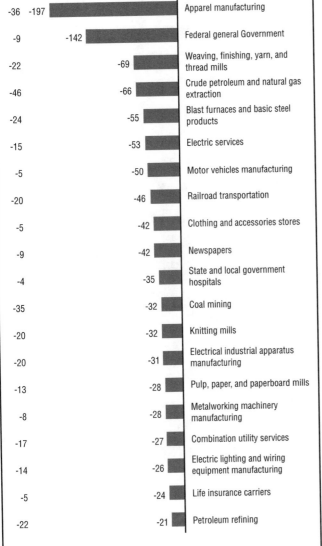

Nonfarm Wage and Salary Employment Decline in Selected Industries, Projected 1998–2008

(Number in thousands)

Employment change

Percent	Number	Industry
-36	-197	Apparel manufacturing
-9	-142	Federal general Government
-22	-69	Weaving, finishing, yarn, and thread mills
-46	-66	Crude petroleum and natural gas extraction
-24	-55	Blast furnaces and basic steel products
-15	-53	Electric services
-5	-50	Motor vehicles manufacturing
-20	-46	Railroad transportation
-5	-42	Clothing and accessories stores
-9	-42	Newspapers
-4	-35	State and local government hospitals
-35	-32	Coal mining
-20	-32	Knitting mills
-20	-31	Electrical industrial apparatus manufacturing
-13	-28	Pulp, paper, and paperboard mills
-8	-28	Metalworking machinery manufacturing
-17	-27	Combination utility services
-14	-26	Electric lighting and wiring equipment manufacturing
-5	-24	Life insurance carriers
-22	-21	Petroleum refining

SOURCE: Occupational Outlook Quarterly, Winter 1999–2000, vol. 43, no. 4

FIGURE 5.10

Nonfarm Wage and Salary Employment Growth in Selected Industries, By Percent, Projected 1998–2008

(Percent)

Industry	Employment change Percent	Thousands
Computer and data processing services	117	1,872
Home health care services	80	541
Residential care facilities	57	424
Security and commodity exchanges and services	55	80
Nonstore retailers, including mail order	55	191
Local and suburban transportation	45	106
Management and public relations services	45	466
Personnel supply services	43	1,393
Museums and botanical and zoological gardens	42	39
Offices of physicians	41	764
Research and testing services	40	247
Freight transportation arrangement	39	71
Security and commodity brokers and dealers	35	175
Federal and business credit institutions	34	50
Water supply and sanitary services	34	67
Personal credit institutions	33	61
Individual, family, and other social services	32	300
Child daycare services	32	196
Credit reporting and collection	32	46
School bus operation	32	45
Total, all industries	15	19,535

SOURCE: Occupational Outlook Quarterly, Winter 1999–2000, vol. 43, no. 4

Services-Producing Industries

Job growth in the services division is greater than all the other divisions within the services-producing sector combined. (The services division includes business services, health services, social services, engineering, management, and educational services.) Wage and salary jobs in the services division over the 1998–2008 period are projected to grow to 11.7 million, a 31 percent increase. (See Figure 5.11.) By 2008, 75 percent of employment gains are expected to take place in the services and retail trade divisions. Figure 5.12 shows the projected change in wage and salary employment within the services division. Business services, the fastest-growing industry group, is led by computer and data processing services and personnel supply services, the fastest-growing industry in the economy. Business services is expected to gain 4.6 million in employment through 2008, a 53 percent increase. Health services follow business services in growth; health services are projected to grow by 29 percent by 2008, representing 2.8 million in employment growth. Factors contributing to growth in the health services industry include the aging population, which will require more services, and the increased use of innovative medical technology. Patients will increasingly be shifted out of hospitals and into outpatient facilities, nursing homes, and home health

FIGURE 5.11

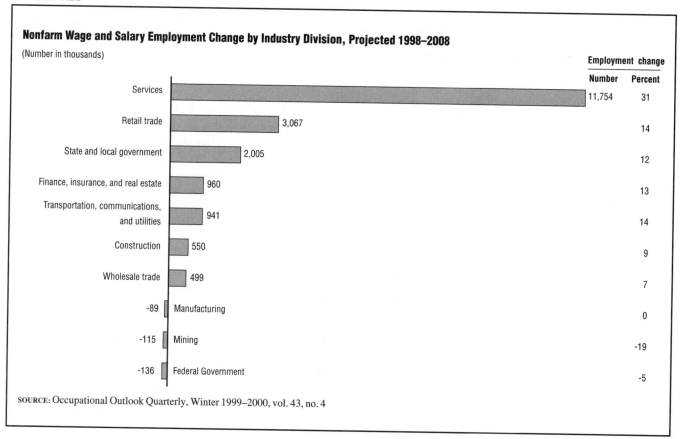

Nonfarm Wage and Salary Employment Change by Industry Division, Projected 1998–2008

(Number in thousands)

SOURCE: Occupational Outlook Quarterly, Winter 1999–2000, vol. 43, no. 4

FIGURE 5.12

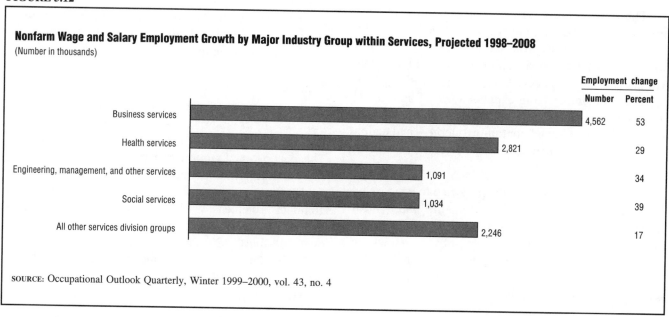

Nonfarm Wage and Salary Employment Growth by Major Industry Group within Services, Projected 1998–2008

(Number in thousands)

SOURCE: Occupational Outlook Quarterly, Winter 1999–2000, vol. 43, no. 4

care in an attempt to contain costs. This will likely lead to a declining hospital service staff, such as licensed practical nurses, since patients will be expected to take care of themselves or hire their own attendants.

Within the services division, engineering, management, and other services as well as social services were projected to add jobs by 2008, though not at the rates of computer and data processing and business services. (See Figure 5.12.) Engineering, management, and other services are expected to comprise 1 million jobs by 2008, a 34 percent increase. Social services will comprise 1 million jobs as well, a 39 percent increase by 2008. The projected increase in the older population is also a driving force in the growth of employment in this industry.

FIGURE 5.13

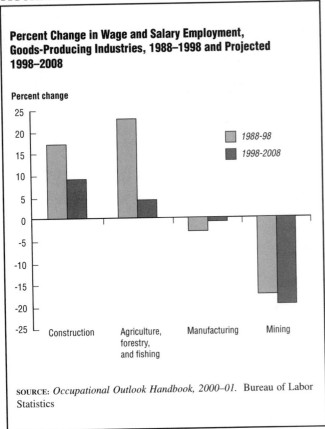

Percent Change in Wage and Salary Employment, Goods-Producing Industries, 1988–1998 and Projected 1998–2008

SOURCE: *Occupational Outlook Handbook, 2000–01.* Bureau of Labor Statistics

The transportation group is projected to have 6.7 million jobs in 2008, an increase of 941,000 over 1998. Jobs in retail trade are projected to increase by 3.1 million. Employment in finance, insurance, and real estate will add 960,000 jobs between 1998–2008. Rising productivity, stemming from expanded use of automated and computerized services that replaced tellers and other bank workers, and continuing mergers and acquisitions will also contribute to the projected decline in employment.

Government employment is projected to increase by 2 million from its 1998 level. All of this employment growth will take place in state and local government, as an increase in teachers will be driven by the growth in school-age population. Federal government employment between 1998–2008 is projected to decline by 136,000, as downsizing continues. (See Figure 5.11.)

Goods-Producing Industries

Employment in the goods-producing sector is projected to vary over the 1998–2008 period. Construction was expected to grow in employment opportunities by 9 percent between 1998 and 2008. Agriculture, forestry, and fishing were also projected to grow by 4 percent. (See Figure 5.13.) Declining employment was projected for manufacturing and mining, by 1 percent and 19 percent, respectively.

EMPLOYMENT BY OCCUPATION

The economy's occupational and industrial structures form a close relationship. Workers in varied occupations provide the skills needed in different industries. Nurses, physicians, orderlies, and medical record technicians are needed in hospitals; cooks, waiters and waitresses, and food preparation workers are needed in restaurants. Consequently, the demand for the occupations concentrated in an industry often rises or falls with the fortunes of that industry. At the same time, it is important to remember that members of the same industry may not share the same concerns. For example, in the health industry, the goals of the hospital administrator, the doctor, and the licensed practical nurse may differ dramatically.

Changes in technology usually affect how industries use workers. For example, technological advances will continue to reduce the need for typists, directory assistance telephone operators, and bookkeeping, accounting, and auditing clerks. Changes in business practices and operations also can affect occupational staffing. For example, many companies are eliminating middle managers, thereby intending to put more authority in the hands of nonmanagerial frontline workers.

The Bureau of Labor analyzes these factors to project employment for more than 500 detailed occupations. These occupations can be grouped in different ways to provide a better understanding of broad occupational employment trends. Two of the grouping methods used are by type of work performed and by education and training usually required.

Types

Employment in professional specialty occupations is projected to grow the fastest of the major occupational groups and to add the most jobs between 1998 and 2008. This occupational group was expected to add 5,343 jobs, representing a rate increase of 27 percent. (See Figure 5.14.) Professional specialty occupations (engineers, architects, scientists, teachers, lawyers, physicians, nurses, writers, artists, and entertainers, etc.) will account for over one-fourth (27 percent) of all new jobs over the 1998–2008 period. This proportion reflects both the group's size (third largest) and its projected growth among the major occupational groups.

The group with the second fastest projected growth rate (22 percent) is technicians and related support occupations (airplane pilots and navigators, computer programmers, legal assistants, radiological technicians, licensed practical nurses, drafting occupations, etc.). This is a small group, however, and is expected to account for the second smallest numerical increase in jobs.

The next fastest growing group (with a 17 percent rate of increase) is service occupations (child care work-

FIGURE 5.14

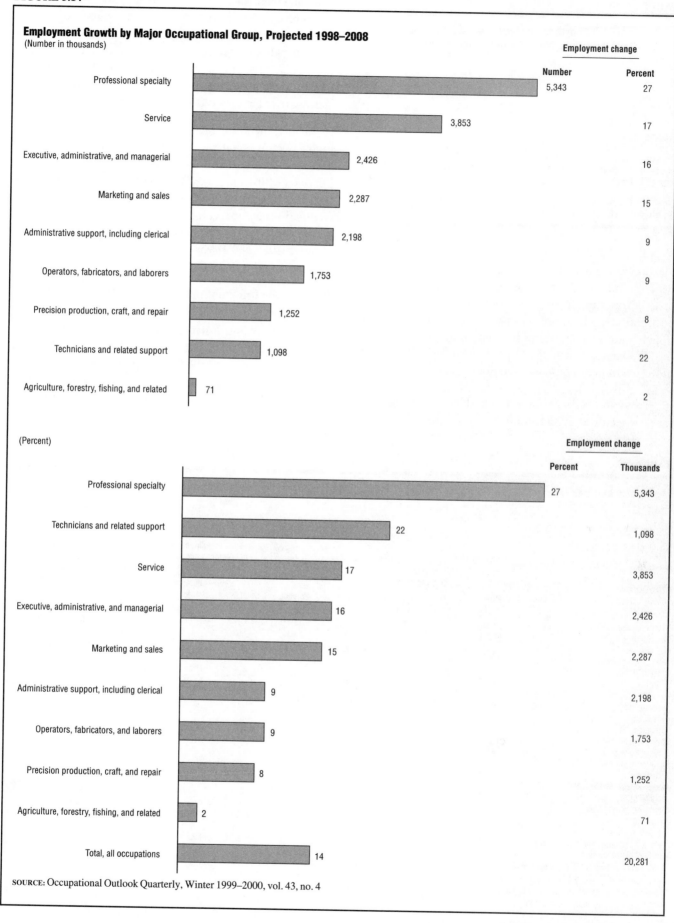

Employment Growth by Major Occupational Group, Projected 1998–2008
(Number in thousands)

Occupational Group	Number	Percent
Professional specialty	5,343	27
Service	3,853	17
Executive, administrative, and managerial	2,426	16
Marketing and sales	2,287	15
Administrative support, including clerical	2,198	9
Operators, fabricators, and laborers	1,753	9
Precision production, craft, and repair	1,252	8
Technicians and related support	1,098	22
Agriculture, forestry, fishing, and related	71	2

(Percent)

Occupational Group	Percent	Thousands
Professional specialty	27	5,343
Technicians and related support	22	1,098
Service	17	3,853
Executive, administrative, and managerial	16	2,426
Marketing and sales	15	2,287
Administrative support, including clerical	9	2,198
Operators, fabricators, and laborers	9	1,753
Precision production, craft, and repair	8	1,252
Agriculture, forestry, fishing, and related	2	71
Total, all occupations	14	20,281

SOURCE: Occupational Outlook Quarterly, Winter 1999–2000, vol. 43, no. 4

TABLE 5.2

BLS Projected Job Growth for Systems Analysts, Computer Engineers and Scientists, and Computer Programmers

Occupation	Numbers of workers in thousands		Percentage change
	1994	2005 (projected)	
IT occupations	1,365	2,184	60
Systems analysts	483	928	92
Computer scientists and engineers	345	655	90
Computer programmers	537	601	12
All other occupations	125,649	142,524	13
Total, all occupations	127,014	144,708	14

SOURCE: *Information Technology Workers*. U.S. General Accounting Office: Washington, D.C.

ers, police and detectives, firefighters, guards, bartenders, waiters and waitresses, dental assistants, hairdressers, etc.). Professional specialty occupations and service occupations, which are on opposite ends of the educational attainment and earnings spectrum, are expected to provide nearly one-half (44 percent) of the 1998–2008 projected total job growth. (See Figure 5.14.)

Two other groups have faster than average growth rates—executive, administrative, and managerial occupa-

tions, and marketing and sales workers. Employment in precision production, craft, and repair occupations; operators, fabricators, and laborers; and administrative support occupations, including clerical, is expected to increase, but at a slower rate than total employment. Employment in agriculture, forestry, fishing, and related occupations will show very little increase over the 1998–2008 period. (See Figure 5.14.)

These different projected growth rates among the major occupational groups will result in changes to the structure of total employment between 1998 and 2008. Service occupations; executive, administrative, and managerial occupations; and technicians and related support occupations are projected to increase their shares of total employment over the 1998–2008 period, as they did between 1986 and 1996.

Demand for Information Technology Workers

Industry reports and numerous newspaper and magazine articles claimed that severe shortages of information technology (IT) workers could cripple the growth of the economy. In response, the U.S. Department of Commerce studied the alleged problem and issued its conclusions in *America's New Deficit: The Shortage of Information Technology Workers* (Washington, DC, 1997).

TABLE 5.3

Employment and Total Job Openings, 1998–2008, and 1997 Median Hourly Earnings by Education and Training Category
[Numbers in thousands of jobs]

Education and training category	Employment				Change		Total job openings due to growth and net replacements, 1998-2008[1]		Median hourly earnings, percent distribution, 1997[2]			
	Number		Percent distribution					Percent distribution	Quartile			
	1998	2008	1998	2008	Number	Percent	Number		1	2	3	4
Total, all occupations	140,514	160,795	100.0	100.0	20,281	14.4	54,622	100.0	25.0	25.0	25.0	25.0
First professional degree	1,908	2,215	1.4	1.4	308	16.1	617	1.1	92.2	7.8	...	...
Doctoral degree	996	1,228	.7	.8	232	23.3	502	.9	100.0	...	...	...
Master's degree	940	1,115	.7	.7	174	18.6	372	.7	97.5	2.5	...	...
Work experience plus bachelor's or higher degree	9,595	11,276	6.8	7.0	1,680	17.5	3,372	6.2	94.1	3.2	2.7	...
Bachelor's degree	17,379	21,596	12.4	13.4	4,217	24.3	7,727	14.1	76.2	19.1	3.3	1.4
Associate degree	4,930	6,467	3.5	4.0	1,537	31.2	2,414	4.4	70.5	25.3	4.2	...
Postsecondary vocational training	4,508	5,151	3.2	3.2	643	14.3	1,667	3.1	7.2	60.5	17.2	15.1
Work experience in a related occupation	11,174	12,490	8.0	7.8	1,316	11.8	3,676	6.7	26.1	50.7	23.1	0.1
Long-term on-the-job training	13,436	14,604	9.6	9.1	1,168	8.7	4,397	8.0	15.9	57.7	7.3	19.1
Moderate-term on-the-job training	20,521	21,952	14.6	13.7	1,430	7.0	6,213	11.4	0.8	55.9	39.8	3.6
Short-term on-the-job training	55,125	62,701	39.2	39.0	7,576	13.7	23,665	43.4	0.7	7.8	35.8	55.8

[1]Total job openings represent the sum of employment increases and net replacements. If employment change is negative, job openings due to growth are zero and total job openings equal net replacements.

[2]The quartile rankings of Occupational Employment Statistics hourly earnings data are presented in the following categories: 1 = very high ($16.25 and over), 2 = high ($10.89 to $16.14), 3 = low ($7.78 to $10.88), and 4 = very low (up to $7.76).

The rankings were based on quartiles using one-fourth of total employment to define each quartile.

NOTE: Detail may not equal total or 100 percent due to rounding.

SOURCE: Douglas Braddock. *Occupational Employment Projections*. Monthly Labor Review, Nov. 1999, pp. 51-77.

In its report, the Department of Commerce presented Bureau of Labor Statistics (BLS) projections that between 1994 and 2005 the United States would require slightly over 1 million additional IT workers, such as computer programmers, systems analysts, and computer scientists and engineers. These workers would fill 820,000 newly created jobs and replace another 227,000 workers who are leaving these fields as a result of retirement, change of profession, or other reasons. The report noted that the number of systems analysts would grow 92 percent. The number of computer engineers and scientists would increase by 90 percent, while the number of computer programmer positions would rise by only 12 percent. (See Table 5.2.)

Since the report was released, the Department of Commerce has issued an update with revised BLS projections showing even stronger growth. The number of IT workers will grow from 1.5 million in 1996 to 2.6 million in 2006, a 42 percent increase. Another 244,000 workers will be needed to replace existing IT professionals.

The Department of Commerce found that 24,553 students earned bachelor's degrees in computer and information sciences in 1994, a decline of more than 40 percent from 1986. As of 1999 data indicates that the decline has come to a halt. There has been modest but steady growth in the number of computer and information science bachelor's degrees awarded between 1993 and 1996, rising to 26,837 in 1996. Despite this, the department concluded that there would be an inadequate supply of IT workers.

The report cites 4 observations upon which their conclusions were based: rising salaries for IT workers, reports of unfilled vacancies for IT workers, the recruiting of foreign workers, and the outsourcing of work to foreign companies. The estimated supply of IT workers (based on students graduating with bachelor's degrees in computer and information sciences) is less than its estimated demand.

For example, the Department of Commerce cites a *Business Week* article, "Forget the Huddled Masses: Send Nerds," to illustrate that companies are searching for IT workers in foreign labor markets. It also reported that India has more than 200,000 programmers and, in conjunction with predominantly U.S. partners, has developed into one of the world's largest exporters of software. In 1996 and 1997 outsourced software development accounted for 41 percent of India's software exports.

The House Committee on Commerce asked the General Accounting Office (GAO) to assess the Department of Commerce's analysis. The GAO study (*Information Technology Workers*, Washington, DC, 1998) concluded that the Department of Commerce failed to provide clear, complete, and compelling evidence for a shortage or a potential shortage of IT workers. First, although some data show ris-

FIGURE 5.15

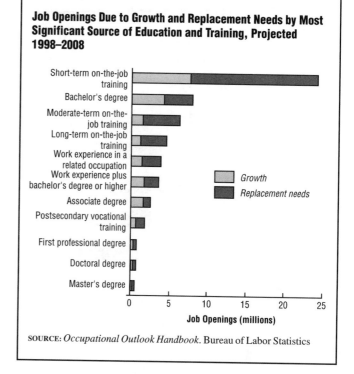

Job Openings Due to Growth and Replacement Needs by Most Significant Source of Education and Training, Projected 1998–2008

SOURCE: *Occupational Outlook Handbook.* Bureau of Labor Statistics

ing salaries for IT workers, other data indicate that those increases in earnings have been commensurate with the rising earnings of all professional specialty occupations. Second, the survey by the Information Technology Association of America (ITAA), a trade association, that the Department of Commerce used to estimate unfilled IT jobs, had an inadequate response rate to form a basis for nationwide estimate of unfilled jobs. Third, although the report cites instances of companies drawing upon talent pools outside the United States to meet their demands for workers, not enough information is provided to determine the magnitude of this phenomenon. Finally, while the report discusses various sources of potential supply of IT workers, it used only the number of students earning bachelor's degrees in computer and information sciences. Workers who receive certifications and degrees in other fields could be qualified, as could large number of workers who have been or will be retrained for these occupations.

The Department of Commerce responded that their report was not a definitive analysis of the labor market for IT workers and that the GAO analysis contained several inaccuracies. The Department of Commerce wrote that its report did not conclude that there would definitely be a shortage of workers, but that the demand for them was increasing, and industry practices showed clear indications of a tight labor market for IT workers. The GAO stood by its conclusions. The debate is important, since many information technology industries have been lobbying Congress to let in more high-skilled foreign workers. Critics say that American workers can be trained to take these jobs.

FIGURE 5.16

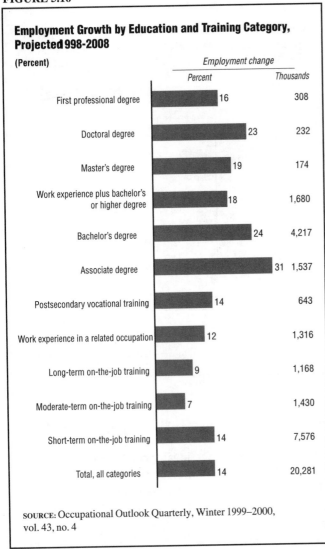

Employment Growth by Education and Training Category, Projected 998-2008

(Percent)

SOURCE: Occupational Outlook Quarterly, Winter 1999–2000, vol. 43, no. 4

FIGURE 5.17

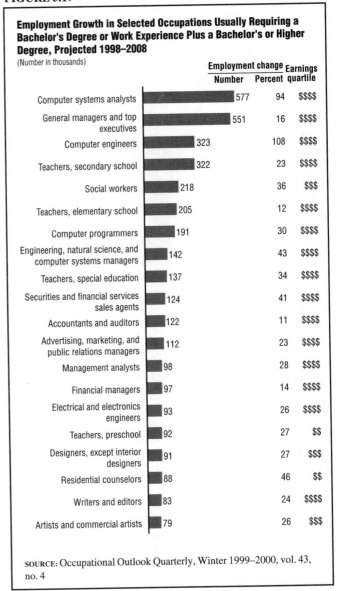

Employment Growth in Selected Occupations Usually Requiring a Bachelor's Degree or Work Experience Plus a Bachelor's or Higher Degree, Projected 1998–2008

(Number in thousands)

SOURCE: Occupational Outlook Quarterly, Winter 1999–2000, vol. 43, no. 4

EDUCATION

Although jobs are available at all levels of education and training, most jobs do not require post-secondary education or training. The economy will produce 20.3 million new jobs between 1998 and 2008, a 14.4 percent increase in employment. Over two-thirds (67 percent) of the growth will be in occupations requiring less education than a bachelor's degree. However, these positions generally offer the lowest pay and benefits. Three of every 4 openings (77 percent) will be in occupations that generally require less than a bachelor's degree. (See Table 5.3 and Figure 5.15.)

However, the five education and training categories with the highest-expected growth (23 percent of all jobs) require at least a bachelor's degree, and the sixth requires an associate's degree. All categories that do not require some college are projected to grow equally or more slowly than average (14 percent). (See Figure 5.16.)

The largest education and training category is short-term on-the-job training in which workers can learn job skills in a few weeks or less. By 2008, 62.7 million workers will be in occupations that usually require short-term on-the-job training. Moderate-term on-the-job training in which workers can generally learn their skills after 1 to 12 months on the job will account for 21.9 million workers.

Occupations in which workers require more than a year of on-the-job experience and formal training will employ 14.6 million workers. An additional 12.5 million workers will be employed in occupations that require experience in another occupation. Almost 112 million workers, representing 69 percent of total employment, will be in jobs that generally require on-the-job training or experience. (See Table 5.3.)

Bachelor's Degree or Higher

Occupations requiring a bachelor's degree or more accounted for 30.8 million jobs in 1998. Over 17 million workers were in jobs that routinely require a bachelor's

FIGURE 5.18

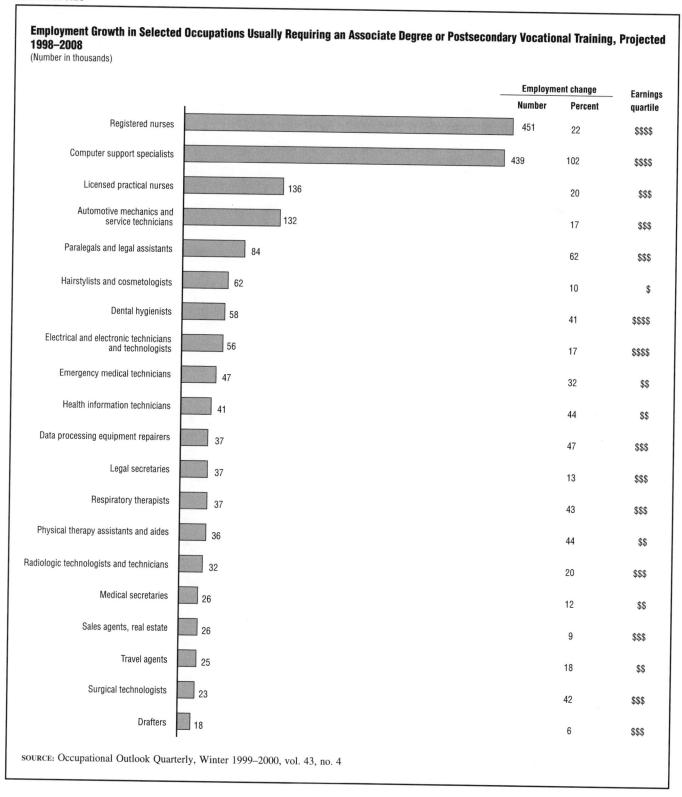

Employment Growth in Selected Occupations Usually Requiring an Associate Degree or Postsecondary Vocational Training, Projected 1998–2008
(Number in thousands)

| | Employment change | | Earnings quartile |
Occupation	Number	Percent	
Registered nurses	451	22	$$$$
Computer support specialists	439	102	$$$$
Licensed practical nurses	136	20	$$$
Automotive mechanics and service technicians	132	17	$$$
Paralegals and legal assistants	84	62	$$$
Hairstylists and cosmetologists	62	10	$
Dental hygienists	58	41	$$$$
Electrical and electronic technicians and technologists	56	17	$$$$
Emergency medical technicians	47	32	$$
Health information technicians	41	44	$$
Data processing equipment repairers	37	47	$$$
Legal secretaries	37	13	$$$
Respiratory therapists	37	43	$$$
Physical therapy assistants and aides	36	44	$$
Radiologic technologists and technicians	32	20	$$$
Medical secretaries	26	12	$$
Sales agents, real estate	26	9	$$$
Travel agents	25	18	$$
Surgical technologists	23	42	$$$
Drafters	18	6	$$$

SOURCE: Occupational Outlook Quarterly, Winter 1999–2000, vol. 43, no. 4

degree. By 2008 more than one-fifth (23 percent) of those employed will be in occupations requiring a bachelor's degree or higher. (See Table 5.3.)

A large amount of employment growth in occupations usually requiring a bachelor's degree or work experience plus a bachelor's degree or higher is projected from 1998–2008. Computer systems analysts, general managers, and top executives are projected to grow by 577,000 and 551,000 employees respectively. (See Figure 5.17.)

Postsecondary Vocational Training

Twenty occupations that usually require post-secondary vocational training will have employment growth

FIGURE 5.19

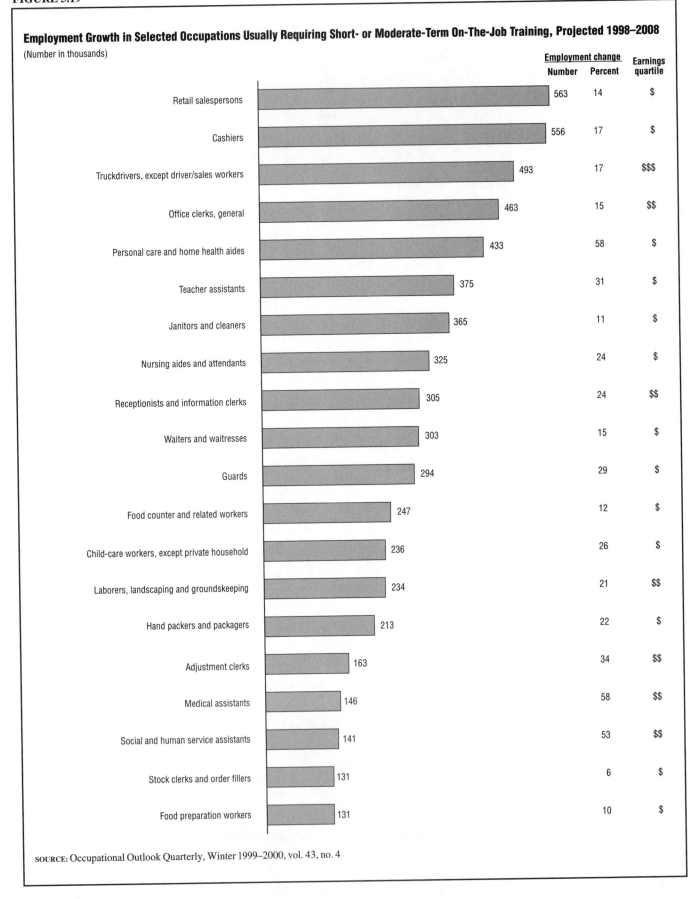

Employment Growth in Selected Occupations Usually Requiring Short- or Moderate-Term On-The-Job Training, Projected 1998–2008

(Number in thousands)

Occupation	Employment change Number	Employment change Percent	Earnings quartile
Retail salespersons	563	14	$
Cashiers	556	17	$
Truckdrivers, except driver/sales workers	493	17	$$$
Office clerks, general	463	15	$$
Personal care and home health aides	433	58	$
Teacher assistants	375	31	$
Janitors and cleaners	365	11	$
Nursing aides and attendants	325	24	$
Receptionists and information clerks	305	24	$$
Waiters and waitresses	303	15	$
Guards	294	29	$
Food counter and related workers	247	12	$
Child-care workers, except private household	236	26	$
Laborers, landscaping and groundskeeping	234	21	$$
Hand packers and packagers	213	22	$
Adjustment clerks	163	34	$$
Medical assistants	146	58	$$
Social and human service assistants	141	53	$$
Stock clerks and order fillers	131	6	$
Food preparation workers	131	10	$

SOURCE: Occupational Outlook Quarterly, Winter 1999–2000, vol. 43, no. 4

TABLE 5.4

Fastest Growing Occupations Projected to have the Largest Numerical Increase in Employment Between 1998 and 2008 by Level of Education and Training

Fastest growing occupations	Education/training category	Occupations having the largest numerical increase in employment
	First-professional degree	
Veterinarians Chiropractors Physicians Lawyers Clergy		Physicians Lawyers Clergy Veterinarians Pharmacists
	Doctoral degree	
Biological scientists Medical scientists College and university faculty Physicists and astronomers		College and university faculty Biological scientists Medical scientists Physicists and astronomers
	Master's degree	
Speech-language pathologists and audiologists Physical therapists Counselors Urban and regional planners Archivists, curators, and conservators		Counselors Physical therapists Speech-language pathologists and audiologists Psychologists Librarians
	Work experience plus bachelor's or higher degree	
Engineering, science, and computer systems managers Medical and health services managers Management analysts Artists and commercial artists Advertising, marketing, and public relations managers		General managers and top executives Engineering, science, and computer systems managers Advertising, marketing, and public relations managers Management analysts Financial managers
	Bachelor's degree	
Computer engineers Computer systems analysts Database administrators Physicians assistants Residential counselors		Computer systems analysts Computer engineers Teachers, secondary school Social workers Teachers, elementary school
	Associate degree	
Computer support specialists Paralegals and legal assistants Health information technicians Physical therapy assistants and aides Respiratory therapists		Registered nurses Computer support specialists Paralegals and legal assistants Dental hygienists Electrical and electronic technicians and technologists
	Postsecondary vocational training	
Data processing equipment repairers Surgical technologists Central office and PBX installers and repairers Emergency medical technicians Manicurists		Licensed practical nurses Automotive mechanics Hairstylists and cosmetologists Emergency medical technicians Data processing equipment repairers
	Work experience in a related occupation	
Private detectives and investigators Detectives and criminal investigators Instructors, adult (nonvocational) education Lawn service managers Office and administrative support supervisors		Office and administrative support supervisors Marketing and sales worker supervisors Blue-collar worker supervisors Food service and lodging managers Teachers and instructors, vocational education and training
	Long-term on-the-job training (more than 12 months)	
Desktop publishing specialists Correctional officers Sheriffs and deputy sheriffs Police patrol officers Telephone and cable TV line installers		Correction officers Cooks, restaurant Police patrol officers Maintenance repairers, general utility Carpenters
	Moderate-term on-the-job training (1 to 12 months)	
Medical assistants Social and human services assistants Electronic semiconductor processors Dental assistants Models, demonstrators, and product promoters		Medical assistants Social and human services assistants Instructors and coaches, sports and physical training Dental assistants Packaging and filling machine operators
	Short-term on-the-job training (up to 1 month)	
Personal care and home health aides Bill and account collectors Ambulance drivers and attendants, except emergency medical technicians Adjustment clerks Teacher assistants		Retail salespersons Cashiers Truck drivers, except driver/sales workers Office clerks, general Personal care and home health aides

SOURCE: *Occupational Outlook Handbook, 2000–01.* Bureau of Labor Statistics

TABLE 5.5

Fastest Growing Occupations, 1998–2008

[Numbers in thousands of jobs]

Occupation	Employment		Change		Quartile rank by 1997 median hourly earnings[1]	Education and training category
	1998	2008	Number	Percent		
Computer engineers	299	622	323	108	1	Bachelor's degree
Computer support specialists	429	869	439	102	1	Associate degree
Systems analysts	617	1,194	577	94	1	Bachelor's degree
Database administrators	87	155	67	77	1	Bachelor's degree
Desktop publishing specialists	26	44	19	73	2	Long-term on-the-job training
Paralegals and legal assistants	136	220	84	62	2	Associate degree
Personal care and home health aides	746	1,179	433	58	4	Short-term on-the-job training
Medical assistants	252	398	146	58	3	Moderate-term on-the-job training
Social and human service assistants	268	410	141	53	3	Moderate-term on-the-job training
Physician assistants	66	98	32	48	1	Bachelor's degree
Data processing equipment repairers	79	117	37	47	2	Postsecondary vocational training
Residential counselors	190	278	88	46	3	Bachelor's degree
Electronic semiconductor processors	63	92	29	45	2	Moderate-term on-the-job training
Medical records and health information technicians	92	133	41	44	3	Associate degree
Physical therapy assistants and aides	82	118	36	44	3	Associate degree
Engineering, natural science, and computer and information systems managers	326	468	142	43	1	Work experience plus bachelor's or higher degree
Respiratory therapists	86	123	37	43	2	Associate degree
Dental assistants	229	325	97	42	3	Moderate-term on-the-job training
Surgical technologists	54	77	23	42	2	Postsecondary vocational training
Securities, commodities, and financial services sales agents	303	427	124	41	1	Bachelor's degree
Dental hygienists	143	201	58	41	1	Associate degree
Occupational therapy assistants and aides	19	26	7	40	2	Associate degree
Cardiovascular technologists and technicians	21	29	8	39	2	Associate degree
Correctional officers	383	532	148	39	2	Long-term on-the-job training
Speech-language pathologists and audiologists	105	145	40	38	1	Master's degree
Social workers	604	822	218	36	2	Bachelor's degree
Bill and account collectors	311	420	110	35	3	Short-term on-the-job training
Ambulance drivers and attendants, except EMTs	19	26	7	35	3	Short-term on-the-job training
Biological scientists	81	109	28	35	1	Doctoral degree
Occupational therapists	73	98	25	34	1	Bachelor's degree

[1] The quartile rankings of Occupational Employment Statistics hourly earnings data are presented in the following categories: 1=very high ($16.25 and over), 2 = high ($10.89 to $16.14), 3 = low ($7.78 to $10.88), and 4 = very low (up to $7.76). The rankings were based on quartiles using one-fourth of total employment to define each quartile.

SOURCE: George T. Silvestri. *Occupational Employment Projections to 2006*. Monthly Labor Review, vol. 120, no. 11

between 1998 and 2008. The fastest growing occupations in this group include computer support specialists, paralegals, and data processing equipment repairers. (See Figure 5.18.)

Twenty selected occupations that usually require short- or moderate-term on-the-job training are projected to increase employment growth between 1998 to 2008. Of the 20 occupations, the fastest growing ones will include personal care and home health aides, medical assistants, and social and human service assistants. (See Figure 5.19.) Retail salespersons and cashiers will provide for the greatest increase in number of jobs between 1998 and 2008.

WHICH WILL BE THE BEST JOBS?

Many criteria are used for determining job quality. Occupational characteristics generally accepted as a mea-sure of future job quality include whether the number of jobs will increase, how much it pays, and whether a high percentage of those in that field are unemployed. In addition, individuals have personal desires and values that bring other factors into play in determining job quality, such as opportunities for self-employment for those who want to be their own boss or the opportunity to travel.

Remember, job growth can be measured both by percentage and numerical change. The fastest growing occupations do not necessarily provide the largest number of jobs. A larger occupation with slower growth may produce more openings than a smaller occupation with faster growth. See Table 5.4 for both the fastest growing occupations and occupations having the largest numerical increase in employment from 1998 to 2008, by level of education and training.

FIGURE 5.20

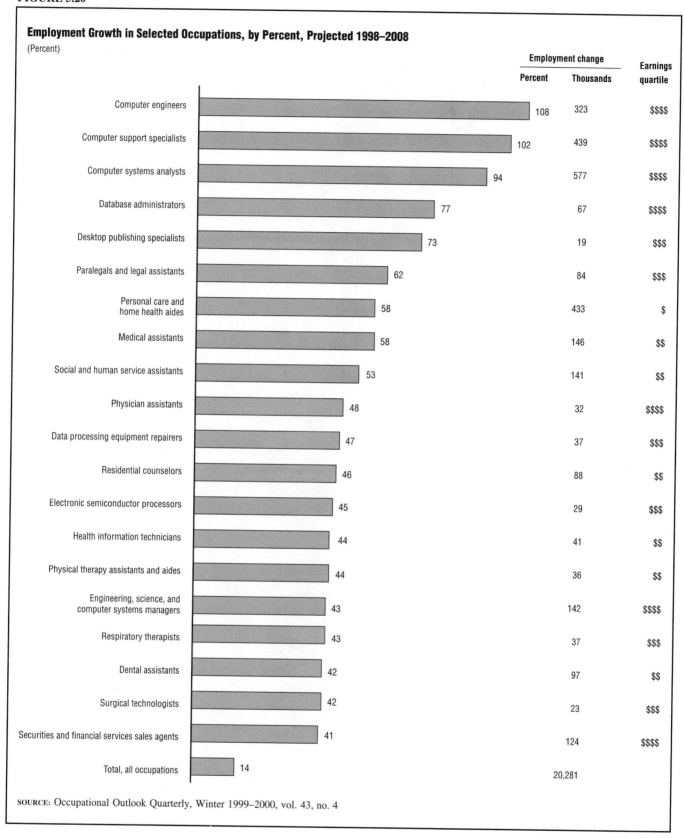

Employment Growth in Selected Occupations, by Percent, Projected 1998–2008

(Percent)

	Percent	Thousands	Earnings quartile
	Employment change		**Earnings quartile**
Computer engineers	108	323	$$$$
Computer support specialists	102	439	$$$$
Computer systems analysts	94	577	$$$$
Database administrators	77	67	$$$$
Desktop publishing specialists	73	19	$$$
Paralegals and legal assistants	62	84	$$$
Personal care and home health aides	58	433	$
Medical assistants	58	146	$$
Social and human service assistants	53	141	$$
Physician assistants	48	32	$$$$
Data processing equipment repairers	47	37	$$$
Residential counselors	46	88	$$
Electronic semiconductor processors	45	29	$$$
Health information technicians	44	41	$$
Physical therapy assistants and aides	44	36	$$
Engineering, science, and computer systems managers	43	142	$$$$
Respiratory therapists	43	37	$$$
Dental assistants	42	97	$$
Surgical technologists	42	23	$$$
Securities and financial services sales agents	41	124	$$$$
Total, all occupations	14	20,281	

SOURCE: Occupational Outlook Quarterly, Winter 1999–2000, vol. 43, no. 4

Fastest Projected Growth

Figure 5.20 shows the 20 occupations with the fastest projected employment growth over the 1998–2008 period. (See also Table 5.5 for 1998–2008 information on fastest-growing occupations, their edu- cation category, and percent and numerical change.) Most have high earnings and low unemployment rates. Eight of these occupations have a large proportion of employment in the health services sector and 8 are in computer-related services.

FIGURE 5.21

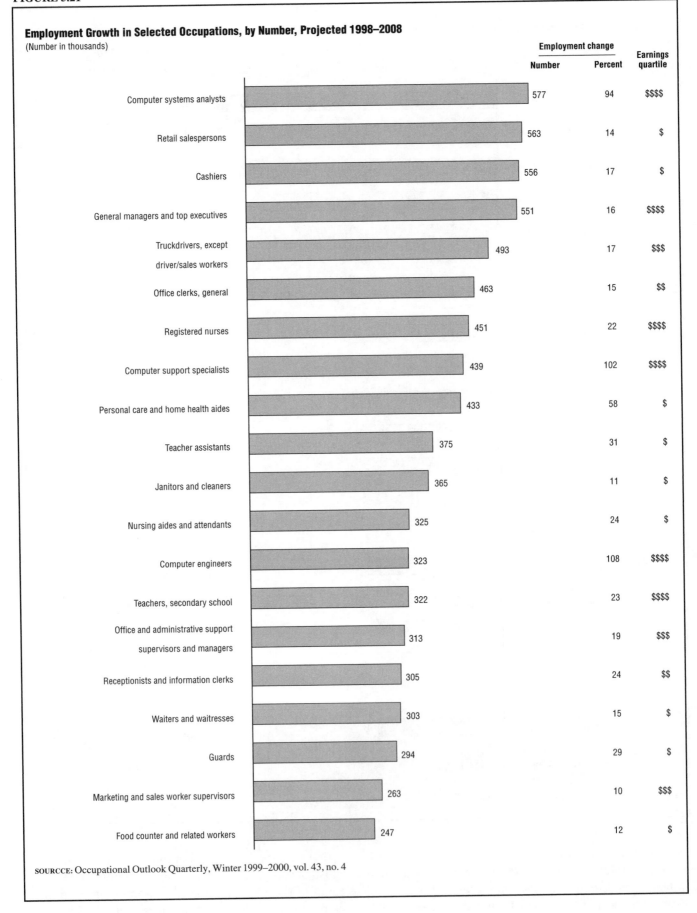

Employment Growth in Selected Occupations, by Number, Projected 1998–2008
(Number in thousands)

Occupation	Employment change		Earnings quartile
	Number	Percent	
Computer systems analysts	577	94	$$$$
Retail salespersons	563	14	$
Cashiers	556	17	$
General managers and top executives	551	16	$$$$
Truckdrivers, except driver/sales workers	493	17	$$$
Office clerks, general	463	15	$$
Registered nurses	451	22	$$$$
Computer support specialists	439	102	$$$$
Personal care and home health aides	433	58	$
Teacher assistants	375	31	$
Janitors and cleaners	365	11	$
Nursing aides and attendants	325	24	$
Computer engineers	323	108	$$$$
Teachers, secondary school	322	23	$$$$
Office and administrative support supervisors and managers	313	19	$$$
Receptionists and information clerks	305	24	$$
Waiters and waitresses	303	15	$
Guards	294	29	$
Marketing and sales worker supervisors	263	10	$$$
Food counter and related workers	247	12	$

SOURCCE: Occupational Outlook Quarterly, Winter 1999–2000, vol. 43, no. 4

TABLE 5.6

Occupations with the Largest Job Growth, 1996–2006

[Numbers in thousands of jobs]

Occupation	Employment		Change		Quartile rank by 1996 median weekly earnings of full-time workers[1]	Education and training category
	1996	2006	Number	Percent		
Cashiers	3,146	3,677	530	17	4	Short-term on-the-job training
Systems analysts	506	1,025	520	103	1	Bachelor's degree
General managers and top executives	3,210	3,677	467	15	1	Work experience plus bachelor's or higher degree
Registered nurses	1,971	2,382	411	21	1	Associate's degree
Salespersons, retail	4,072	4,481	408	10	3	Short-term on-the-job training
Truck drivers light and heavy	2,719	3,123	404	15	2	Short-term on-the-job training
Home health aides	495	873	378	76	4	Short-term on-the-job training
Teacher aides and educational assistants	981	1,352	370	38	4	Short-term on-the-job training
Nursing aides, orderlies, and attendants	1,312	1,645	333	25	4	Short-term on-the-job training
Receptionists and information clerks	1,074	1,392	318	30	4	Short-term on-the-job training
Teachers, secondary school	1,406	1,718	312	22	1	Bachelor's degree
Child care workers	830	1,129	299	36	4	Short-term on-the-job training
Clerical supervisors and managers	1,369	1,630	262	19	2	Work experience in a related occupation
Database administrators, computer support specialists, and all other computer scientists	212	461	249	118	1	Bachelor's degree
Marketing and sales worker supervisors	2,316	2,562	246	11	2	Work experience in a related occupation
Maintenance repairers, general utility	1,362	1,608	246	18	2	Short-term on-the-job training
Food counter, fountain, and related workers	1,720	1,963	243	14	4	Short-term on-the-job training
Teachers, special education	407	648	241	59	1	Bachelor's degree
Computer engineers	216	451	235	109	1	Bachelor's degree
Food preparation workers	1,253	1,487	234	19	4	Short-term on-the-job training
Hand packers and packagers	986	1,208	222	23	4	Short-term on-the-job training
Guards	955	1,175	221	23	3	Short-term on-the-job training
General office clerks	3,111	3,326	215	7	3	Short-term on-the-job training
Waiters and waitresses	1,957	2,163	206	11	4	Short-term on-the-job training
Social workers	585	772	188	32	2	Bachelor's degree
Adjustment clerks	401	584	183	46	3	Short-term on-the-job training
Cooks, short order and fast food	804	978	174	22	4	Short-term on-the-job training
Personal and home care aides	202	374	171	85	4	Short-term on-the-job training
Food service and lodging managers	589	757	168	28	2	Work experience in a related occupation
Medical assistants	225	391	166	74	3	Moderate-term on-the-job training

[1]The quartile rankings are presented in the following four categories, each representing the appropriate quartile from high to low: 1 = very high, 2 = high, 3 = low, 4 = very low. The rankings were based on quartiles using one-fourth of total employment to define each quartile.

SOURCE: George T. Silvestri. *Occupational Employment Projections to 2006.* Monthly Labor Review, vol. 120, no. 11

The health services sector will add over 3 million jobs by 2008. Personal and home care aides and home health aides will be in great demand to provide care for an increasing number of elderly people and for persons who are recovering from surgery and other serious health conditions. This category is increasing, as hospitals and insurance companies require shorter stays for recovery to reduce costs.

Computer engineers and systems analysts jobs are expected to grow rapidly in order to satisfy expanding needs of scientific research and applications of computer technology. The three fastest growing occupations are in computer-related fields. This industry will more than double its employment to 3.2 million workers over the 1998–2008 period.

Largest Job Growth

The 20 occupations with the largest projected employment growth rate account for more than one-third (39 percent) of the projected change in total employment over the 1998–2008 period. Three of these occupations have growth rates that are below average. The fastest growing occupations in this list include computer engineers, computer support specialists, and computer systems analysts. Twelve of the 20 occupations require short-term training on the job; 4 occupations require a bachelor's degree or higher education. (See Figure 5.20.) Figure 5.21 shows the occupations projected to gain the largest number of jobs between 1998–2008. (See also Table 5.6 for 1996–2006 information on fastest-growing occupations, their education category, and percent and numerical change.)

FIGURE 5.22

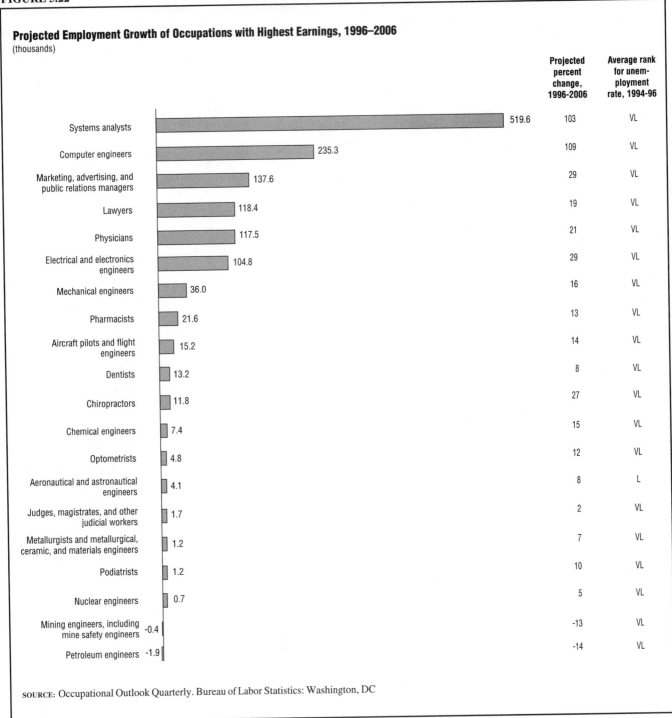

Projected Employment Growth of Occupations with Highest Earnings, 1996–2006
(thousands)

	Projected percent change, 1996-2006	Average rank for unemployment rate, 1994-96
Systems analysts 519.6	103	VL
Computer engineers 235.3	109	VL
Marketing, advertising, and public relations managers 137.6	29	VL
Lawyers 118.4	19	VL
Physicians 117.5	21	VL
Electrical and electronics engineers 104.8	29	VL
Mechanical engineers 36.0	16	VL
Pharmacists 21.6	13	VL
Aircraft pilots and flight engineers 15.2	14	VL
Dentists 13.2	8	VL
Chiropractors 11.8	27	VL
Chemical engineers 7.4	15	VL
Optometrists 4.8	12	VL
Aeronautical and astronautical engineers 4.1	8	L
Judges, magistrates, and other judicial workers 1.7	2	VL
Metallurgists and metallurgical, ceramic, and materials engineers 1.2	7	VL
Podiatrists 1.2	10	VL
Nuclear engineers 0.7	5	VL
Mining engineers, including mine safety engineers -0.4	-13	VL
Petroleum engineers -1.9	-14	VL

SOURCE: Occupational Outlook Quarterly. Bureau of Labor Statistics: Washington, DC

Highest Earnings

Between 1996–2006 the 20 occupations with the highest earnings all require at least a bachelor's degree. Engineering and health occupations dominate the list. Some of these occupations are very small and slow growing and will provide few opportunities for workers in the future. A few are projected to decline, generating openings only from replacement needs. All have low (L) to very low (VL) unemployment rates. (See Figure 5.22.)

LARGEST DECLINE IN EMPLOYMENT

An occupation's employment can decline because it is concentrated in a declining industry or because of changes to occupational staffing patterns. Office automation and other technological advances, declining industry employment, and changing legislation have adversely affected the occupations with the largest projected employment declines. Manufacturing and agriculture-related jobs, such as sewing machine operators and farmers, are examples of occupations that will lose

FIGURE 5.23

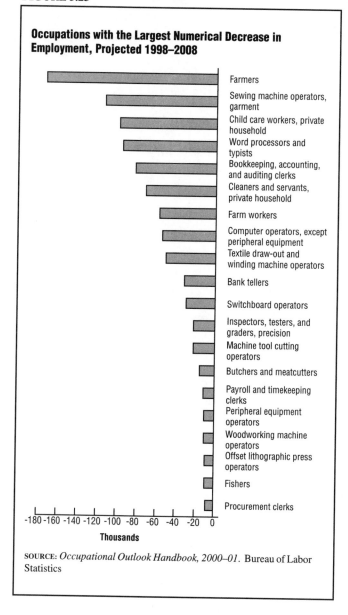

Occupations with the Largest Numerical Decrease in Employment, Projected 1998–2008

SOURCE: *Occupational Outlook Handbook, 2000–01.* Bureau of Labor Statistics

TABLE 5.7

Occupations with the Largest Job Decline, 1996–2006
(Numbers in thousands of jobs)

Occupation	Employment		Change	
	1996	2006	Number	Percent
Sewing machine operators, garment	453	334	-118	-26
Farmers	1,109	997	-112	-10
Bookkeeping, accounting, and auditing clerks	2,250	2,147	-102	-5
Typists, including word processing	653	552	-100	-15
Secretaries, except legal and medical	2,881	2,794	-87	-3
Cleaners and servants, private household	505	421	-84	-17
Computer operators, except peripheral equipment	258	181	-77	-30
Farm workers	873	798	-75	-9
Duplicating, mail, and other office machine operators	196	149	-47	-24
Welfare eligibility workers and interviewers	109	76	-34	-31
Textile draw-out and winding machine operators and tenders	183	155	-28	-15
Station installers and repairers, telephone	37	10	-27	-74
Child care workers, private household	275	250	-25	-9
Inspectors, testers, and graders, precision	634	610	-24	-4
Central office operators	48	26	-23	-47
Machine tool cutting operators and tenders, metal and plastic	127	105	-22	-17
Film strippers, printing	26	7	-20	-75
Peripheral computer equipment operators	33	17	-17	-50
Directory assistance operators	33	18	-16	-47
Custom tailors and sewers	87	73	-15	-17
Textile machine setters and set-up operators	41	27	-14	-34
Highway maintenance workers	171	158	-14	-8
Statistical clerks	78	65	-13	-17
Butchers and meatcutters	217	205	-12	-6
Paste-up workers	15	4	-11	-75
Typesetting and composing machine operators and tenders	14	3	-10	-75
Drilling and boring machine tool setters and set-up operators, metal and plastic	46	36	-10	-22
Proofreaders and copy markers	26	16	-10	-38
Lathe and turning machine tool setters and set-up operators, metal and plastic	71	61	-10	-14
Payroll and timekeeping clerks	161	151	-10	-6

SOURCE: George T. Silvestri. *Occupational Employment Projections to 2006.* Monthly Labor Review, vol. 120, no. 11

employment due to declining employment in some goods-producing industries. The use of typists will decline dramatically because of productivity improvements in office automation and the increased use of word processing equipment by professional and managerial employees. (See Figure 5.23 for 1998–2008 data and Table 5.7 for 1996–2006 data.) In the 1996–2006 data only 5 of the occupations have above average earnings, and 12 have higher than average unemployment rates.

Between 1996–2006 some occupations are projected to decline by 50 percent or more—telephone station installers and repairers, typesetting and composing machine operators, printing film strippers, and peripheral computer equipment operators. The conversion to desktop publishing technology in the printing and publishing industry will affect several of these occupations.

BEST OPPORTUNITIES FOR SELF-EMPLOYMENT

Many types of jobs provide opportunities for self-employment. Between 1996–2006, the largest concentration is made up of occupations requiring creativity, artistic ability, or design skills. Artists, designers, writers, photographers, and architects will account for one-fourth of the projected new jobs for self-employed or unpaid family workers. Fourteen of the 19 occupations with fast growth, high earnings, and low unemployment require at least a bachelor's degree. (See Figure 5.24.)

FIGURE 5.24

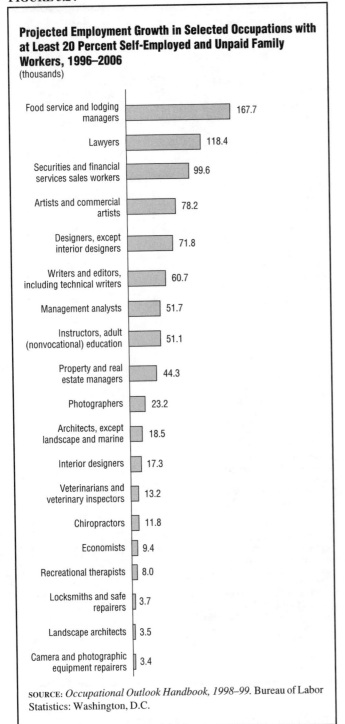

Projected Employment Growth in Selected Occupations with at Least 20 Percent Self-Employed and Unpaid Family Workers, 1996–2006
(thousands)

Food service and lodging managers	167.7
Lawyers	118.4
Securities and financial services sales workers	99.6
Artists and commercial artists	78.2
Designers, except interior designers	71.8
Writers and editors, including technical writers	60.7
Management analysts	51.7
Instructors, adult (nonvocational) education	51.1
Property and real estate managers	44.3
Photographers	23.2
Architects, except landscape and marine	18.5
Interior designers	17.3
Veterinarians and veterinary inspectors	13.2
Chiropractors	11.8
Economists	9.4
Recreational therapists	8.0
Locksmiths and safe repairers	3.7
Landscape architects	3.5
Camera and photographic equipment repairers	3.4

SOURCE: *Occupational Outlook Handbook, 1998–99.* Bureau of Labor Statistics: Washington, D.C.

CHAPTER 6
EARNINGS AND BENEFITS

EARNINGS

The federal government measures both the mean (average) of the nation's workers and the median earnings (one-half earn more than this figure, and one half earn less than this figure) of the nation's workers. Income is the total amount brought in by an individual or family, including earnings and money received from interest, pensions, etc. (See Chapter 4 for information on the relationship between education and income.)

In 1998 the population ages 15 and older had mean (average) earnings of $30,135. Whites earned slightly more ($31,215) than the mean, while blacks ($22,330) and those of Hispanic origin ($21,709) earned less. (See Table 6.1.) Males earned an average salary of $37,180, compared to $22,225 for females. The median earnings were $28,755 for males and $17,716 for females. (See Table 6.2.)

Full-Time, Year-Round Workers

Of the 77.3 million men 15 years old and over who reported working in 1998 (with or without earnings), 74 percent worked full-time, year-round. Of the 68.9 million

women 15 years old and over who reported working in 1998, 56 percent worked full-time, year-round.

In 1998 women working full-time, year-round, earned a median of $25,862, compared to $35,345 for men. Women's median earnings increased 2 percent from 1997 ($25,362), while men's increased 3.4 percent ($34,199). (See Table 6.3.) Figure 6.1 shows that since the mid-1970s through 1996, men's median earnings have generally been declining, while women's earnings have been increasing since the 1960s. These contrasting changes in earnings brought the female-to-male earnings ratio to an all-time high; in 1998 the median earnings for women were about 73 percent of the median for men.

Recent increases in the female-to-male earnings ratio have been due more to declines in the earnings of men than to increases in the earnings of women. (See Figure 6.1.) The last annual increase in men's median earnings was in 1991. Between 1993 and 1996 men's earnings declined by 2.6 percent. Between 1990 and 1996 the earnings of men have declined by 3.3 percent. For women, the change between 1990 to 1996 has been insignificant.

TABLE 6.1

Source of Income in 1998–Number with Income of Specified Type in 1998 of People 15 Years Old and Over by Age
[Numbers in thousands. People 15 years old and over as of March of the following year.]

Source of income	All races Number with income	All races Mean income (dollars)	White Number with income	White Mean income (dollars)	Black Number with income	Black Mean income (dollars)	Hispanic origin Number with income	Hispanic origin Mean income (dollars)
TOTAL, 15 YEARS AND OVER								
Total	193,642	28,236	162,959	29,314	22,048	20,609	18,022	20,105
Earnings	146,141	30,135	122,703	31,215	16,612	22,330	14,683	21,709
Wages and salary	137,209	29,849	114,717	30,914	16,110	22,375	14,058	21,660
Nonfarm self-employment	12,110	24,081	10,787	24,818	771	13,114	790	17,559
Farm self-employment	2,019	8,267	1,868	8,634	101	3,563	58	(B)

SOURCE: *Money Income in the United States: 1998.* U.S. Census Bureau, March 2000

TABLE 6.2

Work Experience in 1998—Total Money Earnings in 1998 of People 15 Years Old and Over by Gender

[Numbers in thousands. People 15 years old and over as of March of the following year.]

| Total money earnings | | Total | Worked | | | | | | | | | Did not work |
| | | | Total | Worked at full-time jobs | | | | Worked at part-time jobs | | | | |
				Total	50 weeks or more	27 to 49 weeks	26 weeks or less	Total	50 weeks or more	27 to 49 weeks	26 weeks or less	
MALE												
Median earnings	dollars	28,755	28,755	31,750	35,345	20,027	5,658	5,179	8,972	6,258	1,874	(B)
Standard error	dollars	233	233	111	133	419	199	127	252	185	49	(B)
Mean earnings	dollars	37,180	37,180	41,268	44,866	28,745	10,542	9,665	14,812	9,934	3,525	(B)
Standard error	dollars	295	295	328	361	1,069	611	330	682	519	235	(B)
Gini ratio		.465	.465	.421	.389	.461	.575	.605	.533	.523	.602	(B)
Standard error		.0049	.0049	.0052	.0057	.0203	.0242	.0171	.0266	.0356	.0354	(B)
FEMALE												
Median earnings	dollars	17,716	17,716	23,047	25,862	16,129	4,715	6,105	9,995	6,284	1,938	(B)
Standard error	dollars	161	161	170	118	320	121	87	146	138	39	(B)
Mean earnings	dollars	22,225	22,225	27,394	30,660	20,752	7,629	9,337	13,300	8,867	3,498	(B)
Standard error	dollars	176	176	217	261	351	259	234	362	485	353	(B)
Gini ratio		.457	.457	.379	.335	.385	.541	.536	.441	.481	.585	(B)
Standard error		.0048	.0048	.0057	.0065	.0152	.0216	.0106	.0145	.0325	.0277	(B)

SOURCE: *Money Income in the United States: 1998*. U.S. Census Bureau, March 2000

Production or Nonsupervisory Earnings

In 1999 production or nonsupervisory workers on private nonfarm payrolls worked an average of 34.5 hours a week and earned a mean salary of $13.24 per hour. Hourly salaries varied by industry. People employed in the services industry worked an average of 32.6 hours and earned close to the total average—$13.38. On the other hand, those in retail trade worked fewer hours (29) and earned an average hourly wage of $9.08. Mining and construction workers earned more than the total average earnings, bringing in $17.04 and $17.13 per hour, respectively. Workers in both categories also worked longer hours per week. (See Table 6.4.)

Occupations

In 1999 full-time wage and salary workers earned a median of $549 per week. Those working in managerial and professional specialties and in precision production, craft, and repair earned more. However, within each occupational grouping, many categories earned significantly more or less than the median wage. Managers in marketing, advertising, and public relations had the highest weekly wages ($1,036) among managerial occupations, while managers of food serving and lodging establishments earned the least ($524). Among professional specialty occupations, physicians ($1,266), chemical engineers ($1,260), and aerospace engineers ($1,201) headed the list of salaries, while prekindergarten and kindergarten teachers ($440) and recreation workers ($416) made the lowest median weekly earnings. (See Table 6.5.)

While those in sales occupations ($523) generally earned less than the median earnings of all workers, sales representatives of commodities, except retail, ($749) earned far more than others. Sales workers in retail and personal services ($329) had the lowest salaries among those in sales occupations. (See Table 6.5.)

Administrative support personnel earned a median salary of $447. Supervisors earned $603, while secretaries received $443. (See Table 6.5.)

In the technical, sales, and administrative support field, airline pilots and navigators ($1,048) and computer programmers ($898) earned far more than the median salaries. Service occupations were among the lowest paid workers. Within the category, child-care workers ($211) and private household workers ($243) earned the lowest salaries. Police and detectives ($817) had the highest. (See Table 6.5.)

In the precision production, craft, and repair grouping, supervisors of mechanics and repairers ($816) and telephone installers and repairers ($770) earned the highest salaries, while several categories in precision jobs were among the lowest. In the operators, fabricators, and laborers category, textile and sewing machine operators ($282) and pressing machine operators ($268) were among the lowest paid. Separating, filtering, and clarifying machine operators earned $648, the highest in this category. Among transportation and material moving occupations, garage and service station-related jobs ($312) were among the lowest paid, while those in railroad transportation earned $816. (See Table 6.5.) See the *Occupational Outlook Handbook* (Bureau of Labor Statistics) for detailed descriptions of each job.

TABLE 6.3

Comparison of Summary Measures of Income by Selected Characteristics, 1989, 1997, and 1998

[Households and people as of March of the following year.]

Characteristics	1998 Median income — Number (1,000)	Value (dollars)	90-percent confidence interval (+/-) (dollars)	Median income in 1997 (in 1998 dollars) — Value (dollars)	90-percent confidence interval (+/-) (dollars)	Median income in 1989[r] (in 1998 dollars) — Value (dollars)	90-percent confidence interval (+/-) (dollars)	Percent change in real income 1997 to 1998 — Percent change	90-percent confidence interval (+/-)	Percent change in real income 1989[r] to 1998 — Percent change	90-percent confidence interval (+/-)
HOUSEHOLDS											
All households	103,874	38,885	378	37,581	286	37,884	344	*3.5	0.6	*2.6	0.8
Type of Household											
Family households	71,535	47,469	410	46,053	394	45,343	413	*3.1	0.6	*4.7	0.8
Married-couple families	54,770	54,276	530	52,486	388	50,702	458	*3.4	0.6	*7.0	0.9
Female householder, no husband present	12,789	24,393	655	23,399	657	22,662	603	*4.2	2.0	*7.6	2.5
Male householder, no wife present	3,976	39,414	1,633	37,205	1,201	39,717	1,607	*5.9	2.8	−0.8	3.5
Nonfamily households	32,339	23,441	467	22,043	347	22,568	363	*6.3	1.3	*3.9	1.6
Female householder	17,971	18,615	462	17,887	428	18,143	474	*4.1	1.8	2.6	2.2
Male householder	14,368	30,414	559	28,022	770	29,489	660	*8.5	1.8	*3.1	1.8
Race and Hispanic Origin of Householder											
All races[1]	103,874	38,885	378	37,581	286	37,884	344	*3.5	0.6	*2.6	0.8
White	87,212	40,912	336	39,579	413	39,852	320	*3.4	0.7	*2.7	0.7
Non-Hispanic White	78,577	42,439	401	41,209	354	40,792	331	*3.0	0.6	*4.0	0.8
Black	12,579	25,351	653	25,440	720	23,950	789	−0.3	1.9	*5.8	2.7
Asian and Pacific Islander	3,308	46,637	2,135	45,954	2,102	47,337	2,007	1.5	3.2	−1.5	3.7
Hispanic origin[2]	9,060	28,330	898	27,043	792	28,631	882	*4.8	1.8	−1.1	2.7
Age of Householder											
15 to 24 years	5,770	23,564	730	22,935	822	24,401	755	2.7	2.4	−3.4	2.6
25 to 34 years	18,819	40,069	696	38,769	755	39,041	603	*3.4	1.3	*2.6	1.5
35 to 44 years	23,968	48,451	730	47,081	637	49,310	675	*2.9	1.0	−1.7	1.2
45 to 54 years	20,158	54,148	877	52,683	727	54,575	893	*2.8	1.1	−0.8	1.4
55 to 64 years	13,571	43,167	989	42,000	763	40,569	878	*2.8	1.5	*6.4	2.0
65 years and over	21,589	21,729	395	21,084	406	20,719	381	*3.1	1.3	*4.9	1.6
Nativity of the Householder											
Native born	92,853	39,677	390	38,229	381	(NA)	(NA)	*3.8	0.7	(X)	(X)
Foreign born	11,021	32,963	1,230	31,806	802	(NA)	(NA)	3.6	2.3	(X)	(X)
Naturalized citizen	4,877	41,028	1,808	(NA)	(NA)	(NA)	(NA)	(X)	(X)	(X)	(X)
Not a citizen	6,143	28,278	1,199	27,379	971	(NA)	(NA)	3.3	2.8	(X)	(X)
Region											
Northeast	19,877	40,634	772	39,535	877	42,780	709	*2.8	1.5	*−5.0	1.5
Midwest	24,489	40,609	600	38,913	747	37,685	642	*4.4	1.3	*7.8	1.5
South	36,959	35,797	500	34,880	580	33,933	471	*2.6	1.1	*5.5	1.3
West	22,549	40,983	661	39,772	910	40,705	696	*3.0	1.4	0.7	1.4
Residence											
Inside metropolitan areas	83,441	40,983	352	39,994	448	40,776	346	*2.5	0.7	0.5	0.7
Inside central cities	32,144	33,151	638	32,039	456	(NA)	(NA)	*3.5	1.5	(X)	(X)
Outside central cities	51,297	46,402	512	45,364	568	(NA)	(NA)	*2.3	0.8	(X)	(X)
Outside metropolitan areas	20,433	32,022	630	30,525	690	29,393	636	*4.9	1.5	*8.9	1.9
EARNINGS OF FULL-TIME, YEAR-ROUND WORKERS											
Male	56,951	35,345	219	34,199	535	35,727	242	*3.4	0.9	*−1.1	0.6
Female	38,785	25,862	194	25,362	259	24,614	270	*2.0	0.7	*5.1	0.9
PER CAPITA INCOME											
All races[1]	271,743	20,120	199	19,541	202	18,280	132	*3.0	0.7	*10.1	0.8
White	223,294	21,394	237	20,743	239	19,385	147	*3.1	0.8	*10.4	0.8
Non-Hispanic White	193,074	22,952	268	22,246	271	(NA)	(NA)	*3.2	0.9	(X)	(X)
Black	35,070	12,957	322	12,543	346	11,406	253	*3.3	1.9	*13.6	2.1
Asian and Pacific Islander	10,897	18,709	1,094	18,510	1,128	(NA)	(NA)	1.1	4.4	(X)	(X)
Hispanic origin[2]	31,689	11,434	410	10,941	393	10,770	294	*4.5	2.3	*6.2	2.7

*Statistically significant change at the 90-percent confidence level.

[r] Revised to reflect the population distribution reported in the 1990 census.

[1] Data for American Indians, Eskimos, and Aleuts are not shown separately. Data for this population group are not tabulated from the CPS because of its small size.

[2] Hispanics may be of any race.

SOURCE: *Money Income in the United States: 1998.* U.S. Census Bureau, March 2000

FIGURE 6.1

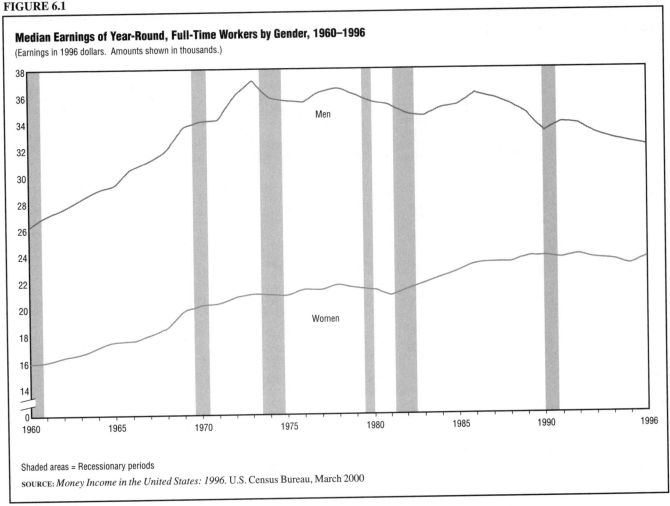

Median Earnings of Year-Round, Full-Time Workers by Gender, 1960–1996

(Earnings in 1996 dollars. Amounts shown in thousands.)

Shaded areas = Recessionary periods

SOURCE: *Money Income in the United States: 1996.* U.S. Census Bureau, March 2000

Starting Salaries for New College Graduates

L. Patrick Scheetz, in *Recruiting Trends: 1997–98* (27 th Edition, Career Services and Placement, Michigan State University, East Lansing, Michigan, December 5, 1997), found that the expanding economy offered recent graduates greater opportunities in the workplace. The engineering fields offered the highest starting salaries for college graduates. Those majoring in education and telecommunications had the lowest starting salaries. (See Table 6.6.) According to the National Association of Colleges and Employers (NACE), starting salaries for liberal arts majors were higher in 1996 than in 1995. For example, the salaries of journalism graduates went up 14.9 percent to an average of $22,897. Political science majors had a 9.2 percent rise in their salaries, starting with an average of $26,924.

EMPLOYEE BENEFITS

Medium and Large Private Establishments

In 1997, the most recent year for such data, most workers at medium and large private establishments had paid holidays (89 percent) and paid vacations (95 percent). The proportion has gone down somewhat from

1984 when 99 percent had paid holidays and paid vacations. Over one-half (56 percent) of these employees had paid sick leave, down from the 67 percent of 1984, but only 20 percent got paid personal leave. Unpaid family leave has become a major benefit. Ninety-three percent of 1997 full-time employees got unpaid family leave, compared to 84 percent in 1995. (See Table 6.7.)

Three of four employees (76 percent) in medium and large private establishments had employer-provided medical care plans, down significantly from 97 percent in 1984. In addition, in 1984 only 36 percent had to contribute to their own insurance coverage. By 1997, 69 percent had to contribute. The average monthly contribution rose from about $12.00 in the mid-1980s to $39.14 in 1997. Almost nine of ten of these employees were participants in life insurance plans; however, only two of five (43 percent) had long-term disability insurance plans. (See Table 6.7.)

Small Private Establishments

In 1996 a smaller proportion of employees who worked for small private establishments had paid holidays (80 percent). Only 50 percent of these workers got

TABLE 6.4

Average Hours and Earnings of Production or Nonsupervisory Workers[1] on Private Nonfarm Payrolls by Major Industry, 1990–1999

Year and month	Total private[1]			Mining			Construction		
	Weekly hours	Hourly earnings	Weekly earnings	Weekly hours	Hourly earnings	Weekly earnings	Weekly hours	Hourly earnings	Weekly earnings
ANNUAL AVERAGES									
1990	34.5	10.01	345.35	44.1	13.68	603.29	38.2	13.77	526.01
1991	34.3	10.32	353.98	44.4	14.19	630.04	38.1	14.00	533.40
1992	34.4	10.57	363.61	43.9	14.54	638.31	38.0	14.15	537.70
1993	34.5	10.83	373.64	44.3	14.60	646.78	38.5	14.38	553.63
1994	34.7	11.12	385.86	44.8	14.88	666.62	38.9	14.73	573.00
1995	34.5	11.43	394.34	44.7	15.30	683.91	38.9	15.09	587.00
1996	34.4	11.82	406.61	45.3	15.62	707.59	39.0	15.47	603.33
1997	34.6	12.28	424.89	45.4	16.15	733.21	39.0	16.04	625.56
1998	34.6	12.78	442.19	43.9	16.90	741.91	38.8	16.59	643.69
1999	34.5	13.24	456.78	43.8	17.04	746.35	39.0	17.13	668.07
MONTHLY DATA, NOT SEASONALLY ADJUSTED									
1999:									
April	34.3	$13.16	$451.39	43.3	$16.93	$733.07	38.6	$16.85	$650.41
May	34.6	13.19	456.37	44.2	17.00	751.40	39.3	17.02	668.89
June	34.6	13.14	454.64	44.2	16.93	748.31	39.8	17.08	679.78
July	34.7	13.15	456.31	44.7	17.12	765.26	39.9	17.22	687.08
August	35.1	13.20	463.32	44.5	17.01	756.95	40.0	17.26	690.40
September	34.3	13.38	458.93	44.4	17.10	759.24	38.6	17.41	672.03
October	34.6	13.41	463.99	44.6	17.00	758.20	40.0	17.49	699.60
November	34.5	13.43	463.34	44.7	16.95	757.67	39.5	17.37	686.12
December	34.6	13.47	466.06	44.4	17.13	760.57	38.7	17.42	674.15
2000:									
January	34.4	13.58	467.15	44.3	17.24	763.73	38.3	17.34	664.12
February	34.2	13.58	464.44	44.2	17.13	757.15	38.6	17.37	670.48
March[p]	34.2	13.60	465.12	43.9	17.17	753.76	38.8	17.48	678.22
April[p]	34.6	13.71	474.37	44.7	17.22	769.73	39.1	17.60	688.16

Year and month	Manufacturing				Transportation and public utilities			Wholesale trade		
	Weekly hours	Hourly earnings	Hourly earnings, excluding overtime	Weekly earnings	Weekly hours	Hourly earnings	Weekly earnings	Weekly hours	Hourly earnings	Weekly earnings
ANNUAL AVERAGES										
1990	40.8	10.83	10.37	441.86	38.4	12.92	496.13	38.1	10.79	411.10
1991	40.7	11.18	10.71	455.03	38.1	13.20	502.92	38.1	11.15	424.82
1992	41.0	11.46	10.95	469.86	38.3	13.43	514.37	38.2	11.39	435.10
1993	41.4	11.74	11.18	486.04	39.3	13.55	532.52	38.2	11.74	448.47
1994	42.0	12.07	11.43	506.94	39.7	13.78	547.07	38.4	12.06	463.10
1995	41.6	12.37	11.74	514.59	39.4	14.13	556.72	38.3	12.43	476.07
1996	41.6	12.77	12.12	531.23	39.6	14.45	572.22	38.3	12.87	492.92
1997	42.0	13.17	12.45	553.14	39.7	14.92	592.32	38.4	13.45	516.48
1998	41.7	13.49	12.79	562.53	39.5	15.31	604.75	38.4	14.06	539.90
1999	41.7	13.91	13.18	580.05	38.7	15.67	606.43	38.4	14.59	560.26
MONTHLY DATA, NOT SEASONALLY ADJUSTED										
1999:										
April	41.6	$13.80	$13.10	$574.08	38.6	$15.57	$601.00	38.3	$14.48	$554.58
May	41.7	13.85	13.14	577.55	38.8	15.55	603.34	38.6	14.53	560.86
June	41.8	13.91	13.17	581.44	39.0	15.56	606.84	38.4	14.44	554.50
July	41.2	13.92	13.20	573.50	38.9	15.66	609.17	38.4	14.55	558.72
August	41.8	13.95	13.20	583.11	39.4	15.67	617.40	38.7	14.65	566.96
September	41.7	14.11	13.33	588.39	38.5	15.78	607.53	38.3	14.73	564.16
October	42.0	14.04	13.27	589.68	38.4	15.76	605.18	38.6	14.78	570.51
November	42.2	14.08	13.31	594.18	38.3	15.87	607.82	38.4	14.82	569.09
December	42.5	14.21	13.41	603.93	38.4	15.94	612.10	38.5	14.91	574.04
2000:										
January	41.6	14.19	13.47	590.30	38.2	15.95	609.29	38.5	15.06	579.81
February	41.5	14.19	13.47	588.89	38.1	16.02	610.36	38.2	14.95	571.09
March[p]	41.5	14.22	13.50	590.13	38.0	16.01	608.38	38.2	14.94	570.71
April[p]	41.7	14.30	13.56	596.31	38.7	16.14	624.62	38.9	15.13	588.56

TABLE 6.4

Average Hours and Earnings of Production or Nonsupervisory Workers[1] on Private Nonfarm Payrolls by Major Industry, 1990–1999

[CONTINUED]

Year and month	Retail trade			Finance, insurance, and real estate			Services		
	Weekly hours	Hourly earnings	Weekly earnings	Weekly hours	Hourly earnings	Weekly earnings	Weekly hours	Hourly earnings	Weekly earnings
				ANNUAL AVERAGES					
1990	28.8	6.75	194.40	35.8	9.97	356.93	32.5	9.83	319.48
1991	28.6	6.94	198.48	35.7	10.39	370.92	32.4	10.23	331.45
1992	28.8	7.12	205.06	35.8	10.82	387.36	32.5	10.54	342.55
1993	28.8	7.29	209.95	35.8	11.35	406.33	32.5	10.78	350.35
1994	28.9	7.49	216.46	35.8	11.83	423.51	32.5	11.04	358.80
1995	28.8	7.69	221.47	35.9	12.32	442.29	32.4	11.39	369.04
1996	28.8	7.99	230.11	35.9	12.80	459.52	32.4	11.79	382.00
1997	28.9	8.33	240.74	36.1	13.34	481.57	32.6	12.28	400.33
1998	29.0	8.73	253.17	36.4	14.06	511.78	32.6	12.85	418.91
1999	29.0	9.08	263.32	36.2	14.61	528.88	32.6	13.38	436.19
				MONTHLY DATA, NOT SEASONALLY ADJUSTED					
1999:									
April	28.7	$9.03	$259.16	35.9	$14.61	$524.50	32.4	$13.32	$431.57
May	29.1	9.03	262.77	36.4	14.72	535.81	32.7	13.34	436.22
June	29.4	9.02	265.19	35.9	14.50	520.55	32.6	13.23	431.30
July	29.8	9.02	268.80	36.2	14.53	525.99	32.8	13.20	432.96
August	29.9	9.04	270.30	36.9	14.61	539.11	33.2	13.25	439.90
September	28.8	9.18	264.38	36.0	14.63	526.68	32.3	13.48	435.40
October	28.8	9.20	264.96	36.1	14.68	529.95	32.7	13.54	442.76
November	28.7	9.21	264.33	36.0	14.73	530.28	32.7	13.60	444.72
December	29.3	9.25	271.03	36.2	14.75	533.95	32.6	13.69	446.29
2000:									
January	28.5	9.33	265.91	36.7	14.97	549.40	32.7	13.81	451.59
February	28.5	9.34	266.19	36.1	14.92	538.61	32.6	13.80	449.88
March[p]	28.6	9.36	267.70	35.9	14.96	537.06	32.5	13.81	448.83
April[p]	29.0	9.42	273.18	36.7	15.15	556.01	32.9	13.89	456.98

[1]Data relate to production workers in mining and manufacturing; construction workers in construction; and nonsupervisory workers in transportation and public utilities; wholesale and retail trade; finance, insurance, and real estate; and services.

[p] = preliminary.

NOTE: Establishment survey estimates are currently projected from March 1998 benchmark levels. When more recent benchmark data are introduced, all unadjusted data from April 1998 forward are subject to revision.

SOURCE: *Current Employment Statistics.* Bureau of Labor Statistics, May 2000

paid sick leave. Even fewer (14 percent) got paid personal leave. Less than half (48 percent) of employees of small private firms received unpaid family leave. Approximately two-thirds were participants in medical-care plans, with 52 percent contributing a monthly contribution of $42.63. A majority of the workers (62 percent) participated in employer-provided life insurance plans, but only 15 percent of those working for small business firms had pension plans. (See Table 6.8.)

State and Local Governments

About three-fourths (73 percent) of employees of state and local governments had paid holidays in 1994. However, most (94 percent) received paid sick leave. One in four (38 percent) got paid personal leave. Unpaid family leave was a benefit that 93 percent of state and local government employees received. Most (87 percent) participated in employer-provided life insurance plans and medical-care plans with 47 percent of the participants contributing a monthly contribution of $30.20 to the

health plan. Nine of ten (91 percent) were provided with a pension plan. (See Table 6.8.)

TYPES OF EMPLOYEES. In 1996 blue-collar and service employees of small private establishments were less likely than other types of employees to participate in employee benefit programs. For example, while 56 percent of blue-collar and service employees had medical care benefits, 69 percent of clerical and sales employees and 76 percent of professional and technical employees did. Nearly three-fourths (71 percent) of the blue-collar and service workers got paid holidays, compared to 91 percent of clerical and sales employees and 86 percent of professional and technical employees. (See Table 6.9.)

Blue-collar and service employees of state and local governments in most cases fared better than did other state and local government employees. More of them (91 percent) got paid holidays and vacations than did the white-collar employees (86 and 84 percent, respectively). Only one-third of the teachers got paid holidays, and only 9 per-

TABLE 6.5

Median Weekly Earnings of Full-Time Wage and Salary Workers by Detailed Occupation and Gender

(Numbers in thousands)

Occupation	1999					
	Both sexes		Men		Women	
	Number of workers	Median weekly earnings	Number of workers	Median weekly earnings	Number of workers	Median weekly earnings
Total, 16 years and over	97,626	$549	55,181	$618	42,444	$473
Managerial and professional specialty	30,704	797	15,537	952	15,167	681
Executive, administrative, and managerial	14,973	792	7,981	967	6,992	652
Administrators and officials, public administration	610	877	300	1,007	310	725
Administrators, protective services	55	889	44	([1])	11	([1])
Financial managers	697	878	344	1,154	353	703
Personnel and labor relations managers	181	831	74	1,014	108	742
Purchasing managers	139	803	74	989	65	699
Managers, marketing, advertising, and public relations	695	1,036	441	1,241	254	800
Administrators, education and related fields	703	913	282	1,076	420	819
Managers, medicine and health	602	759	139	1,006	462	714
Managers, food serving and lodging establishments	946	524	498	617	449	461
Managers, properties and real estate	338	600	149	679	189	578
Management-related occupations	4,026	704	1,677	847	2,349	630
Accountants and auditors	1,362	723	549	891	813	651
Underwriters	119	744	39	([1])	80	653
Other financial officers	684	758	324	923	360	615
Management analysts	244	908	126	1,080	118	790
Personnel, training, and labor relations specialists	475	674	149	727	326	653
Buyers, wholesale and retail trade, except farm products	140	643	75	675	65	588
Construction inspectors	67	730	63	748	4	([1])
Inspectors and compliance officers, except construction	234	755	161	772	73	707
Professional specialty	15,731	800	7,556	939	8,175	707
Engineers, architects, and surveyors	2,084	1,033	1,865	1,052	219	907
Architects	129	918	108	983	21	([1])
Engineers	1,945	1,041	1,749	1,058	197	933
Aerospace engineers	84	1,201	74	1,202	10	([1])
Chemical engineers	75	1,260	62	1,312	13	([1])
Civil engineers	255	965	229	984	25	([1])
Electrical and electronic engineers	618	1,073	564	1,087	55	956
Industrial engineers	259	970	216	991	43	([1])
Mechanical engineers	324	1,035	304	1,041	19	([1])
Mathematical and computer scientists	1,638	983	1,117	1,056	522	876
Computer systems analysts and scientists	1,348	1,008	959	1,079	390	907
Operations and systems researchers and analysts	242	864	128	952	115	781
Natural scientists	514	873	370	939	143	731
Chemists, except biochemists	131	970	100	1,002	31	([1])
Physical scientists, n.e.c	50	987	38	([1])	12	([1])
Biological and life scientists	95	762	52	801	42	([1])
Medical scientists	93	724	54	800	38	([1])
Health diagnosing occupations	539	1,192	389	1,342	150	888
Physicians	460	1,266	335	1,364	125	852
Health assessment and treating occupations	2,219	760	368	887	1,851	746
Registered nurses	1,585	750	141	791	1,443	747
Pharmacists	165	1,159	88	1,222	77	1,105
Dietitians	55	577	8	([1])	47	([1])
Therapists	356	728	101	793	256	707
Respiratory therapists	69	689	31	([1])	38	([1])
Physical therapists	86	877	28	([1])	58	808
Speech therapists	65	780	5	([1])	61	770
Physicians' assistants	58	908	29	([1])	29	([1])
Teachers, college and university	638	953	397	1,038	241	859
Teachers, except college and university	4,259	688	1,130	768	3,129	659
Teachers, prekindergarten and kindergarten	432	440	9	([1])	423	442
Teachers, elementary school	1,837	710	308	785	1,529	697
Teachers, secondary school	1,179	756	521	803	658	722
Teachers, special education	326	677	53	744	273	664
Counselors, educational and vocational	207	786	62	902	144	742
Librarians, archivists, and curators	210	701	39	([1])	171	684
Librarians	183	700	32	([1])	151	684
Social scientists and urban planners	306	740	142	847	164	682
Economists	120	863	57	977	63	774
Psychologists	141	673	55	760	86	623

See footnotes at end of table.

TABLE 6.5

Median Weekly Earnings of Full-Time Wage and Salary Workers by Detailed Occupation and Gender [CONTINUED]

(Numbers in thousands)

	1999					
	Both sexes		Men		Women	
Occupation	Number of workers	Median weekly earnings	Number of workers	Median weekly earnings	Number of workers	Median weekly earnings
Social, recreation, and religious workers	1,177	596	542	654	634	557
Social workers	705	601	220	661	485	579
Recreation workers	85	416	27	(1)	58	417
Clergy	295	657	256	676	38	(1)
Lawyers and judges	613	1,198	412	1,369	201	971
Lawyers	577	1,168	386	1,340	191	974
Writers, artists, entertainers, and athletes	1,327	681	722	748	604	605
Technical writers	63	861	25	(1)	38	(1)
Designers	453	642	233	757	220	512
Actors and directors	65	784	45	(1)	20	(1)
Painters, sculptors, craft artists, and artist printmakers	93	595	52	647	41	(1)
Photographers	56	617	47	(1)	9	(1)
Editors and reporters	212	750	113	803	98	709
Public relations specialists	155	735	58	881	97	684
Athletes	54	613	46	(1)	8	(1)
Technical, sales, and administrative support	27,388	488	10,525	626	16,863	431
Technicians and related support	3,550	618	1,802	728	1,749	528
Health technologists and technicians	1,304	511	292	594	1,011	489
Clinical laboratory technologists and technicians	292	623	77	709	215	593
Radiologic technicians	139	619	40	(1)	99	596
Licensed practical nurses	259	498	16	(1)	243	492
Engineering and related technologists and technicians	874	662	716	673	158	625
Electrical and electronic technicians	412	690	348	701	64	649
Drafting occupations	212	665	177	663	35	(1)
Surveying and mapping technicians	51	557	44	(1)	7	(1)
Science technicians	250	582	150	656	100	480
Biological technicians	86	500	36	(1)	50	388
Chemical technicians	71	677	46	(1)	25	(1)
Technicians, except health, engineering, and science	1,122	761	643	902	479	624
Airplane pilots and navigators	99	1,048	97	1,050	3	(1)
Computer programmers	564	898	405	935	159	788
Legal assistants	313	589	43	(1)	270	581
Sales occupations	9,728	523	5,402	666	4,326	399
Supervisors and proprietors	3,275	587	1,924	691	1,351	454
Sales representatives, finance and business services	1,817	708	1,019	821	798	589
Insurance sales	391	622	201	750	190	539
Real estate sales	364	657	173	767	191	585
Securities and financial services sales	399	791	276	979	123	616
Advertising and related sales	155	747	66	892	88	626
Sales occupations, other business services	508	721	302	809	206	611
Sales representatives, commodities, except retail	1,279	749	968	792	311	610
Sales workers, retail and personal services	3,324	329	1,475	423	1,849	296
Sales workers, motor vehicles and boats	268	665	240	679	29	(1)
Sales workers, apparel	148	298	43	(1)	104	286
Sales workers, shoes	57	302	33	(1)	24	(1)
Sales workers, furniture and home furnishings	118	511	62	536	57	497
Sales workers, radio, television, hi-fi, and appliances	213	495	157	512	56	413
Sales workers, hardware and building supplies	204	426	163	473	41	(1)
Sales workers, parts	146	400	132	403	15	(1)
Sales workers, other commodities	645	333	249	392	396	315
Sales counter clerks	94	335	34	(1)	60	303
Cashiers	1,289	280	301	296	989	275
Street and door-to-door sales workers	117	431	47	(1)	70	387
Administrative support, including clerical	14,109	447	3,322	539	10,788	427
Supervisors	650	603	282	701	368	560
General office	348	595	115	706	233	539
Financial records processing	77	678	15	(1)	62	622
Distribution, scheduling, and adjusting clerks	207	590	140	668	67	511
Computer equipment operators	298	525	128	610	170	485
Computer operators	292	528	124	612	168	485
Secretaries, stenographers, and typists	2,629	446	47	(1)	2,582	446

TABLE 6.5

Median Weekly Earnings of Full-Time Wage and Salary Workers by Detailed Occupation and Gender [CONTINUED]

(Numbers in thousands)

Occupation	1999 Both sexes Number of workers	Both sexes Median weekly earnings	Men Number of workers	Men Median weekly earnings	Women Number of workers	Women Median weekly earnings
Secretaries	2,162	443	26	([1])	2,136	443
Stenographers	67	490	4	([1])	63	488
Typists	400	454	17	([1])	382	455
Information clerks	1,467	393	182	497	1,285	386
Interviewers	120	408	17	([1])	103	396
Hotel clerks	89	315	22	([1])	67	308
Transportation ticket and reservation agents	218	486	70	527	147	464
Receptionists	727	374	30	([1])	697	373
Records processing, except financial	753	440	171	513	582	421
Order clerks	249	493	70	629	179	460
Personnel clerks, except payroll and timekeeping	58	523	10	([1])	49	([1])
Library clerks	58	434	15	([1])	43	([1])
File clerks	206	361	43	([1])	162	349
Records clerks	174	437	32	([1])	142	423
Financial records processing	1,480	440	157	489	1,322	435
Bookkeepers, accounting, and auditing clerks	1,084	443	107	478	977	440
Payroll and timekeeping clerks	127	474	16	([1])	111	459
Billing clerks	145	428	14	([1])	131	428
Billing, posting, and calculating machine operators	74	404	10	([1])	63	400
Communications equipment operators	117	384	29	([1])	88	367
Telephone operators	107	377	24	([1])	83	365
Mail and message distributing	829	629	504	665	325	575
Postal clerks, except mail carriers	298	687	156	701	142	670
Mail carriers, postal service	301	697	218	714	82	646
Mail clerks, except postal service	135	389	50	414	85	382
Messengers	96	453	80	457	16	([1])
Material recording, scheduling, and distributing clerks	1,652	448	953	485	700	417
Dispatchers	232	487	107	583	125	441
Production coordinators	181	592	71	734	109	474
Traffic, shipping, and receiving clerks	572	411	409	419	163	388
Stock and inventory clerks	398	470	242	505	156	438
Expediters	191	393	65	487	126	364
Adjusters and investigators	1,596	473	400	536	1,196	453
Insurance adjusters, examiners, and investigators	416	528	112	660	304	501
Investigators and adjusters, except insurance	925	452	219	511	706	435
Eligibility clerks, social welfare	98	481	13	([1])	85	468
Bill and account collectors	157	451	56	489	101	429
Miscellaneous administrative support occupations	2,593	409	448	483	2,145	399
General office clerks	511	419	98	461	412	413
Bank tellers	288	346	21	([1])	267	343
Data-entry keyers	594	422	110	433	484	420
Statistical clerks	80	432	17	([1])	63	401
Teachers' aides	368	315	28	([1])	341	314
Service occupations	10,841	336	5,209	402	5,632	304
Private household	384	243	17	([1])	367	240
Child care workers	157	211	1	([1])	156	212
Cleaners and servants	220	259	15	([1])	205	255
Protective services	2,138	592	1,791	613	347	492
Supervisors	180	759	156	815	23	([1])
Police and detectives	100	817	84	889	16	([1])
Firefighting and fire prevention	221	740	216	742	5	([1])
Firefighting	204	744	202	745	3	([1])
Police and detectives	1,079	657	898	681	181	574
Police and detectives, public service	602	751	519	766	83	650
Sheriffs, bailiffs, and other law enforcement officers	179	628	153	645	27	([1])
Correctional institution officers	298	521	226	540	72	492
Guards	659	393	521	402	138	335
Guards and police, except public service	618	398	501	403	118	368
Service occupations, except private household and protective	8,318	313	3,400	336	4,918	302
Food preparation and service occupations	3,189	298	1,583	311	1,607	286

See footnotes at end of table.

TABLE 6.5

Median Weekly Earnings of Full-Time Wage and Salary Workers by Detailed Occupation and Gender [CONTINUED]

(Numbers in thousands)

	1999					
	Both sexes		Men		Women	
Occupation	Number of workers	Median weekly earnings	Number of workers	Median weekly earnings	Number of workers	Median weekly earnings
Supervisors	276	342	120	415	156	310
Bartenders	167	334	97	334	70	334
Waiters and waitresses	652	302	172	325	480	294
Cooks, except short order	1,311	302	800	317	511	279
Food counter, fountain, and related occupations	108	252	46	([1])	62	247
Kitchen workers, food preparation	135	297	41	([1])	94	295
Waiters' and waitresses' assistants	229	286	119	290	110	282
Miscellaneous food preparation occupations	312	268	188	266	124	270
Health service occupations	1,791	324	217	368	1,574	320
Dental assistants	127	377	5	([1])	123	373
Health aides, except nursing	246	318	49	([1])	196	317
Nursing aides, orderlies, and attendants	1,418	322	163	367	1,255	318
Cleaning and building service occupations	2,188	321	1,303	363	885	292
Supervisors	153	407	97	472	55	317
Maids and housemen	472	296	87	330	385	289
Janitors and cleaners	1,496	324	1,054	351	442	293
Pest control	59	450	56	450	2	([1])
Personal service occupations	1,150	321	298	379	852	310
Supervisors	56	470	24	([1])	32	([1])
Hairdressers and cosmetologists	310	322	47	([1])	263	323
Attendants, amusement and recreation facilities	140	384	83	384	57	384
Public transportation attendants	58	604	11	([1])	47	([1])
Welfare service aides	54	310	6	([1])	49	([1])
Early childhood teachers' assistants	266	275	10	([1])	256	274
Precision production, craft, and repair	11,927	594	10,861	606	1,066	428
Mechanics and repairers	4,263	621	4,057	622	206	592
Supervisors	262	816	232	820	30	([1])
Mechanics and repairers, except supervisors	4,001	613	3,824	615	176	555
Vehicle and mobile equipment mechanics and repairers	1,455	594	1,436	594	18	([1])
Automobile mechanics	635	555	628	555	7	([1])
Bus, truck, and stationary engine mechanics	301	588	300	588	1	([1])
Aircraft engine mechanics	146	737	142	740	4	([1])
Small engine repairers	54	420	53	419	2	([1])
Automobile body and related repairers	123	584	121	586	1	([1])
Heavy equipment mechanics	145	667	144	669	1	([1])
Industrial machinery repairers	546	608	530	612	16	([1])
Electrical and electronic equipment repairers	889	698	785	703	104	616
Electronic repairers, communications and industrial equipment	201	621	184	630	17	([1])
Data processing equipment repairers	281	689	233	707	48	([1])
Telephone line installers and repairers	55	755	51	760	3	([1])
Telephone installers and repairers	240	770	210	761	30	([1])
Miscellaneous electrical and electronic equipment repairers	74	693	70	694	4	([1])
Heating, air conditioning, and refrigeration mechanics	310	580	308	579	2	([1])
Miscellaneous mechanics and repairers	790	607	754	612	36	([1])
Millwrights	72	697	70	700	2	([1])
Construction trades	4,143	566	4,059	571	85	423
Supervisors	504	720	495	722	9	([1])
Construction trades, except supervisors	3,639	540	3,563	545	76	417
Brickmasons and stonemasons	128	546	125	564	3	([1])
Tile setters, hard and soft	58	440	56	443	2	([1])
Carpet installers	62	507	62	507	-	-
Carpenters	962	518	950	518	12	([1])
Drywall installers	126	483	121	486	5	([1])
Electricians	739	645	723	651	17	([1])
Electrical power installers and repairers	134	731	133	730	1	([1])
Painters, construction and maintenance	331	427	317	432	14	([1])
Plumbers, pipefitters, steamfitters, and apprentices	417	595	408	596	9	([1])
Concrete and terrazzo finishers	87	501	85	501	2	([1])
Insulation workers	51	546	49	([1])	2	([1])
Roofers	147	467	146	469	1	([1])
Structural metalworkers	55	634	55	634	-	-
Extractive occupations	128	716	126	717	2	([1])
Precision production occupations	3,393	583	2,619	630	774	403
Supervisors	1,121	668	904	704	217	515

See footnotes at end of table.

TABLE 6.5

Median Weekly Earnings of Full-Time Wage and Salary Workers by Detailed Occupation and Gender [CONTINUED]

(Numbers in thousands)

Occupation	1999					
	Both sexes		Men		Women	
	Number of workers	Median weekly earnings	Number of workers	Median weekly earnings	Number of workers	Median weekly earnings
Precision metalworking occupations	869	634	809	646	60	442
Tool and die makers	139	785	134	792	5	(1)
Machinists	489	604	461	610	28	(1)
Sheet-metal workers	128	628	120	635	8	(1)
Precision woodworking occupations	75	457	65	481	11	(1)
Cabinet makers and bench carpenters	58	454	54	465	4	(1)
Precision textile, apparel, and furnishings machine workers	115	402	65	421	50	350
Precision workers, assorted materials	460	423	203	513	257	369
Optical goods workers	64	465	26	(1)	38	(1)
Electrical and electronic equipment assemblers	290	391	97	476	193	359
Precision food production occupations	380	400	242	440	138	342
Butchers and meat cutters	237	400	174	428	64	322
Bakers	110	394	61	475	49	(1)
Precision inspectors, testers, and related workers	131	618	100	657	32	(1)
Inspectors, testers, and graders	123	619	94	654	30	(1)
Plant and system operators	241	688	233	689	9	(1)
Water and sewage treatment plant operators	56	625	53	635	4	(1)
Stationary engineers	109	621	109	620	-	-
Operators, fabricators, and laborers	15,182	429	11,685	472	3,498	337
Machine operators, assemblers, and inspectors	6,814	423	4,371	487	2,444	340
Machine operators and tenders, except precision	4,368	416	2,829	481	1,538	326
Metalworking and plastic working machine operators	369	509	307	534	62	410
Punching and stamping press machine operators	101	458	74	505	27	(1)
Grinding, abrading, buffing, and polishing machine operators	113	490	97	507	16	(1)
Metal and plastic processing machine operators	142	454	110	471	32	(1)
Molding and casting machine operators	97	452	74	473	23	(1)
Woodworking machine operators	138	385	119	398	19	(1)
Sawing machine operators	81	386	71	393	10	(1)
Printing machine operators	325	491	251	526	74	366
Printing press operators	256	477	208	513	48	(1)
Textile, apparel, and furnishings machine operators	745	298	211	348	534	282
Textile sewing machine operators	416	282	94	326	322	273
Pressing machine operators	67	268	17	(1)	50	260
Laundering and dry cleaning machine operators	139	294	48	(1)	90	266
Machine operators, assorted materials	2,622	437	1,813	487	809	350
Packaging and filling machine operators	341	361	129	416	212	327
Mixing and blending machine operators	129	491	112	497	16	(1)
Separating, filtering, and clarifying machine operators	58	648	50	657	8	(1)
Painting and paint spraying machine operators	186	462	161	480	25	(1)
Furnace, kiln, and oven operators, exc. food	69	591	67	597	2	(1)
Slicing and cutting machine operators	153	430	115	473	38	(1)
Photographic process machine operators	69	342	34	(1)	35	(1)
Fabricators, assemblers, and hand working occupations	1,781	444	1,192	495	589	365
Welders and cutters	527	520	496	525	32	(1)
Assemblers	1,158	412	637	463	521	368
Production inspectors, testers, samplers, and weighers	665	424	349	506	316	369
Production inspectors, checkers, and examiners	487	456	256	530	231	395
Production testers	53	520	39	(1)	14	(1)
Graders and sorters, except agricultural	120	305	52	347	69	288
Transportation and material moving occupations	4,401	513	4,083	522	317	394
Motor vehicle operators	3,184	514	2,927	524	257	389
Supervisors	78	585	61	621	17	(1)
Truck drivers	2,493	527	2,409	532	85	412
Drivers—sales workers	130	534	122	555	8	(1)
Bus drivers	284	428	166	498	119	384
Taxicab drivers and chauffeurs	149	427	127	441	22	(1)
Transportation occupations, except motor vehicles	154	761	152	772	2	(1)
Rail transportation	108	816	107	820	1	(1)

See footnotes at end of table.

TABLE 6.5

Median Weekly Earnings of Full-Time Wage and Salary Workers by Detailed Occupation and Gender [CONTINUED]

(Numbers in thousands)

| | 1999 | | | | | |
| | Both sexes | | Men | | Women | |
Occupation	Number of workers	Median weekly earnings	Number of workers	Median weekly earnings	Number of workers	Median weekly earnings
Material moving equipment operators	1,063	498	1,005	503	58	415
Operating engineers	229	575	223	579	6	(1)
Crane and tower operators	69	580	67	586	2	(1)
Excavating and loading machine operators	81	571	79	577	2	(1)
Grader, dozer, and scraper operators	63	480	61	477	2	(1)
Industrial truck and tractor equipment operators	513	448	474	451	39	(1)
Handlers, equipment cleaners, helpers, and laborers	3,967	363	3,230	377	737	314
Helpers, construction and extractive occupations	106	329	103	330	3	(1)
Helpers, construction trades	93	336	92	335	2	(1)
Construction laborers	804	414	776	413	28	(1)
Production helpers	53	357	42	(1)	11	(1)
Freight, stock, and material handlers	1,287	361	996	375	291	318
Stock handlers and baggers	578	314	389	320	189	300
Machine feeders and offbearers	75	395	45	(1)	30	(1)
Garage and service station related occupations	134	314	131	313	3	(1)
Vehicle washers and equipment cleaners	199	312	173	315	26	(1)
Hand packers and packagers	253	317	107	338	147	305
Laborers, except construction	1,107	373	879	393	229	315
Farming, forestry, and fishing	1,583	331	1,364	341	218	283
Farm operators and managers	72	499	61	525	11	(1)
Farm managers	67	499	56	543	11	(1)
Other agricultural and related occupations	1,441	321	1,237	329	204	277
Farm occupations, except managerial	603	311	512	317	91	268
Farm workers	531	304	463	311	68	259
Related agricultural occupations	838	330	725	342	113	288
Supervisors, related agricultural	87	514	81	539	6	(1)
Groundskeepers and gardeners, except farm	657	322	614	322	44	(1)
Forestry and logging occupations	58	503	55	508	2	(1)

[1] Data not shown where base is less than 50,000.

NOTE: Beginning in January 1999, data reflect revised population controls used in the household survey.

SOURCE: *Employment and Earnings.* Bureau of Labor Statistics, Jan. 2000

cent got paid vacations. (Teachers are typically paid to work a specific number of days per year.) Health care benefits appear to be a basic benefit for all government workers since about the same proportion of blue-collar and service employees, teachers, and white-collar employees participated in health care benefits. (See Table 6.10.)

FIRMS PROVIDING BENEFITS

For more than 50 years, the U.S. Chamber of Commerce has surveyed a cross section of businesses as to the benefits offered. The average benefit payment expended by the approximately 600 firms who replied to the survey in 1998 amounted to 37.2 percent of their total payroll, down from 41.3 percent in 1996. In 1965 benefits were 21.5 percent of payroll.

Benefits As Percentage of Total Payroll

Table 6.11 breaks down the types of benefits for all employees as a percent of payroll. Almost 9 percent were legally required payments, such as Social Security, unem-

ployment insurance, and workers compensation. Medical benefits (10 percent) and payment for vacations, holidays, and sick leave (10 percent) accounted for one-fifth as a percent of payroll. Legally required benefits as a percentage of payroll for hourly workers were slightly more than for salaried workers, while retirement benefit percentages were significantly higher for salaried workers. (See Table 6.12.)

Distribution of Benefit Spending

Figure 6.2 shows how the benefit dollars were spent in 1996. More than one-fifth of all benefit dollars went to legally required benefits; another 23 percent were for medical benefits. Companies paid almost one-fourth of benefit dollars for paid leave and holidays. Life insurance took only 1 percent of the benefit dollars.

According to the U.S. Chamber of Commerce 1996 survey, average annual benefits per employee amounted to $14,086. The 802 firms responding to the survey paid an average annual wage of $29,371; this, along with payroll taxes, etc., made the total gross payroll $34,109. Benefits were 41.3 percent of the total gross payroll. The entire pay package for an employee was $43,457, of which 32.4 percent were employee benefits. (See Figures 6.3 and 6.4.)

Based upon its 1996 questionnaire, the survey estimated that benefits amounted to a total of $1.5 trillion. In 1975 benefits were $244.4 billion, 30 percent of the gross payroll. Some of the increase came from rising health insurance costs, and paid vacations and holidays, but almost half came from the growth of mandated benefits, such as Social Security.

Employee Benefits Policy at the Beginning of the Twenty-first Century

Initiatives that were pursued by the U.S. government during 2000 promised to impact the realm of employee benefits. Debate continued through June 2000 concerning a policy that would finance voluntary family leave for employees with funds from unemployment insurance. The new policy, crafted by the Federal Department of Labor, would allow states to use unemployment insurance trust funds to pay for employees taking leave for instances like the birth or the adoption of a child. According to the Employment Policy Foundation (EPF), a research group in Washington, D.C., half of employees received full pay during these leaves and an additional one of five employees receive partial pay on such leaves. The EPF argued that the policy would cause state unemployment insurance trust funds to decrease below solvency levels by 2003. Additionally, the group projected that payroll taxes would need to be increased by 145 percent to implement the policy. According to the EPF, the cost of running the unemployment insurance system could be expected to increase by two times.

Congressional debate concerning legislation (the Norwood-Dingell Bill, H.R. 2723) that had the capacity to greatly impact employer-sponsored health insurance continued through mid-2000. The bill would make it possible for employees to sue health plans, insurers, and employers for personal injury or death under state tort law. Such legislation would increase employers' costs by an estimated $16.7 billion per year. Employers who were surveyed noted that these rising costs would result in reduced benefits coverage and lower wage increases.

EMPLOYER-SPONSORED HEALTH INSURANCE

Health insurance became a major issue during the late 1990s. Many employees do not change jobs because they fear losing their health coverage. Welfare recipients often stay on welfare to avoid losing Medicaid coverage. If they took a job, it may not offer health insurance.

Health care has been debated at all levels of government. As of 1995, 45 states had passed legislation

TABLE 6.6

Estimated Average Starting Salaries and Ranges for New College Graduates in 1997–1998

Bachelor's Degree Graduates Academic Majors	Estimated Average Starting Salary	Percentile	
		10th	90th
Chemical Engineering	$44,557	$39,558	$48,719
Electrical Engineering	$41,167	$35,394	$46,845
Mechanical Engineering	$39,857	$34,353	$45,492
Industrial Engineering	$39,462	$33,728	$44,763
Computer Science	$38,741	$31,230	$45,388
Physics	$36,692	$29,412	$43,344
Materials and Logistics Mgt. (purchasing, operations, and transportation)	$36,190	$25,875	$43,470
Packaging Engineering	$36,089	$29,148	$45,804
Chemistry	$35,227	$20,640	$53,664
Civil Engineering	$34,385	$28,732	$41,224
Mathematics	$33,180	$22,704	$42,353
Financial Administration	$32,430	$24,323	$41,400
Nursing	$31,802	$24,685	$41,280
Geology	$31,273	$24,768	$40,248
Accounting	$31,209	$24,840	$36,225
General Business Admin.	$30,373	$21,735	$40,365
Marketing/Sales	$29,012	$20,700	$36,225
Human Resources Management	$28,003	$20,700	$36,018
Agriculture	$27,710	$20,700	$36,225
Human Ecology/Home Economics	$27,339	$21,466	$34,056
Retailing	$26,650	$22,704	$30,960
Cornmunications	$26,392	$19,608	$35,088
Natural Resources	$26,035	$17,595	$33,120
Hotel, Rest. Inst. Mgt.	$25,938	$22,770	$30,015
Advertising.	$25,485	$18,576	$31,992
Journalism	$24,588	$18,576	$31,992
Liberal Arts/Arts & Letters	$24,578	$15,480	$31,992
Social Science	$24,170	$15,480	$34,056
Education	$23,837	$18,576	$29,515
Telecommunications	$22,563	$15,480	$31,992

Advanced Degree Graduates	Estimated Starting Salary	Percentile	
		10th	90th
MBA	$44,666	$31,500	$58,800
Masters	$43,645	$31,370	$49,995
Ph.D.	$58,109	$49,790	$73,325

SOURCE: L. Patrick Scheetz. *Recruiting Trends 1997-98*. 27th Edition. Michigan State University: East Lansing, MI

regulating the small-employer health insurance market, and 44 states included premium rate restrictions as part of reforms. Almost all reforms included portability of health insurance (in which employees who had coverage at their previous place of employment are immediately eligible at their next jobs) and preexisting condition limitations (in which an insurer could not deny coverage because of a preexisting physical ailment). Since passage of the 1996 Health Care Portability and Accountability Act (PL 104-191), such reforms apply to all states.

While Congress was debating the 1993 Health Security Act (which failed to pass), the President's Task Force on Health Care Reform identified a number of unanswered questions on employer-sponsored health insurance. The *National Employer Health Insurance Survey (NEHIS)* was developed to gather data for policymakers

TABLE 6.7

Percent of Full-Time Employees Participating in Employer-Provided Benefit Plans and in Selected Features Within Plans, Medium and Large Private Establishments, Selected Years 1984–1997

Item	1984	1986	1988	1989	1991	1993	1995	1997
Scope of survey (in 000's)	21,013	21,303	31,059	32,428	31,163	28,728	33,374	38,409
Number of employees (in 000's):								
With medical care	20,383	20,238	27,953	29,834	25,865	23,519	25,546	29,340
With life insurance	20,172	20,451	28,574	30,482	29,293	26,175	29,078	33,495
With defined benefit plan	17,231	16,190	19,567	20,430	18,386	16,015	17,417	19,202
Time-off plans								
Participants with:								
Paid lunch time	9	10	11	10	8	9	–	–
Average minutes per day	26	27	29	26	30	29	–	–
Paid rest time	73	72	72	71	67	68	–	–
Average minutes per day	26	26	26	26	28	26	–	–
Paid funeral leave	–	88	85	84	80	83	80	81
Average days per occurrence	–	3.2	3.2	3.3	3.3	3.0	3.3	3.7
Paid holidays	99	99	96	97	92	91	89	89
Average days per year[1]	9.8	10.0	9.4	9.2	10.2	9.4	9.1	9.3
Paid personal leave	23	25	24	22	21	21	22	20
Average days per year	3.6	3.7	3.3	3.1	3.3	3.1	3.3	3.5
Paid vacations	99	100	98	97	96	97	96	95
Paid sick leave	67	70	69	68	67	65	58	56
Unpaid maternity leave	–	–	33	37	37	60	–	–
Unpaid paternity leave	–	–	16	18	26	53	–	–
Unpaid family leave	–	–	–	–	–	–	84	93
Insurance plans								
Participants in medical care plans	97	95	90	92	83	82	77	76
Percent of participants with coverage for:								
Home health care	46	66	76	75	81	86	78	85
Extended care facilities	62	70	79	80	80	82	73	78
Physical exams	8	18	28	28	30	42	56	63
Percent of participants with employee contribution required for								
Self coverage	36	43	44	47	51	61	67	69
Average monthly contribution	$11.93	$12.80	$19.29	$25.31	$26.60	$31.55	$33.92	$39.14
Family coverage	58	63	64	66	69	76	78	80
Average monthly contribution	$35.93	$41.40	$60.07	$72.10	$96.97	$107.42	$118.33	$130.07
Participants in life insurance plans	96	96	92	94	94	91	87	87
Percent of participants with:								
Accidental death and dismemberment insurance	74	72	78	71	71	76	77	74
Survivor income benefits	–	10	8	7	6	5	7	6
Retiree protection available	64	59	49	42	44	41	37	33
Participants in long-term disability insurance plans	47	48	42	45	40	41	42	43
Participants in sickness and accident insurance plans	51	49	46	43	45	44	–	–
Participants in short-term disability plans[2]	–	–	–	–	–	–	53	55
Retirement plans								
Participants in defined benefit pension plans	82	76	63	63	59	56	52	50
Percent of participants with:								
Normal retirement prior to age 65	63	64	59	62	55	52	52	52
Early retirement available	97	98	98	97	98	95	96	95
Ad hoc pension increase in last 5 years	47	35	26	22	7	6	4	10
Terminal earnings formula	54	57	55	64	56	61	58	56
Benefit coordinated with Social Security	56	62	62	63	54	48	51	49
Participants in defined contributions plans	–	60	45	48	48	49	55	57
Participants in plans with tax deferred savings arrangements	–	33	36	41	44	43	54	55
Other benefits								
Employees eligible for:								
Flexible benefits plans	–	2	5	9	10	12	12	13
Reimbursement accounts[2]	–	5	12	23	36	52	38	32
Premium conversion plans[3]	–	–	–	–	–	–	5	7

[1]Methods used to calculate the average number of paid holidays were revised in 1995 to count partial days more precisely. Average holidays for 1995 and 1997 are not comparable to those reported in 1991 and 1993.

[2]Prior to 1995, reimbursement accounts that were part of flexible benefit plans were tabulated separately.

[3]Included in reimbursement accounts prior to 1995.

NOTE: Dash indicates data not available.

SOURCE: *The American Workforce.* Bureau of Labor Statistics, Nov. 1999

TABLE 6.8

Percent of Full-Time Employees Participating in Employer-Provided Benefit Plans and in Selected Features within Plans, Small Private Establishments and State and Local Governments, Selected Years 1987–1996

Item	Small private establishments			State and local governments			
	1992	1994	1996	1987	1990	1992	1994
Scope of survey (in 000's)	34,360	35,910	39,816	10,321	12,972	12,466	12,907
Number of employees (in 000's):							
With medical care	24,396	23,536	25,599	9,599	12,064	11,219	11,192
With life insurance	21,990	21,955	24,635	8,773	11,415	11,095	11,194
With defined benefit plan	7,559	5,480	5,883	9,599	11,675	10,845	11,708
Time-off plans							
Participants with:							
Paid lunch time	9	–	–	17	11	10	–
Average minutes per day	37	–	–	34	36	34	–
Paid rest time	49	–	–	58	56	53	–
Average minutes per day	26	–	–	29	29	29	–
Paid funeral leave	50	50	51	56	63	65	62
Average days per occurrence	3.0	3.1	3.0	3.7	3.7	3.7	3.7
Paid holidays	82	82	80	81	74	75	73
Average days per year[1]	9.2	7.5	7.6	10.9	13.6	14.2	11.5
Paid personal leave	12	13	14	38	39	38	38
Average days per year	2.6	2.6	3.0	2.7	2.9	2.9	3.0
Paid vacations	88	88	86	72	67	67	66
Paid sick leave	53	50	50	97	95	95	94
Unpaid leave	18	–	–	57	51	59	–
Unpaid paternity leave	8	–	–	30	33	44	–
Unpaid family leave	–	47	48	–	–	–	93
Insurance plans							
Participants in medical care plans	71	66	64	93	93	90	87
Percent of participants with coverage for:							
Home health care	80	–	–	76	82	87	84
Extended care facilities	84	–	–	78	79	84	81
Physical exam	28	–	–	36	36	47	55
Percent of participants with employee contribution required for:							
Self coverage	47	52	52	35	38	43	47
Average monthly contribution	$36.51	$40.97	$42.63	$15.74	$25.53	$28.97	$30.20
Family coverage	73	76	75	71	65	72	71
Average monthly contribution	$150.54	$159.63	$181.53	$71.89	$117.59	$139.23	$149.70
Participants in life insurance plans	64	61	62	85	88	89	87
Percent of participants with:							
Accidental death and dismemberment insurance	76	79	77	67	67	74	64
Survivor income benefits	1	2	1	1	1	1	2
Retiree protection available	25	20	13	55	45	46	46
Participants in long-term disability insurance plans	23	20	22	31	27	28	30
Participants in sickness and accident insurance plans	26	26	–	14	21	22	21
Participants in short-term disability plans[2]	–	–	29	–	–	–	–
Retirement plans							
Participants in defined benefit pension plans	22	15	15	93	90	87	91
Percent of participants with:							
Normal retirement prior to age 65	50	–	47	92	89	92	92
Early retirement available	95	–	92	90	88	89	87
Ad hoc pension increase in last 5 years	4	–	–	33	16	10	13
Terminal earnings formula	54	–	53	100	100	100	99
Benefit coordinated with Social Security	46	–	44	18	8	10	49
Participants in defined contributions plans	33	34	38	9	9	9	9
Participants in plans with tax deferred savings arrangements	24	23	28	28	45	45	24
Other Benefits							
Employees eligible for:							
Flexible benefits plans	2	3	4	5	5	5	5
Reimbursement accounts[2]	14	19	12	5	31	50	64
Premium conversion plans[3]	–	–	7	–	–	–	–

[1]Methods used to calculate the average number of paid holidays were revised in 1994 to count partial days more precisely. Average holidays for 1994 are not comparable to those reported in 1990 and 1992.

[2]Prior to 1996, reimbursement accounts that were part of flexible benefit plans were tabulated separately.

[3]Included in reimbursement accounts prior to 1996.

NOTE: Dash indicates data not available.

SOURCE: *The American Workforce.* Bureau of Labor Statistics, Nov. 1999

TABLE 6.9

Participation[1] in Selected Employee Benefit Programs, Full-Time Employees, Small Private Establishments, 1996

Benefit	All employees	Professional, technical, and related employees	Clerical and sales employees	Blue-collar and service employees
Paid time off:				
Holidays	80	86	91	71
Vacations	86	90	95	79
Personal leave	14	21	18	8
Funeral leave	51	60	60	42
Jury duty leave	59	74	68	47
Military leave	18	25	22	12
Family leave	2	3	3	1
Unpaid family leave	48	53	52	43
Disability benefits[2]:				
Paid sick leave	50	66	64	35
Short-term disability	29	32	33	25
Long-term disability insurance	22	39	30	10
Survivor benefits:				
Life insurance	62	72	68	54
Accidental death and dismemberment	49	59	53	42
Survivor income benefits	1	(3)	1	1
Health care benefits:				
Medical care	64	76	69	56
Dental care	31	40	35	24
Vision care	12	14	11	12
Outpatient prescription drug coverage	57	67	61	50
Retirement income benefits:				
All retirement[4]	46	56	53	37
Defined benefit	15	12	16	15
Defined contribution[5]	38	51	46	28
Savings and thrift	23	32	29	16
Deferred profit sharing	12	13	17	9
Employee stock ownership	1	2	2	1
Money purchase pension	4	6	3	3
Stock bonus	(3)	(3)	(3)	(3)
Simplified employee pension	1	2	1	1
Other	(3)	(3)	(3)	(3)

See footnotes at end of table.

TABLE 6.9

Participation[1] in Selected Employee Benefit Programs, Full-Time Employees, Small Private Establishments, 1996 [CONTINUED]

Benefit	All employees	Professional, technical, and related employees	Clerical and sales employees	Blue-collar and service employees
Cash or deferred arrangements:				
With employer contributions	24	30	31	17
Salary reduction	24	30	31	17
Savings and thrift[6]	21	28	26	14
Deferred profit sharing	2	1	3	2
Other	1	1	1	1
Deferral of profit sharing allocation	(3)	-	1	(3)
No employer contributions	4	8	4	3

[1]Participants are workers covered by a paid time off, insurance, or retirement plan. Employees subject to a minimum service requirement before they are eligible for benefit coverage are counted as participants even if they have not met the requirement at the time of the survey. If employees are required to pay part of the cost of a benefit, only those who elect the coverage and pay their share are counted as participants. Except for family leave, benefits for which the employees must pay the full premium are outside the scope of the survey. Only current employees are counted as participants; retirees are excluded.

[2]The definitions for paid sick leave and short-term disability (previously sickness and accident insurance) were changed for the 1996 survey. Paid sick leave now only includes plans that either specify a maximum number of days per year or unlimited days. Short-term disability now includes all insured, self-insured, and state-mandated plans available on a per disability basis as well as the unfunded per disability plans previously reported as sick leave. Sickness and accident insurance, reported in years prior to this survey, only included insured, self-insured, and state-mandated plans providing per disability benefits at less than full pay.

[3]Less than 0.5 percent.

[4]Includes defined benefit pension plans and defined contribution retirement plans. The total is less than the sum of the individual items because many employees participated in both types of plans.

[5]The total is less than the sum of the individual items because some employees participated in more than one type of plan.

[6]Participants in savings and thrift plans usually are allowed to make pretax contributions. In the 1996 survey, provisions governing pretax contributions were not determinable for about one-tenth of the employees with savings and thrift plans.

NOTE: Because of rounding, sums of individual items may not equal totals. Where applicable, dash indicates that no data were reported.

SOURCE: *Employee Benefits in Small Private Establishments.* U.S. Department of Labor, April 1999

and researchers to use in developing and evaluating alternative health care policies.

Employer-sponsored health insurance is a major source of private health care coverage in the United States. At the end of 1993, 40 percent of private sector establishments, employing 80.3 percent of all private workers, offered health insurance to their employees. (See Table 6.13.) About 68 percent were eligible for health benefits, and 58 percent participated in their employer-sponsored health plans. (The *NEHIS* found that 99 percent of public employees had health insurance available at their jobs.) By 2000 two-thirds of all American employees obtained employer-sponsored health insurance.

Firm size was one of the most important determinants of whether a business offered health insurance. One-third (33 percent) of firms with less than ten employees offered heath insurance, compared to 96 percent of establishments with 100 or more employees. (See Tables 6.13 and 6.14.) The percent of establishments offering health insurance at the end of 1993 varied widely by state, ranging from 40 percent in Montana to 86 percent in Hawaii. Most of the variation across states occurred among firms with fewer than 50 employees.

Types of Establishments

Table 6.14 and Figure 6.5 show that provision of health insurance also varies by type of industry. Over 60 percent of private establishments in mining; transportation, communication, and utilities; wholesale trade; and finance, insurance, and real estate offered health benefits to workers. Employers in agriculture, forestry, and fishing and in construction were least likely to offer health benefits to employees.

TABLE 6.10

Participation¹ in Selected Employee Benefit Programs, Full-Time Employees, State and Local Governments, 1994

Benefit	All employees	White-collar employees, except teachers	Teachers	Blue-collar and service employees	Benefit	All employees	White-collar employees, except teachers	Teachers	Blue-collar and service employees
Paid time off:					Health care benefits:				
Holidays	73	86	33	91	Medical care	87	89	84	86
Vacations	66	84	9	91	Dental care	62	62	59	66
Personal leave	38	30	58	31	Vision care	35	36	30	37
Funeral leave	62	59	58	70	Outpatient prescription drug coverage	86	89	84	84
Jury duty leave	94	94	94	93					
Military leave	75	80	61	82	Retirement income benefits:				
Family leave	4	4	3	6					
					All retirement²	96	96	97	95
Unpaid family leave	93	93	96	90					
					Defined benefit	91	90	93	91
Disability benefits:									
					Defined contribution³	9	10	7	9
Short-term disability protection	95	94	97	96	Savings and thrift	2	3	1	2
Paid sick leave	94	93	96	94	Money purchase pension	7	7	5	7
Sickness and accident insurance	21	24	11	26					
					Cash or deferred arrangements:				
Long-term disability insurance	30	31	37	23	With employer contributions	7	8	5	8
					Salary reduction	2	3	1	2
Survivor benefits:					Savings and thrift	2	3	1	2
					Money purchase pension	(⁴)	(⁴)	(⁴)	(⁴)
Life insurance	87	87	85	87	Other⁵	5	5	3	6
Accidental death and dismemberment	56	55	53	59					
Survivor income benefits	2	1	3	2	No employer contributions	17	18	18	16

¹Participants are workers covered by a paid time off, insurance, or retirement plan. Employees subject to a minimum service requirement before they are eligible for benefit coverage are counted as participants even if they have not met the requirement at the time of the survey. If employees are required to pay part of the cost of a benefit, only those who elect the coverage and pay their share are counted as participants. Benefits for which the employee must pay the full premium are outside the scope of the survey. Only current employees are counted as participants; retirees are excluded.

²Includes defined benefit pension plans and defined contribution retirement plans. The total is less than the sum of the individual items because many employees participated in both types of plans.

³Includes defined contribution plans not shown separately.

⁴Less than 0.5 percent.

⁵Includes required contributions made to money purchase pension plans on a pretax basis.

NOTE: Because of rounding, sums of individual items may not equal totals. Where applicable, dash indicates no employees in this category.

SOURCE: *Employee Benefits in State and Local Governments*. Bureau of Labor Statistics: Washington, D.C., 1994

The seasonality of agricultural workers and the contractual nature (involving site-specific jobs) of construction workers may discourage these employers from offering health benefits. Agricultural and construction establishments were also more likely to be small businesses. Finally, these trades often employ less-educated workers and recent immigrants who are less likely to expect or ask for health coverage. Only 51 percent of service establishments and 44 percent of retail trade establishments offered health insurance. Retail and service industries likely offered less health insurance because they tend to be smaller businesses, often employing many part-time workers, low-wage workers, and recent immigrants.

Workforce Characteristics

The likelihood of a firm offering health benefits depends not only on employer characteristics, such as size, industry, age, and corporate structure of the firm, but also on employee demand for health benefits. Employer-sponsored health insurance is attractive because it is the least expensive way to obtain health insurance. Employees with lower incomes, however, may not even be able to afford to pay the employee share of the premium. Thus they may choose not to enroll in, or even to ask for, employer-sponsored health insurance. Firms with many low-wage employees and fewer full-time employees tended not to have health insurance. Firms with union employees were most likely to have insurance. (See Figure 6.6.)

Employee Contributions Rising

By the late twentieth century, employees were paying more for their medical insurance than ever before. The proportion of those required to pay more rose between 1991 and 1997. In 1991, 51 percent of the employees who purchased medical-care coverage through their employers were required to contribute for single coverage

TABLE 6.11

Types of Benefits for All Employees as a Percent of Payroll

	Benefits as a Percent of Payroll All Employees		
	Year		
Types of Benefits	1994	1995	1996
Legally required payments	8.9	8.9	8.8
Retirement and savings	7.2	7.5	6.3
Life insurance and death benefits	0.4	0.4	0.4
Medical and medically related benefits	10.4	10.5	9.6
Paid rest periods, lunch periods, etc.	2.2	2.2	3.7
Payment for vacations, holidays, sick leave, etc.	9.7	10.2	10.2
Miscellaneous benefits	1.9	2.2	2.3
Total	**40.7**	**42.0**	**41.3**

SOURCE: *The Hidden Payroll*, in Employee Benefits. U.S. Chamber of Commerce: Washington, D.C., 1997

TABLE 6.12

Comparison of Benefits for Salaried Workers with Hourly Paid Employees

	Benefits as a % of Payroll		
	Salaried	Hourly	Difference
Total	**42.9**	**41.2**	**+1.7**
Legally required	8.3	8.9	-0.6
Retirement	10.6	6.0	+4.6
Life insurance	0.6	0.3	+0.3
Medically related	8.6	9.7	-1.1
Paid rest periods*		4.0	
Payment for time not worked	12.4	10.0	+2.4
Miscellaneous	2.5	2.3	+0.2

*Since salaried workers are not paid strictly on time, payments for rest periods are not used for salaried workers

SOURCE: *The Hidden Payroll*, in Employee Benefits. U.S. Chamber of Commerce: Washington, D.C., 1997

FIGURE 6.2

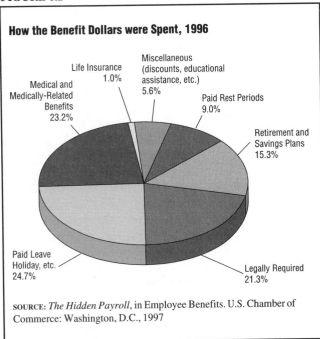

How the Benefit Dollars were Spent, 1996

Life Insurance 1.0%
Miscellaneous (discounts, educational assistance, etc.) 5.6%
Medical and Medically-Related Benefits 23.2%
Paid Rest Periods 9.0%
Retirement and Savings Plans 15.3%
Paid Leave Holiday, etc. 24.7%
Legally Required 21.3%

SOURCE: *The Hidden Payroll*, in Employee Benefits. U.S. Chamber of Commerce: Washington, D.C., 1997

and more than two-thirds (69 percent) paid for family coverage. By 1997, with the employer picking up the balance, 2 of 3 (69 percent) full-time employees with medical insurance contributed to the cost of a single coverage. More than three-fourths (80 percent) of employees contributed to the cost of family coverage. (See Table 6.15.)

Blue-collar and service workers were less likely to contribute towards either single or family coverage than their white-collar counterparts. In 1995, 56 percent of blue-collar and service workers helped pay for single coverage, and 67 percent did so for family coverage. Among white-collar workers, 78 percent contributed towards single coverage, and 87 percent did so for family coverage. In 1995 average monthly employee contribu-

tions were $34 for single coverage and over $118 for family coverage.

PARTICIPATION IN SAVINGS AND THRIFT PLANS

The *Survey of Consumer Finance*, prepared by the Federal Reserve Board, showed that from 1989 to 1992, mean, or average, family net worth (in 1992 dollars) rose 11.7 percent, from $197,200 to $220,300. The median family net worth remained about the same (about $52,000). The composition of assets held by families also changed during the 1989–92 period. The proportion of families owning retirement accounts, including individual retirement accounts (IRAs), Keogh accounts, and employer-sponsored defined contribution plans, increased from 35.4 percent to 39.3 percent. The median value of these accounts (in 1992 dollars) increased by 33.9 percent, from $11,200 to $15,000.

In 1993 the *Employee Benefits Survey*, prepared by the Bureau of Labor Statistics (BLS), showed that 29 percent of full-time employees in medium and large private establishments were currently participating in savings and thrift plans with employer matching contributions. Ninety-nine percent of the savings and thrift plan participants were in 401(k) plans, where employee contributions are made with pretax dollars. (The employee's taxable income is reduced by the amount of the contribution. However, taxes are deferred, not eliminated—when the employee starts withdrawing funds from the plan, taxes must be paid on the pretax contributions, any employer matching contributions, and any earnings on these contributions.)

All savings and thrift plans require a basic employee contribution, which may be matched by the employer. However, not all employers make matching contributions. Some 26 percent of full-time employees participating in

FIGURE 6.3

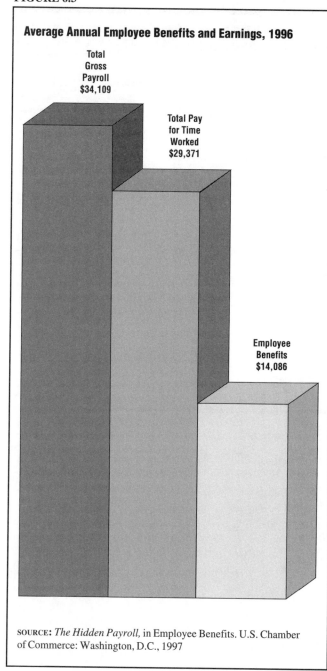

Average Annual Employee Benefits and Earnings, 1996

Total
Gross
Payroll
$34,109

Total Pay
for Time
Worked
$29,371

Employee
Benefits
$14,086

SOURCE: *The Hidden Payroll,* in Employee Benefits. U.S. Chamber of Commerce: Washington, D.C., 1997

FIGURE 6.4

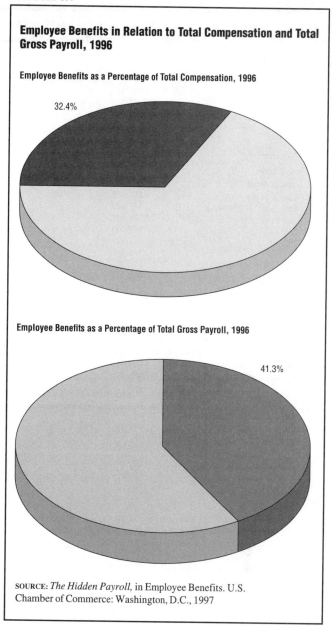

Employee Benefits in Relation to Total Compensation and Total Gross Payroll, 1996

Employee Benefits as a Percentage of Total Compensation, 1996

32.4%

Employee Benefits as a Percentage of Total Gross Payroll, 1996

41.3%

SOURCE: *The Hidden Payroll,* in Employee Benefits. U.S. Chamber of Commerce: Washington, D.C., 1997

savings and thrift plans did not receive matching contributions from their employers. Many plans allow an additional contribution by the employee in excess of the maximum amount matched by the employer. This is called a voluntary employee contribution.

Who Participates?

The 1993 *Employee Benefits Survey of Medium and Large Private Establishments* examined the relationship between selected savings and thrift plan provisions and employee participation in such plans. Overall, 69 percent of employees participated in available programs. Employees who were offered a plan with an employer matching contribution (80 percent) were much more likely to participate than one with no employer matching contribution (51 percent). Professional, clerical, and sales employees were more likely than blue-collar employees to participate in such plans. (See Table 6.16.)

TABLE 6.13

Number and Percent Distribution of Private Establishments and Percent Offering Health Insurance, and Number and Percent Distribution of Employees and Percent of Employees in Establishments Offering Health Insurance and Percent Enrolled in Employer's Health Plan by Firm Size, 1993

Firm size[2]	Private establishments[1]			Private employees			
	Number of establishments	Percent distribution	Percent offering health insurance	Number of employees	Percent distribution	Percent working in establishments that offer health insurance	Percent enrolled in employer's health plan
Total, United States	**11,210,800**	**100.0**	**40.0**	**103,257,100**	**100.0**	**80.3**	**56.1**
1 employee (SENE's[3])	4,934,000	44.0	25.2	4,934,000	4.8	25.2	25.2
SENE's 18–64 years	4,456,600	39.8	27.9	4,456,600	4.3	27.9	27.9
SENE's 65 years and over	477,400	4.3	[4]	477,400	0.5	[4]	[4]
2 or more employees	6,276,800	56.0	51.6	98,323,100	95.2	83.1	57.6
2–9	3,914,400	34.9	33.2	15,725,700	15.2	39.2	25.8
10–24	870,800	7.8	67.1	10,726,800	10.4	68.8	44.3
25–99	596,400	5.3	83.0	16,250,000	15.7	84.2	53.8
100–999	406,800	3.6	94.6	20,910,700	20.3	95.9	65.0
1,000 or more	488,400	4.4	96.7	34,710,000	33.6	99.3	73.4

[1] Establishments are defined as single business locations.

[2] Number of employees nationwide as reported by respondent.

[3] Self-employed with no employee (SENE) businesses. For these businesses, those who directly purchase health insurance for themselves or those who obtain health insurance through union, association, or business arrangements were considered as "offering health insurance."

[4] Since virtually all SENE's 65 years old or older are covered by Medicare, other supplementary health plans (for example, Medigap) that were privately purchased were not counted as "offering health insurance."

NOTES: Estimates in this table are based on a December 31, 1993, reference period. Figures may not add to totals because of rounding.

SOURCE: Allen K., Park C. *Health Insurance Coverage for the Self-Employed With No Employees*. National Center for Health Statistics: Hyattsville, MD, 1999

TABLE 6.14

Percent of Private Establishments Offering Health Insurance by Firm Size, According to Selected Characteristics, 1993

Establishment characteristics	All firm sizes	Firm size[1]					
		Less than 10 employees	10-24 employees	25-99 employees	100 or more employees	Less than 50 employees	50 or more employees
		Percent of establishments offering health insurance*					
United States	51.6	33.2	67.1	83.0	95.7	42.2	94.3
Industry group							
Agriculture, forestry, and fishing	30.2	21.8	60.9	85.5	93.6	29.1	84.7
Mining	67.3	40.4	87.8	98.0	99.2	53.2	98.7
Construction	40.4	31.7	62.9	80.0	94.5	37.6	91.5
Manufacturing	60.8	36.8	75.5	89.3	99.2	49.8	97.4
Transportation, communication, and utilities	65.8	41.0	75.4	86.4	97.6	52.3	95.6
Wholesale trade	64.9	43.3	79.9	94.5	99.2	55.6	98.8
Retail trade	43.6	22.5	48.1	69.3	95.5	29.9	93.2
Finance, insurance, and real estate	64.8	38.9	85.1	96.2	97.6	49.9	97.4
Services	51.3	36.9	70.4	82.0	91.5	45.4	90.5
Ownership							
For profit	52.3	34.3	68.0	83.2	97.1	43.1	95.4
Incorporated	66.0	45.2	73.0	85.7	97.5	55.6	96.3
Unincorporated	28.4	23.6	47.2	64.1	90.8	26.2	84.5
Nonprofit	66.1	48.6	70.5	86.5	89.2	58.0	89.9
Other	65.3	37.8	76.6	94.1	89.3	52.1	91.2
Age of firm							
Less than 5 years	34.8	26.8	48.2	68.2	91.1	31.3	88.5
5-9 years	41.2	29.7	59.0	75.8	92.5	36.4	89.0
10-24 years	50.0	35.7	70.0	83.3	94.4	44.4	93.2
25 years or more	71.8	45.7	78.8	90.8	97.0	58.1	96.3
Location of establishments in firm							
1 location only	40.9	33.1	66.8	80.5	92.2	39.7	89.9
2 or more locations, all in same State	73.5	35.4	66.8	85.7	94.4	62.2	92.4
2 or more locations, multiple States	93.0	54.9	78.7	87.7	96.8	74.5	96.4
Metropolitan area indicator							
Metropolitan area	53.7	34.9	69.0	83.4	96.0	44.2	94.6
Nonmetropolitan area	43.7	27.7	59.0	81.5	94.3	35.3	92.8
Percent of employees that are full-time							
Less than 25 percent	26.6	10.7	20.0	52.5	84.7	15.6	79.9
25-49 percent	41.0	23.0	46.4	64.4	92.0	29.6	89.3
50-74 percent	43.5	27.9	63.0	78.0	95.4	34.7	94.0
75 percent or more	59.4	40.0	77.7	90.2	97.7	50.6	96.7
Presence of union employees							
No union employees	51.9	34.7	67.9	83.4	95.2	43.6	93.8
Has union employees	84.0	62.1	85.7	97.0	98.5	74.7	98.2
Percent of low-wage employees[3]							
50 percent or more of employees are low-wage	25.2	15.4	26.9	49.4	83.9	18.5	79.7
50 percent or more of employees are not low-wage	58.3	40.9	74.0	88.2	96.5	50.8	95.5

[1] Number of employees nationwide as reported by respondent.

[2] An establishment is defined as a business at a single physical location.

[3] Low-wage employees earned less than $5 per hour or less than $10,000 per year.

NOTES: Estimates in this table are based on a December 31, 1993, reference period.

SOURCE: *Employer-Sponsored Health Insurance*. National Center for Health Statistics: Hyattsville, MD

FIGURE 6.5

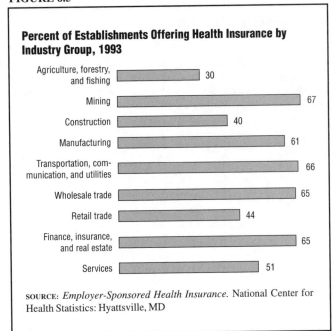

Percent of Establishments Offering Health Insurance by Industry Group, 1993

Industry Group	Percent
Agriculture, forestry, and fishing	30
Mining	67
Construction	40
Manufacturing	61
Transportation, communication, and utilities	66
Wholesale trade	65
Retail trade	44
Finance, insurance, and real estate	65
Services	51

SOURCE: *Employer-Sponsored Health Insurance*. National Center for Health Statistics: Hyattsville, MD

FIGURE 6.6

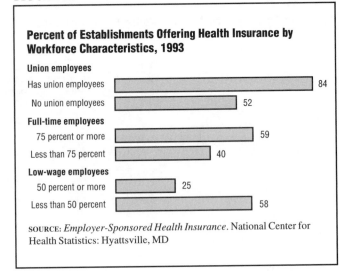

Percent of Establishments Offering Health Insurance by Workforce Characteristics, 1993

Union employees
	Percent
Has union employees	84
No union employees	52

Full-time employees
	Percent
75 percent or more	59
Less than 75 percent	40

Low-wage employees
	Percent
50 percent or more	25
Less than 50 percent	58

SOURCE: *Employer-Sponsored Health Insurance*. National Center for Health Statistics: Hyattsville, MD

TABLE 6.15

Percent of Full-Time Employees Participating in Employer-Sponsored Medical Benefits by Type of Medical Plan and Requirement for Employee Contributions, Medium and Large Private Establishments, 1991, 1993, 1995, and 1997

Type of plan and contribution requirement	1991	1993	1995	1997
Type of plan				
Total	100	100	100	100
Traditional fee-for-service plans[1]	67	50	37	27
Preferred provider organizations[2]	16	26	34	40
Health maintenance organizations[3]	17	23	27	33
Other[4]	(5)	1	1	1
Requirement to contribute for single coverage				
Total	100	100	100	100
Employee contribution not required	49	37	33	31
Employee contribution required	51	61	67	69
Not determinable	(5)	2	-	-
Requirement to contribute for family coverage				
Total	100	100	100	100
Employee contribution not required	31	21	22	20
Employee contribution required	69	76	78	80
Not determinable	(5)	3	-	(5)

[1] These plans pay for specific medical procedures as expenses are incurred.

[2] Groups of hospitals and physicians that contract to provide comprehensive medical services at prearranged prices. To encourage use of organization members, the health plan limits reimbursement rates when participants use nonmember services.

[3] Includes Federally qualified and other HMOs that deliver comprehensive health care on a prepayment rather than fee-for-service basis.

[4] Includes exclusive provider organizations, which are groups of hospitals and physicians that contract to provide comprehensive medical services. Participants are required to obtain services from members of the organization in order to receive plan benefits.

[5] Less than .5 percent.

NOTE: Because of rounding, sums of individual items may not equal totals. Dash indicates no data were reported.

SOURCE: *Employee Benefits in Medium and Large Private Industry Establishments*. Bureau of Labor Statistics, 1997

TABLE 6.16

Employee Participation in Savings and Thrift Plans, by Presence or Absence of Employer Matching Contribution, Medium and Large Private Establishments, 1993

Plan	All employees	Professional, technical, and related employees	Clerical and sales employees	Blue-collar and service employees
	Percent			
All plans	**69**	**73**	**75**	**62**
Employer matching contribution	80	83	81	77
No employer matching contribution	51	56	59	44

SOURCE: *Employee Participation in Savings and Thrift Plans, 1993*. Family Economics and Nutrition Review, vol. 9, no. 4

CHAPTER 7
GETTING A JOB

A journey of a thousand miles begins with a single step
— A Chinese proverb.

Being out of work, changing careers, or trying to get one's first job can be a very scary experience. It takes some people a great deal of time and effort to find a job they will enjoy. Others may walk right into an ideal employment situation. In any case, the journey to a career begins with the single step of doing something to get a job.

Many job counselors recommend to their clients to "get on your mark" by researching the job market for what you want to do. Next, "get ready" with the information and training you need to do the work you want to do. Then "get set" by finding out about companies that can use your skills and places where you want to work. Finally "go" for the job, by putting together a good resume that tells possible employers about your talents and skills. Be prepared to meet prospective employers with courteous manners, a good appearance, and sound interview skills.

SOURCES OF CAREER INFORMATION
Personal Contacts

Families and friends can be extremely helpful in providing career information. While they may not always have the information you need, they may know other people who do and can put you in touch with them. These contacts can lead to an "information interview," where talking to someone can give you information about a company or career. This person should have the experience to tell you how he or she trained for the job and got promotions or what he or she likes or dislikes about the job. Not only can the person tell you what to do, but also he or she can tell you what not to do.

Libraries and Career Centers

Libraries have a lot of information about careers and job training. Begin with the card catalog or computer listings under "vocations" or "careers" and then look under

specific fields of work. For instance, for those who like working with animals, there are veterinarians and veterinarian assistants, zoologists, animal trainers, breeders, groomers, and many other careers that involve working with animals. Check trade publications and magazines that describe and discuss the kind of work you want to do.

In addition the Bureau of Labor Statistics of the U.S. Department of Labor publishes the *Occupational Outlook Handbook*, which describes about 250 occupations in detail. School career centers often offer individual counseling and testing, guest speakers, field trips, and career days. Information in career guidance materials should be current. Try to find a number of sources, since one resource might glamorize the occupation, overstate the earnings, or exaggerate the demand for the occupation.

Counselors

Counselors are professionals trained to help you discover strengths and weaknesses, guide you through an evaluation of goals and values, and help determine what you want in a career. Counselors can be found in

- High school guidance offices,

- Placement offices in private vocational/technical schools,

- College career planning and placement offices,

- Vocational rehabilitation agencies,

- Counseling service offices offered by community organizations,

- Private counseling agencies, and

- State employment service offices.

The Internet

The career information available on the Internet provides much of the same information available through

TABLE 7.1

Where to Learn About Job Openings

- Personal contacts
- College career planning and placement offices
- Classified ads
    - National and local newspapers
    - Professional journals
    - Trade magazines
- Internet networks and resources
- State employment service offices
- Federal Government
- Professional associations
- Labor unions
- Employers
- Employment agencies and career consultants
- Community agencies

SOURCE: *Occupational Outlook Handbook, 2000–01.* Bureau of Labor Statistics

libraries, career centers, and guidance offices. However, no single network or resource will contain all the desired information. As in a library search, one must look through various lists by field or discipline or by using particular keywords.

Organizations

Professional societies, trade associations, labor unions, business firms, and educational institutions offer a variety of free or inexpensive career material. *The Guide to American Directories, The Directory of Directories*, and *The Encyclopedia of Associations*, found at local libraries, are useful resources. Trade organizations are particularly important if you already have a job and are seeking another one or fear being "downsized" by your present employer.

Education and Training Information

Every job requires some kind of training, even one that uses simple, everyday skills. Most people get some kind of training in life during the process of growing up. For example, just keeping your room clean, making the bed, and vacuuming the carpet teach skills. However, someone who has never used a telephone might not be a good choice for answering the company phone. On the other hand, phone skills can be taught and learned in a relatively short period of time.

Most jobs, however, require more training than just learning to use the telephone or vacuum a carpet. Free training may be available through vocational courses in public schools, local branches of state employment offices, or on-the-job training in apprenticeship programs. Some occupations require a few months of training, while others may take many years of education and cost a lot of money. Physicians, for instance, may spend

as many as 15 years and many tens of thousands of dollars to learn a specialty in medicine.

Colleges, schools, and training institutes readily reply to requests for information about their programs. Professional and trade associations have lists of schools that offer career preparation in their fields. Information on financial aid for study or training is available from a variety of sources—high school guidance counselors, college financial aid officers, banks and credit unions, and state and federal governments. Directories and guides to sources of student financial aid can be found in guidance offices and public libraries.

JOB SEARCH METHODS

Table 7.1 lists sources of information about job openings.

Personal Contacts—Networking

A good place to start collecting information is from family, friends, and acquaintances. Do not be afraid to ask friends or relatives if they know of an available job. While it might be embarrassing, many jobs are gotten through personal contacts. Although it may be difficult, they also may put you in touch with someone else who can help you. Such networking can lead to meeting with someone who is hiring for his/her firm or who knows of specific job openings.

Classified Ads

The "Help Wanted" ads in newspapers list hundreds of jobs, although many job openings are not listed. Also, classified ads sometimes do not give all important information. Many offer little or no description of the job, working conditions, or pay. Some ads do not identify the employer. They may simply give a post office box for sending a resume. This makes follow-up inquiries very difficult. Furthermore, some ads advertise employment agencies rather than actual employment openings. Some helpful hints on using classified ads include:

- Do not rely solely on the classified ads to find a job; follow other leads as well.

- Answer ads promptly since openings may be filled quickly, even before the ad stops appearing in the paper.

- Read the ads every day, particularly the Sunday edition, which usually includes the most listings.

- Know that "no experience necessary" ads often signal low wages, poor working conditions, or commission work. On the other hand, you have to start somewhere.

- Keep a record of all ads to which you have responded, including the specific skills, educational background, and personal qualifications required for the positions.

Internet Networks and Resources

A variety of information is available on the Internet, including job listings and job search resources and techniques. Internet resources are available 7 days a week, 24 hours a day. No single network or resource will contain all information on employment or career opportunities, so be prepared to search for what you need. Job listings may be posted by field or discipline, so begin your search using keywords.

A good place to start your job search is *America's Job Bank* (http://www.ajb.dni.us/). *America's Job Bank*, run by the U.S. Department of Labor's Employment and Training Administration, provides information on preparing resumes and using the Internet for job searches, as well as trends in the U.S. jobs market and approximately 1.4 million job openings. The Internet is completely unregulated, so if you come across a job offer that seems too good to be true, it probably is.

Public Employment Services

States operate employment services, sometimes called the Job Service, in coordination with the U.S. Employment Service of the U.S. Department of Labor. About 1,700 local offices help job seekers find jobs and employers find qualified workers at no cost to themselves. Telephone listings, under "Job Service" or "Employment," under the state government telephone listings, will show the nearest offices.

Private Employment Agencies

These agencies can be helpful, but they are in business to make money. Most agencies operate on a commission basis, with the fee dependent upon a percentage of the salary paid to a successful applicant. The newly hired employee or the hiring company will have to pay a sizable fee. Job seekers should find out the exact cost and who is responsible for paying the fees before using the service.

College Career Planning and Placement Offices

College placement offices facilitate job placement for their students and alumni. They set up appointments and provide facilities for interviews with recruiters. Placement offices usually list part-time, temporary, and summer jobs offered on campus. They also list jobs in regional business, nonprofit, and government organizations. Students can receive career counseling and testing, job search advice, and use of the career resource library. The last time a young person will likely have valuable services available for "free" are these college placement offices. (They are generally included in tuition and fees, so it is wise to make use of as many of them as needed.)

Community Agencies

Many nonprofit organizations, including churches, synagogues, and vocational rehabilitation agencies, offer coun-

TABLE 7.2

What Goes Into a Resume

- Name, address, and telephone number.
- Employment objective. State the type of work or specific job you are seeking.
- Education, including school name and address, dates of attendance, curriculum, and highest grade completed or degree awarded.
- Experience, paid and volunteer. Include the following for each job: Job title, name and location of employer, and dates of employment. Briefly describe your job duties.
- Special skills, proficiency in foreign languages, achievements, and membership in organizations.
- References, when requested.

SOURCE: *Occupational Outlook Handbook, 2000–01*. Bureau of Labor Statistics

seling, career development, and job placement services. These are often targeted to a particular group, such as women, youth, minorities, ex-offenders, or older workers.

Employers

It is possible to apply directly to employers without a referral. Potential employers can be found in the Yellow Pages, directories of local chambers of commerce, and in other directories that provide information about employers.

APPLYING FOR A JOB

Resumes and Application Forms

Resumes (summary of a job applicant's previous employment, education, and skills) and application forms are two ways to provide employers with written evidence of your qualifications. Some employers prefer that prospective employees present a resume, while others require that job seekers fill out an application form.

There are many ways to organize a resume. A variety of books are available in local libraries and bookstores. See Table 7.2 for the basic information that is included in a resume. The company to which the job seeker is applying usually supplies an application form. Job seekers need to fill out application forms completely and follow all instructions.

Cover Letters

A cover letter is sent with a resume or application form as a way to introduce the job seeker to prospective employers. It should capture the employer's attention, follow a business letter format, and include the following information:

- The name and address of the specific person to whom the letter is addressed,

- The reason for the applicant's interest in the company and type of job the applicant is seeking,

- A brief list of qualifications for the position including education, job experience, and unpaid experience,

TABLE 7.3

Job Interview Tips

Preparation:
- Learn about the organization.
- Have a specific job or jobs in mind.
- Review your qualifications for the job.
- Prepare answers to broad questions about yourself.
- Review your resume.
- Practice an interview with a friend or relative.
- Arrive before the scheduled time of your interview.

Personal Appearance:
- Be well groomed.
- Dress appropriately.
- Do not chew gum or smoke.

The Interview:
- Relax and answer each question concisely.
- Respond promptly.
- Use good manners. Learn the name of your interviewer and shake hands as you meet.
- Use proper English—avoid slang.
- Be cooperative and enthusiastic.
- Ask questions about the position and the organization.
- Thank the interviewer when you leave and, as a follow up, in writing.

Test (if employer gives one):
- Listen closely to instructions.
- Read each question carefully.
- Write legibly and clearly.
- Budget your time wisely and don't dwell on one question

Information to Bring to an Interview:
- Social Security number.
- Driver's license number.
- Resume. Although not all employers require applicants to bring a resume, you should be able to furnish the interviewer information about your education, training, and previous employment.
- References. An employer usually requires three references. Get permission before using anyone as a reference. Make sure they will give you a good reference. Try to avoid using relatives.

SOURCE: *Occupational Outlook Handbook, 2000–01.* Bureau of Labor Statistics

- Any special skills,

- References (if requested),

- A request for an interview, and

- Home and work phone number.

Interviewing

An interview showcases qualifications to an employer. Table 7.3 provides some helpful hints. The prepara-tion, personal appearance, and information you bring to the interview are all very important. Being prepared is perhaps the most important part of the interview. Preparation will show the interviewer that you are knowledge-able and confident, and you will also feel more at ease and have a "clear head" for answering questions and tak-ing any tests required.

No matter what the job, go to the interview as well groomed as possible and present yourself with polish and confidence. It is always better to be overdressed than underdressed. Never smoke, chew gum, or accept an alcoholic beverage. If, after the interview, you are still interested in the job, tell the interviewer.

Whether you get the job or not, it is important to fol-low through with a brief note of thanks to the person who interviewed you. The note is not just one of thanks, but another opportunity to "sell" your strong qualities. This is a courtesy that many people forget or fail to do, but smart job seekers always follow through. It almost always leaves a positive impression on a potential employer. If another job becomes available, the interviewer may remember that you were thoughtful enough and cared enough to say "thanks."

Testing

Many employers require prospective employees to take drug, alcohol, and/or psychological tests. See Chap-ter 8 for some information on testing.

EVALUATING A JOB OFFER

When a job is offered, the job seeker needs to evalu-ate the offer carefully. There are many issues to consider. Will the organization be a good place to work? Will the job be interesting? Are the people easy to work with? How are opportunities for advancement? Is the salary fair? Does the employer offer good benefits? Rarely will you ever find the perfect job, especially the first time out. Don't cut off possibilities because the job offered is not exactly the job you wanted or trained for.

CHAPTER 8
WORKERS' RIGHTS

Over the past 100 years, federal, state, and local governments have created a body of laws, rules, and regulations to protect the rights of workers. These laws cover many aspects of work. As it is impossible to review all of these elements and the many situations to which they apply, the following covers some of the major work-related laws. Most of this material was based on an article by Larry Drake and Rachel Moskowitz, "Your Rights in the Workplace," *Occupational Outlook Quarterly,* volume 41, number 2, Summer 1997.

WAGES AND HOURS

Passed in 1938, the Fair Labor Standards Act (FLSA-52 Stat 1060) is the most important wage and hour law. It applies to all businesses involved in interstate commerce and established rules covering minimum hourly wages, overtime pay, and the work of children. Many states also have statutes that set higher standards than the FLSA. Employers must abide by the more stringent rules.

The minimum wage was increased to $5.15 an hour on September 1, 1997. With a few minor exceptions, the FLSA requires that workers earning an hourly wage be paid overtime pay at least one and one half times the regular pay rate for all hours worked in the workweek after the first 40 hours.

The FLSA also contains provisions that regulate the wages at which young people may work and the hours they may work. Employers may pay youth under 20 years of age a minimum wage—$4.25 an hour during their first 90 consecutive calendar days of employment with an employer. Individuals under the age of 16 may work only under certain conditions. Youths 14 and 15 years old may work outside of school hours in various nonmanufacturing, nonmining, nonhazardous jobs. They may work up to 3 hours on a school day or 8 hours on a nonschool day for a total of 18 hours in a school week and 40 hours in a nonschool

week. In addition, work must be performed between the hours of 7 a.m. and 7 p.m., except from June 1 through Labor Day, when evening hours are extended to 9 p.m.

Although the federal minimum wage remained at $5.15 an hour in 2000, an initiative called the Living Wage Campaign proposed a national minimum wage rate of $8.00 per hour, or enough to support a family of four at the local poverty level. Even though federal policymakers were debating whether to raise the federal minimum wage $1.00 over 2–3 years, many county and city governments across the United States adopted living wage minimums of their own, which ranged from $6.25 to $10.75 per hour. However, estimates placed employees covered by living wage ordinances as a fairly small proportion of total U.S. employees.

UNEMPLOYMENT

The Social Security Act of 1935 (49 Stat 620) created a federal unemployment compensation system. Shortly afterward, the federal government decided to allow states to create their own unemployment systems. Every state has done so.

While there are minimum federal standards every state must meet, each state has its own and is responsible for determining who is eligible for benefits, how much unemployed workers will receive, and how long the benefits will last. Unemployment insurance benefits are paid entirely by taxes on employers, except in three states (Alaska, New Jersey, and Pennsylvania), where the employee also contributes.

During the late 1990s changes in the economy, workforce, and workplace prompted the U.S. Department of Labor to reassess the unemployment insurance system to better ensure that it met the needs of the changing U.S. employment realm. The Department invited peer comment on unemployment insurance issues. Generally, participants agreed that the program accomplished its goals and provided incentive for the unemployed to return to work. Furthermore, it would continue to fulfill these goals with consistent funding.

However, policy during 2000 was proposed by the Clinton administration that would fund employee family leave using unemployment insurance funds. Opponents claimed that such policy could draw any state unemployment insurance programs below solvency and could raise payroll taxes an average of 145 percent.

Benefits

Unemployment insurance pays benefits to qualified workers who are unemployed and looking for work. Most states pay a maximum of 26 weeks of benefits. People may be disqualified from receiving benefits for various reasons, such as voluntarily leaving work without good cause or being fired for misconduct. Another reason is the refusal of suitable work without good cause. "Good cause" must be connected with the job, rather than with the individual's personal life. Also, with few exceptions, workers are not eligible for benefits if their unemployment is caused by a labor dispute.

ON-THE-JOB SAFETY

In 1970 Congress passed the Occupational Safety and Health Act (PL 91-596). This law set up a comprehensive national policy to guarantee workers a safe and healthy workplace. The Labor Department's Occupational Safety and Health Administration (OSHA) enforces this statute.

Under the law, employers must furnish employment "free from recognized hazards" that are "likely to cause death or serious physical harm." OSHA has established hundreds of detailed occupational safety and health standards that regulate specific workplace hazards so employers will know what is required of them. Things covered include personal protective equipment, machine protections, structural protections, fire protection, and protection against hazardous materials, such as flammable gases.

While OSHA has established many required standards, it also issues nonbinding regulations. For example, in April 1998 OSHA recommended that retail outlets, such as convenience stores with a history of crime, use bulletproof glass or employ at least two clerks at night. It also suggested that such stores keep a minimum amount of cash on hand, use drop safes (the cashier can put money in but cannot take the money out) and security cameras, be well lit, and train workers how to behave during an armed robbery.

The act also gives workers the right to information about the kinds of hazards to which they are exposed in the workplace. Workers may be entitled to recover dam-

ages if they are harmed by unsafe and unhealthy workplace conditions. In certain rare circumstances, workers can walk off the job rather than expose themselves to an imminently dangerous situation.

At the beginning of the twenty-first century OSHA proposed an ergonomics standard. According to OSHA, 33 percent of all work-related injuries and illnesses are a result of work-related musculoskeletal disorders (MSDs). In 1997 compensation for such injuries comprised $1 out of every $3 spent on workers' compensation. Costs of MSDs were expected to rise from $20 billion to $54 billion per year. Ergonomic programs incorporate seating and office furniture that minimize the occurrence of MSDs such as repetitive stress disorder. The Employment Policy Foundation (EPF) criticized the OSHA proposed standard, claiming that it would cost business up to $100 billion annually and override any benefits. EPF claimed that companies had already made good progress in implementing ergonomic changes, and that the federal proposal was an unwise expenditure of taxpayer dollars.

For young people, workplace safety is covered by FLSA, in addition to the OSHA regulations covering all workers. FLSA prohibits employing minors under age 18 to work at 17 hazardous nonfarm jobs. These prohibited jobs include driving a motor vehicle, being an outside helper on a motor vehicle, operating various power-driven machines, and performing roofing operations. Limited exemptions are provided for apprentices and student-learners under specified conditions.

COMPENSATION FOR WORK-RELATED INJURIES AND ILLNESSES

If a person is injured on the job or becomes ill because of the work environment, he or she will likely come in contact with the workers' compensation program (workers' comp). Workers' comp is an insurance program that pays injured workers to compensate them for their lost wage-earning capability. It also pays workers' medical and rehabilitation expenses and provides benefits for dependents of workers who are killed on the job.

This program is financed primarily by insurance premiums paid by employers. Both workers and employers benefit from this program. Workers receive compensation in the event they are injured and unable to work. Employers benefit because the program makes the costs of workers' compensation a predictable business expense that can be included in production costs. Each state administers its own workers' comp programs.

For workers' comp to apply, there needs to be an "injury by accident." Generally, the accident must occur when the person is working. The injured worker and the workers' comp insurance company, or state insurance fund, tries to reach a settlement. If they cannot, there is an appeal process. Many states have a payment schedule that specifies definite amounts for particular injuries. In most cases, workers' comp will pay a worker a weekly amount equal to a percentage of his or her average weekly pay, up to a maximum set by law.

DISCRIMINATION AND HARASSMENT

Employers are not allowed to discriminate on the basis of sex, race, religion, national origin, or disability. Furthermore, they must ensure that workers are not subjected to sexual harassment.

Discrimination

There are many national laws protecting employees from discrimination in the workplace with respect to hiring, compensation, terms, conditions, and privileges of employment. These laws cover employees of all types of businesses, from very large to very small. They also apply to employment agencies and labor organizations.

The Equal Pay Act of 1963 (PL 88-38) established that employers cannot pay lower wages to an employee based on gender. Equal pay must be paid to workers for equal work if the jobs they perform require "equal skill, effort, and responsibility and are performed under similar working conditions."

The Civil Rights Act of 1964 (PL 88-352) makes it unlawful for an employer to discriminate against individuals on the basis of race, color, religion, national origin, or sex. This law was amended (PL 95-555) in 1978, making it unlawful for an employer to discriminate on the basis of pregnancy, childbirth, or a related medical condition. This law not only applies to hiring but also to promotion and termination. In 1997 the Supreme Court ruled in *Robinson v. Shell Oil Company* (No. 95-1376) that the Civil Rights Act of 1964 protected workers from retaliation for filing complaints about discrimination on the job. This ruling included forbidding retaliation in the form of a bad job recommendation after the worker is no longer employed.

The Age Discrimination in Employment Act of 1967 (PL 90-202) makes it unlawful for an employer to discriminate against individuals age 40 or older with respect to hiring, compensation, and employment on the basis of age.

The Americans with Disabilities Act (ADA) of 1990 (PL 101-336) makes it unlawful for an employer to discriminate in hiring, compensating, or employing individuals with disabilities. This law applies to companies that have 15 or more employees. The law requires reasonable accommodation for disabled applicants and employees. For example, if an employee cannot fit his or her wheelchair through the entrance to the workplace, the employer may be required to alter that entrance or provide a different work area. The ADA affected 43 million Americans at the beginning of the twenty-first century.

State and local laws extend the coverage of the federal statutes in different ways. Some state laws extend federal protections to employers who are covered by those statutes because of their small size, for example. Other states protect against discrimination based on factors not covered by federal law, such as sexual preference.

Sexual Harassment

Workers have the right to be free from sexual harassment—unwelcome sexual advances or conduct—from supervisors and coworkers, as well as from customers and clients. There are two main forms of sexual harassment. One is demanding sexual favors in return for job benefits over which the individual has some control, such as promotions. This is known as quid pro quo sexual harassment. Another type is "hostile work environment" sexual harassment. When individuals use obscene language, post lewd pictures, make unwelcome sexual advances, or talk about sex in an offensive manner, they are creating a hostile work environment.

Sexual harassment is a violation of the 1964 Civil Rights Act, as amended in 1972 (PL 92-261). Under the Civil Rights Act of 1991 (PL 102-166), victims of sexual harassment are entitled to damages for pain and suffering, as well as to lost pay. The Equal Employment Opportunity Commission defines sexual harassment as unwelcome sexual advances, requests for sexual favors, and other verbal or physical conduct of a sexual nature.

THE RIGHT TO JOIN A UNION

The National Labor Relations Act of 1935 (49 Stat 449) guarantees nonsupervisory employees the right to organize a union, choose their own representatives, and bargain collectively with their employer for higher pay, better benefits, improved working conditions, and more relaxed work rules. Workers have the right to join a union, if one exists, or to help organize one, if one does not exist. The law prohibits employers from punishing employees who exercise their right to join a union and participate in union activities. Workers in a company who want to form a union must ask a federal or state agency, such as the National Labor Relations Board, to hold an election to determine if a majority of workers want to be represented by a union.

Workers may be required to join a union after they are hired; such workplaces are called union shops. Twenty-one states have enacted right-to-work laws that prohibit the union shop. This means that to get or hold a job, workers do not have to join a union if one exists. Closed shops, in which only union members in good standing could be hired to begin with, are illegal.

By law, all workers in a bargaining unit are entitled to the benefits gained through union collective bargaining,

TABLE 8.1

National Estimates of the Prevalence of Drug and Alcohol Testing Among Worksites and Employees, by Selected Characteristics of the Worksite, 1992–1993

[In percent]

Characteristic	Worksites[1]			Employees		
	Total (in thousands)	Test for drug use	Test for alcohol use	Total (in thousands)	In worksites that test for drug use	In worksites that test for acohol use
All worksites	162.8 (-)	48.4 (1.2)	23.0 (1.0)	41,127 (1,271)	62.3 (1.6)	32.7 (2.1)
Worksites size						
50-99 employees	61.6 (1.7)	40.2 (2.1)	16.5 (1.6)	4,319 (124)	40.7 (2.2)	16.7 (1.6)
100-249 employees	66.0 (1.8)	48.2 (1.9)	22.9 (1.7)	9,612 (265)	48.9 (1.9)	23.2 (1.7)
250-999 employees	29.0 (.9)	61.4 (2.1)	32.7 (2.1)	12,520 (404)	62.8 (2.1)	33.5 (2.2)
1,000 employees or more	6.2 (.3)	70.9 (3.4)	42.1 (3.5)	14,675 (1,282)	77.1 (3.4)	43.0 (5.0)
Type of industry						
Manufacturing	54.0 (1.0)	60.2 (2.2)	28.3 (2.0)	14,058 (554)	73.5 (2.2)	37.5 (2.8)
Wholesale and retail	32.2 (1.1)	53.7 (3.3)	22.1 (2.7)	4,901 (236)	57.3 (3.0)	27.7 (3.2)
Communications, utilities, and transportation	13.5 (.8)	72.4 (3.3)	34.9 (3.0)	4,202 (435)	85.8 (2.6)	43.9 (5.3)
Finance, insurance, and real estate	14.2 (0.5)	22.6 (2.1)	7.8 (1.3)	4,369 (563)	50.2 (6.7)	12.2 (3.1)
Mining and construction	5.6 (.4)	69.6 (4.1)	28.6 (3.5)	801 (49)	77.7 (3.2)	32.2 (3.1)
Services	43.3 (1.2)	27.9 (2.0)	17.4 (1.7)	12,796 (998)	47.5 (4.5)	32.7 (5.2)
Region						
Northeast	33.0 (1.5)	33.3 (2.4)	12.9 (1.7)	9,356 (617)	49.1 (3.6)	19.3 (2.6)
Midwest	40.7 (1.8)	50.3 (2.5)	24.0 (2.1)	10,190 (616)	62.4 (3.1)	34.4 (3.2)
South	59.1 (1.9)	56.3 (2.0)	26.3 (1.8)	14,986 (1,168)	71.8 (2.6)	36.9 (4.4)
West	30.0 (1.6)	46.8 (2.9)	26.0 (2.5)	6,594 (460)	59.4 (3.3)	39.7 (3.9)

[1] Worksites of private nonagricultural firms with more than 50 full-time employees at the time of survey.

NOTE: Standard errors appear in parentheses.

SOURCE: Tyler D. Hartwell et al. *Prevalence of Drug Testing in the Workplace.* Monthly Labor Review, vol. 119, no. 11

whether they are union members or not. Nonunion workers employed by a unionized company get the same benefits as union members, even if they do not join the union.

While unions historically represented the working class, they also have a growing presence in professional specialties. As an example, medical doctors began organizing unions during 2000. Their initiative to organize was driven partly by policy that made it possible for patients to sue for malpractice under state laws. An unresolved issue remained as of June 2000—whether doctors in organized labor unions should have the right to strike.

EMPLOYER TESTING

Employers may administer various tests to potential or current employees in order to determine their fitness to perform the duties of a position. Recently, many companies have introduced testing for the use of drugs and are administering polygraph (lie detector) exams and psychological tests.

Drug and Alcohol Testing

Growing concern over the impact of drug and alcohol abuse in the workplace has led to an increase in the number of employers who test for drug and alcohol abuse. These tests are performed on employees and, increasingly, on job applicants. Workers in some jobs, such as air-

line pilots, are required by law to submit to drug and alcohol testing, but an increasing number of employers are requiring employees to submit to testing as a condition of employment.

Some programs use mandatory and random testing. Others test only on the basis of reasonable suspicion. Workers in jobs that are particularly related to safety or security concerns are more likely to be tested. Workers in some occupations, such as those who operate airplanes, buses, and large trucks, are required to take a drug and alcohol test upon employment. They also must submit to testing if they have been involved in an accident.

Tyler D. Hartwell, Paul D. Steele, Michael T. French, and Nathaniel F. Rodman, in "Prevalence of Drug Testing in the Workplace" (*Monthly Labor Review,* Bureau of Labor Statistics, November 1996), surveyed the nation's companies with 50 or more employees to determine how many tested for alcohol and/or drug abuse. They found about 48 percent tested for drug abuse, and 23 percent tested for alcohol abuse. (See Table 8.1.)

The larger the company, the more likely employees were tested. Among smaller companies with 50 to 99 workers, 40 percent tested for drug use and 16.5 percent for alcohol use. Among larger companies with 1,000 employees or more, 71 percent tested for drug use and 42 percent for alcohol use. Those working in communications, mining and construction, manufacturing, and wholesale and retail were more likely to be tested than those in finance and services. Those working in the Northeast were less likely to be tested than those living in other regions. (See Table 8.1.)

While 48 percent of the companies had drug testing, only 24 percent examined all their employees. Fourteen percent tested only job applicants, 4 percent inspected only employees that the Department of Transportation requires be analyzed, 1 percent assessed only safety or security employees, and 6 percent tested various combinations of types of employees.

What happens to job applicants or employees who refuse to take drug tests? That depends on where they work and the state law, if there is one. In many cases refusal to take the test is grounds for not getting a job or being fired.

If a job applicant takes the test and tests positive, he or she may not get the job. If a worker tests positive on a random drug test, treatment and counseling sponsored by the company may be given, or employment may be terminated.

These tests have led to controversy throughout the country because many people think the tests invade personal privacy. By 1998, 17 states had some type of regulation to control drug testing in the private sector. Some states ban or restrict random drug testing, while others require that a second, confirmatory drug test be given if the first one is positive. Some states require that the results of these tests be kept confidential, while others limit the type of discipline employers can mete out to employees who fail drug tests.

Polygraph Exams

At one time it was popular among many employers to use polygraph tests on their employees. Many workers resented these tests, and their aversion eventually led a number of states to pass laws limiting their use. In 1988 Congress passed the Employee Polygraph Protection Act (PL 100-347), which prohibits most private employers from using lie detector tests either for preemployment screening or during the course of employment. In most circumstances employers are prohibited from requiring or requesting any employee or job applicant to take a lie detector test. Employers are also prevented from discharging, disciplining, or discriminating against an employee or prospective employee for refusing to take a test or for exercising other rights under this act.

Still, many employers may administer these tests. Federal, state, and local governments are exempt from the Employee Polygraph Protection Act, and the law does not apply to tests given by the federal government to certain private individuals engaged in national security-related activities. Furthermore, the act permits polygraph tests to be administered in the private sector to certain prospective employees of security service firms and pharmaceutical manufacturers, distributors, and dispensers.

The act also permits polygraph testing of certain employees who are reasonably suspected of involvement in a workplace incident, such as theft or embezzlement, that resulted in economic loss to the employer. Some restrictions may apply in these cases, and state or local law or collective bargaining agreements may be more restrictive.

Where polygraph tests are permitted, they are subject to numerous strict standards concerning the conduct and length of the test. Persons who take polygraph tests have a number of specific rights, including the right to a written notice before testing, the right to refuse or discontinue a test, and the right not to have test results disclosed to unauthorized persons.

In cases where employers cannot legally administer polygraph testing, they may instead be able to administer what is known as honesty testing, discussed below. Honesty testing has opponents, including some labor unions and others that are concerned about where to draw the line regarding privacy. On the other hand, such methods sustain interest from employers, who wish to make the best hiring decisions and minimize, in some cases, company theft. Employers may also request information such as applicants' credit reports or criminal records.

Psychological Testing

Concerned about the high costs and legal problems that can result from hiring the wrong person for the job, some employers are administering psychological tests to prospective employees and to employees who are under consideration for promotions. In 1997 the American Management Association International, a 90,000 member organization in New York, found that 38.6 percent of 906 companies surveyed said they gave psychological exams to job applicants. These tests ranged from "honesty testing" and career directions to analytical thinking. According to Rochelle Kaplan, legal counsel for the National Association of Colleges and Employers and a specialist in employment and labor law, any requested psychological test results should relate directly to the job being applied for. Additionally, access to such test results should be limited to those making the hiring decision.

CHAPTER 9
BUSINESS OPPORTUNITIES

Starting or acquiring a business has long been considered an American dream. For many, this dream has become a reality. The Dun & Bradstreet Corporation (D & B) compiles data on entrepreneurial activity in the United States. Every year, people start thousands of businesses. Other firms fail, discontinue, are sold, or continue operating. According to D & B, over 700,000 changes are made daily to its database of over 11 million businesses.

The number of small businesses reported by Dun and Bradstreet, a company of The Dun and Bradstreet Corporation, and the Bureau of the Census 1992 Economic Survey differ dramatically. D & B listed 11 million businesses, while the Bureau of the Census counted 17 million. D & B counts small businesses that become part of its database through an application for credit at a bank or other lending facility. They also might respond to mailers sent out by D & B requesting a business owner to voluntarily become part of the D & B database. Companies that did not apply for credit, did not want anyone to know their affairs, or ignored the mailer would not be included in the D & B database and therefore would not be counted.

As indicated in the footnote below, the Bureau of the Census counted Schedule C businesses (individual proprietorship or self-employed person) and Subchapter S corporations. It does not count the large number of small businesses incorporated as standard corporations.

As a result, both surveys undercount the number of small businesses in the United States. Recognizing this, both surveys are used as indicators. While neither survey may be completely accurate, a base of 11 or 17 million is certainly large enough upon which to base observations.

In addition, every 5 years in years ending in "2" and "7," the Bureau of the Census surveys business enterprises. Any business that filed an IRS form 1040, Schedule C (individual proprietorship or self-employed persons), form 1065 (partnership), or form 1120S (Subchapter S corpora-

tion—usually small corporations in which the profits pass through to the owners without being taxed first) was counted. The latest Bureau of the Census survey with available data is the *1992 Economic Census*. Although the*1997 Economic Census* has been carried out, data for these studies is not normally available until several years after the study.

BUSINESS STARTS

In 1998, according to D & B, business starts decreased by 7 percent to total 155,141 (down from 166,740 startups in 1997). The 1998 startups employed 906,105 people. D & B speculated that startups declined due to the strong U.S. economy; startups are assumed to increase when people face unemployment and consider other methods of earning a living.

The largest percentages of business startups in 1998 were in the service and retail sectors; together they comprised 53 percent of 1998 startups and 54 percent of 1998 jobs created by startups. However, these represented declines from 1997 figures, and figures in almost every industry sector declined. For 1998, business startups increased over 1997 in agriculture, forestry, and fishing, as well as finance, insurance, and real estate. On a regional basis, 1998 business startups increased employment only in the southeast part of the United States. By mid 2000, 2,394 businesses in the U.S. were started weekly, down from 3,009 weekly businesses at the same time in 1999. (See Table 9.1.) Figure 9.1 illustrates the overall decline of business startups from 1994 through 1997.

Most businesses that start up are very small. In 1997, 54 percent of the new businesses employed just two people or less. Only 10 percent of the firms employed more than 11 people. (See Table 9.2 and Figure 9.2.)

BUSINESS FAILURES

In 1997 D & B found that 83,384 business failed. The failure rate of 88 per 10,000 businesses listed with D & B

TABLE 9.1

Weekly Business Starts—2000 vs. 1999

	2000 Week Ending	1999 Week Ending	2000 Weekly Starts	1999 Weekly Starts	2000 13-week Moving Average	2000 52-week Moving Average	2000 Year-to-date Starts	1999 Year-to-date Starts	Change 2000 vs 1999
21	5/26/00	5/28/99	2,394	3,009	2,495	2,718	50,912	58,372	-12.8%
20	5/19/00	5/21/99	2,311	2,920	2,478	2,729	48,518	55,363	-12.4%
19	5/12/00	5/14/99	2,223	2,811	2,469	2,741	46,207	52,443	-11.9%
18	5/5/00	5/7/99	2,230	2,713	2,498	2,752	43,984	49,632	-11.4%
17	4/28/00	4/30/99	2,436	3,089	2,506	2,762	41,754	46,916	-11.0%
16	4/21/00	4/23/99	2,254	3,397	2,495	2,774	39,318	43,830	-10.3%
15	4/14/00	4/16/99	2,632	3,096	2,502	2,796	37,064	40,433	-8.3%
14	4/7/00	4/9/99	2,765	2,939	2,519	2,805	34,432	37,337	-7.8%
13	3/31/00	4/2/99	2,546	3,409	2,436	2,808	31,667	34,398	-7.9%
12	3/24/00	3/26/99	2,686	2,534	2,463	2,825	29,121	30,989	-6.0%
11	3/17/00	3/19/99	2,323	2,765	2,458	2,822	26,435	28,455	-7.1%
10	3/10/00	3/12/99	2,635	2,588	2,557	2,831	24,112	25,690	-6.1%
9	3/3/00	3/5/99	3,006	2,644	2,621	2,830	21,477	23,102	-7.0%
8	2/25/00	2/26/99	2,169	2,729	2,633	2,823	18,471	20,458	-9.7%
7	2/18/00	2/19/99	2,189	2,201	2,640	2,834	16,302	17,729	-8.0%
6	2/11/00	2/12/99	2,609	2,245	2,757	2,834	14,113	15,528	-9.1%
5	2/4/00	2/5/99	2,333	2,784	2,813	2,827	11,504	13,283	-13.4%
4	1/28/00	1/29/99	2,294	2,816	2,885	2,835	9,171	10,499	-12.6%
3	1/21/00	1/22/99	2,344*	2,451*	3,010	2,845	6,877	7,683	-10.5%
2	1/14/00	1/15/99	2,843	2,420	3,089	2,848	4,533	5,232	-13.4%
1	1/7/00	1/8/99	1,690*	2,812	3,131	2,839	1,690	2,812	-39.9%

* Four-day week

Note: The 13-week moving average represents the average level of starts for a period of approximately one quarter ending with the current week. This average presents a better measure of the trend in new business activity by eliminating the volatility often associated with monthly or weekly comparisons of data. The 52-week moving average column indicates change in business starts over the course of a year and hence is a useful indicator of the relative level of activity. Comparisons of year-to-date figures in the first few weeks of the year are not conclusive.

SOURCE: Economic Analysis Department, The Dunn and Bradstreet Corp., May 31, 2000

FIGURE 9.1

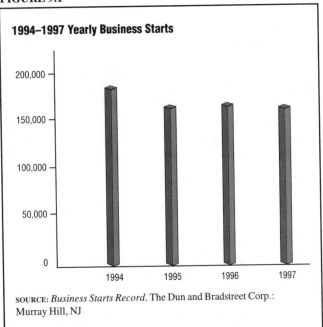

1994–1997 Yearly Business Starts

SOURCE: *Business Starts Record.* The Dun and Bradstreet Corp.: Murray Hill, NJ

TABLE 9.2

Business Starts Distribution by Employment Size

	1996		1997	
	Firms	Percent	Firms	Percent
Employees				
2 or less	98,671	57.9%	89,927	53.9%
3 to 5	38,129	22.4%	40,304	24.2%
6 to 10	18,135	10.6%	19,393	11.6%
11 to 20	8,727	5.1%	9,402	5.6%
21 or more	6,813	4.0%	7,714	4.6%
Total	170,475	100.0%	166,740	100.0%

SOURCE: *Business Starts Record.* The Dun and Bradstreet Corp.: Murray Hill, NJ

that 71.7 percent of discontinued businesses attributed their failure to inadequate cash flow or low sales. Another 8.2 percent thought they were unsuccessful because of lack of access to business loans or credit.

NUMBER OF BUSINESSES

The Bureau of the Census identified almost 17.3 million individual proprietors, partnerships, and Subchapter S corporations in 1992, with sales and receipts of $3.3 trillion. Nonminority males owned a majority (59 per-

was well below a high of 120 in 1986. Before that the previous high was 150 per 10,000 failures in 1932, a Great Depression year. In 1997 each failed firm owed an average liability (debt) of $448,970. (See Table 9.3 and Figure 9.3.) The *1992 Economic Census* survey reported

cent) of the firms, while women owned 34 percent, and minorities operated 11 percent. (See Table 9.4.) The Census Bureau reported that while the nonminority male- and female-owned firms were spread across all states, more than half of all minority-owned firms were located in just four states: California, Texas, Florida, and New York. Approximately 47 percent of the minority population is concentrated in these four states.

Most of these firms were concentrated in the service industries. Forty-five percent of all U.S. firms, 48 percent of the minority-owned firms, 54 percent of the firms owned by women, and 41 percent of the firms owned by nonminority males were classified as services. Retail trade had the next largest share—14 percent of all U.S. firms, 16 percent of the minority-owned firms, and 19 percent of the women-owned firms. However, construction had the second largest share (15 percent) of the nonminority male-owned firms.

HOW OWNERS ACQUIRED THEIR BUSINESSES

Most (69 percent) owners founded their own businesses. About 10 percent had the businesses transferred to them, generally as a gift, while another 10 percent bought the businesses. About 3 percent inherited their firms. (See Table 9.5.)

REASONS FOR BECOMING A BUSINESS OWNER

One-fifth (21.3 percent) of owners reported that they became an owner to have a primary source of income, while one-fourth (25.6 percent) wanted to have a secondary source of income. Another one-fifth (21.5 percent) wanted to be their own boss. Less than 3 percent wanted to bring a new idea to the marketplace. Approximately 8 percent wanted to have more freedom to meet family responsibilities. (See Table 9.5.)

CAPITAL REQUIREMENTS

Most 1992 business owners (57 percent) started their enterprises with less than $5,000. In fact, one-fourth (25 percent) required no capital. (See Table 9.5.) Forty-four percent of the owners did not borrow their starting capital but used money or assets of their own or from their families. Only 19 percent used capital based on a personal loan, which could have included borrowing against the home mortgage, using credit cards, or borrowing from a family member.

PROFITABILITY

In 1992, 35 percent of business owners reported that 75 percent or more of their personal income was produced as a result of their business, while 36 percent reported that none or less than 10 percent of their income came from the business. (See Table 9.6.)

FIGURE 9.2

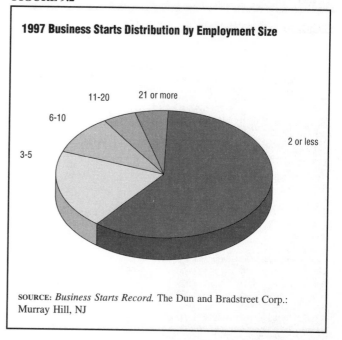

1997 Business Starts Distribution by Employment Size

SOURCE: *Business Starts Record.* The Dun and Bradstreet Corp.: Murray Hill, NJ

Thirty-nine percent of businesses reported a net profit of less than $10,000 from their businesses, while 21 percent claimed a profit of $10,000 or more. On the other hand, 20 percent of the businesses reported experiencing a net loss in 1992. (See Table 9.6.)

HOME-BASED BUSINESSES

In 1992 approximately half (50 percent) of all businesses were home-based. Not surprisingly, the percentage of firms operated from a home tended to be higher for smaller firms. Fifty-seven percent of businesses with receipts less than $25,000 were home-based, compared to 26 percent of firms with receipts of $25,000 to $199,999, 16 percent of firms with receipts of $200,000 to $999,000, and only 5 percent of firms with receipts of $1,000,000 or more.

Of the home-based businesses, male-owned firms were most likely to use the residence to do clerical work only or for phone calls or e-mail. In contrast, home-based women-owned firms were more likely to use their residences to produce goods or services on the premises. (See Table 9.7.)

OWNER'S WORK EXPERIENCE

Sixty-six percent of the business owners stated that the business they owned in 1992 was the first one they had owned. Approximately 69 percent of the business owners reported that they were the original founders of the business. About 21 percent purchased their share of the business or received a transfer of ownership in the business. For a firm with $50,000 or more in receipts in 1992, the larger the receipts, the less likely the business

TABLE 9.3

Business Failures, 1927–1997

	Number of failures	Total failure liabilities	Failure rate per 10,000 listed concerns	Average liability per failure		Number of failures	Total failure liabilities	Failure rate per 10,000 listed concerns	Average liability per failure
1927	23,146	$ 520,105,000	106	$22,471	1962	15,782	$ 1,213,601,000	61	$ 76,898
1928	23,842	489,559,000	109	20,534	1963	14,374	1,352,593,000	56	94,100
1929	22,909	483,252,000	104	21,094	1964	13,501	1,329,223,000	53	98,454
1930	26,355	668,282,000	122	25,357	1965	13,514	1,321,666,000	53	97,800
1931	28,285	736,310,000	133	26,032	1966	13,061	1,385,659,000	52	106,091
1932	31,822	928,313,000	154	29,172	1967	12,364	1,265,227,000	49	102,332
1933	19,859	457,520,000	100	23,038	1968	9,636	940,996,000	39	97,654
1934	12,091	333,959,000	61	27,621	1969	9,154	1,142,113,000	37	124,767
1935	12,244	310,580,000	62	25,366	1970	10,748	1,887,754,000	44	175,638
1936	9,607	203,173,000	48	21,148	1971	10,326	1,916,929,000	42	185,641
1937	9,490	$ 183,253,000	46	$19,310	1972	9,566	$ 2,000,244,000	38	$ 209,099
1938	12,836	246,505,000	61	19,204	1973	9,345	2,298,606,000	36	245,972
1939	14,768	182,520,000	70	12,359	1974	9,915	3,053,137,000	38	307,931
1940	13,619	166,684,000	63	12,239	1975	11,432	4,380,170,000	43	383,150
1941	11,848	136,104,000	55	11,488	1976	9,628	3,011,271,000	35	312,762
1942	9,405	100,763,000	45	10,713	1977	7,919	3,095,317,000	28	390,872
1943	3,221	45,339,000	16	14,076	1978	6,619	2,656,006,000	24	401,270
1944	1,222	31,660,000	7	25,908	1979	7,564	2,667,362,000	28	352,639
1945	809	30,225,000	4	37,361	1980	11,742	4,635,080,000	42	394,744
1946	1,129	67,349,000	5	59,654	1981	16,794	6,955,180,000	61	414,147
1947	3,474	$ 204,612,000	14	$58,898	1982	24,908	$15,610,792,000	88	$ 626,738
1948	5,250	234,620,000	20	44,690	1983	31,334	16,072,860,000	110	512,953
1949	9,246	308,109,000	34	33,323	1984	52,078	29,268,646,871	107	562,016
1950	9,162	248,283,000	34	27,099	1985	57,253	36,937,369,478	115	645,160
1951	8,058	259,547,000	31	32,210	1986	61,616	44,723,991,601	120	725,850
1952	7,611	283,314,000	29	37,224	1987	61,111	34,723,831,429	102	568,209
1953	8,862	394,153,000	33	44,477	1988	57,097	39,573,030,341	98	693,084
1954	11,086	462,628,000	42	41,731	1989	50,361	42,328,790,375	65	840,507
1955	10,969	449,380,000	42	40,968	1990	60,747	56,130,073,898	74	923,996
1956	12,686	562,697,000	48	44,356	1991	88,140	96,825,314,741	107	1,098,539
1957	13,739	615,293,000	52	44,784	1992	97,069	94,317,500,288	110	971,653
1958	14,964	728,258,000	56	48,667	1993	86,133	47,755,514,259	109	554,438
1959	14,053	692,808,000	52	49,300	1994	71,558	28,977,866,378	86	404,956
1960	15,445	938,630,000	57	60,772	1995	71,128	37,283,550,627	82	524,175
1961	17,075	1,090,123,000	64	63,843	1996	71,931	29,568,731,719	80	411,071
					1997p	83,384	37,436,934,664	88	448,970

Due to a statistical revision, data prior to 1984 are not directly comparable with the new series.

p = preliminary

SOURCE: *Business Failure Record*. The Dun and Bradstreet Corp.: Murray Hill, NJ

was to be owned by the "original founder." Prior to beginning or acquiring the business, half (49.9 percent) the owners had close relatives who owned a business or who had been self-employed.

Two-thirds (65.5 percent) had never owned another business. About one-fifth (21.3 percent) reported having worked for relatives. Fifty-two percent of business owners had 10 or more years of work experience prior to starting or acquiring their businesses. More than one-third (33.9 percent) had no managerial experience when they started their businesses. One-fifth (19.6 percent) had 10 or more years of managerial experience. (See Table 9.8.)

Fifty-one percent of the business owners managed or worked in their business the entire year (48 weeks or more). About 35 percent of business owners averaged more than 40 hours per week in their business, while 36 percent worked less than 20 hours per week. The percent-age of business owners working less than 20 hours per week was highest in the finance, insurance, and real estate sector. (See Table 9.9.)

OWNER CHARACTERISTICS

In 1992 half (50 percent) of the business owners in each group were between the ages of 35 and 54 years of age, and over half of those individuals were in the 35- to 44-year age bracket. Seven of ten (71.9 percent) of the owners were married when they began or acquired their business. Most (84.1 percent) were born in the United States, 9 percent were born outside the United States, and 7 percent did not report their status. (See Table 9.10.) Asians and Pacific Islanders dominated the foreign-born percentages. (See Figure 9.4.)

Fewer than 10 percent (9.4 percent) of business owners had less than a high school education; 22.6 percent

FIGURE 9.3

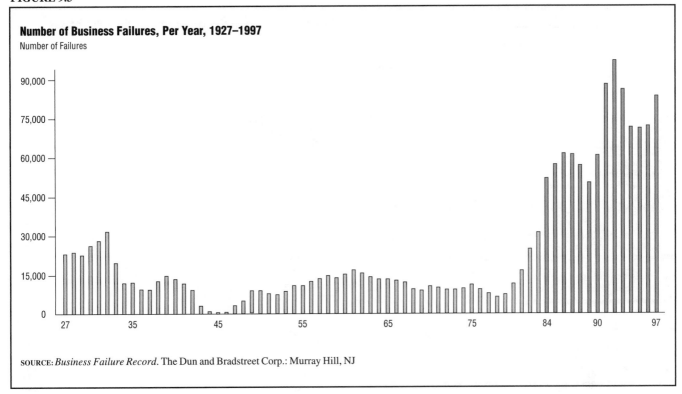

Number of Business Failures, Per Year, 1927–1997

Number of Failures

SOURCE: *Business Failure Record*. The Dun and Bradstreet Corp.: Murray Hill, NJ

had completed high school or had a GED equivalency. About one-fifth (20.2 percent) had attained a bachelor's degree. Another 15 percent had attained an advanced degree. One of six (17.3 percent) business owners who had attended school beyond high school studied business; another 11.7 percent had a liberal arts/general studies education. (See Table 9.11.)

Minority Business Owners

A survey by Dun & Bradstreet, conducted in early 1999, showed that minorities were becoming less optimistic about the performance of their small businesses. Minority business owners showed lowered expectations for customer growth, revenue growth, profit growth, and economic outlook, among others. The biggest challenge to minorities in running their businesses was keeping good employees. Future challenges that concerned minorities included government regulations and cash flow. Previously, minority attitudes about their businesses had tended to be more optimistic than the rest of the small business population in the United States.

IMPACT OF THE INTERNET

A Dun & Bradstreet 2000 survey indicated that between 1999 and 2000, the proportion of small business owners with Internet access jumped 57 percent. By 2000, 70 percent of small businesses had online access. Regardless, half of these businesses claimed that the Internet had no significant impact on their business. The data showed that the use of the Internet for marketing and research had actually declined. According to Dun & Bradstreet, this seemed to indicate that small businesses were proceeding cautiously into the realm of e-commerce. Only 26 percent of businesses used the Internet to sell or market products. The top use of online access was e-mail (71 percent). (See Table 9.12.)

Small businesses were increasingly maintaining an online presence through website development. Small business websites increased 10 percent between 1998 and 1999 for businesses overall. Sixty-five percent of businesses with 26–100 employees indicated that they had a web page or site in 2000. Businesses with 6–25 employees showed the slowest growth in website development between 1999 and 2000. (See Table 9.13.)

TABLE 9.4

Business Ownership Group, 1992

Ownership group	Firms (number)	Sales and receipts ($1,000,000)
All businesses[1]	17,253,143	3,324,200
All minorities[1]	1,965,565	202,011
Hispanic	771,708	72,824
Black.	620,912	32,197
Asian, Pacific Islander, American Indian, and Alaska Native (APVAIAN or referred to as Other minority)	606,426	99,709
Women	5,888,883	642,484
Nonminority male	10,114,456	2,526,942

[1]Detail does not add to total because of inclusion of some firms in more than one group. Firms that were equally owned by two or more minorities are included in the data for each minority group, but counted only once at total levels.

SOURCE: *Characteristics of Business Owners, 1992 Economic Census.* U.S. Census Bureau: Washington, D.C.

TABLE 9.5

Characteristics of Business Owners and Their Businesses—Start–Up Issues
[Detail may not add to total due to rounding]

Item	All businesses
HOW THE OWNER ACQUIRED THE BUSINESS	
Founded	68.9
Received transfer of ownership/gift	10.5
Purchased	10.1
Inherited	2.7
Other means	2.2
Not reported	5.6
REASON FOR BECOMING AN OWNER IN THE BUSINESS	
To have a primary source of income	21.3
To have a secondary source of income	25.6
To have work which conforms to owner's health limitations	1.6
To have work not available elsewhere in the job market	1.5
To have more freedom to meet family responsibilities.	7.6
To bring a new idea to the marketplace	2.6
To advance in my profession	6.2
To be my own boss	21.5
Other reason	6:7
Not reported	5.5
TOTAL CAPITAL NEEDED BY OWNER TO START/ACQUIRE THE BUSINESS	
None	25.0
Less than $5,000	32.0
$5,000 to $9,999	9.6
$10,000 to $24,999	11.4
$25,000 to $49,999	5.7
$50,000 to $99,999	4.6
$100,000 to $249,999	3.0
$250,000 to $999,999	1.4
$1,000,000 or more	.5
Not reported	6.8

SOURCE: *Characteristics of Business Owners, 1992 Economic Census.* U.S. Census Bureau: Washington, D.C.

TABLE 9.6

Characteristics of Business Owners and Their Businesses—Profits and Income
[Detail may not add to total due to rounding.]

Item	All businesses
BUSINESS'S NET PROFIT (OR LOSS) BEFORE TAXES AS REPORTED ON ITS TAX RETURN	
Net Profit	
$100,000 or more	2.2
$25,000 to $99,999	8.0
$10,000 to $24,999	8.3
Less than $10,000	38.5
Net Loss	
Less than $10,000	15.6
$10,000 to $24,999	2.6
$25,000 to $99,999	1.5
$100,000 or more	.7
Not reported	22.5
DURING 1992, THE PERCENT OF OWNER'S TOTAL PERSONAL INCOME PRODUCED AS A RESULT OF THE BUSINESS	
None	12.9
Less than 10 percent	22.9
10 to 24 percent	8.4
25 to 49 percent	6.7
50 to 74 percent	5.5
75 to 99 percent	11.1
100 percent	24.1
Not reported	8.5

SOURCE: *Characteristics of Business Owners, 1992 Economic Census.* U.S. Census Bureau: Washington, D.C.

TABLE 9.7

Summary Characteristics of Business Owners and Their Businesses—Business Location, 1992

Detail may not add to total due to rounding.

Item	All businesses	Hispanic-owned businesses	Black-owned businesses	Other minority-owned businesses	Women-owned businesses	Nonminority male-owned businesses	Standard error of estimate for column-				
	A	B	C	D	E	F	A	B	C	D	E
OPERATED PRIMARILY FROM OR IN A HOME WHEN FIRST ESTABLISHED											
Yes	52.1	46.2	48.7	34.3	55.2	51.7	.6	1.4	1.2	1.0	.8
No	40.0	43.4	36.7	56.9	35.4	41.7	.6	.8	1.0	1.1	.4
Don't know	1.7	2.0	2.1	3.3	1.7	1.8	.3	.3	.2	.2	.3
Not reported	6.2	8.4	12.5	5.5	7.7	5.0	.3	.9	.4	.2	.7
OPERATED PRIMARILY FROM OR IN A HOME DURING 1992											
Yes	49.6	44.2	47.2	33.8	53.2	46.8	.6	1.6	1.1	1.0	.7
No	43.2	45.7	37.7	59.9	38.2	45.2	.4	1.0	.9	1.1	.4
Not reported	7.2	10.1	15.1	6.3	8.6	6.0	.4	I.0	.4	.5	.8
HOME-BASED BUSINESSES' PRIMARY USE OF THE HOME											
To produce goods/services on the on the premises	20.2	17.4	18.5	15.8	26.4	17.3	.6	1.2	.8	1.1	.8
To do clerical work (goods/services produced off the premises)	23.7	18.9	21.2	13.9	22.6	24.9	.7	1.0	.7	.7	.8
To telecommute (outside employment doing office work at home)	8.2	8.1	8.1	7.0	6.8	9.0	.4	.2	.4	.7	.5
Not reported	13.1	17.8	21.8	13.1	14.3	11.9	.5	1.3	.8	.5	.8
Not applicable	34.9	38.1	30.3	50.3	30.0	36.8	.4	.6	.9	.9	.5

SOURCE: *Characteristics of Business Owners, 1992 Economic Census.* U.S. Census Bureau: Washington, D.C.

TABLE 9.8

Summary Characteristics of Business Owners and Their Businesses—Work Experience, 1992

Detail may not add to total due to rounding.

Item	All businesses	Hispanic-owned businesses	Black-owned businesses	Other minority-owned businesses	Women-owned businesses	Nonminority male-owned businesses	Standard error of estimate for column-					
	A	B	C	D	E	F	A	B	C	D	E	F
YEARS OF WORK EXPERIENCE PRIOR TO STARTING/ACQUIRING THE BUSINESS												
None (did not work)	7.6	12.8	9.7	13.7	9.0	6.3	.4	.5	.6	.9	.7	.5
Less than 2 years	6.3	7.8	6.4	8.5	6.9	5.7	.4	.6	.3	.8	.8	.5
2 to 5 years	14.2	16.5	12.7	18.9	13.8	14.1	.5	.7	.5	1.1	.5	.8
6 to 9 years	14.1	13.0	13.2	14.7	13.4	14.5	.5	.6	.4	.8	.6	.9
10 to 19 years	26.4	25.4	26.2	23.6	27.6	26.0	.6	.9	.6	.6	.8	1.0
20 years or more	25.9	17.7	22.3	14.8	23.3	28.3	.9	.5	.3	.6	1.2	1.6
Not reported	5.5	6.7	9.4	5.8	6.0	5.0	.3	.5	.4	.5	.5	.5
PREVIOUS YEARS OF WORK EXPERIENCE IN A MANAGERIAL CAPACITY												
None	33.9	35.1	40.6	28.1	36.0	32.7	.7	.8	.7	.9	.8	1.1
Less than 2 years	8.0	7.9	7.4	9.1	7.9	7.9	.5	.4	.6	.4	.6	.6
2 to 5 years	13.8	12.6	12.1	16.0	13.2	14.2	.4	.6	.5	1.0	.6	.7
6 to 9 years	9.0	7.9	6.7	9.4	9.0	9.0	.3	.5	.4	.8	.6	.5
10 to 19 years	11.4	9.3	8.3	10.3	10.2	12.3	.6	.6	.5	.5	.5	.9
20 years or more	8.2	4.5	3.6	4.6	5.8	10.0	.5	.5	.2	.5	.3	.8
Not sure	2.4	2.9	2.4	3.1	2.5	2.3	.2	.5	.1	.5	.4	.2
Not reported	5.7	7.0	9.1	5.7	6.5	5.1	.3	.5	.6	.5	.4	.5
Not applicable	7.6	12.8	9.7	13.7	9.0	6.3	.4	.5	.6	.9	.6	.5
PREVIOUS YEARS OF WORK EXPERIENCE AS THE OWNER OF ANOTHER BUSINESS												
None	65.5	65.5	69.9	56.9	67.8	64.6	.7	1.3	1.0	.8	.5	1.2
Less than 2 years	3.0	2.6	2.7	4.4	3.3	2.7	.2	.2	.3	.4	.5	.3
2 to 5 years	5.6	4.8	4.3	7.4	4.9	5.9	.3	.4	.3	.8	.4	.4
6 to 9 years	3.3	2.4	1.5	3.9	2.4	3.9	.2	.2	.2	.4	.2	.4
10 to 19 years	4.8	2.9	1.6	4.7	3.2	5.9	.4	.3	.2	.5	.3	.5
20 years or more	3.9	1.6	.8	2.1	2.3	5.1	.5	.2	.2	.2	.1	.7
Not sure	.8	1.0	.8	1.6	.8	.9	.1	.2	.2	.2	.1	.2
Not reported	5.4	6.3	8.7	5.4	6.3	4.8	.3	.6	.5	.4	.3	.5
Not applicable	7.6	12.8	9.7	13.7	9.0	6.3	.4	.5	.8	.9	.6	.5

SOURCE: *Characteristics of Business Owners, 1992 Economic Census.* U.S. Census Bureau: Washington, D.C.

TABLE 9.9

Weeks and Hours Owner Spent Managing or Working by Industry Division, 1992
[All data are shown as percents, except firms.]

Type of firm and industry division	Firms (number)	Number of weeks spent managing or working in the business							Average number of hours per week spent managing or working in the business			
		None	Less than 12	12 to 23	24 to 35	36 to 47	48 or more	Not reported	None	Less than 10	10 to 19	20 to 29
	A	B	C	D	E	F	G	H	I	J	K	L
1 All businesses	17 253 143	8.4	12.4	6.2	6.4	7.1	51.3	8.3	8.4	17.1	10.5	8.9
2 Agricultural services, forestry, fishing, and mining	53 253	14.2	9.9	7.7	9.1	6.9	41.4	10.9	13.5	13.8	10.2	9.4
3 Construction	1 829 620	8.6	8.6	5.4	7.1	8.1	56.8	5.5	8.5	9.4	6.3	8.9
4 Manufacturing	517 714	10.6	11.2	5.6	6.6	4.7	55.7	5.6	10.8	12.6	10.1	7.9
5 Transportation, communications, and utilities	698 903	5.6	7.3	6.9	6.7	9.4	54.3	9.8	5.5	13.1	8.1	6.3
6 Wholesale trade	538 339	6.3	8.7	5.0	3.7	4.4	64.7	7.1	6.4	11.9	8.3	5.5
7 Retail trade	2 470 045	5.3	9.1	6.6	6.6	6.7	57.1	8.6	5.8	14.2	11.2	9.2
8 Finance, insurance, and real estate	1 941 029	20.7	19.7	3.2	3.3	4.5	41.4	7.2	20.7	29.1	5.2	5.3
9 Services	7 784 016	4.6	12.6	7.1	7.4	8.1	52.1	8.2	4:6	16.9	13.9	10.7
10 Industries not classified	882 224	7.4	12.7	8.9	6.0	7.7	39.9	17.3	7.4	17.5	8.6	8.6

SOURCE: *Characteristics of Business Owners, 1992 Economic Census.* U.S. Census Bureau: Washington, D.C.

TABLE 9.10

Characteristics of Business Owners and Their Businesses—Age, Citizenship, and Marital Status
[Detail may not add to total due to rounding.]

Item	All businesses
AGE AS OF DECEMBER 31, 1992	
Under 25	2.3
25 to 34	14.2
35 to 44	27.1
45 to 54	22.9
55 to 64	17.5
65 Or over	10.4
Not reported	5.7
BORN IN THE UNITED STATES	
Yes	84.1
No	8.7
Not reported	7.2
MARITAL STATUS WHEN THE BUSINESS WAS STARTED/ACQUIRED	
Never married	12.2
Married	71.9
Divorced/separated	8.3
Widowed	1.8
Not reported	5.8

SOURCE: *Characteristics of Business Owners, 1992 Economic Census.* U.S. Census Bureau: Washington, D.C.

FIGURE 9.4

Foreign Born Business Owners, 1992

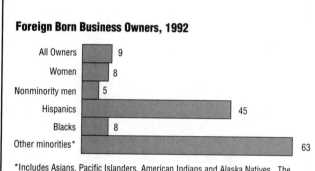

*Includes Asians, Pacific Islanders, American Indians and Alaska Natives. The foreign-born percentages are dominated by Asians and Pacific Islanders.
SOURCE: *Census and You.* U.S. Census Bureau: Washington, D.C.

TABLE 9.11

Summary Characteristics of Business Owners and Their Businesses—Educational Attainment, 1992

Detail may not add to total due to rounding.

Item	All businesses	Hispanic-owned businesses	Black-owned businesses	Other minority-owned businesses	Women-owned businesses	Nonminority male-owned businesses	Standard error of estimate for column					
	A	B	C	D	E	F	A	B	C	D	E	F
HIGHEST LEVEL OF EDUCATION COMPLETED OR DEGREE RECEIVED WHEN BUSINESS WAS STARTED/ACQUIRED												
Less than 9th grade	3.7	14.8	6.0	5.3	3.2	3.3	.2	.7	.3	.4	.4	.2
Some high school, but no diploma	5.7	10.6	10.4	6.4	4.9	5.7	.2	.6	.4	.6	.5	.4
High school graduate or GED equivalency	22.6	18.2	21.3	14.8	22.4	23.2	.6	.7	.5	.6	.7	.8
Technical, trade, or vocational school	7.0	7.9	8.6	4.7	7.6	6.7	.2	.7	.5	.5	.4	.4
Some college, but no degree	16.1	16.6	16.6	12.9	17.7	15.4	.6	.9	.4	.8	.8	.8
Associate Degree	4.0	4.1	4.9	4.4	4.7	3.5	.4	.4	.4	.3	.6	.5
Bachelor's Degree	20.2	11.9	11.9	23.7	20.6	20.6	.6	.7	.6	1.5	.9	1.0
Master's Degree	5.8	3.9	6.7	8.9	7.0	5.0	.3	.2	.6	.7	.5	.5
Professional School or Doctorate	8.9	5.4	6.0	12.1	5.2	10.8	.2	.4	.4	.9	.5	.4
Not reported	6.1	6.6	7.7	6.5	6.7	5.6	.3	.4	.5	.8	.3	.5
IF ATTENDED COLLEGE OR OTHER SCHOOL BEYOND HIGH SCHOOL, AREA OF CONCENTRATION												
Architecture/Engineering	5.0	4.9	2.6	9.6	3.3	5.7	.2	.4	.3	.5	.3	.3
Biological/Medical Science	6.9	5.6	5.8	11.8	6.9	6.7	.3	.5	.2	.9	.4	.5
Business	17.3	14.2	14.2	17.6	16.0	18.3	.4	.6	.5	.9	.5	.8
Computer Science	1.0	1.5	1.5	2.8	1.1	.8	.1	.2	.1	.4	.2	.2
Construction Trade/Industrial Arts	1.9	1.6	1.9	1.2	1.3	2.3	.2	.2	.1	.3	.3	.2
Law and Legal Studies	3.5	2.2	2.4	2.2	2.0	4.4	.2	.2	.2	.3	.2	.4
Liberal Arts/General Studies	11.7	7.6	10.1	7.7	14.9	10.5	.5	.5	.5	.8	.5	.8
Mathematics	.8	.5	.9	1.3	.8	.8	.1	.1	.1	.2	.1	.2
Military Technologies	.5	.2	.3	.3	.1	.7	.1	.1	.1	.1	.1	.2
Other college	5.9	3.8	5.5	5.3	8.2	4.9	.3	.4	.3	.4	.6	.5
Other vocational	5.5	5.0	7.5	5.1	6.2	5.1	.3	.5	.5	.5	.4	.6
Not reported	8.0	9.1	9.8	8.5	8.6	7.6	.3	.5	.4	.8	.5	.6
Not applicable	32.0	43.6	37.6	26.5	30.5	32.2	.6	1.0	.4	.6	.9	.9

SOURCE: *Characteristics of Business Owners, 1992 Economic Census.* U.S. Census Bureau: Washington, D.C.

TABLE 9.12

Small Businesses, Use of the Internet

Used Internet for . . .	in 1999	in 1998
E-Mail	71%	76%
Business Research	58%	71%
Personal Research	50%	64%
Purchase Goods/Services (business use)	43%	38%
Purchase Goods/Services (personal use)	31%	35%
Sell/Market Products	26%	29%

SOURCE: Economic Analysis Department, The Dunn and Bradstreet Corp., May 25, 2000

TABLE 9.13

Small Business Presence on the Web

Has Web Page/Site	All Small Businesses	1-5 empl.	6-25 empl.	26-100 empl.	Home-Based	Women-Owned	Minority-Owned
2000	38%	28%	47%	65%	24%	41%	40%
1999	28%	22%	45%	43%	16%	22%	30%

SOURCE: Economic Analysis Department, The Dunn and Bradstreet Corp., May 25, 2000

IMPORTANT NAMES
AND ADDRESSES

AFL-CIO
American Federation of Labor—Congress of
Industrial Organizations
815 16th St. NW
Washington, DC 20006
(202) 637-5000
FAX: (202) 637-5058
E-mail: feedback@aflcio.org
URL: http://www.aflcio.org

Center on Budget and Policy Priorities
820 First St. NE, Suite 510
Washington, DC 20002
(202) 408-1080
FAX: (202) 408-1056
E-mail: bazie@cbpp.org
URL: http://www.cbpp.org

Dun & Bradstreet
One Diamond Hill Rd.
Murray Hill, NJ 07974-1218
(908) 665-5000
FAX: (908) 665-5803
URL: http://www.dnb.com

**Employment and Training
Administration**
U.S. Department of Labor
Unemployment Insurance Service
200 Constitution Ave. NW, #S4231
Washington, DC 20210
(202) 219-5922
FAX: (202) 219-8506
(800) US-2JOBS
URL: http://www.doleta.gov

Employment Policy Foundation
1015 15th St. NW, Suite 1200
Washington, DC 20005
(202) 789-8685
FAX: (202) 789-8684
E-mail: info@epf.org
URL: http://www.epf.org

Employment Standards Administration
U.S. Department of Labor
200 Constitution Ave. NW, Room S-3325

Washington, DC 20210
(202) 693-0023
URL: http://www.dol.gov/dol/esa

**Equal Employment Opportunity
Commission**
1801 L St. NW, #10006
Washington, DC 20507
(202) 663-4900
FAX: (202) 663-4494
URL: http://www.eeoc.gov

**House Committee on Education and the
Workforce**
Room 2181 Rayburn House Office Bldg.
Washington, DC 20515
(202) 225-4527
FAX: (202) 225-9571
TTY: (202) 226-3372
URL: http://www.house.gov/ed_workforce/

National Alliance of Business
1201 New York Ave. NW, #700
Washington, DC 20005
(202) 289-2888
FAX: (202) 289-1303
(800) 787-2848
E-mail: info@nab.com
URL: http://www.nab.com

**National Association of Manufacturers
Employment Policy**
1331 Pennsylvania Ave. NW
Suite 600
Washington, DC 20004-1790
(202) 637-3000
FAX: (202) 637-3182

**National Association of Temporary and
Staffing Services**
Suite 200, 277 South Washington St.
Alexandria, VA 22314
(703) 253-2050
FAX: (703) 253-2053
E-mail: asa@staffingtoday.net
URL: http://www.natss.org

National Center for Health Statistics
U.S. Department of Health
6525 Belcrest Rd., #1064
Hyattsville, MD 20782-2003
(301) 436-4636
FAX: (301) 436-5202
URL: http://www.cdc.gov/nchs/default.htm

National Labor Relations Board
1099 14th St. NW
Washington, DC 20570-0001
(202) 273-1790
FAX: (202) 273-4276
URL: http://www.nlrb.gov

National Safety Council
1025 Connecticut Ave. NW #1200
Washington, DC 20036
(202) 293-2270
FAX: (202) 293-0032
URL: http://www.nsc.org

**Occupational Safety and Health
Administration**
U.S. Department of Labor
200 Constitution Ave. NW #N3647
Washington, DC 20210
(202) 693-1999
URL: http://www.osha-slc.gov

**Senate Committee on Health, Education,
Labor, and Pensions**
428 Dirksen Senate Office Bldg.
Washington, DC 20510-6300
(202) 224-5375
TDD (202) 224-1975
URL: http://www.senate.gov/~labor

**Society for Human Resource
Management**
1800 Duke St.
Alexandria, VA 22314
(703) 548-3440
FAX: (703) 535-6490
(800) 283-7476

E-mail: shrm@shrm.org
URL: http://www.shrm.org

U.S. Bureau of Labor Statistics
U.S. Department of Labor
2 Massachusetts Ave. NW, #2860
Washington, DC 20212
(202) 691-5200
FAX: (202) 606-7890
E-mail: blsdata_staff@bls.gov
URL: http://www.bls.gov

U.S. Bureau of the Census
U.S. Department of Commerce
4700 Silver Hills Rd.
Suitland, MD 20746
(301) 457-4608

FAX: (301) 457-3761
(301) 763-2800 (Public Information)
E-mail: comments@census.gov
URL: http://www.census.gov

U.S. Chamber of Commerce
1615 H St. NW
Washington, DC 20062-2000
(202) 659-6000
FAX: (202) 463-3190
URL: http://www.uschamber.org

U.S. Department of Commerce
Main Commerce Building
14th and Constitution Ave. NW
Washington, DC 20230
(202) 482-2000

FAX: (202) 482-3610
URL: http://www.doc.gov

U.S. Department of Education
400 Maryland Ave. SW
Washington, DC 20202-0498
(202) 401-2000
FAX: (202) 401-0689
(800) USA-LEARN
E-mail: CustomerService@inet.ed.gov
URL: http://www.ed.gov

U.S. Department of Labor
200 Constitution Ave. NW, Room S-1032
Washington, DC 20210
(202) 693-4650
URL: http://www.dol.gov

RESOURCES

The Bureau of Labor Statistics (BLS), a branch of the U.S. Department of Labor, is the most important source of information on employment and unemployment in the United States. *Employment and Earnings*, a monthly BLS publication, gives complete statistics on employment in the United States. The BLS also releases special reports, such as *A Profile of the Working Poor, 1997* (Report 936, 1999).

The BLS also publishes the *Monthly Labor Review*, which contains articles on issues having to do with jobs and how workers are affected by changes in the labor market. The *Monthly Labor Review* also provides historical data and supplies information on employee benefits, including medical and life insurance, disability insurance, and retirement.

The monthly *BLS News* provides information on employment situations. The BLS also puts out *Issues in Labor Statistics*, such as "How Long Is the Workweek?" (1997), "Workers Are on the Job More Hours over the Course of the Year" (1997), and "Are Workers More Secure?" (1998). The BLS periodically surveys employee benefits. *Employee Benefits in Small Establishments: 1994* (1996) and *Employee Benefits in State and Local Governments: 1994* (1996) are two of the surveys on benefits. Information on employee benefits was also provided by the Employment Policy Foundation, including the topics of paid family leave, unemployment insurance, and employer-sponsored medical coverage.

The BLS annual *Occupational Handbook* is the most complete source on jobs available. The handbook outlines future job projections. It also provides complete information on most jobs and directs the reader to further information. Any consideration of a job should include the *Occupational Handbook* as a resource. The Bureau of Labor Statistics *Occupational Outlook Quarterly* contains valuable articles on employment and the labor market.

The quarterly *Family Economics and Nutrition Review*, prepared by the Agricultural Service of the U.S. Department of Agriculture, contains articles on family living, including articles on jobs and workers. "Employee Participation in Savings and Thrift Plans, 1993" (vol. 9, no. 4, 1996) discusses workers who save through company plans.

The Bureau of the Census, a branch of the U.S. Department of Commerce, is the major source of information about the American people. Some of its studies concern employment and how much people earn. Helpful publications from the Bureau of the Census include *Money Income in the United States, 1998* (1999) and *1992 Economic Census, Characteristics of Business Owners* (1997).

The U.S. Department of Education also publishes valuable information on educational levels and their relationship to career opportunities in its *Digest of Education Statistics: 1999* (2000), *Condition of Education, 1999* (1999), and *Projections of Education Statistics to 2009* (1999).

The General Accounting Office reported its findings on information technology workers to the House Committee on Commerce in its *Information Technology: Assessment of the Department of Commerce's Report on Workforce Demand and Supply* (1998). The National Center for Health Statistics (Hyattsville, Maryland) provided information on health insurance in its *Employer-Sponsored Health Insurance* (1997).

The Society for Human Resource Management's (Alexandria, Virginia) *1996 Issues Management Survey* is based on a poll of its membership. The series included the *1996 Workplace Violence Survey* (1996) and the *1996 Job Security and Layoff Survey* (1996). The Gale Group is grateful to SHRM for allowing use of its tables and figures.

The Gale Group also thanks Dun and Bradstreet, a company of The Dun and Bradstreet Corporation, (Murray Hill, New Jersey) for allowing use of materials from its annual *Business Starts Records* (1998 and 1999–2000) and *Business Failure Records* (1997). Dun and Bradstreet also provided information on business Internet use and minority business owners' attitudes toward their businesses. The Center on Budget and Policy Priorities, a private research group, provided information on employment and earnings of former welfare recipients. The National Association of Colleges and Employers as well as the Greenwood Publishing Group provided information on psychological testing of employees. The Career Services and Placement Office of Michigan State University granted permission to use material from its *Recruiting Trends: 1997–1998* (December 1997). The Gale Group thanks the U.S. Chamber of Commerce (Washington, DC) for consent to use graphics from its *Employment Benefits—1997 Edition—The Hidden Payroll*. The National Association of Temporary and Staffing Services allowed use of material from its survey published in *Contemporary Times* magazine (spring 1998 issue). Online sources from the Department of Labor, the Access Board of the Americans with Disabilities Act, and OSHA provided information on current topics such as reassessing the ADA and proposing an ergonomics standard. The Gale Group also gratefully thanks the Gallup Poll for use of its tables.

INDEX

Page references in italics refer to photographs. References with the letter t following them indicate the presence of a table. The letter f indicates a figure. If more than one table or figure appears on a particular page, the exact item number for the table or figure being referenced is provided.

A

ADA (Americans with Disabilities Act), 151

Age

    alternative work arrangements, 53t

    college enrollment, 77, 78t–79t, 79f

    contingency employment, 50, 51t

    displaced workers, 60t

    education, 76t–77t

    employment status, 3t, 4t–5t

    income averages, 125t

    job holdings, multiple, 48 (t2.8)

    job searching, 14–15, 27f, 27t, 73 (t3.12)

    jobs held, number of, 26t

    labor force, 1, 85t, 101–102, 102t, 103 (f5.2)

    poverty, 14t

    small business owners, 163 (t9.10)

    tenure, 13, 23t, 24t

    unemployment, 63, 65t, 66, 67t, 71 (t3.10), 73 (t3.13), 86t

    union membership, 28t

    work hours, 45 (t2.4)

    working poor, 6

Age Discrimination in Employment Act of 1967, 151

Agricultural industry, 44t

Alcohol testing, 152–153, 152t

Alternative work arrangements, 50, 52t, 53t, 54t

Americans with Disabilities Act (ADA) of 1990, 151

America's Job Bank (http:// www.ajb.dni.us/), 147

America's New Deficit: The Shortage of Information Technology Workers (Department of Commerce), 110–111

At-home work, 51–52, 55f, 56t, 57t, 157, 161t

B

Benefits, 126–144, 136t, 137t, 141f

    average spending, 134–135, 140f

    company size, 126–128

    comparison for salaried and hourly workers, 140 (t6.12)

    full-time employment, 138t

    government employment, 139t

    savings and thrift plans, 140–141

    types, 134, 140 (t6.11)

    unemployment, 149–150

    See also Health insurance

Business failures, 155–156, 158t, 159f

    See also Small businesses

Business start-ups, 155, 156f, 156t, 157f

    See also Small businesses

C

Career guidance, 145–146

Career placement offices, 147

Citizenship of small business owners, 163f, 163 (t9.10)

Civil Rights Act of 1964, 151

Civil Rights Act of 1991, 151

Classified advertisements, 146–147

Colleges

    career placement offices, 147

    degrees conferred, 82f, 83t, 84t, 87t

    enrollment, 78t–79t, 79f, 80t–82t

    graduates, 93t, 94f, 94t, 95f, 96t, 126, 135t

    See also Education

Compensation. *See* Benefits; Income

Contingency employment, 48 (t2.9), 49–51, 50t, 51t

D

Department of Commerce, 110–111

Discrimination, 151

Displaced workers, 53–54, 60t, 61t, 62t

Drug testing, 152–153, 152t

Duration of unemployment, 66–68, 70t, 71 (t3.9), 72t

    See also Unemployment

E

Earnings. *See* Income

Economic growth, 103–104, 104 (f5.6)

Education, 75–100

    alternative work arrangements, 54t

    contingency employment, 50, 51t

    employment status, 7t, 90f

    income, 85–87, 88–91, 91f, 92t, 97t–98t, 98f, 99t

    job growth, 112–116, 112 (t5.16)

    job searching, 15, 27t

    jobs held, number of, 14, 26t

    labor force, 5, 82–85

    poverty, 15t, 92, 100t

    small business owners, 164 (t9.11)

    tenure, 13

    unemployment, 65, 66t, 86t, 87f

    working poor, 8

    years completed, 75–77, 75f, 76t–77t, 85t

    See also Colleges; Training

Employee Polygraph Protection Act, 153

Employees' rights, 149–153

Employer testing, 152–153, 152t

Employment agencies and services, 147

Employment decline, 106 (f5.9), 120–121, 121f, 121t

    See also Employment shifts

Employment growth. *See* Job growth